WALKING THROUGH ELYSIUM

Vergil's Underworld
and the Poetics of Tradition

EDITED BY BILL GLADHILL AND
MICAH YOUNG MYERS

Walking through Elysium: Vergil's Underworld and the Poetics of Tradition

UNIVERSITY OF TORONTO PRESS
Toronto Buffalo London

Toronto Buffalo London
utorontopress.com

ISBN 978-1-4875-0577-6 (cloth) ISBN 978-1-4875-3264-2 (PDF)
ISBN 978-1-4875-3265-9 (ePUB)

Library and Archives Canada Cataloguing in Publication

Title: Walking through Elysium : Vergil's underworld and the poetics of tradition / edited by Bill Gladhill and Micah Young Myers.
Names: Gladhill, Bill, editor. | Myers, Micah Young, 1979– editor.
Series: Phoenix. Supplementary volume; 59.
Description: Series statement: Phoenix supplementary volumes; 59 | Includes bibliographical references.
Identifie s: Canadiana (print) 20190232323 | Canadiana (ebook) 20190232552 | ISBN 9781487505776 (hardcover) | ISBN 9781487532642 (PDF) | ISBN 9781487532659 (EPUB)
Subjects: LCSH: Virgil – Influenc . | LCSH: Virgil – Themes, motives. | LCSH: Virgil. Aeneis. Liber 6. | LCSH: Voyages to the otherworld in literature.
Classification: LCC PA6825 .W35 2020 | DDC 873/.01 – dc23

University of Toronto Press acknowledges the financial assistance to its publishing program of the Canada Council for the Arts and the Ontario Arts Council, an agency of the Government of Ontario.

Canada Council for the Arts Conseil des Arts du Canada

Funded by the Government of Canada Financé par le gouvernement du Canada

CONTENTS

ACKNOWLEDGMENTS

Many hands aided in the publication of this volume. We would like to thank the participants of "*Aeneid* Six and Its Cultural Reception," held at the Harry Wilks Study Center at the Villa Vergiliana, Cuma, Italy, and the University of Naples Federico II in June 2013, including Craig Kallendorf, Emily Gowers, Massimo Giuseppetti, Jelena Pilipovic, Fabio Stok, Francisco Edi Sousa, Ioannis Ziogas, Lauren Curtis, Alessandro Schiessaro, Sarah Spence, Alison Keith, John Schafer, Emily Pillinger, Damien Nelis, Serena Fusco, Moa Elisabeth Ekbom, Gaetano Bevelacqua, Gabriela Ryser, Jacob Mackey, Anna Jourbina, Adrian Mihai, Séverine Clément-Tarantino, Luigi Galasso, Nandini Pandey, Ourania Molyviati, Linda Robertson, Matteo Soranzo, Valentina Prosperi, Ippokratis Kantzios, Hallie Marshall, Alessandro Barchiesi, Arturo De Vivo, Valeria Viparelli, Marisa Squillante, Giancarlo Abbamonte, Concetta Longobardi, Grant Parker, Joseph Farrell, Maggie Kilgour, and Philip Hardie. We would also like to thank the Vergilian Society, the Harry Wilks Study Center, Dipartimento di Studi Umanistici at the University of Naples Federico II, British Virgil Society, McGill University, Accademia Virgiliana di Mantova, Social Sciences and Humanities Research Council of Canada, and Fonds de recherche du Québec – Société et culture for their support during the conference and the publication of the proceedings. In addition, we are grateful to Antimina Sgariglia and the rest of the staff at Villa Vergiliana for their efforts before and during the symposium. Lastly, we would like to thank the anonymous readers of the University of Toronto Press for their insightful feedback and suggestions, and Suzanne Rancourt, Charles Stuart, Michaela Drouillard, and Donald McCarthy for their help in editing and formatting the volume.

CONTRIBUTORS

Alessandro Barchiesi is Professor of Classics at New York University.

Lauren Curtis is Associate Professor of Classics at Bard College.

Bill Gladhill is Associate Professor of Classics at McGill University.

Emily Gowers is Professor of Latin Literature at the University of Cambridge and a Fellow of St. John's College.

Miguel Herrero de Jáuregui is Profesor Titular de Filología Griega at Universidad Complutense de Madrid.

Alison Keith is Professor of Classics at the University of Toronto.

Maggie Kilgour is Molson Professor of English Language and Literature at McGill University.

Jacob L. Mackey is Assistant Professor of Classics at Occidental College.

Micah Young Myers is Associate Professor of Classics at Kenyon College.

Grant Parker is Associate Professor of Classics at Stanford University.

Emily Pillinger is Lecturer in Latin Language and Literature at King's College London.

Matteo Soranzo is Associate Professor of Italian at McGill University.

Fabio Stok is Professore Ordinario di Lingua e Letteratura Latina at Università di Roma Tor Vergata.

WALKING THROUGH ELYSIUM

Vergil's Underworld and the Poetics of Tradition

Introduction

BILL GLADHILL AND MICAH YOUNG MYERS

This volume represents a select grouping of papers on the theme of *Aeneid* 6 and its reception, delivered during the summer of 2013 at the Villa Vergiliana, a short walk from the Antro della Sibilla.[1] The original call for papers for that year's Vergilian Society Symposium Cumanum hoped to answer a fundamental question: how does the conceptualization of *Aeneid* 6 as a product of reception and as a formative model for later reception illuminate the complex interplay of texts and their mediations across time and cultures? *Aeneid* 6 stands as a deeply significant artefact of the reception of prior Greek and Roman literary and material culture, while itself becoming a crucible in which later artists, scholars, and thinkers mingled, mixed, and shaped their own productions on the underworld (among other things). Of the nearly 130 abstracts submitted in response to the call for papers, few attempted to address Vergil's own reception of Greek literature and art in *Aeneid* 6. Quite unexpectedly, there were no abstracts that centred on foundational responses to *Aeneid* 6, such as Dante's *Divina Commedia* or Melville's *Moby Dick*.[2] Scholarship on *Aeneid* 6 and its reception in material culture were largely (though not entirely) absent.[3] The vast majority of abstracts – and the papers delivered at the Villa – focused on the reception of *Aeneid* 6 in the Latin literary tradition from Tibullus to Augustine, along with a number of reassessments of this tradition in the Renaissance and early modern period. The papers presented at the symposium as well as the ones that form *Walking through Elysium* reflect therefore, a particular moment in Vergilian scholarship. But this volume also emphasizes that more collaborative and interdisciplinary research ought to be conducted on *Aeneid* 6 (and works like it), whose literary, artistic, philosophical, religious, and spiritual themes raise fundamental questions about the role of literature and art in the mediation of life, death, and the human experience.

At the time of the conference, *Aeneid* 6 was already undergoing an intense re-evaluation across a number of domains. The conference occurred just months prior to the publication of a new text, translation, and commentary on *Aeneid* 6 by Nicholas Horsfall (who passed away during the writing of this introduction). Nearly a month after the conference Seamus Heaney descended, only to return in 2016 with the posthumous publication of his unfinished translation of *Aeneid* 6.[4] At the conference Linda Robertson delivered "To Pull History through to the Present: The *Aeneid* and Artistic Design of the National September 11 Memorial and Museum." Robertson showed and discussed a series of interviews with 9/11 Memorial planners, who, in addition to incorporating a quotation of *Aeneid* 9.447, deliberately modelled the entry into the museum at Ground Zero on Aeneas' *katabasis* in *Aeneid* 6. In fact, the description of Memorial Plaza on The National September 11 Memorial & Museum website reads like an echo of Vergilian geopoetics:

> [The] memorial plaza is punctuated by the linear rhythms of rows of deciduous trees, forming informal clusters, clearings and groves … surrounding the pools on bronze parapets are the names … Standing there at the water's edge, looking at a pool of water that is flowing away into an abyss, a visitor to the site can sense that what is beyond this parapet edge is inaccessible.[5]

Even the Memorial Jury's remarks on Michael Arad's winning design for the Memorial show Vergilian reminiscences:

> Of all the designs submitted, we have found that "Reflecting Absence" by Michael Arad, in concert with landscape architect Peter Walker, fulfills most eloquently the daunting but absolutely necessary demands of this memorial. In its powerful, yet simple articulation of the footprints of the Twin Towers, "Reflecting Absence" has made the voids left by the destruction the primary symbols of our loss. By allowing absence to speak for itself, the designers have made the power of these empty footprints the memorial.[6]

"Reflecting Absence" or "allowing absence to speak for itself" could be read as succinct distillations of the final panel on the doors to the temple of Apollo, left unfinished by Daedalus (*Aen.* 6.30–4; trans. Heaney 2016):

> tu quoque magnam
> partem opere in tanto, sineret dolor, Icare, haberes.
> bis conatus erat casus effingere in aur ,
> bis patriae cecidere manus. quin protinus omnia

perlegerent oculis ...

In which grand design
You too would figure significant ,
Icarus, had sorrow allowed it. Twice
Dedalus tried to model your fall in gold, twice
His hands, the hands of a father, failed him.
The Trojans would have kept standing, fascinated
By all on display ...[7]

Walking through Elysium does not claim to occupy the same intellectual, artistic, or emotional spaces as the underworlds of Horsfall, Heaney, or the 9/11 Memorial. These are powerfully pivotal reassessments, enactments, and performances of the legacy of Vergil's underworld. One represents the most recent articulation of a long development of exegesis and scholarship on Vergil. Another is a poet's translation of a single book, itself an act of literary revelation and communion that cannot be uncoupled from prior literary engagements with *Aeneid* 6. The last stands as a monumental memorialization of a profoundly deep *dolor* that interfaces with the poetics of mourning and memory.[8] The falling of Daedalus' hands means something wholly different now.

The purpose of the present volume is one step removed from these particularly intense and direct meditations on and mediations of *Aeneid* 6. As noted earlier, *Walking through Elysium* studies the reception of *Aeneid* 6 in primarily the Latin literary tradition, broadly defined as both Vergil's own reception of prior traditions and the reception of *Aeneid* 6 in later texts. In many ways the contributions hope to "reflect absences" in the tradition of *Aeneid* 6 in a way that is evocative of Vergil's famous ecphrasis of Daedalus' doors quoted above. Vergil builds into his text a prior work of art by the "fi st" artist, and then fills the absent space intended for Icarus on the doors, while the internal viewers – the Trojans – see only the unfinished door. The culmination of the door's artistic design is only gleaned through this *fictional* act of reception (behind which is the literary reception of Catullus 64), as Vergil himself depicts the death of Icarus in the falling hands of Daedalus (*patriae cecidere manus*, 6.32). In this moment the *Aeneid* itself signals that reception happens in the gaps, voids, and empty spaces between literary and material arts across temporal, spatial, and cultural domains, interweaving complex patterns of artistic appreciation and interpretation, simultaneously focusing and distorting meaning and significanc . The process never ends; it has no beginning. The plummeting Icarus becomes a void, which becomes a pantomime performance of Daedalus that, in turn, inaugurates Vergil's ecphrasis of the underworld, as Icarus' death anticipates Death itself. The void on Daedalus' doors becomes *Aeneid* 6 as it revels in its intermedial, fi - tive receptions of Daedalus' work.

Studies on classical reception have risen dramatically, especially over the last thirty years.[9] These studies encompass micro- and macro-receptions of literature, art, architecture, and intellectual history across cultural, temporal, and geographic domains. The bibliography on the reception of Vergil is particularly vast, as reflected in the resources collected in Niklas Holzberg's Vergil bibliographies or in Jan Ziolkowski and Michael Putnam's *The Virgilian Tradition: The First Fifteen Hundred Years.*[10] This is not the place to rehearse the hermeneutic tradition of reception studies and their impact on the study of literature and art. The reception turn has occurred and we are its beneficiarie . There are many good explorations of this development that can be consulted, such as Hans Robert Jauss's *Toward an Aesthetic of Reception,* Charles Martindale's *Redeeming the Text,* Lorna Hardwick and Christopher Stray's *A Companion to Classical Receptions,* Craig Kallendorf's *A Companion to the Classical Tradition,* or the collection of papers in Martindale and Richard Thomas' *Classics and the Uses of Reception* and in Philip Goldstein and James Machor's *New Directions in American Reception Study*. This is not to mention focused explorations on a single author. Within Latin literature consider Richard Thomas' *Virgil and the Augustan Reception* and Aude Doody's *Pliny's Encyclopedia: The Reception of the* Natural History, to take two examples of studies of very different Roman authors. Our field of course, is far from the only one to have embraced reception. John Nash's *James Joyce and the Act of Reception* and Lucia Aiello's *After Reception Theory: Fedor Dostoevskii in Britain, 1869–1935* are important examples of reception outside of Classics.

In particular, Philip Hardie's scholarship on the reception of Vergil provides an important model for this collection. Hardie's article, "In the Steps of the Sibyl: Tradition and Desire in the Epic Underworld," offers a thoughtful and succinct analysis of the influence of Vergil's Parade of Heroes on Spenser, Milton, Silius Italicus, and Petrarch. *Rumour and Renown: Representations of* Fama *in Western Literature,* which traces the notion of *fama* from Homer and Hesiod via Vergil to Alexander Pope, represents a watershed moment in big scholarship, where the scope of the classical tradition is viewed in its totality. Additionally, Hardie's *The Last Trojan Hero: A Cultural History of Virgil's* Aeneid explores the reception of Vergil's epic. His chapter on *Aeneid* 6 surveys its reception across a variety of texts, including many major works, such as those by Dante, Petrarch, and Milton, in a manner that complements and contextualizes *Walking through Elysium.*

In the case of *Aeneid* 6 and its reception, *Walking through Elysium* argues that Vergil's underworld is an inflection point, to which authors time and again return in order to meditate on life, death, and rebirth. *Aeneid* 6 was a revolutionary literary event, in which Vergil incorporated diverse traditions and myriad ideas and expressions on death and the afterlife, and then arranged a wholly new discourse, which in turn became the source model for an expansive assemblage of literary themes and episodes. Literary underworlds and afterlives from the Augustan age to late antiquity, from Renaissance poetry to twenty-fi st-century literature and scholarship, are filtered through and enriched by the sixth book of the *Aeneid*. Given the long shadow of *Aeneid* 6, *Walking through Elysium* does not pretend total and complete coverage of its influenc . Many volumes could be (and ought to be) published on the reception of *Aeneid* 6 in the visual arts, in late antique and Renaissance poetry and epic – from Prudentius and Dracontius to Petrarch, Pontano, and beyond – or in the works of Christian theologians or in scholarship and intellectual history from Servius to Horsfall. This is the work for other researchers in future volumes and publications. Each paper in *Walking through Elysium* interrogates a precise moment of literary reception and refraction, offering a deep analysis of the dynamics of reception. Yet they all share a common thread: Vergil provided poets and thinkers a way to imagine death and the afterlife in literary terms. Like his Daedalus, he provided an empty panel (after empty panel after empty panel ...) to be filled by later authors and interpreters. The contributions in this volume stress the subtle and intricate ways writers wove *Aeneid* 6 into their works. These allusions operate on many levels, from the literary and political to the religious and spiritual. *Aeneid* 6 reshaped prior philosophical, religious, and poetic traditions of *katabasis*, while offering a universalizing account of the spiritual that could accommodate prior as well as emerging religious and philosophical systems. *Aeneid* 6 became an archetype, a model flexible enough to be employed across genres and periods and among differing cultural and religious contexts.

The chapters of *Walking through Elysium* individually and collectively reflect new perspectives on *Aeneid* 6 and speak to Vergil's incorporation of and influence on literary representations of *katabaseis*, underworlds, souls, afterlives, prophecies, journeys, and spaces, from sacred and profane to wild and civilized. So, as chapters in the volume demonstrate, Horace's *Carmen Saeculare* recalls the choral dancing in Vergil's Elysium, while Seneca's tragic space uses *Aeneid* 6 as a sort of literary *skene*, designed to infuse Roman drama with the dark resonances of Vergil's underworld. Likewise, in *Confessions* 9 Augustine and Monnica interface with Anchises and Aeneas' Elysian conversations as they contemplate the nature of spirituality. In turn, some fifteen hundred years later, Mary Shelley mediates her husband's death through Vergil and *Aeneid* 6, showing a deep awareness that the Bay of Naples has become a metaliterary space infused with the hazy mirage of Vergil's netherworld. Similarly, the closer Statius comes to Cumae, the greater the echo of *Aeneid* 6 in his poetry. *Aeneid* 6 becomes the archetypal model for subsequent underworlds in the Western tradition. The examples of its influence are many and manifold

The volume is not organized chronologically. While something is gained in reading the reception of *Aeneid* 6 through its influence over linear time, this overemphasizes time as the pivotal and most important element of reception. *Aeneid* 6 has existed in ponderous simultaneity from its composition to the present moment. It has always been *present* since its publication. It was present for Ovid, for Servius, and for W.F. Jackson Knight. They breathed over its words and touched its pages, just as we have and others will. The act of reception does not happen only along a temporal continuum. It also occurs in the present moment of its observation and the recognition that an act of allusive reception has occurred. To this end the contributions follow the steps of the Sibyl and Aeneas in *Aeneid* 6. They begin with the Trojans' arrival in Cumae, and then move in parallel to Aeneas' descent through the underworld and his release through the Gate of Ivory, albeit with the wandering back and forth across the verses and spaces of *Aeneid* 6 that the literary fractalization of reception so often requires. By organizing the contributions in this manner, the volume stresses the centrality of *Aeneid* 6 as the overarching, organizational principle of its reception. We are privileging the work of art in its own reception.

The contributions begin, like *Aeneid* 6, above ground in the spaces that lead to the underworld. Alessandro Barchiesi's exploration in chapter 1 of *siluae* in *Aeneid* 6 demonstrates that Vergil renders his underworld episode as a proto-colonial narrative, innovating upon and departing from earlier epic traditions of woods and hellish landscapes – especially those found in Homer and Apollonius – to create a new vision of wild spaces that in turn becomes a model in its own right. In Barchiesi's reading Vergil reactivates earlier epic traditions that conflate woods and underworlds, transforming the landscape of Cumaean Italy into a katabatic space that represents something wholly novel and new, while also participating in a wider network of geographic and topographic changes to the Cumaean landscape during the Augustan period.

In chapter 2, Emily Pillinger moves us through another sort of *siluae* influenced by *Aeneid* 6: Statius' *Siluae* 4.3. Pillinger investigates how Statius uses the dynamics of time, distance, and speed, as experienced by travellers along the Via Domitiana from Rome to Cumae, to describe his own navigation of Roman literary history. This itinerary is in part presided over by Vergil's Cumaean Sibyl, with the journeys taken by her and Aeneas in *Aeneid* 6 offering a model onto which Statius plots his own progress.

In chapter 3 Maggie Kilgour traces the reception of *Aeneid* 6 via the Sibyl through Dante, Ariosto, Spenser, Abraham Cowley, and Milton to Mary Shelley, whose engagements with Vergil are reflected especially in her letters, her journals, and her post-apocalyptic novel *The Last Man* (1826). Themes of prophecy and teleology in *Aeneid* 6, refracted through Renaissance and early modern literary responses to the Vergilian tradition and the death of Shelley's husband, Percy, become, for Shelley, touch points for explaining both personal loss and the worldwide cataclysm of *The Last Man.* Kilgour's wide-ranging survey highlights how Vergil's underworld reverberates across times and cultures in complex and deep ways.

From Cumae and the Sibyl the volume moves to the golden bough in chapter 4, where Matteo Soranzo discusses Baptista Mantuanus and Giles of Viterbo, two Mendicant friars and Vergil enthusiasts from early Renaissance Italy, whose allegorical interpretations of the golden bough reflect its crucial role in the negotiation of European cultural heritage. Soranzo shows that "[w]hether they took Vergil's golden bough to be the unpredictable manifestation of divine inspiration before the coming of Christ, or rather the result of a forgotten Etruscan fringe of a Biblical legacy, Mantuanus and Giles used Vergil as part of an act of cultural identity grounded in their respective views of tradition."

We then descend into the underworld in chapter 5. Drawing on a broad range of source material from Homer to Plutarch, Miguel Herrero de Jáuregui puts a spotlight on the often overlooked passages that describe Aeneas' movement through the underworld. Herrero analyses these passages in terms of ritual descent, reflected especially in "Orphic" gold tablets. Aeneas' manner of motion – characterized in Book 6 by resolution, firmnes , and urgency – is, in Herrero's reading, deeply implicated in a broader network of ideas connecting locomotion, error, and redemption within ritualized, katabatic traditions.

The reader then enters the *lugentes campi* in chapter 6, where Micah Myers argues that Vergil's depiction of the dead lovers here and his presentation of the "Poets' Corner" in Elysium responds to Roman love elegy – especially Tibullus 1.3 – and, in turn, influences subsequent elegiac descriptions of the afterlife.

In chapter 7 Alison Keith explores the broad influence of *Aeneid* 6 across Ovid's works, as the elegiac master returns again and again to the *Aeneid*'s underworld, even as his poetics transform from elegy to epic and back again.

Chapter 8 shifts from Ovidian poetics and the Augustan age to Senecan tragedy and the late Julio-Claudian period. Bill Gladhill discusses the pervasive influence of *Aeneid* 6 on Seneca's *Hercules Furens*, *Phaedra*, and *Oedipus*. Vergil provides an elaborate and sophisticated vision of the underworld that Seneca could activate at every register of language and narrative. *Aeneid* 6 impregnates Senecan tragedy with a profound dramatic experience, which absorbs the dark and haunting milieu of Vergil's hell.

Vergil's underworld continues to expand in chapter 9, where Fabio Stok contextualizes Servius' references to Lucretius in his interpretation of Vergil's list of sinners and punishments in Tartarus. In Stok's view, Servius positions his Lucretian reading of *Aeneid* 6 in relation to Neoplatonic sources. Stok then situates Vergil's punishment of sinners within a broader Christianizing exegetical tradition, including Ambrose, Augustine, and Paulinus of Nola, suggesting that Servius, too, had an audience that included Christians in mind when he composed his commentary on Vergil.

From Tartarus the volume shifts to Elysium. In chapter 10 Lauren Curtis brings the collection back into an Augustan context, arguing that the chorus of boys and girls in Horace's *Carmen Saeculare* is modelled on the Elysian chorus of *Aeneid* 6. Curtis argues that "by harnessing the pragmatic potential of lyric song ... in the context of Rome's ritual renovation, the children's choral voice in the *CS* can be described as 'foundational' in a way that is very different from, but closely in dialogue with, the paeans of Vergil's underworld." Essentially, Horace builds Vergil's Elysian chorus into his own choral performance in the *Carmen Saeculare*, in order to reappropriate the Roman reception of Greek *choreia* from epic back into lyric.

In chapter 11 Emily Gowers discusses the relationship between *Aeneid* 6 and the pre-existing epic tradition, investigating Homer's absence from Vergil's Elysium. Gowers finds that the representations of time, temporal cycles, and reincarnation in *Aeneid* 6 displace previous epic notions of metempsychosis, highlighting a deep awareness on Vergil's part of Ennian chronology in the *Annales*.

In chapter 12 Jacob Mackey argues that Monnica and Augustine's contemplation of the saints in *Confessions* 9 is closely modelled on Aeneas' and Anchises' viewing of the parade of Roman souls in *Aeneid* 6, but filtered directly through Plotinus. In effect, Augustine displaces *Aeneid* 6 by substituting for Anchises' cosmological, psychological, and eschatological speech a Latin translation of Plotinus' *Enneads*. In Mackey's reading Augustine exemplifies a profound moment in the reception of *Aeneid* 6 in which the receptions of Vergil and Plato merge within a Christianized context.

In chapter 13, the final one in this collection, Grant Parker brings us to the Gates of Sleep at the end of *Aeneid* 6. Parker illustrates the various scholarly approaches to the famous conundrum of the Gate of Ivory in order to explore the particular philology of spiritualist receptions of *Aeneid* 6 by W.F. Jackson Knight and T.J. Haarhoff.

This introduction, along with the papers in the volume, are cumulative acts of scholarly engagement, in which each contributor has read *Aeneid* 6 through the lens of Ovid, Augustine, Shelley, or others in iterative and reflective processes of analysis and assessment. Receptions flow from these cumulative acts of reading and interpretation. The iterative process of analysis has resulted in a punctual, perfective moment of reception. The recognition of Seneca's incorporation of Vergil in his tragedies changes how we read Seneca (and Vergil). In the same way, Ovid is no longer simply Ovid. Augustine is no longer simply Augustine. But Ovidian reception *is* fundamentally different than Augustinian reception. Each work is changed through the recognition of reception. But this recognition is not an inert process; it is formed through a bewildering number of possible interpretive acts, which are themselves implicated in an equally bewildering number of social, cultural, and historical contingencies, what Charles Martindale describes as "interpretations of ancient texts … constructed by the chain of receptions through which their continued readability has been effected."[11] This is to say nothing of the role of serendipity and intuition in the exploration of reception. Ultimately, this "chain of reception" is part of the joy and pleasure of interpretation.

Eight chapters in the volume focus on the reception of *Aeneid* 6 by Roman poets. This tradition, from Vergil's inclusion of prior literature through to Statius's reception of *Aeneid* 6, reflects a deep *literary* engagement with Greek and Roman texts. Roman poets were in an intense intertextual engagement with Vergil's underworld. But outside of Horace's choral *Carmen Saeculare,* which effectively merges Augustus' Rome with Vergil's Elysium, the interactions within the poetic tradition largely remained a function of textuality. While this Roman tradition often displays a complex literary engagement with *Aeneid* 6, it often uses Vergil's underworld to interface with the power of the emperor and the imperial family. So, Horace's *Carmen Saeculare* imbues the rituals of the Augustan *saeculum* with the Elysian imprimatur of *Aeneid* 6, while Senecan tragedy encodes the Julio-Claudians with a powerfully Tartarean charge. Each work emphasizes in its own way the continual and sustained influence of *Aeneid* 6 on Roman literature, yet there is no evidence within this tradition that *Aeneid* 6 became "spiritual." The five remaining chapters focus on prose authors from late antiquity to the twentieth century. These chapters represent a marked reorientation of the meaning and influence of *Aeneid* 6. As the collection moves into late antiquity, the Renaissance, and the modern period,

Aeneid 6 is situated within a broader complex of religious and metaphysical discourses, including reflective and spiritualist receptions of Vergil's underworld. *Aeneid* 6 becomes part of broader debates among Christians and Neoplatonists. One can see the continued development of this more spiritually charged interpretation of Vergil's underworld in the works of Shelley and Jackson Knight, whose receptions undergo more personal and romantic distillations and impressions. This mode of reception is still active in the works of Heaney and in The National September 11 Memorial. The reasons for this development will become poignantly clear in the course of the volume. There are still many empty spaces in this tradition that have yet to be filled *hoc opus, hic labor est*. It is understood that this volume both is a study of reception and a product of reception. In five hundred years, scholars and intellectual historians may wonder why at the turn of the second millennium *Aeneid* 6 was in the air. There is no way for any of us now to know what might be said of Vergil or of us at that time, or what broad currents of history, religion, and culture might give coherence to the historian or critic of literature. What is clear is that *Aeneid* 6 continues to resonate at a deep level, and we are still only beginning to ask why.

NOTES

1 Miguel Herrero de Jáuregui was unable to present his paper at the symposium, while Alessandro Barchiesi gave his paper near the antro itself.

2 Two invited speakers, Philip Hardie ("Some Early Modern Afterlives of the Vergilian Underworld") and Joseph Farrell ("Reading the Vergilian Underworld through Dante and Homer"), did address *Aeneid* 6 and its relationship to Dante and the broader epic tradition. While Dante, among other Renaissance and early modern authors, was notably absent in the abstracts, several such authors, including Dante, are treated by Soranzo and Kilgour in this volume. Nor does the paucity of abstracts on these topics suggest an absence in scholarship. Witness, to take one recent example, *The Virgil Encyclopedia* (published in 2014, itself a massive tome of continued Vergilian influence and reception) which has 250 entries on ancient, medieval, and Renaissance receptions, along with another 174 on early modern and modern receptions (notably, Melville is absent). On *Moby-Dick; or The Whale* and its reception of classical underworlds, see the excellent study of Treichel 2009. The work of Vergilian reception in this tradition is vast and it can hardly be addressed adequately in any cursory or summarizing way.

3 See Pandey 2014, which was the lone paper at the conference that engaged directly with Vergil and intermediality.

4 For Heaney's engagements with *Aeneid* 6 throughout his career, see Hardie 2014: 46–9; Heaney's introduction to his 2016 translation; Ware 2018.

5 https://www.911memorial.org/design-competition.

6 https://www.911memorial.org/design-competition.

7 See Ware 2018 on Heaney's translation of Vergil's Daedalus into Joyce's Dedalus and its broader implications.

8 For the complexities of The National September 11 Memorial & Museum's engagements with Vergil, see Alexander 2011; Dunlap 2014; Pandey 2017: 24–5.

9 See especially Comparetti 1895; Fagiolo and Luchinat 1981; Suerbaum 1981 and 2008; Macdonald 1987; Kallendorf 1989, 2007a, and 2007b; Jacoff and Schnapp 1991; Hardie 1993, 2012 and 2014; Martindale 1993 and 1997; Spence 2001; Thomas 2001; Heil 2002; Rees 2004; Hinds 2005; Martindale and Thomas 2006; Graziosi and Greenwood 2007; Carver 2007; Ford 2007; Hardwick and Stray 2007; Ossa-Richardson 2008; Caruso and Laird 2009; Ziolkowski and Putnam 2008; Farrell and Putnam 2010; Grafton, Most and Settis 2010; Wilson-Okamura 2010; *Classical Receptions Journal*; *International Journal of the Classical Tradition*.

10 www.niklasholzberg.com/Homepage/Bibliographien.html. See also www.virgil.org/bibliography/.

11 Martindale 1993: 7.

1

Into the Woods (*Via Cuma 320, Bacoli*)

ALESSANDRO BARCHIESI

I.

This will be a very embodied kind of paper. It shows traces of its informal performed version, an unfinished and rough feel for which I apologize, and this is a reason why I have included the street address of the location after the title: the Villa Vergiliana at Cuma. The paper only exists because it was written for and performed in Cuma(e). But even more influential on the paper was the idea by Bill Gladhill:[1] instead of having delivering my paper on the premises of the Villa, we walked out, on a balmy evening in late June 2013, and went to the Sibyl's cave. My paper was performed in front of the gaping space, with its tunnel, and we could see and smell the overgrown area all around, and hear the rustling of foliage and see the wood getting darker and darker. When I finished it was even clearer that we were surrounded by what remains of an ancient forest, or maybe the ghost of it: and this is actually what this paper will talk about, the natural space between the citadel of Cumae and Lake Avernus, and Aeneas in the woods. But let me add a few words about the landscape as it is today.

The recent police discovery that the *camorra,* the organization of crime and drugs in the territory of Naples and Caserta, de facto controls and exploits Lake Avernus has added a different shade of dark to the history of this surprising place. (There is a relevant video on YouTube entitled "Casalesi: sequestrato il lago d'Averno" [https://www.youtube.com/watch?v=NUbCmXVZZQ] where everybody is wearing black ski masks: this is because they are special agents, not narcos.) It is darkness without romanticism, as people who know the *camorra* or at least the harrowing book *Gomorra* by Roberto Saviano can confirm On the other hand, a dark romanticism has been promoted by the *Aeneid* and has created a lasting fame around Lake Avernus and the strange place that Vergil calls Cumae. We could choose many nodes in this tradition, but it is best to start from the early twentieth century and then work our way back. J.G. Frazer's *Golden Bough* was a title designed to connect with the whole Classical/Romantic tradition, illustrated by J.M.W. Turner's *Golden Bough,* with the intention of following as a *fil rouge* the mysterious ritual of the King of the Wood at Lake Nemi, and of later getting lost in a worldwide maze of stories and rituals. This is an example of the lyric style of the very fi st pages, before Frazer launches into his campaign for a universal library of myths and rituals (Frazer, *The Golden Bough,* 1922, 1.9–10):

His eyes probably acquired that restless, watchful look which, among the Esquimaux of Bering Strait, is said to betray infallibly the shedder of blood; for with that people revenge is a sacred duty, and the manslayer carries his life in his hand. To gentle and pious pilgrims at the shrine the sight of him might well seem to darken the fair landscape, as when a cloud suddenly blots the sun on a bright day. The dreamy blue of Italian skies, the dappled shade of summer woods, and the sparkle of waves in the sun, can have accorded but ill with that stern and sinister figur . Rather we picture to ourselves the scene as it may have been witnessed by a belated wayfarer on one of those wild autumn nights when the dead leaves are falling thick, and the winds seem to sing the dirge of the dying year. It is a sombre picture, set to melancholy music – the background of forest showing black and jagged against a lowering and stormy sky, the sighing of the wind in the branches, the rustle of the withered leaves under foot, the lapping of the cold water on the shore, and in the foreground, pacing to and fro, now in twilight and now in gloom, a dark figure with a glitter of steel at the shoulder whenever the pale moon, riding clear of the cloud-rack, peers down at him through the matted boughs.

Conveniently for someone who started writing in late nineteenth-century Cambridge, the connection between Avernus and Nemi is underwritten by the visual art of Turner, who had dedicated twin paintings to the two *nemora.* But what matters in this extract is not only Turner, it is Vergil's Avernus forest too.[2] At a crucial juncture of his project Frazer establishes the setting at Nemi with the help of Turner (a painter who was already in a complex negotiation with Avernus).[3] Then with the help of Vergil's Avernus he "dims the lights," a fade to black – the final goal, as you know, is to enable his reader to see not only Avernus in Nemi, but even the Eskimo blade runner in a Classical Italian setting. Precisely when we think that he is being quintessentially Romantic, Frazer actually turns to Vergil: Vergil's *Aeneid,* working in dialogue with Turner's painting, provides him with an antidote to typical sunny and bountiful imaginations of Italy in the Grand Tour, a reinvention of Italy as a heart of darkness, instead of Turner's much-admired "golden glow" of the Italian landscape ("golden glow" is Frazer's own definition of Turner's Avernus at the incipit of his long work).

What can we say about the origins and significance of this imagination of the place? Well, it is very woodsy, so let me start from a point made by Philip Hardie about forests in the *Aeneid* (Hardie 1994: 141 on *Aen.* 9.381–3):

An ecphrasis of a forest, one of the many scenes in the *Aeneid* set amidst dark woods, which constantly hover on the edge of becoming *selva oscura*. Woods are places of perplexity and error … the habitations of the numinous and monstrous … the locus for primitivism hard or soft, for hunting … and for regression … associated with journeys into the Underworld. They may also be places of privileged return to the past, of reintegration … Here the dark spaces of the *fallax silua* (392) are the setting for a failure of reason … and perhaps also symbolize the return of Euryalus and Nisus from the world of war to the adolescent world of the hunt, under the sign of Diana.

Hardie is focusing on the episode of Euryalus and Nisus in Book 9, but he broadens the discussion[4] to the significance of forests in the *Aeneid*. This is the art of commentary at its best, but David West thought otherwise. In his famous and explicitly titled Presidential Address to the Classical Association of England, *Cast Out Theory* (1995), West singled out this passage to exemplify the excessively theoretical jargon, which was changing, he claimed, the healthy empirical nature of Anglo-Saxon classical scholarship, and had been generated by deference to the model of French anthropology and structuralism. It is no metaphor to say that West wanted to see the trees not the forest: I shall explain later that my own view of the *Aeneid* is closer to the approach of Philip Hardie, who apparently privileges the forest over the trees.

Now if we accept some measure of generalization, and if we take seriously the presence of dark woods (and I could also mention mountains, gorges, and caves), we begin to realize that there is a fundamental difference between the *Aeneid* and Homeric landscapes. The constant presence of landscape features that are wild and impenetrable is not a feature of Homeric war narrative, nor of course is it common in the Ithacan half of the *Odyssey*, while even during the travels of Odysseus very exotic and unexplored locations do not regularly look like a *fluuius opacus* (7.36) or *iuga longa … solorum nemorum* (11.545) or *tenebrae ramorum* (9.384) or a *silua … horrida* (9.381–2) or a *densis frondibus atrum … latus* (11.523–4) or a place surrounded and enclosed by *arboribus … atque horrentibus umbris* (1.311) or a *siluam immensam* (6.186). (I do not need to recall here the narratological aspect: for the narrator and the audience, all those woods and mountainsides and shadowy rivers and dark branches are present in the story while they are being focalized by characters who are in a recurring state of emotional tension, and this subjectivity heightens the pathos.)

In Homer, Circe of course lives in a densely shaded and mysterious wood, mentioned as "wood" but not described and only briefly focalized (*Od.* 10.150 and 197: "the thick brush and the wood"; 10.210: "the house of Circe in the forest glades"; 10.275: "through the sacred glades"; 10.308: "through the forested island"), but the other scenes in Odysseus' travelogue are rather short on focalized wild places. Often, we wonder what to do with our modern perception of "wild" while reading Homer: the exotic in the *Odyssey* has strong connotations of productivity and fertility. Calypso has an exotic orchard in the island at the edges of the earth (5.63–75), so pleasant to be irresistible to viewers (cave, luxuriant grove, alder, poplar, sweet-smelling cypress, birds, garden vine with grape, flowery meadow with violets and celery), and the Phaeacians proudly sport an orchard (7.112–32), another object of marvel, enclosed, luxuriant, full of fruit, and a vineyard, all in constant bloom and productivity; the Cyclopes do not practise agriculture (9.105–20), but theirs is a bountiful landscape, not only made of caves and crags, but endowed with spontaneous wheat and barley and wine, not to mention flocks and cheese; the Laestrygonians are cannibals, but they have a *polis,* as well as plazas, a harbour, fountains, and a lumber trade (10.103–16): in fact, one of the horrors of the situation is that before getting to the money shot of the story we see their smooth road and wagons and a girl collecting water from a fountain, not really the stuff of a *Texas Chainsaw* atmosphere; the Cimmerians, who look so promising even by their name, have a *demos,* a *polis,* and tons of mist, but no wilderness, or perhaps we don't get to see it (11.13–15). The only description in the *Odyssey* that would satisfy our Roman poetics of wilderness is the flashback about hunting in the Parnassus in the Eurykleia episode. But even there the place is just remote rather than alien or frightening (see *Od.* 18.428 ff.), a place where it is interesting to ask, why do we encounter wilderness precisely in this not very outlandish context? Because in that juvenile episode the hero Odysseus for the only time in this epic is physically penetrated by an aggression?[5] The *Odyssey* gives a great impulse to the epic tradition of landscape ecphrasis (Hoelscher 1988), but the element of mystery and primitivism is not exactly the main key there. It is also significant that where we do have an important tradition of surviving pictorial landscapes in Rome, precisely in the area of *Odyssey* illustration and in the age of Vergil, there is certainly no comparable emphasis on mystery and danger: the conventional label "idyllic-sacral" landscapes does indeed point to aspects that are shared with the sense of place typical of the *Aeneid,* like the incorporation of man-made but obsolete buildings into nature and the reference to the sacred, but there is no comparable interest in *selva oscura* and rugged mountains. Nor does the inclusion of small-scale herdsmen in the landscapes truly create an atmosphere of sinister mystery. The *Odyssey* frieze should not be forgotten in this discussion, since after all for us it is the earliest extant example of landscape painting in the Western tradition, and it is true that the picture of the Cimmerian land is less misty than in Homer: but it is hard to find a specific connection to the Vergilian Avernus.

II.

The general difference vis-à-vis Homer's text holds true even in the case of Vergil's Avernus, where we have a potential model in the *Odyssey* that is indeed dark and remote, for who would not agree that the land of the Cimmerians is such a place? When Circe begins her instructions to the hero at the end of Book 10, we seem to hear notes of promising mystery – a travel across the Ocean, the groves of Persephone (508–9), the dank house of Hades and the crossing of two infernal streams; yet the topographical detail is not accompanied by notes of wilderness: "tall poplars, and willows that shed their fruit" is all we hear about, no "*selva oscura*" motif, and when we get to the fi st-person account at the start of Book 11, even the trees are absent. We are lost in the mist and fog, and the place is quite simply "the *demos* and *polis* of Cimmerian men," covered in mist and cloud, and a dock for the visit to the underworld (*Od.* 11.14–15). No wonder few scholars have tried to identify the Cimmerians (with one influential exception in antiquity, on which more below). They appear as the quintessential people of the far north and west as seen by the Greeks, and the story does not embrace the opportunity of a dark, primeval, and mysterious forest.

Now a dark, primeval, and mysterious forest is precisely what the Trojans encounter in the Cumae and Avernus area.[6] This is indeed how the prophet Helenus had announced the place back in 3.442: *diuinosque lacus et Auerna sonantia siluis*. The scene, which forms the prologue to the underworld exploration, is important inter alia because this is indeed (with the exception of a short encounter at 3.521–47) the fi st Italian place visited by the Trojans after their difficult quest.[7] At the start of Book 6 they disembark full of enthusiasm and plunge into forests that are the haunts of wild beasts (6.5–8). In a short while they will meet the very civilized Euboean colony of Cumae and its lavishly decorated temple of Apollo, but for now we have a fi st contact with what will turn out to be the forest of Avernus. I do not have time to discuss the entire episode, but I want to focus on its dynamics, which have been well analysed by Ray Clark, one of the key figures in the history of the Vergilian Society (note especially Clark 1992).[8] The visit of Aeneas to Cumae starts from a highland, with a sacred grove and sanctuary, dynamically followed by a descending pattern: from a Cumaean, Hellenized, Apolline acropolis down to an underground chamber then down into a "katabatic, chthonian forest" and *bois sacré,* down to lake Avernus, then to a cave, a fissure in the ground, the throat of Dis, the vertical entrance to Hell. (And Hades from now on will have of course its own forests and lakes, partly similar, partly different.) More generally, *terris iactatus et alto* in the prooemium of the *Aeneid* (1.3), with that striking syllepsis, hints at a significant innovation in the poem. Some of the maritime dangers and labours in the *Odyssey* and the *Argonautica* tend to become land peripeties in Vergil,[9] and the Avernus episode is one of them. This is per se a new imagination of Avernus and *katabasis,* the new equivalent of the "water obstacles" in the marine setting of the Odyssean entrance to the underworld.

The best way for us to approach imaginations of the underworld outside literature is to look at the so-called Orphic Tablets or golden leaves,[10] and they as a rule do not mention any forest or rough landscape – only an isolated tree perhaps as a point of reference, the odd willow or elm (e.g., Edmonds 2010). There is no sense that approaching the underworld means crossing a wild place in those Greek texts or rituals. Even the surviving Greek poet who has the strongest credentials as a narrator of travels in wild lands and exotic landscapes, Apollonius Rhodius, has not contributed to Vergil something like the Avernus forest. On one occasion, in *Arg.* 2, the Argonauts approach a place that is in fact an entrance to the netherworld, the Acherusian headland (728–51). The place is promising for our discussion because on the one hand it is associated with Hades, on the other it has a place in important Greek colonization traditions in the Black Sea, and in this context the episode has been well discussed, especially by William Thalmann (2011). The link with colonization narratives is also important, as we shall see, for the *Aeneid* and its approach to Italy. Now in this Hellenistic and Ptolemaic epic the whole vision of the land offers nothing like a wild trackless forest: Apollonius only has a couple of words for a glen covered by rocks and *hyle* (2.736), and a naturalistic indication of some tall plane trees (2.733), but his entire description concentrates on a different and very original kind of horror. The sublime horror of the place is about sound and wind, acoustic and tactile reaction; what we experience is wind and cold vapour and din and sea waves crashing and underground winds, and the abyss of the Acheron River. Of course a poet like Apollonius is perfectly aware of the possibilities of a topothesia of wilderness when combined with colonization narratives, and the narrator hastens to add that the river mouth of the Acheron is, rather unexpectedly, celebrated by the Greek settlers heading from Megara into the land of the barbarian Mariandyni as the saviour of sailors, *Soonautes* (2.746 ff.): so the wild and sublime place has been at some point converted and domesticated from menace to accomplice in a typical story of colonization. But even here, as in the *Odyssey*, like in so many Greek representations of nature, we see the tree, not the forest.[11]

I am no professor of creative writing but, by the way, if you care for my advice, once you know you have the intention of describing emotional *selva oscura*, you had better stay away from botanic species, and even from naming trees, and keep descriptive language under control. A willow, a tall plane tree, two oaks: those specifics inevitably destroy the intended effect of my - tery and identity loss, and make the atmosphere descriptive and controlled. If you need emotion, just follow Vergil's forest path and use *tenebrae ramorum, fallax silua, luce maligna,* and the like. Even Ovid's influential *incaedua silua* (*Am.* 3.1.1; *Fast.* 1.213) is a tad too technical to have the same impact, and his *lucus … niger ilicis umbra* (*Fast.* 3.295) is pictorial, but not mysterious and emotional in the Vergilian way: it is *niger*, not *ater*. Apollonius, who is a powerful influence on Vergil and has so many things to say about a hero who goes to visit wild places and approaches Hekate in a foreign setting, has nothing comparable when Jason and Medea find their way to what may be thought of as the Argonautic equivalent of the Golden Bough, the Golden Fleece protected by the dragon of Ares: all we see is a "path to a sacred wood" (4.123–4), then a "huge oak" (ibid.), and when they are done they leave the "very shaded grove" (4.167). We are far from Vergil's *lacu nigro nemorumque tenebris* (6.238) or from the *lucus* enclosed by *obscuris … conuallibus umbrae* (6.139).

In any case, up to now we have established the importance of the Vergilian redefinition of Cumae-cum-Avernus: a katabatic forest followed by a chthonian forest, and the whole geography unified by an emotional undercurrent. Now we should examine this construction step by step. First, Vergil's underworld is equipped with a Sibyl: a Sibyl who, as many have realized, was perhaps never really at Cumae, and in any case is a product of memory and local legend. If we want to understand the Vergilian Sibyl, as Damien Nelis (2004) has stressed, it is fundamental that she combines the roles of a priestess of Apollo, as in the Sibylline oracles tradition, and of a priestess of Hecate, as chiefly Medea in Colchis. Only this double-faced situation makes sense of what happens in Book 6, where she plays a pivotal role in shifting from prophet to scout, while Aeneas shifts from oracle customer to a sort of initiate: fi st she predicts the future, then she becomes the guide for Avernus and the underworld.

At this point, in spite of the riddling tradition of oracles, the Sibyl describes the underworld very clearly in terms of space, although the clarity of the explanation does not destroy the dark horror of the itinerary (6.131–2): *tenent media omnia siluae | Cocytusque sinu labens circumuenit atro,* a situation well explained by Clark (1992: 169): "the pathless forest is or begins in the upper world." At 6.8 the Trojans had been confronted with undefined *siluae,* the haunts of wild beasts (this being, as I stressed, their fi st contact with the land and the landscape of Italy); at 6.13 we learn about the Sibyl in Trivia's grove, and this initially looks like a typical, domesticated *lucus* surrounding a sanctuary. But if we pause for reflection Trivia is already suggesting a chthonic place, not the expected Apolline sacred enclosure, as the Delphic tradition would seem to suggest. Then the Sibyl appears and she is the priestess of Apollo and Trivia (6.35: one might have expected Diana), and Aeneas initially invokes Apollo (6.56), but later promises a marble temple for Apollo and Trivia (6.69) as well as a future for the Sibyl in the Trojan colony in Latium; a second speech by Aeneas, however, entirely focuses on entering the underworld, and here he mentions the fact that the Cumaean Sibyl has been appointed by Hecate (which clarifies the previous references to Trivia) to oversee the Avernus forest (6.118: *te ... lucis Hecate praefecit Avernis),* and asks for admission to Hades.

The text emphasizes that Aeneas must find his way in the wood without direct guidance from the Sibyl. When he finally gets to the Golden Bough the situation is, as Conington 1876 *ad loc.* puts it, "as if the whole forest conspired to hide it" (cf. 6.188: *nemore in tanto*). So the fi st important point is that Aeneas is an explorer while he approaches the task of a *katabasis;* this is rather different from Odysseus, who just uses the land of the Cimmerians as a "dock" to the underworld. Even within the underworld, the narrative is rich in natural details that appear to be a continuation of the dark, wild landscape above: muddy, eddying waters from the deep (6.296–7), Charon walking *per tacitum nemus* (6.386), a slippery riverbank with pale grass (6.416), the *silua ... magna* where Dido wanders around (6.451). Only as we progress towards the Elysian fields we find a less wild nature, and the choice seems to be between two urban settings: a bifurcation between a grim city of punishment (6.540 ff.) and the *amoena uirecta | fortunatorum nemorum* (6.638–9), the gymnasia and Campus Martius of the more fortunate souls.

III.

Part of this tradition will eventually lead to Dante, but in the *Commedia* the *selva oscura* is detached from any earthly location, abstract in its physical appearance, and strongly allegorical. This is not exactly the poetics of wilderness in Vergil. The very fi st activity that engages the Trojans on Italian land (6.176–82) is *deforestation*: the occasion is typical of epic

(6.179 *itur in antiquam siluam*; see Hinds 1998: 11–14 for the metapoetics in this moment), a grand funeral for a fallen comrade, but the preparations for the pyre of Misenus occur in a very peculiar kind of forest. It could be termed, as we saw, a katabatic forest. Building on Servius and Silius Italicus, Matthew Leigh (2010) has brilliantly shown that the intervention of the Trojans on wild nature is the anticipation of the domestication of the Avernus area by Agrippa, as a preparation to the war against Sextus Pompey. Significantl , no such action is recorded by Vergil when the Trojans are on Greek or African land – modification and taming of wild and even hellish landscape is their approach to Italy, as opposed to other colonial encounters they have experienced. Strabo's account, an Augustan account, is perfect if we want to understand the contrast (Strabo 5.4.5, tr. Roller 2014):

> Aornos is encircled by steep brows that rise up on all sides except where one sails in. *Today* these have been laboriously cultivated, although *formerly* they were thickly shaded by a wild and impassable forest of large trees, which, because of superstition, made the gulf shadowy … such are the stories told before our time, *but now* the forest around Aornos has been cut down by Agrippa and the land has been built on, the underground passageway has been cut from Aornos as far as Kyme.

Duane Roller's translation "because of superstition" is slightly odd, but it helps focus on the fusion between landscape and religious horror: this is what Silius means in his astonishing episode where Hannibal wants to see Avernus, *Pun.* 12.125: *religione sacer saeuum retinebat honorem.* The "superstition" protects the place from human intervention, and this in turn makes the wood even wilder as time passes. The contrast between the deep past and the present is a contrast between a religiously (*kata deisidaimonian*) wild forest and the imperial intervention of Agrippa, taming the wilderness, cutting passages, setting the stage for cultivation, the economy (cf. Lake Lucrinus, "Lake Profit") and the navy (cf. Verg. *Georg.* 2.161–4). This being Strabo, we expect that the deep past, the "former landscape," might coincide with the authority of Homer, and we will not be disappointed, as I discuss in the next section.

In Vergil, then, the landscape of the Ploutonion is a forest, the pathless forest that begins in the upper world, leads to the underworld, and is an obstacle that needs to be explored and tamed. Aeneas, who is consulting the oracle in the guise of a typical Greek settler, is also an explorer, not only a typical *theoros* who consults an oracle. He must find his way in the wood, without direct guidance from the Sibyl. He is an explorer of a new land while he performs a *katabasis*. In Dante, the *selva oscura* is abstract and strongly allegorical – but in Vergil we have strong pointers towards a realistic geography, precisely when we encounter mystery and wilderness, and the search for a magical device. (Dante in fact separates the two strands, the pathless forest and the search for a talisman: the pathless forest is the place of error in *Inferno* 1, while the Golden Bough surfaces in *Purgatorio* 1 as the supernatural reed, in a landscape that does not look like a forest at all.) The contrast is not quite different from the effect of the fi st landing in Latium (Jenkyns 1998: 469–70 on 7.25–36: *ingentem ex aequore lucum ... fluuio succedit opaco*), where the territory ahead is experienced as *terra incognita* precisely when the plot of the *Aeneid* approaches its most familiar location, "one of the most busy and populous spots in all Italy" (one should add a "façade maritime"[12] and a trade hub). We may want to contrast, for various reasons, the arrival at the Phasis in Apollonius, *Arg.* 2.1260 ff.: "they rowed into the great stream of the river ... on their left was ...": there we have visibility as if in a map, then a "thick marsh" where the heroes anchor, then "hide out of sight in the dense reeds" (3.6), but again we gather very little sense that this is a dark, mysterious terra incognita, and there is no reference to taming or transforming the landscape. The emphasis on transformative work in Vergil is implicitly confirmed at the end of the book,[13] where the final action of Aeneas is written: *ille uiam secat ad nauis sociosque reuisit. | tum se ad Caietae recto fert limite portum* ("he cuts the road to the ships and reconnects with his companions. Then, in a straight line, he travels to the harbour of Caieta," 6.899–900) and where the language used makes us wonder whether the movement is only traversing the landscape or else creating connections and links (*uiam secat, recto ... limite*).

Finally, when Aeneas crosses over and down to the underworld we find an extraordinary moment: the walk into Hell[14] is "like" walking in a dark forest, so that what was previously the narrative instantly becomes simile once Aeneas has entered the sylvan threshold of Hell (6.268–72):

> ibant obscuri sola sub nocte per umbram
> perque domos Ditis uacuas et inania regna:
> quale per incertam lunam sub luce maligna
> est iter in siluis, ubi caelum condidit umbra
> Iuppiter, et rebus nox abstulit atra colorem.

In the shadow they walked, through the darkness, under a solitary night, and through the empty home of Dis and the hollow kingdom: just as under a failing light, with a dim moon, we travel in the woods, once Jupiter has covered the sky in shadows, and black night has removed the colour of things.

It is here that we have an anticipation of Frazer's anthropological wood (section 1, above). The extraordinary experience of walking into the netherworld is accompanied by one exceptional innovation in the highly codified tradition of epic narrative:[15] the simile, which by definition should import into the narrative an outside field often a natural field (wild, or georgic), a strategy which operates through analogy but also difference, is just for once directly relevant to the story world, and almost a prolongation of the previous narrative: seriously, we do not know where we are anymore. They were hiking in a forest in a dusk, and now "it is like when one walks through a forest at night." Our world or the other world? Narrative or simile? Precisely at the transition between Avernus as a terrestrial place and Avernus as a supernatural, or rather infranatural, space, we lose the stable boundary between narrated action and simile: "just like when (subject? somebody, or we) walk into a forest at dusk, and every colour is fading away." On the way back, we will find the Gate of Dream .

The forest landscape in the *Aeneid* is endowed with emotional undertones that resonate with the idea of a native resistance – an idea with a powerful future in Rome's expanding frontiers, be it Caligula's Germanic charades or the army camp at Vindolanda (in both situations, we know about people who quoted or adapted the *Aeneid*). This is not simply romanticism or emotional fallacy: the mesh between the narrative and the treatment of landscape is a very intense one. We are so used to colonial narratives and to European descriptions of the new world that we sometimes fail to recognize the uncommon originality of this aspect of Vergilian epic. Italy is at the same time early and primitive, and wild and new: both approaches are not entirely natural within the epic tradition, and they can be intensified respectively by the antiquarian approach (the "Rome before Rome" idea) and by narrative focalization on the Trojan settlers, whenever they are allowed to dictate the rules of engagement between humans and landscape.

Just a final (truly final) word about Aeneas. His recurring contact with wilderness and forests and *luci* is a marked feature of the *Aeneid*, as we saw: he has even been constructed as a King of the Wood (Dyson 2001). Is this related to his destiny and very special end? "The Laurentine wilderness," writes Nicholas Purcell (1998: 10), "was a setting for uncanny events such as the disappearance of Aeneas: the shrine that recorded this was at the heart of the landscape of fen and forest on the banks of the Numicus below Lavinium." The recent (2017) re-opening of the sacred area at Lavinium is oriented on a rediscovery of hoary hero-cults, looking back at a misty cult of Aeneas in sixth-century BCE Latium: this is important, but one is also interested in the revamping of the Lavinium area in the generation of Vergil and Augustus: a recuperation of *lucus*, wilderness, and hero-cult. *Lucus* and wilderness are not synonyms, but Purcell shows how the two are connected in the Lavinium area. In his n. 49 he mentions the disappearance of Aeneas as it is featured in the elogium from Pompeii (ILS 63): in a text certainly representative of the official elogium of Aeneas in the Forum Augustum, Aeneas vanishes "in a Laurentine war or on Laurentine soil" (Purcell 1998: n. 49). Now the new reconstruction of the elogium of Aeneas in the Forum Augustum by Jonathan Edmondson (forthcoming) makes it likely that the standard text – a text likely to be connected with the *Aeneid*, and made to be frequently replicated throughout the empire of Octavian – actually read *in luco Laurenti subito non comparuit*. Aeneas has an end, and a future cult, in a grove.

IV.

Such are the stories told before our time, but now the forest around Aornos has been cut down by Agrippa and the land has been built on, the underground passageway has been cut from Aornos as far as Kyme, and everything has been shown to be a myth, although the Cocceius who made the tunnel there … rather understood the story just told about the Kimmerians, and perhaps he believed that it was an ancestral custom at this place for roads to be tunnelled.

(Strabo 5.4.6, tr. Roller 2014)

But it is not over yet with Strabo and Vergil. The other interesting aspect is that Strabo brings us into two opposite approaches to the Campanian landscape, the primitive and the modern, and that both interact with the text of the *Aeneid*.

Lucius Cocceius Auctus we know from epigraphic sources and has made a mark on histories of Roman engineering;[16] he certainly was no Homeric scholar. A *libertus* in charge of many works about 38–35 BCE, he operates under Agrippa during the war effort against Sextus Pompey: the Cumaean Peninsula, Misenum, the water system of Lucrinus and Avernus are redesigned, in a process that turns the western Bay of Naples into the main port for the Roman navy (cf. Verg. *Georg*. 2.161–4), and transforms a couple of suggestively named water basins, "Lake Profit and "Lake Hell." Paradoxically, perhaps not without irony, Strabo (above) saw the technician Cocceius as reinstating the romance of the Cumaean landscape: tunnels and underground passages are bringing back a Cimmerian past. But even irony may be a false impression: the landscape where Cocceius and Vergil were busy, each in their own way, is by now inseparable from the memory of the

Odyssey, and this is not purely a literary or scholarly matter: it has to do with identity and prestige.

In fact, the *laudes Italiae* in the *Georgics* offer already a full template of a certain encounter between the romance of engineering and the waterworks at hell's gate (2.161–4, trans. Fairclough 1999):

an memorem portus Lucrinoque addita claustra
atque indignatum magnis stridoribus aequor,
Iulia qua ponto longe sonat unda refuso
Tyrrhenusque fretis immittitur aestus Auernis?

Shall I tell of her harbours, and the barrier thrown across the Lucrine, and how Ocean clamours aloud in anger, where the Julian waters echo afar as the sea is flung back, and the Tyrrhenian tide pours into the channels of Avernus?

The traditional landscape of Lake Profit and Lake Hell, Lucrinus and Avernus, is now enriched with a new body of water boldly designated *Iulia unda* – a paradox, since a Roman magistrate could at a maximum attach his name to an aqueduct or fountain or haven, and Octavian will of course go further in this direction, as in Aqua Augusta, or in Portus Iulius, but now the name of Octavian is paradoxically inscribed on the water of the new military harbours. The new harbour work now is ready for explicit competition with Alexandria,[17] the rival capital boasting her famous twin harbours (and *portus* must be a real plural at 2.161): whether you like the breakthrough or not depends on how you react to the alarming confusion of Tyrrhenian tide and Avernus overflow (2.164). Is the sea now, thanks to Julian innovation, blended with the underworld?

There is in fact another crucial contribution made by Strabo to our "forest-and-underworld" problem. Right after mentioning the deforestation at Aornos and the sulphuric and infernal atmosphere of the Ploutonion, the Stygian and Acherusian waters, and before getting to the tunnels of Cocceius, the geographer wheels in the crucial text of Ephoros (Strab. 5.4.5; Ephoros fr. 134A). According to this fourth century historian, the Odyssean underworld must be located around Avernus, because this is where the mysterious race of the Cimmerians used to live. Cimmerians: mysterious people of cave dwellers, living in subterranean dwellings connected by a network of tunnels, working the mines, welcoming strangers to an underground oracle, abhorring the sun, and emerging only at night. All is lost now, except the oracle that has been moved elsewhere: they were destroyed by a certain king, unsatisfied with their underground oracle .

Now we begin to see the whole picture – the landscape of Cumae and the oracle were once the same thing with the *Odyssey*. This is where Odysseus landed, searching for the underworld: the sunny and fertile landscape of Cumae and Baiae, at fi st sight such a bad fit for the darkness of Homeric Cimmeria, is the cover of a hidden underworld; indeed, it begins to look as if Avernus is an *overworld*. The Homeric connection now helps us to reorganize the entire landscape, consisting of a coast, mountains, and lakes darkened by impenetrable woods, a Phlegraean area of underground fires and exhalations, oracles, and air that poisons the birds. In one word, Nekyia, or Ploutonion.[18]

At least some of Ephoros' original agenda can still be reconstructed.[19] A historian of the Greek West, he was able to connect one important area of Greek colonization (Cumae and Neapolis) with the foundational text of Greek diaspora, the *Odyssey*. He worked with pleasure the customs and secrets of the Cimmerians into the underground, with Herodotean gusto and a passion for the ethnography of barbarian people. From now on, the headland will have its primitive *verso*, and the Odyssean intertext will provide a good platform of cultural exchange between Greeks and Italic peoples, and later the Romans. One crucial factor in the mix was the idea that Cumae was the earliest official Greek *apoikia* in the West, and for a long time the westernmost area settled by Greek-speaking colonists: all this in a culture where West is also Erebos and in close proximity to the dead.[20] In Italy and in Greece Cumae is thought to be as ancient as Rome, at least when the Romans and the Western Greeks start experimenting with intercultural chronology (Feeney 2008: 97); its Greek name Kyme recreates the home of the Euboean settlers and also resonates (Strabo 5.4.4; cf. perhaps Lycophron 695–6) with Greek *kyma* ("swell, wave"), and also no doubt with "Kimmerian," encapsulating the whole migration: from Kyme, through the waves, to the Kimmerian land. This must have been interesting for a historian born at Euboean Kyme: Ephoros had found a way to explain the darkness of the Kimmerian *polis* of Homer, the Erebos associations of Campania, and to boost the nobility of his own birthplace in a colonial setting.

As we have seen, there are many innovations, textual and material, in the territory of Cumae and Avernus in *Aeneid* 6. The geopoetics of Vergil (for the approach, see Barchiesi 2017)[21] is no less intense and drastic than the interventions of Agrippa and Octavian on the landscape.[22] With their works they modify or recreate the stuff of epic, but the presence of epic is still felt: the *Odyssey* "owns" the Phlegraean fields Octavian disturbs the waters of Avernus; Agrippa rebuilds the road once paved by Hercules (Strabo 5.4.6). When Aeneas gets there in Vergil, the Greeks have recently started the palaeo-colony of Cumae (*Euboicus* is repeated twice, at 6.2 and 42; *Chalcidicus* at 6.17). The Greek temple of Apollo is crafted by master engineer Daedalus (6.14–33), a fitting start for a place that will become a triumph of Roman engineering.

The connection between Vergil and the tradition of Homeric scholarship that locates the Nekyia at Avernus becomes even clearer if we can accept the information, mediated by Varro, that in the *Bellum Poenicum* by Naevius there was mention of a Cimmerian Sibyl, located in Italy. This precious snippet (fr. 12 Strz.: *quartam [sc. Sibyllam] Cimmeriam in Italia, quam Naeuius in libris belli Punici, Piso in annalibus* [L. Calpurnius Piso Frugi *FRH*]) deserves a fuller discussion, one that cannot be anticipated here but has relevance to our argument, since it is likely that this Sibyl was evoked in connection to Aeneas' travels along the coast of Campania towards Latium.[23] I must conclude for now, but I do so keeping in mind the possibility of Naevius as a mediator between Hellenistic universal/local histories and the tradition of Roman epic.

Vergil has combined his underworld with the idea of a fi st contact with wild Italy, and his construction of the place has important links with his whole idea of Italy as a powerful and threatening land. It is impressive that the fi st close encounter of the Trojans with Sicily had offered a long, and unusually unmotivated in the narrative economy, ecphrasis of the Sicilian Volcano (3.571 *portus ... sed horrificis iuxta tonat Aetna ruinis*), a model of a colonial "fi st encounter." Our Italic underworld episode is also a proto-colonial episode, and in spite of the many Greek colonial and ktistic narratives that have been explored by Horsfall (1989) in his influentia paper *Aeneas the Colonist*, it is intertextual with Greek narratives at the level of content and form of content but not deeply influenced by the emotional style of Greek traditions of colonization narratives. It is closer, to quote just one example, to Fracastoro's split vision of the New World in the *Siphylis*[24] than to the aetiological narratives of Apollonius Rhodius or Callimachus.

We come back from our evening walk around the Villa Vergiliana with two approaches that need to be kept in mind. The fi st is based on local knowledge: the shape of a volcanic lake, the reflection of dense woods in the water, hollow spaces and sulphurous underground, hot springs and cracks, adventures in Homeric interpretation, the never-ending works of the Roman military, rumours about oracles of the dead, all welded into one memorable topography. The second approach is broader, and takes into account Vergil's subjective style as well as the special construction of Italy in the *Aeneid*, the geopoetics of the *Aeneid*.

NOTES

1 I also thank Bill Gladhill for a number of reactions and suggestions on a fi st draft. Thanks also to Simone Marchesi for his comments on Dante.
2 For the forest description and perception in the *Aeneid* see below, and note also the comparative approach of Harrison 2009.
3 On the connection of Lake Nemi and Lake Avernus as mediated by Turner, see the important essay by Beard 1993 ("Frazer et ses bois sacrés").
4 For an even broader overview, see Harrison 2009.
5 On the importance of this episode, see Purves 2013, who points out that the wilderness of Parnassus is reminiscent of the world of Homeric similes more than of standard Homeric narrative and description.
6 This episode is part of a wider web of Italic imagery in Vergil, the systematic representation of Italy as a wild and antique land, but I will return to this topic in a book based on my 2011 Sather Lectures, entitled *The War for Italia*. For the tension between the landscape at Cumae and the transformative works of the Roman Empire, see also Pillinger in this volume, with important contributions to Vergil from the angle created by Statian reception.
7 As is well known, no Roman definition of Italia ever included Sicily or the islands, so the landing at Cumae is the fi st extended contact of the expedition with the promised land of Italy (or Hesperia, 6.6). On the rigorous distinction between islands and the mainland, see e.g., Cornell 2013: 3.196.
8 See also Clark 1979 and Della Corte 1985.
9 If we look at texts that for Vergil and his audience represented the canon for early Roman epic, we have evidence for a storm in Naevius, *Bellum Poenicum* (14 Strz.), but as far as I can say in the fragments and *testimonia* there is no specific evidenc of a war in Italy in the Aeneas legends as narrated by Naevius and Ennius.
10 For other ways to use the Orphic tablets and leaves in research on *Aeneid* 6, see Herrero in this volume (with bibliography, complementing the commentary by Horsfall 2013a).
11 For a comparative treatment of nature in Vergil's opus and of landscapes in Greek poetry, see Jenkyns 1998: 21–72, who uses the idea of "pathetic fallacy" and Vergil's background as a Transpadane Roman as the two main parameters for his analysis.
12 Purcell 1996.
13 For a similar emphasis on *uiam secat*, see Pillinger in this volume.
14 Herrero in this volume is complementary to my reading, and well brings out the importance of movement and active progress in the underworld narrative.
15 The innovation is reinforced by the universal implication of *est iter*: the simile, again unconventionally, has no recognizable individual subject, and so

attracts the collective participation of the audience, who is now sucked into the experience of walking in(to) the night.

16 Ulrich and Quenemoen 2014: 132–3.

17 On competition with Egypt in the whole section of the *laudes Italiae*, see the illuminating paper by Hunter 2001.

18 The whole discussion of Stärk 1995 is extremely valuable. He also points to the importance of Silius Italicus, who offers a vision of the landscape sandwiched between Homer and Vergil, and significantly resorts to strategies of duplication two different visits by Hannibal and Scipio, and two different Sibyls at Cumae and Avernus.

19 For scepticism about a direct reworking of the *Odyssey* into Ephoros' account, see Roller 2018: 274.

20 See Ustinova 2009: 76–81, with bibliography.

21 Note also Connors 2011 on the possibilities of "environmental criticism" applied to the text of Strabo.

22 By the way, the Marcellus episode that closes the book sets a date for Book 6 and the rest of the work not only in celebrating Marcellus but de facto in opening the way to Agrippa as a successor. This political effect is enhanced by the implication of Agrippa in the descriptive section of Cumae and Avernus that opens the book. It is interesting to speculate about the significance of those elements if we imagine for a moment an alternative world where Agrippa not Tiberius, after triumphing in the civil war of *Aen.* 8.682 *parte alia uentis et dis Agrippa secundis* and acquiring special powers in 23 BCE, is now the second emperor of Rome. Note that Agrippa circulated an autobiographical text and wrote about geography.

23 My discussion will also include fr. 13 Strz., which mentions a relative of Aeneas giving her name to the island of Prochyta, very close to Cumae and clearly visible from the sanctuary of Apollo. Both fragments are also connected to the work on the Aeneas legend and on Italian city foundations by republican historians and antiquarians, operating after Naevius and before Vergil.

24 On the striking combination of Eden and of the Vergilian Harpies' episode in Fracastoro, see Hardie 2004b.

2

A Walk in Vergil's Footsteps: Statius on the Via Domitiana[1]

EMILY PILLINGER

I. The Road

At the end of Statius' *Thebaid*, the poet bids his opus goodbye with the instruction that it should take care to walk several steps behind Vergil's *Aeneid* (*Theb.* 12.816–17):

> uiue, precor; nec tu diuinam Aeneida tempta,
> sed longe sequere et uestigia semper adora.

> Live, I pray; yet do not challenge the divine *Aeneid*,
> but follow it at a distance and always worship its footsteps.

This gesture of humble deference to the masterpiece of the Augustan age appears to play perfectly into the rhetoric of post-Augustan decline: when Statius' epic walks into the literary tradition it is belated, and behind.[2]

Such deferential posturing is not quite so marked when Statius slips "into the woods" of the *Siluae*.[3] The poems are too busy jostling with each other, with their different meters, different addressees, different settings, buildings, and objets d'art all crowding into the five books of observation and praise.[4] This chapter explores the way in which one of these poems sees Statius taking a more nuanced and confident approach to his tracking of Vergil's footsteps. *Siluae* 4.3 is poem in which 163 hendecasyllabic lines describe and celebrate the emperor Domitian's construction of a new road. Statius uses the dynamics of time, distance, and speed, as they are experienced by a traveller on this road, to describe his own navigation of literary history – specificall , literary history as it had been shaped over the past century by both the infrastructure and the cultural politics of Roman imperial power.[5] The process is presided over by Vergil's Cumaean Sibyl, and the journeys taken by her and Aeneas in *Aeneid* 6 offer a model against which Statius plots his own progress.

The work and travels Statius describes take place on the Via Domitiana, which was built in 95 CE. It branched off the Via Appia, connecting Sinuessa to Puteoli (modern Pozzuoli), and passing by Cumae with the cave of its famous sibylline resident.[6] The road's construction meant that travellers journeying from Rome to the Bay of Naples no longer had to go via Capua inland, but could proceed directly down the west coast of Italy. Making full use of the mobility facilitated by this new road, Statius' entire fourth book of *Siluae* shuttles between Rome and Naples in its settings, reflecting the divided loyalties of the Neapolitan poet whose career was made in Rome, but who was in the process of retiring to his hometown at the time of the book's composition.[7] The third poem of the book celebrates the completion of the road that had made the journey between the two cities that much quicker and easier, cementing Statius' role as both a beneficiary (in practice) and a champion (in poetry) of Domitian's investments in imperial infrastructure.[8]

Siluae 4.3 describes the building of the Via Domitiana in full technical detail. Despite the apparent mundanity of the object of praise, the narrative of the roadworks becomes the fundament on which the rest of the poem is built.[9] The poet cuts no corners in his depiction of the road-building process, pointing out the ditches, curbs, excavations, foundations, and paving, as well as the human effort expended on its construction (*Silu.* 4.3.49): *o quantae pariter manus laborant.*[10] Beyond this account of the building work, the poem is divided into roughly three parts, which map points on the route of the completed road southwards like a Roman itinerary.[11] A similar poetic version of an itinerary may be found in Horace *Satires* 1.5, in which the poet describes a trip all the way down the Via Appia to Brundisium, partly in the company of Vergil. There are also extant fragments of a satire by Lucilius about a trip to Sicily, which may have been Horace's model.[12] But Statius is not describing a specific episode of his own travel, at least not in the purportedly autobiographical mode of those earlier satirists. Statius begins the poem in his own voice, introducing the road's construction with references to Domitian's manifold qualities and explaining the benefits of the road to all travellers from Latium (1–66). The second part of the poem is delivered in large part through the voice of the river Volturnus, which was situated halfway between Sinuessa and Puteoli and had been bridged to carry the new road (67–113). The river offers thanks to the emperor for transforming it from a dangerously wild torrent into a clean and well-controlled watercourse. The third and final part of the poem begins when the narrator is startled to see that the Sibyl of Cumae has turned up – or, rather, the narrator has turned up in Cumae to find the Sibyl in front of him, standing on the road (114–end).[13] Statius gracefully gives way to her as speaker, citing her superior claim to poetic authority as a *uates sanctior* (*Silu.* 4.3.120), and her fulsome praises of Domitian complete the poem.[14]

With the arrival of the Sibyl on the recently completed road Statius reminds his audience of Vergil's Sibyl in *Aeneid* 6, and all the journeys that she facilitates in that book. The appearance of Statius' Sibyl on a road, rather than in a temple, cave, or the underworld, signals her transportation into Domitian's newly "industrial" landscape. At the same time, it is also a reminder that even in the *Aeneid* the prophet is a guide not only to the tracks of the underworld, but also to the new land that the Trojans are about to colonize – a colonization that will ultimately lead to the infrastructure works that will support Statius' freewheeling career between Rome and Naples.[15] At the midpoint of the *Aeneid,* as Aeneas' wanderings across the Mediterranean Sea are brought to an end and his helmsman Palinurus is sacrificed to Neptune, the Trojans are beginning their transformation from sea travellers to land travellers.[16] This is hinted at in the fi st line of *Aeneid* 6, in which Aeneas is described as racing full sail to the Italian shore with the image of giving a horse its head (*classique immittit habenas, Aen.* 6.1), and the Sibyl marks the transition more firmly still: *o tandem magnis pelagi defuncte periclis* | (*sed terrae grauiora manent*) ("O you who have at last escaped great dangers of the sea | [but still more terrible struggles await you on land]," 6.83–4).

In another indication of this new existence for the Trojans, Aeneas no sooner sets foot on the Italian mainland for the fi st time than he proceeds to undertake several expeditions back and forth around the area of Avernus from his camp on the beach: he travels to the Sibyl's cave, into the forest to fetch the golden bough, and to the underworld and the Elysian Fields. In counterpoint with the smooth southward journey Statius will describe in *Siluae* 4.3, these preliminary trips by the Trojans in the *Aeneid* show their fi st halting steps on the historical pathway that will lead forwards through time and northwards through Italy to Augustan Rome.[17]

Aeneid 6 opens with the artwork of Daedalus on the doors to the temple of Apollo. This ecphrastic tour de force tells the story of its creator's journey across the Mediterranean, from the surreal nightmare of Minos' labyrinthine Crete (an underworld in its own right), through the strange route of the sky (*insuetum … iter, Aen.* 6.16), to the as-yet trackless Italy. Fitzgerald has unpacked much symbolic spatial and temporal activity in this ecphrasis and its context, noting that it evokes journeys "whose main object is to sever rather than to connect," in literal, psychological, and historical terms.[18] Whether or not this severance is really achieved for Daedalus or Aeneas, the image of the labyrinth at the heart of Daedalus' work emphasizes the dangers and rewards of travel in the teleological *Aeneid*.[19] In its paradigm form the maze is designed to ensure that the Minotaur and his victims never escape back into the world outside. It is a space in which a road is no more than a perverse deceit. In its successful reworkings, the image of the maze becomes about the imposition of order, about avoiding endless circularity, and about finding a safe way to proceed forwards through history (in, for example, the weaving patterns of the boys on horseback in the *lusus Troiae* at *Aen.* 5.545–603, with the Cretan labyrinth explicitly evoked at 5.588–93). This labyrinthine road may not be direct, but it is trustworthy. For Aeneas in *Aeneid* 6, one space after another (the woods containing the golden bough, the underworld itself) will be figured as a labyrinth that is designed to baffle and entrap, but ends up revealing to the hero a hidden road that constitutes both a safe return and a move onwards and upwards.

Daedalus' visual autobiography, culminating with his escape to Italy, is a reflection of Aeneas' own long flight westwards. After this ecphrastic episode Vergil sends Aeneas on multiple short return journeys. The hero is now criss-crossing the land, making progress with each step he takes backwards and forwards across his new homeland. Firstly he visits the Sibyl's cave (*Aen.* 6.9–13), in the strange grove dedicated to the goddess Diana-Hecate "Trivia" – "of the crossroads" (6.156–7). Hecate is a chthonian goddess who, the Sibyl later explains, was the Sibyl's own guide to the underworld: *sed me cum lucis Hecate praefecit Auernis, | ipsa deum poenas docuit perque omnia duxit* ("but when Hecate placed me in charge of the groves of Avernus | she taught me the punishments of the gods and led me through everything," 6.564–5). Hecate's association with the underworld serves as an early hint at the otherworldly journey Aeneas will undertake later in the book. At the same time, her title "Trivia" reminds the audience that one of the several divine forces at work in *Aeneid* 6 is a figur , often represented with two or three faces, who presides over the point of diverging and converging roads.[20]

After finding the body of Misenus floating in the sea and initiating his burial, a process that involves "returning" him to his resting place, according to the Sibyl's instructions (*sedibus hunc refer ante suis, Aen.* 6.152), Aeneas' next journey is to fetch the golden bough. Though his steps are hesitant, Venus' doves guide him directly to the tree as Aeneas had requested: *este duces o, si qua uia est, cursumque per auras | derigite in lucos* ... ("Be our guides and, if there is a route, direct a path into the grove | by flying through the air ..." 6.194–5). The doves offer the bird's-eye perspective that opens up nature's secrets to reveal a route, in a way that echoes Daedalus' aerial travel and the craftsman's own revelation of the secrets of his labyrinth to Theseus and to the viewers of his artwork at Cumae: *Daedalus ipse dolos tecti ambagesque resoluit*

("Daedalus himself reveals the deceptions and ambiguities of the building," 6.29). Aeneas then brings the bough straight back out of the forest to the Sibyl, before returning to the shore to complete the burial of Misenus. In the process he turns yet one more Trojan hero from being lost at sea to rooted in the land.

After these short but significant preliminary journeys, Aeneas finally undertakes his journey to the underworld, a trip that combines elements of the literal, the mystical, and the metaphorical. This is not a difficult journey in itself, but one that Aeneas is told is miraculous when achieved as a round trip (*Aen.* 6.126–9):

> Tros Anchisiade, facilis descensus Auerno …
> sed reuocare gradum superasque euadere ad auras
> hoc opus, hic labor est.

> Trojan son of Anchises, the descent to Avernus is easy …
> but to recall your step and escape into the breezes above –
> this is the challenge, this is the real task.

The process by which Aeneas actually leaves the underworld is obscured by the reference to the Gates of Sleep that bring the meaning – even the reality status – of the entire episode into question.[21] Yet instead of resolving this issue, Vergil whisks Aeneas back to his camp on the shore, and both he and the epic's audience are brought back to earth. Aeneas is described as returning to the place from which he had set out with a prosaic idiom that faintly evokes the imposition of a new road on the landscape: *ille uiam secat ad nauis sociosque reuisit* ("he cuts a path through to the ships and rejoins his comrades," 6.899).[22]

Statius picks up on this busy coming and going when in *Siluae* 4.3 he has his Sibyl summarize Vergil's underworld scene with extreme, even ludicrous, laconicism (*Silu.* 4.3.131–3):

> praescios Auerni
> Aeneas auide futura quaerens
> lucos et penetrauit et reliquit.

> Aeneas, eagerly seeking knowledge of the future
> both entered and left
> the prophetic groves of Avernus.

With Aeneas' adventures in *Aeneid* 6 absurdly reduced to a hop down to and up from the underworld, Statius' Sibyl travesties Vergil's great episode of national self-discovery. Aeneas' own haste to discover his future (*auide futura quaerens,* 132), matches his eagerness to grasp the golden bough in the *Aeneid* (*auidus,* 6.210), but in the epic he was slowed down by solemn ritual demands (not to mention the bough's resistance) and by his own growing fascination with the underworld and its inhabitants. Statius has removed all of Vergil's rich delays and distracting details in order to focus on the road, shifting the emphasis from the metaphysical to the banally concrete, from the savouring of the journey to its successful and speedy completion.

The road shapes even the visual effect of the poem. Morgan has pointed out that the layout of the short hendecasyllabic lines down the page constructs a slim track that evokes a *carmen figuratum.*[23] At the same time, it is also a very long track, at 163 lines; *Siluae* 4.3 could run anywhere from four to seven columns in a bookroll.[24] One might imagine a bookroll whose layout highlighted the points of transition down the Via Domitiana as they appear in the poem. Following Schafer's remarkable work on Roman authorial pagination, an approximately forty-line model (as Schafer proposes for Vergil's *Georgics*) creates the image of a poetic road in four columns, if *Siluae* 4.3 starts at the top of a column.[25] Each column break is motivated by one of the twists and turns encountered on the road and immortalized in the poem. Column two begins as the road construction begins, with the demarcation of channels: *hic primus labor incohare sulcos* ("The fi st job here was to lay out the furrows," *Silu.* 4.3.40). The shift from column two to three is negotiated at the point where Volturnus acknowledges that his newly controlled windings are owed to Domitian: *amnis esse coepi* (*Silu.* 4.3.80). Toward the bottom of column three the Sibyl is spotted "at the very end of the new road" (*fine uiae recentis imo,* 4.3.114), and column four, beginning with the deictic *en!* at line 121, is devoted to her speech, which "fills the road" (*uiamque replet,* 4.3.122). This longer final column of forty-three lines mimics the strange expansion of time found in the last lines of the poem (see discussion below).[26] The poem thus has a strong claim to being an example of what classicists would call a *technopaegnion,* though it should perhaps more appropriately be given the term used by scholars of modern literature: "concrete poetry."

As Statius makes his marks on paper, so the road makes its marks on the Italian landscape. This clash of environmental worlds exposes the poem's unstraightforward poetics – particularly those associated with Callimachus – and potentially unstraightforward politics.[27] Statius gestures toward a celebration of the broad epic highway that Callimachus rejects in *Epigram* 28 ("I hate the cyclic poem, nor do I like the road that ferries many people back and forth"), but in celebrating the taming of the roaring Volturnus Statius also celebrates the pure stream that defines Apollo's poetic priorities in Callimachus' *Hymn to Apollo* (*Hymn* 2.107–12).[28] So too politically: the poem's description of the road dominating wild nature may be read as Statius signalling a problematically aggressive or even hubristic kind of imperialism.[29] This explains Volturnus' account of his earlier muddy but exuberant existence, Statius' references to the builders felling forests and stripping mountains, and his risky identification of Domitian with Xerxes attempting to bridge the Hellespont (*Silu.* 4.3.57–8).[30] Critics of this reading argue that it attributes too much ecological sensibility to the Romans and offers too narrow a political reading of Callimachean poetics.[31] Reitz balances this poetic and political ambiguity in her reading of the poem's aural world. From the beginning Statius draws his audience's attention toward the tremendous noise created by the road's construction, *immanis sonus* (*Silu.* 4.3.2), to which the voices of the poet, Volturnus, and the Sibyl, contribute over the rest of the poem. As Reitz notes, loudness is traditionally opposed to the restraint required by Callimacheanism, but Statius appears to have rejigged the system: "for praise poetry such as the *Siluae*, the 'noise' of fulsome rhetoric and unrestrained hyperbole is an integral feature. Statius requires a new literary aesthetic, which allows speed and loudness where they are appropriate to poetic content and context, and he employs the description of fast, noisy construction to convey it."[32]

The building works of *Siluae* 4.3 are certainly tied firmly to the emperor Domitian, as both the commissioner of the road and the focus of the poem's praise.[33] As Purcell puts it, "the *display* of the power of the conqueror to grasp the landscape, human and physical, and change it, is what is essential to Roman imperialism."[34] The river Volturnus leans significantly against the bridge on which the emperor's actions were inscribed (*maximoque | pontis Caesarei reclinis arcu, Silu.* 4.3.69–70).[35] Domitian is also the poem's implicit addressee – indeed, its explicit addressee once the Sibyl begins to speak – and its ideal audience. As *dominus et deus* in real life and in Statius' *Siluae*, Domitian permeates and dominates the natural world, the world of material construction, and the world of literary endeavour; there is no sound or space that is not under imperial control, whether for praise or implicit critique.[36] However, while this sound and space belongs to the single figure of the emperor, it is navigable by other individuals in different ways. As Purcell has pointed out, the way in which imperial ideology appropriates geographical features is not a purely top-down process, but rather part of a discourse that engages with a range of participants. "Changing the order of the world was undoubtedly one of the resonant challenges in such undertakings [canal-building and road-engineering], but the excuse was always to improve communications. And if communications were fi st for Roman rulers and their agents, they could hardly exclude a wide range of uses by

Rome's subjects, whose passage patterned the identity of the new routes."[37] The road and *Siluae* 4.3 both allow for subjective journeys through the objectively despotic and flattery-fille world that Statius describes and in which he participates.

The poetics and politics of *Siluae* 4.3 remain inscrutable when Statius introduces the Sibyl at Cumae. The immediacy of the short lines, the unmuffled racket of the road's construction, the directness of the road, and the new purity of the Volturnus are now all complemented by the strangely straightforward speech of Statius' Sibyl. She is completely untroubled by the layers of ambiguity that normally guarantee the authenticity of a sibyl's pronouncements, and abandons without explanation her hexameters – customary both from her association with the Greek hexametric sibylline oracles and from Vergil's *Aeneid* – for Statius' hendecasyllables.[38] This leaves her flattery of the emperor unsettlingly transparent. The role of the Sibylline Books at the heart of the Roman state makes the voice of their purported author, the Cumaean Sibyl, always inherently political, but not uncomplicatedly so. Newlands suggests that the overblown praise of Domitian, placed in the mouth of Statius' Sibyl, proves that the poet is possessed of equivocal feelings toward Domitian: since any sibyl's voice must always be open to radically resistant meanings, even this apparently fulsome praise is marked as full of sibylline *ambages*.[39] Smolenaars and Morgan argue the opposite: that the directness of Statius' Sibyl is designed to show how Domitian's rule engenders the kind of praise that overrides poetic, cultural, and religious traditions, including the tradition of sibylline obscurity.[40]

In Vergil's *Aeneid* the difficulties surrounding the Sibyl's communications are circumvented, but only after careful planning and pleading on the part of her petitioners. Vergil begins by emphasizing the layers of confusion normally associated with the Sibyl's prophecies. The problems identified with her mythical role are explained most clearly by Helenus in his instructions to Aeneas in *Aeneid* 3.441–60. This is where Aeneas fi st learns of the *insana uates* and her *carmina uolitantia,* the prophecies written on leaves that fly around in the breeze blowing through the many mouths of her cave until their disorder defies sense.[41] This passage displays the poetic Sibyl's initial affiliation with Callimacheanism within Vergil's epic: according to Helenus the wind is "light" or "fine – a *tenuis uentus* (448) – which excites the "delicate leaves" – *teneras frondes* (449). The Sibyl is not interested in producing the "single work of continuous poetry" condemned by Callimachus in his *Aetia* (fr. 1.3) – *nec … iungere carmina curat* (*Aen.* 4.451) – nor does she care that the larger body of people who come to consult her leave unsatisfied

These communicative challenges are replayed in Aeneas' effort to forestall them by means of the prayer he addresses to the Sibyl at *Aeneid* 6.65–76, including a request that she not write down her poetry on leaves that are vulnerable to confusion: *foliis tantum ne carmina manda, | ne turbata uolent rapidis ludibria uentis* (*Aen.* 6.74–5). In this prayer the hero also gestures toward the obscurity that continues to define the voice of the Sibyl in Augustan Rome. The problematic fragility of her leaves foreshadows the secrecy and indeterminacy of the Sibylline Books at Rome, a connection that is reinforced by Aeneas' vow to offer her a sacred space at Rome in which her *sortes* may rest, and to found a priesthood of *quindecimuiri* dedicated to interpreting her verses (6.71–4):[42]

te quoque magna manent regnis penetralia nostris:
hic ego namque tuas sortis arcanaque fata
dicta meae genti ponam, lectosque sacrabo,
alma, uiros.

Magnificent sacred inner shrines wait you in our realm:
for here I shall lay your predictions and hidden fates,
spoken to my people, and I shall appoint chosen men as priests,
dear protector.

The Sibyl of the *Aeneid* ultimately agrees to deliver her prophecies in a one-off oral performance, though it transpires that she can reveal little Aeneas either does not know or will not soon discover over the course of the following six books of Vergil's epic. More importantly, this performance is clearly the exception to her rule. Uncommunicative wanderings (*ambages*) have been marked as central to her characterization and authority under normal circumstances, and these obfuscations are preserved in texts buried in the most august religio-political space in Augustan Rome.

In Statius' poem, although the Sibyl also delivers an oral performance, and although she too is emerging from an arboreally themed writing project (not leaves, but *Woods*), she projects quite different priorities from Vergil's Sibyl.[43] On the road outside her cavern she launches into song, acknowledging the presence not of the privileged poet who has already caught sight of her, but the emperor whom she sees in her visions. To this emperor she turns and spontaneously announces that she has no interest in crumbling texts or priests' rituals (*Silu.* 4.3.141–4):[44]

nec iam putribus euoluta chartis
sollemni prece Quindecim Virorum

perlustra mea dicta, sed canentem
ipsam comminus ut mereris audi.

And do not wade through my words
unrolled on crumbling bookrolls
to the solemn prayer of the *quindecimuiri*, but come close
and listen to me singing, as you deserve.

This Sibyl has become the kind of sibyl Aeneas would have liked to meet with back in the *Aeneid*. She cuts through the need for cajoling speeches, bypasses the historical attentions of the *quindecimuiri*, and tramples all over the untrodden road: *nouisque late | bacchatur spatiis uiamque replet* ("and she goes bacchic-wild all over | the new route and fills the road," 4.3.121–2). Above all, Statius' Sibyl offers a strong assertion of the power of her contemporary voice over text: *audi* (144). Where Vergil's private, even exclusive, Sibyl sang only reluctantly to Aeneas and pronounced prophecies that went no further than the scope of the *Aeneid*'s own narrative, Statius' Sibyl invites the attentions of an ever widening and amplifying circle of listeners. The *immanis sonus* of the road's construction at the beginning of the poem gives way to her penetrating voice that dominates the end of the poem and the end of the road. Domitian is her immediate addressee, apparently next to her (*comminus*, 144), and the poet Statius has already situated himself on the road near her (them) as he records her words. Then, by dispensing with the secrecy normally guaranteed by the *quindecimuiri*, which Aeneas had promised the Sibyl that she would be granted after her prophecy to him in *Aeneid* 6, Statius' Sibyl implicitly welcomes a wider audience: the audience attending any recitation of the poem, or the readership of the written book – not to mention the book's specific dedicatee, Vitorius Marcellus. This Sibyl "fills (*replet*, 122) space, sound, the poem's final column, and the book's literary scene, mirroring the way that Domitian fills the landscape and its poetry: she too governs the order of her world, while also being subject to the public's independent (if circumspectly unexpressed) reading of her words.

To conclude this section: on the one hand, *Siluae* 4.3 describes a single road, commissioned by a single and all-powerful emperor, and celebrated in a single poem. On the other hand, the poem reveals a degree of carefully managed fragmentation: the Via Domitiana connects two cities (Rome, Naples) and two texts (the *Aeneid*, the *Siluae*), three voices (Statius, Volturnus, the Cumaean Sibyl), four columns of poetry (perhaps), and an infinite number of future travellers. Above all, it permits of two-way and frequent traffic Along with the freedom of travel permitted by the road comes each traveller's subjective, layered, and repeatable experience of its various spatial, sonic, and temporal dimensions.

The rest of this chapter will explore what this subjective experience means for Statius as a poet. His focus on the road reveals his fascination with the workings of the literary canon and with the poetic and political significance of his relationship with Vergil in particular. As he did at the end of the *Thebaid,* Statius in *Siluae* 4.3 uses the image of the road as a way of mapping the progress of literary tradition, and placing himself on that map. The following sections will consider how Statius' poetics are shaped by his feel for the physical dynamics of distance, time, and speed on the Via Domitiana, and how Statius tackles the notion of a "return" journey in literary history by bringing Vergil's Sibyl back from Augustan Rome to Flavian Cumae.

II. Distance

Siluae 4.3 is a poem primarily about distance: the distance between Rome and Cumae, and the fact that Domitian has effectively lessened it (*Silu.* 4.3.24–6):[45]

> gaudens Euboicae domum Sibyllae
> Gauranosque sinus et aestuantis
> septem montibus admouere Baias.

> Rejoicing in moving the home of the Euboean Sibyl
> and the lakes of Mt. Gaurus and the steaming baths of Baiae
> towards the seven hills [of Rome].

The natural (Mt. Gaurus and its lakes), the man-made (Baiae's natural springs, which had been channelled into hot baths), and the historical and literary (Cumae, identified with its Greek colonize s from Euboea as well as with the prophet made most famous by Vergil), are all jumbled together and then brought into closer contact with Rome, the centre of power. Of course this is an illusion: the geography of Italy has not changed. But distance is experienced through travel, and the experience of travelling between Rome and the exotic locales of Puteoli *has* changed. The empire seems to be contracting as the journey between its centre and external regions gets quicker and easier.[46]

It is, then, the bodily experience of an individual that guarantees the effect of Domitian's work. In the case of *Siluae* 4.3, the presence of the author at different spots down the road gestures toward that bodily experience. However, Statius does not mark his movement down the road autobiographically, as in the satires of Horace and Lucilius. Instead, Statius has one authorial voice displace another: his introduction gives way to the voice of the river Volturnus and then to that of the Sibyl, each contributing to a polyphony of praise for Domitian that splits and displaces the authorial voice. Statius makes this explicit when he allows the overbearing Sibyl to take over from his song: *cedamus; chely, iam repone cantus: | uates sanctior incipit, tacendum est* ("Let us give way; lyre, put aside your song now: | a more holy visionary is beginning her song, and we must be silent," 119–20). This does not mean that Statius is left behind. The poet is clearly on the spot – indeed, on each and every spot down the road – acting as the fi st witness to the second and third voices and conveying their words to the wider audience of the *Siluae*. Though the narrative technique whereby the poet quotes knowledgeable and serendipitously met interviewees is that of Callimachus' *Aetia* and Ovid's *Fasti*, Statius uses it to replay scenes from *Aeneid* 6 in multiple ways. Introducing the Sibyl, he professes surprise at her appearance: *quam… cerno… uisu fallimur?* ("whom do I see… do my eyes deceive me...?," 4.3.114–17). Through his characterization as a witness to the Sibyl's epiphany, Statius begins the scene by playing a version of Aeneas. Aeneas is always profoundly moved by visuals in Vergil's epic, and this is emphasized in *Aeneid* 6. The hero is transfixed by Daedalus' decoration of Apollo's temple at Cumae, such that the Sibyl rebukes him for wasting time staring at it (*Aen.* 6.37), and his whole role in the underworld scene is as a fascinated observer of phenomena that are essentially dreamlike. Statius rightly ponders: *uisu fallimur?*

Statius also becomes a proxy figure reflecting the tension between physical and metaphysical existence in *Aeneid* 6, with its shadows of divinities above and underground and its apparitions of humans out of time. Much of this is established through Statius' play with space and presence on the Via Domitiana, and with the distance, real or conceptual, between individuals. When Statius' Sibyl suddenly moves into the second person, she makes Statius a stand-in for the emperor Domitian *salue, dux hominum et parens deorum, | prouisum mihi cognitumque numen* ("Greetings, leader of men and father of gods, | divinity already foreseen and known to me," 4.3.139–40). Domitian is the ostensible addressee, but he is not there in person. Instead, it is Statius who receives and records this address.[47] The emperor is praised to the skies, but he remains insubstantial compared to the poet. This is emphasized by the intertextuality Statius builds with two scenes from *Aeneid* 6. When Statius' Sibyl fi st announces her vision of Domitian with *en! hic est deus* ("Look! This man is a god," 4.3.128) she evokes Anchises introducing a pre-mortal, predivine Augustus to Aeneas in the underworld parade of heroes: *hic uir, hic est* (*Aen.* 6.791).[48] Augustus is both there and not there in Vergil's text. So, too, Domitian is both present in and absent from Statius' text, as the poet creates a world that is rooted in Domitian's contemporary history and technology but infused with mythic otherworldliness, and escalated to evoke the ghostly presence of not a man (*uir*), but a god (*deus*).

The other Vergilian scene evoked involves the triangular dynamics surrounding Vergil's Sibyl when she is inspired by Apollo and voyeuristically observed by Aeneas. When the Sibyl of Statius' poem cries *en! hic est deus*, she also echoes Vergil's Sibyl crying out to Apollo *deus, ecce, deus!* ("The god, look, the god!" *Aen.* 6.46). Like Domitian to Statius' Sibyl, Apollo is invisible to all but the Sibyl in *Aeneid* 6. However, Apollo also makes his presence known to her through his physicalized – indeed sexualized – inspiration of her (*Aen.* 6.46–51, 77–80):[49]

... cui talia fanti
ante fores subito non uultus, non color unus,
non comptae mansere comae; sed pectus anhelum,
et rabie fera corda tument, maiorque uideri
nec mortale sonans, adflata est numine quand
iam propiore dei ...
at Phoebi nondum patiens immanis in antro
bacchatur uates, magnum si pectore possit
excusisse deum; tanto magis ille fatigat
os rabidum, fera corda domans, fingitque premend .

... as she said this
in front of the doors suddenly her expression, her complexion, fluctuated
her hair sprang out wildly; but her chest was panting,
and her wild heart swelled with frenzy, and she seemed to grow larger
making inhuman noises, breathed into by the rapidly approaching
spirit of the god ...
But no longer suffering Phoebus, the visionary went bacchic-wild
in the huge cave, as if she were trying to shake the great god
from her chest; all the more did he keep pressing on against her
maddened mouth, conquering her wild heart, and he shaped her by force.

Although these scenes influence Statius' description of his Sibyl's inspiration (e.g., *bacchatur*, 4.3.122), if Domitian is playing Apollo he is certainly not a sexual aggressor in the same way: Statius hastens to assure his audience of this with the unnecessary explanation that his Sibyl's prophecies fall from a "chaste mouth" (*uirgineo... ore*, 123). At the same time, insofar as Domitian is identified with the road he has imposed on the landscape, his power of inspiration is as physical in its expression as that of Apollo. If

Apollo "fills up" Vergil's Sibyl as he gets closer to her – *adflata est numine* (6.50) – Statius' Sibyl "fills Domitian's road as she rampages across it: *uiamque replet* (4.3.122). Domitian in *Siluae* 4.3 is as powerful, immanent, and inspirational as Apollo in *Aeneid* 6, but he is also as strange a combination of the material and the incorporeal.

Meanwhile, the evocation of Apollo's influenc , the god who inspires the ambiguous words of both poets and prophets, encourages the audience of *Siluae* 4.3 to spot one further place-swapping game: that between Statius and the Sibyl, the poet and prophet of this poem. The sharing of words between these characters is important. While the Sibyl offers a buffer behind whose extravagant and apparently disinterested praise Statius can shelter, the poet also gains prestige from his association with the prophet's voice.[50] Vergil had foregrounded the vatic ground he shares with his Sibyl when he had her prophesy *horrida bella* (*Aen.* 6.86), *horrida bella* that Vergil would then re-announce in the following book (7.41). The Vergilian Sibyl's prophecy continues (6.83–97) by summarizing the very events that the poet will outline in his broader programmatic appeal to the muse Erato (7.37–45), and which he will go on to narrate in the second half of his epic.

Statius' Sibyl is aligned with her poet-creator even more closely. Firstly, by dismissing the crumbling texts of the treasured Sibylline Books (*putres chartae*, 4.3.141) in favour of the immediacy of her voice, she shows that she shares Statius' anxiety about what happens when occasional, even improvised, poems are written down and collected into fixed anthologies. Statius spells out his concern directly in the preface to his fi st book of *Siluae* (*Silu.* 1, preface):

diu multumque dubitaui, Stella ... an hos libellos, qui mihi subito calore et quadam festinandi uoluptate fluxerunt cum singuli de sinu meo pro<dierint>, congregatos ipse dimitterem.

I have hesitated much and for a long time, Stella ... whether I should collect together and publish these little pieces, which poured out of me with a sudden feverishness and with a kind of delight in the speed, emerging from my breast one by one.

The fluent oral delivery of the Sibyl in her inspiration mirrors Statius' purported compositional style, with the heat and joyful rush (*festinandi uoluptas*) of inspiration.[51] In their joint suspicion of the transformation of voice into text, the two move away from the model of written composition that characterizes the Sibyl when she fi st appears in Helenus' prophecy in *Aeneid* 3, and from the famously slow and painstaking production of epic such as Vergil's *Aeneid* itself, or indeed Statius' *Thebaid* (his twelve sleepless years of work mentioned, like his deferential walking behind Vergil, in the epic's final sphragis: *Theb.* 12.811–12). Instead, here in the *Siluae*, Statius and his Sibyl collaborate in a celebration of speedy poetry and the highway to which it is so well suited.[52]

In a less explicit but more fundamental move to close the distance between himself and his prophet, Statius has his Sibyl join him in rejecting the hexameters normally associated with sibylline prophecy.[53] Vergil's epic Sibyl abandoned her Greek language but kept its hexameter; Statius' sylvan Sibyl abandons both Greek and Latin *epos* for hendecasyllables.[54] While Statius has handed over the solo voice fi st to Volturnus and then to the Sibyl in order to mark the variegated experience of journeying down the road from Rome to Cumae, he reaffirms his association with the production of those voices by wresting the meter of the Sibyl's prophecies into his own form. Statius and his Sibyl effectively stand together on the Via Domitiana, rattling out their praise, registering their physical and poetic closeness to each other and to Vergil's characters at Cumae, but in a modern Cumae that is now just that much closer to Rome, and that much further from the world of epic.

III. Speed × Time

Distance is calculated by multiplying a journey's speed by the time it takes, and Statius has already been seen in this poem to be linking questions of space and displacement with his speedy compositional practices. Statius also focuses on the speed of the traveller when he introduces the poem in the preface to the fourth book of *Siluae*, noting both there and in the poem itself that Domitian has removed the delays caused by sand dunes (*Silu.* 4, preface and *Silu.* 4.3.21–3):[55]

uiam Domitianam miratus sum, qua grauissimam harenarum moram exemit, cuius beneficio tu quoque maturius epistulam meam accipies, quam tibi in hoc libro a Neapoli scribo.

I have admired the Via Domitiana, by which he [Domitian] has cut the extremely tiresome delay caused by the sand dunes, and whose benefaction means that you will also receive all the more quickly my letter, which I am writing to you in this book from Naples.

hic segnis populi uias grauatus
et campos iter omne detinentis

longos eximit ambitus nouoque
iniectu solidat grauis harenas.

This man, frustrated by the people's slow roads
and by plains that hold back every journey
is cutting the lengthy detours and making solid
the swampy sands with fresh surfacing.

It is to highlight the importance of speed that Statius introduces his audience to another, anonymous, traveller down the Via Domitiana.[56] Statius' own progress is fixed to that of the poem, but this other traveller changes his pace according to the changes that have been made in the road. Early in the poem the traveller is "sluggish," a *piger uiator* struggling down the Via Appia despite his fast vehicle:[57] *hic quondam piger axe uectus uno | nutabat cruce pendula uiator* ("Here once the sluggish traveller, carried on a single axle, | used to bounce around on a lurching carriage-pole," 4.3.27–8). By the middle of the poem, where the Via Domitiana branches off from the Via Appia at the river Volturnus, the traveller has speeded up, becoming a *citus uiator* (*Silu.* 4.3.101–6):

illic flectit iter citus uiato ,
illic Appia se dolet relinqui.
tunc uelocior acriorque cursus
tunc ipsos iuuat impetus iugales,
ceu fessis ubi remigum lacertis
primae carbasa uentilatis, aurae.

There the swift traveller directs his course,
there Appia laments at being left behind.
Then the pace becomes more fast and furious
and the rush delights the very teams of carriage animals,
in the same way as when you, breezes, fi st fill the sail
when the rowers' arms are exhausted.

Statius notes that the animals enjoy the new ease of movement on this road, drawing a comparison with rowers enjoying the wind filling their sails that blurs the difference between land travel and sea travel. This in turn evokes not just Aeneas' progression from sea to land, but also Daedalus' technological advances in locomotion, for the novelty of his invention forced Vergil to confuse different elements in his description of the new form of travel, the craftsman's "oarage of wings" (*remigium alarum, Aen.* 6.19).

The acceleration of Statius' anonymous traveller as he leaves the Via Appia contrasts with the relaxed pace of Horace in his satirical version of such a trip southwards. There the poet's own journey along the earlier part of the Via Appia is determinedly leisurely, as he takes two days to cover the ground that others might achieve within a day: *hoc iter ignaui diuisimus, altius ac nos | praecinctis unum: minus est grauis Appia tardis* ("Lazy as we are, we split this part of the journey, which more energetic travellers manage in one day: the Via Appia is less difficult for those who take it slowly," *Sat.* 1.5.5–6). As Gowers writes of this pedestrian poem: "walking is the natural pace for satire."[58] Statius' hendecasyllabic effusion speeds things up relative to Horace's hexametric satire (a satire that itself "rejects the high road of continuous epic"), just as Statius' traveller speeds up when he drives his animals down the new road leading off the Appian Way.[59] Now even this journey down to Naples, considerably longer than the short stretch of the Via Appia that Horace took at such a relaxed pace, has become achievable within a single day (*Silu.* 4.3.111–13):

qui primo Tiberim relinquit ortu,
primo uespere nauiget Lucrinum.
nil obstat cupidis, nihil moratur

He who leaves the River Tiber as the sun is just rising,
can sail the Lucrine Lake as it is just setting.
Nothing gets in the way of those eager to travel, nothing delays them.

With the acceleration of the nameless traveller comes a contraction in their journey time, and it is in playing further on this temporal dimension to the poem that Statius introduces some of his boldest moves in relation to Vergil's *Aeneid.* To an extent Statius has picked up on a theme of acceleration that is found in *Aeneid* 6 as well: Vergil's Sibyl vigorously speeds up the action whenever Aeneas seems to be dawdling.[60] Shortly after snapping at Aeneas for gazing at Daedalus' artwork, she incites the hero to push on with his prayer to Apollo: *"cessas in uota precesque, | Tros" ait "Aenea? cessas?"* (*Aen.* 6.51–2). Once in the underworld the Sibyl chivvies Aeneas on when he risks spending too much time discussing with Deiphobus the events surrounding the fall of Troy (*Aen.* 6.537–9):

et fors omne datum traherent per talia tempus,
sed comes admonuit breuiterque adfata Sibylla est:
"nox ruit, Aenea; nos flendo ducimus horas ...

And perhaps they would have spent all the allotted time on such things,

but his companion the Sibyl warned him and briefly explained
"The night is passing, Aeneas; we are wasting hours with weeping …"

Finally, the Sibyl ensures that Aeneas speeds up yet further after she has described the horrors in Tartarus and she and the hero are at last on the verge of the Elysian Fields (*Aen.* 6.628–30):

haec ubi dicta dedit Phoebi longaeua sacerdos,
"sed iam age, carpe uiam et susceptum perfice munus
acceleremus" ait.

After she had made this speech the long-lived priestess of Phoebus said,
"but come now, hit the road and finish the job you h ve undertaken;
let us speed up."

Despite the emphasis that the Sibyl has placed on Aeneas fulfilling his destiny without delay, this final quotation highlights an element of paradox in Vergil's presentation of the prophet. The Sibyl's visions command stretches of time that reach far beyond normal human limits of understanding. In parallel with this, according to legend, the Cumaean Sibyl inhabits a body that endures through abnormally long periods of time. Vergil nods to this tradition when he acknowledges that his Sibyl is *longaeua* ("long-lived"), but her insistence that Aeneas must hurry through his travels and experiences in *Aeneid* 6 suggests that, far from being slowed down by extreme old age, she is full of youthful vigour.

Vergil's inconsistency on this matter is fi st exposed by Ovid, the master of Vergilian re-reading, when he retells the story of the *Aeneid* at the end of his *Metamorphoses*. Throughout the books in which Ovid responds to the *Aeneid* he targets and magnifies Vergil's omissions, whilst eliding Vergil's more elaborate episodes.[61] Ovid focuses closely on the narratives of *Aeneid* 3 and *Aeneid* 6, and he makes the extreme old age of the Sibyl a crucial part of his characterization. Ovid's Sibyl dwells on the myth that she bargained for a thousand years of life from Apollo. She is now seven hundred years old and unsteady of step (*Met.* 14.142–4):

… sed iam felicior aetas
terga dedit, tremuloque gradu uenit aegra senectus,
quae patienda diu est.

… but now my happier youth has fled
and with tottering step weak old age approaches,
which must be endured for a long time.

Ovid's Sibyl looks forward to the time when her body will give way to her voice: *usque adeo mutata ferar nullique uidenda, | uoce tamen noscar; uocem mihi fata relinquent* ("I will be so much changed and visible to nobody, | however, I shall be known by my voice; the fates will leave me my voice," 14.152–3). In the move from the *Aeneid* to the *Metamorphoses* there has been no shift in the narrative time frame: Aeneas meets the Sibyl at the same point in his, and presumably her, life story. The main difference is that Ovid lingers on the return journey from the underworld, in an exact inversion of Vergil's narrative. Vergil's Aeneas and his Sibyl had conversed most during the preamble to their underworld visit and on the way to the Elysian Fields, with their return achieved brusquely and obscurely. Ovid moves the extended exchange between hero and prophet to a slow and fatigued return: *inde ferens lassos auerso tramite passus | cum duce Cumaea mollit sermone laborem* ("From there, dragging his weary footsteps along the path back | he eased the effort through conversation with his Cumaean guide," 14.120–1). The exhaustion of both characters on their way back amplifies the more fundamental exhaustion of the Sibyl who has "returned" to her epic travels, and whose age is now her defining feature. This age cannot be a result of the passing of narrative time between Vergil's plot and that of Ovid, since they address the same mythic moment. Yet in allowing the Sibyl to grow old between her appearance in one epic and another, Ovid uses the elastic age of the Sibyl to reflect the passage of literary history. The Sibyl is, by the time of Ovid's *Metamorphoses,* a tired old trope.

The question that remains, then, is how this Sibyl is still going strong in Domitian's era, one hundred years on from Ovid and Vergil's lifetime. By any calculation, ancient or modern, the mythic narrative with which Vergil and Ovid are concerned happened a good millennium before the construction of the Via Domitiana. No matter how young the Cumaean Sibyl really was when she met Aeneas, she should not be alive in Statius' era. If Statius were following Ovid's lead in letting the Sibyl's age measure the passing of a more fluid literary time, rather than mytho-historical time, then he could have made a case for his Sibyl being just a century older than the figure found in the *Aeneid* or the *Metamorphoses.* To do this, however, Statius would have needed to produce an even more aged or insubstantial Sibyl to mark the distance between the eras of the Augustan and the Flavian poets. Instead, while Statius' Sibyl may have white hair (*albam crinibus,* 4.3.116), she is snappy of step, of poetry, and of language.[62] Statius also rejects the possibility that the Sibyl has undergone a more fundamental transformation, the kind that both Vergil and Ovid had hinted would lie in the Sibyl's future. Her physical presence could by now have been identified with the Sibylline Books, which is what Vergil's Aeneas had implied that the Sibyl would become when she was moved to *penetralia* at Rome. This transformation into text may also be what Ovid was referring to when his Sibyl claimed that she would gradually turn into a disembodied voice over the final three hundred years of her life. Statius' Sibyl rejects both of these narratives. She scorns writing, implying that paper lacks the endurance of her own voice, while in bearing witness to her visual appearance Statius also makes it clear that she is not just a voice, either.

Statius' ebullient Sibyl does more than just defy the future that was mapped out for her by earlier texts; she even starts to amend the previous versions of her character. She and Statius are both addicted to the prefix "re-" in this section of the poem, as the two *uates* return to and rework her character. The words are not always about literal repetition, but their clustering creates a sense of reflective commentary on her past voice: *repone, replet, relinquit, renatae,* even the echo in *regente.*[63] Moreover, the Sibyl's fi st word, *dicebam* ("I used to say," 124), corrects the tradition that she was habitually a writer. Or, perhaps, the verb slyly alludes to the fact that even when poetic representations of her gesture towards the tradition of her writing, they consistently overrule it and end up granting her voice full rein regardless. At the same time, the reference to her delivery of prophecies in the past grants this contemporary Sibyl an authority that is not just that of a prophet, but that of a prophet proven truthful. The opening lines of her speech are not prophecy, but statement of present fact that is prophetic only through the retrospective construction of "I told you so."

The temporal twists and turns continue through to the very end of the Sibyl's speech, at which point she enters a truly prophetic mode. Here, in the last lines of the poem, the passage of time gets even more bizarrely interrupted and transcended, as the Sibyl suggests that Domitian will thrive until the Via Domitiana grows to be older than the Via Appia (*Silu.* 4.3.158–63):

et laudum cumulo beatus omni
scandes belliger abnuesque currus;
donec Troicus ignis et renatae
Tarpeius pater intonabit aulae,
haec donec uia te regente terras
annosa magis Appia senescet.

and blessed with all the heaping on of praise
you will climb some chariots in martial mode and reject others;
as long as there remains the Trojan fire and the Tarpeian father
continues to thunder in his restored temple,
until, while you rule the earth,
this road grows older than the ancient Via Appia.

Statius is clearly playing with Horace's prophecy at the end of his third book of *Odes* (*Carm.* 3.30.7–9):[64]

> ... usque ego postera
> crescam laude recens dum Capitolium
> scandet cum tacita uirgine pontifex.

> ... I will keep on growing,
> staying young through future praise, as long as
> a priest continues to climb the Capitol alongside a silent virgin.

The tension between these intertextual passages comes through the shifting roles played within the triangular configuration of poet, priest/priestess, and imperial power. Horace predicted that future audiences' praise of his poetry would grant him immortality, and keyed this to the enduring imperial monuments and religious rituals of Rome. By contrast, Statius' words of praise are delivered by the Sibyl and directed at Domitian, with the poet relegated to the background. Domitian climbs upwards, instead of the Roman priest. Statius has no silent virgin priestess in his scene, but a defiantly talkative one (recall *uirgineo... ore, Silu.* 4.3.123). Instead of performing rituals to guarantee the continued success of her city and its poetry, she composes the poetry, and specifically the temporal clause (162–3), that measures and celebrates the endurance of the *princeps*.

The temporal clause itself, however, seems to be a contradiction in terms. How can a road only just built become older than a road that has already long been in existence? Coleman rationalizes the line as an adynaton, while Shackleton Bailey takes it as "until the road becomes older than the Via Appia is *now*."[65] Both explanations make a kind of sense of the lines in the context of Roman imperial panegyric, but there is no denying the fact that the lines are perversely phrased. The contorted logic is compounded by the confusion of age and youth that Statius' Sibyl locates in Domitian's own family. Just a few lines earlier, the Sibyl had prophesied that Domitian would outlive his children and other descendants (*Silu.* 4.3.148–50):

> natis longior abnepotibusque
> annos perpetua geres iuuenta
> quos fertur placidos adisse Nestor ...

> longer-lived than your children and more distant descendants
> in eternal youth you will achieve the same number of peaceful years
> as Nestor is said to have experienced ...

For Domitian, whose only son had died a decade before the composition of this poem, these lines seem a tactless way to praise the emperor's divinity, but they fit the broader pattern of temporal distortions within the poem.[66] Domitian's unnatural longevity aligns the emperor with his sibylline panegyrist, who also seems to have found eternal youth in this poem.[67] Disregarding Statius' claims to immortality, though they are hinted at by the evocation of Horace's *sphragis*, Statius' Sibyl and Domitian instead perform the symbiotic relationship of patron and poet whose mutual support bestows fame and youth upon both figure . The ageless Sibyl composes the timeless poetry that voices Domitian's praise, while the ageless Domitian constructs the timeless road on which the Sibyl performs.[68] Prophet, *princeps*, and pathway all prove capable of transcending straightforward processes of temporal precedence.

IV. Comings and Goings

In this final section it is time to return to the notion of return journeys, and to rediscover what is happening to Statius' age and precedence as a poet while the Sibyl and Domitian negotiate their own immortality. The *Aeneid* constructs a forward-driving narrative in which Augustan Rome is the ultimate spatial and temporal goal, but it cannot ignore the anxiety of "what comes next?" in its teleological conception of history.[69] This is particularly pointed in *Aeneid* 6, where Anchises' account of the parade of heroes relies heavily on the reader's understanding of Rome's historical development. Is there really no danger that Rome will become one of the many cities that rise and fall, like Troy and Carthage before it?[70] And what of its imperial leadership? Who will follow Augustus, when the last historical moment mentioned in *Aeneid* 6, and indeed in the whole *Aeneid*, is the death of the emperor's heir, Marcellus?

At the central point of *Aeneid* 6 Rome has begun to appear as a real political and physical entity, and in the face of legitimate Augustan concerns about the future of Rome and its governance, the theme of "returning" works in the epic to create a sense of satisfying resolution and homecoming, rather than uncertain exploration, invasion, or colonization with undefined spatial or temporal ends. Vergil's decision to foreground Aeneas' back-and-forth trips in *Aeneid* 6 becomes part of his broader effort to set up the migration of the Trojans as a *nostos*, a return to the land of Dardanus. This legitimizes the Trojans' claim to Italian land, taps into the Greek *nostos* narratives, and fits the new Roman epic into a temporal framework that reaches even further back than the Trojan War. Meanwhile, the push-and-pull forces being identified with the city of Rome from before its very foundation provide a paradigm for the centripetal pull of contemporary Augustan imperial power, allied with its centrifugal expansionist agenda.[71] Statius builds on Vergil's lead in turning the dangerous theme of cities rising and falling over time into the rather safer issue of peoples coming and going through space; where Vergil focused on the significance of this for Rome, Statius focuses on what this means for individuals moving around the contemporary Roman empire – including himself.

Vergil had already established a connection between Rome and Cumae when his Sibyl recommended, in her final words of prophecy, that Aeneas seek his fi st alliance with those living in Pallanteum, the city founded by Evander on the site of future Rome (*Aen.* 6.95–7):

tu ne cede malis, sed contra audentior ito,
qua tua te Fortuna sinet. uia prima salutis
(quod minime reris) Graia pandetur ab urbe.

Do not give in to your troubles, but go forth all the more boldly in defianc ,
as far as your Fortune allows. The fi st road to safety
(though you may least expect it) will be opened to you from a Greek city.

Although she is herself a Greek figure explicitly based in a Greek colony (*Aen.* 6.2; 6.42), it is still surprising to find that the Sibyl defines Rome by its Hellenic origins. She is linking the Greek-founded cities in Italy to provide a pre-trodden pathway for the incoming Trojans, and to soften the impression of an Italy that exists simply "before" and "after" the foundational efforts of Aeneas. There are, rather, layers of foundation stories, with settlers marking the movement of humanity from one space to another as much as from one era to another.

Statius also explores the experience of those travelling between Rome and Cumae, and particularly the experience of writers on the move. The metaphorical road to safety (*uia ... salutis*, *Aen.* 6.96) that the Sibyl exhorts Aeneas to follow has been literalized in the form of the road that facilitates Roman imperial push and pull: the Via Domitiana. Statius takes the theme of the "return" found in *Aeneid* 6, but describes a journey down the road in the opposite direction to Aeneas, and further return journeys are implied by references to characters beyond the poem who live, travel, and send writings along the empire's roads. These characters include the poets Statius, Vergil, and the Sibyl herself.

Aeneas' promise that the Sibylline Books would find a home in the temple to Apollo on the Palatine imagined Vergil's Sibyl as having been reduced to text and transplanted to Rome by the time of the Augustan era. The situation appears to have changed in Statius' poem. The Via Domitiana may have brought Cumae closer to Rome than ever before, but in his role as the Sibyl's scribe at Cumae, Statius as poet-narrator is actually helping the prophet to resist her transformation into textual form and to resist the lure of Rome. He makes it unnecessary for her to travel, as his poetry conveys her voice to the city in her stead through the medium of the *Libri Siluarum,* rather than the *Libri Sibyllini.* In other words, the Sibyl's authority appears to have moved up to Rome for the Augustan poets, and returned to her long-established home at Cumae for the Flavians.

Statius also explores the mobility of the historical Vergil and his writings. Vergil's epic was to find its honorary home in Augustus' library on the Palatine, joining the Sibylline Books in the same complex. This is not, however, where Vergil's own journey ended. The poet was buried just outside Naples, not far from Cumae (a return journey of sorts too, as the *sphragis* of the *Georgics* reminds Vergil's audience of the time the poet spent in Naples or "Parthenope": *me... dulcis alebat | Parthenope, Georg.* 4.563–4). Like the Sibyl, Vergil ended up with a text in Rome and a body in Campania. Statius draws out the significance of this in his structuring of the fourth book of *Siluae,* which finds its author in the process of retiring to Naples.[72] Immediately following the poem on the Via Domitiana comes a verse letter written by Statius to a friend in Rome. In this hexametric poem Statius is apparently now established in Naples and using letters to help him traverse the distance between his home and Rome. Adopting the tactics used by Ovid in his exile poetry, Statius makes this travelling poem an extension of his authorial voice – and a speedy one at that, on account of the new Via Domitiana (*Silu.* 4.4.1–3):

> curre per Euboicos non segnis, epistula, campos,
> hac ingressa uias qua nobilis Appia crescit
> in latus ...

> Run as fast as you can across the Euboean plains, letter,
> setting off on your journey from this spot, where the famous Via Appia
> branches out sideways ...

Like the *Aeneid,* like the Sibylline Books, this poem reveals that Statius' book is submitting to the pull of Rome and its noble inhabitants. And like those other texts, the letter marks a detachment from the physical body of its original author. Indeed, this letter announces the fact that its author has just achieved a *nostos* that takes him in the opposite direction from his poetry, for he was born in Campania.[73] His return was long planned and fi - ted to his own aging, as he explains to his less enthusiastic wife in the final poem of the previous book. He questions the reason for her gloom: *anne quod Euboicos fessus remeare penates | auguror et patria senium componere terra?* ("Is it because, worn out as I am, I propose to return home to my Euboean household gods and to spend my declining years in my home country?" *Silu.* 3.5.12–13).

The tension between the direction of Statius and Vergil and the direction of their texts illustrates a more general poetic aspect of the peculiar push and pull associated with Rome's force field The attraction of Rome as a space that guarantees poetic immortality through its physical monuments, its cultural and ritual performances, and above all its political structures, draws in poets from across Italy and the wider empire.[74] But these poets identify their formative experiences – their education, leisure, retirement, or exile – with other parts of the empire, such that for them the city's gravitational pull generates traction. Autobiographical references to Sabine farms (Horace), Getic towns (Ovid), Spanish rivers (Martial), estates in Verona (Catullus), Mantua (Vergil), or Graeco-Roman Campania (Statius), all draw attention to the separation of poets from their poetic productions – the latter being more firmly tied to Rome. This division is fostered with care, particularly in the case of praise poets like Statius, whose works depend upon the Roman political epicentre for support and yet require some appearance of dispassionate distance for their praise to carry weight.[75]

What is striking about Statius's negotiation of this theme is that for him the relationship between poetic authority and carefully sustained distance operates in the realm of canon formation as well as that of political praise. In fact, in following Vergil to Naples towards the end of his career, Statius is performing an odd literalization of the final lines of his *Thebaid*, from which this chapter began. In those final lines of the *Thebaid* Statius defers politely to Vergil, as he does to the Sibyl's voice in *Siluae* 4.3. However, in *Siluae* 4.3 the temporal and spatial positioning of the characters on the Via Domitiana offers a more complex exploration of Statius' belief in how literary history operates. This exploration is modelled upon the dynamics of empire: imperial power emanates out in concentric circles from Rome, down its radial roads, whilst it demands feedback in the form of tributes in appreciative response, an influx of cultural productivity.[76] In the context of this political and poetic ebb and flo , Statius appears to feel less intimidated by Vergil's influence than he does at the end of the *Thebaid*. Indeed, Statius shows that he approaches the idea of sustained distance between people and places rather more confidently than even Vergil himself had done during Rome's fi st tentative steps into imperial praise. Where Vergil had used the concept of the labyrinth and the return, particularly in *Aeneid* 6, to make his Augustan foundation narrative a homecoming in the face of troubling challenges to his epic's teleological drive, Statius gestures to the direct and endlessly elastic nature of Rome's reach through time and space, and to the human "circulation" that takes place within this system on both a local and an imperial scale.[77] The mechanics and the discourses of empire now make negotiating distance from the city of Rome a familiar necessity, rather than an exotic danger; Statius has the freedom to send a book or to roam in person up and down the Via Domitiana, with his poetic outputs and his autobiographical narrative equally comfortably aligning themselves with Rome's pulsating radii.[78]

For Statius, Rome is central, and it is everywhere: all roads lead to Rome. The perspective offered by *Siluae* 4.3 undercuts the expression of humility that appeared to characterize the final lines of the *Thebaid*, where Statius had set his epic walking in the footsteps of Vergil's *Aeneid*. In the *Siluae*'s world of Flavian imperial praise, time and space are newly flexibl , with the notional boundaries of lives or regimes or landscapes replaced by representations of Rome's eternal and global – even cosmic – reach. Because of the empire's objective dominance over all dimensions, the subjective experience and status of its poets is freed from conventional hierarchies and rankings. In a world where Rome and its emperors are all-powerful, omnipresent, and immortal, no poet operating within those forces is ever precisely *behind* another poet, either in time or space. Each poet and his poetry are simply (and temporarily) facing in one direction or another.[79]

NOTES

1 I would like to express my gratitude to the participants of the Symposium Cumanum 2013, who generously offered many thoughtful suggestions in response to my paper. Particular thanks to Bill Gladhill for organizing the event, and to him and Micah Myers for their editorial help as the paper turned into this chapter. I am also grateful to John Schafer for a fascinating conversation on the Roman bookroll.

2 The rhetoric of post-Augustan decline is exposed and exploded in Hinds 1998: 83–91. Ziolkowsky and Putnam 2008: 59 note that the notion of walking behind used here by Statius not only alludes to a hierarchy of literary prestige, but also appropriates the speech of Aeneas telling Dido about the decision to have Creusa walk behind him as he left Troy (Verg. *Aen.* 2.711). On these final lines of the *Thebaid*, see McNelis 2007: 23; Ganiban 2007: 2–3, with bibliography.

3 On the title *Woods*, see Wray 2007.

4 Henderson 1998: 102–7.

5 On the fictionality of the *deixis* in the poem, see Nauta 2002: 359–61. Hulls 2010 points out that throughout the fourth book of *Siluae* Statius is preoccupied by reworking other literary genres into a more occasional mode: epic in *Siluae* 4.2 and 4.3, but also lyric in 4.5 and 4.7. Rosati 2002 discusses Statius' self-consciousness as a poet more generally.

6 Dio 67.14.1.

7 Coleman 1988: xx–xxii; Nauta 2008; Newlands 2012: 136–59.

8 Morzadec 2004: 85 notes the "triptyque" that constitutes the fi st three praise poems of *Siluae* 4. This tripartite division repeats within 4.3, split as it is between the voices of Statius, Volturnus, and the Sibyl.

9 Reitz 2012. For more on the complexities of Statius' praise of imperial and other elite *luxuria* and *aedificatio*, see Myers 2000; Bodel 1997: 16.

10 Statius' text is from Coleman 1988 throughout; translations are my own.

11 On the geography of the poem, see Smolenaars 2006: 226–7; more generally on Roman landscape and imperial power, see Purcell 1990 and 2012.

12 Gowers 1993 and 2011.

13 Nauta 2008: 148–9 exposes the staginess of this scene.

14 Hardie 1983: 141 argues that Statius' reference to the Sibyl as a *uates sanctior* (*Silu.* 4.3.120) is part of a more general reluctance on his part to lay claim to the status of *uates* as poets did in the Augustan era, though Nauta 2008: 149 points out that Statius is still essentially "playing" the *uates*. Gladhill notes (personal correspondence) that Vergil never uses the term *uates* of himself until after *Aeneid* 6, so Statius may be aligning himself with the Vergil of the early books of the *Aeneid*. See further Lovatt 2007: 146, also addressing the connection with the Sibyl's appearance as a poetic *uates* in *Siluae* 5.3.

15 Barchiesi in this volume notes how the Trojans are already beginning to map and tame the wilderness around Avernus in Vergil's *Aeneid*, partly to reflect the engineering works in the region undertaken by Agrippa.

16 Nicoll 1988. In this volume see Barchiesi.

17 "Halting steps" in the sense that these trips repeatedly stop and start, but Herrero in this volume rightly notes how Aeneas' and the Sibyl's actual gait is determined, firm and speedy, especially in contrast with that of the dead in the Underworld.

18 Fitzgerald 1984: 52.

19 On Vergil's inclusion of the Minotaur myth, and its significance for Seneca see Gladhill in this volume.

20 Cf., e.g., Mart. 9.64.3; *OCD* sv. Hecate.

21 Hom. *Od.* 19.562–7. On the ambiguities of Vergil's version of this, see (among many) Otis 1959; Tarrant 1982; Molyviati-Toptsis 1995. On the Gates, see also Parker in this volume.

22 See also Barchiesi in this volume.

23 Morgan 2000: 114–15; Newlands 2002: 300; Morgan 2010: 54–6. The visual appearance of the poem may not have made much impact in recitation, but it complements the poem's noisy aural dimension (discussed below): this is a poem designed to trigger a range of senses in a variety of reading contexts.

24 Van Sickle 1980: 6 and Winsbury 2009: 46 identify as the norm 25–45 lines per column, based on calculations in Kenyon 1932: 55–7. Johnson 2004: 122–5 observes that papyrus column heights increase (at Oxyrhynchus, at least) from the second century CE, and identifies the verage range of lines as 25–50, with some rare examples reaching anywhere from 18 to 64 lines.

25 Schafer 2017. The assumption that 4.3 begins at the top of a column is a big one, particularly as the prose preface to *Siluae* 4 complicates any attempt to establish a layout that works for the whole book. However, even if each poem did not begin at the top of a new column, a rough calculation based on word counts suggests that the preface could fit neatly into one single column with the fi st two poems of the book filling three more approximately forty-line columns (114 lines of verse, with a little extra space needed to mark the mid-column division between *Silu.* 4.1 and 4.2). This layout would still leave 4.3 to start at the top of column 5.

26 An intriguing comparandum is the 110-line Latin epigraphic poem with strong Statian echoes that is unevenly inscribed over three columns on a funerary monument in North Africa (*CIL* VIII.212–13; CLE 1552 A and B). It displays marks that appear to reveal a more systematic original layout on papyrus. See Force 1993, with Pillinger 2013: 184.

27 As Morgan 2000: 118 notes, the very couching of a panegyrical poem in informal hendecasyllables creates a tension between form and function. This reflects a more general ambiguity in the *Siluae* that is embedded in the work's title. Wray 2007 notes that, after the Greek ὕλη on which it is modelled, the word suggests a meditation upon the form and values of "wood" (timber, things constructed out of wood), "the woods" (untamed forest, trees), and "material" (matter, including rough drafts of poems and man-made artefacts). When these poems focus on man-made constructions and their relation to the natural world, as in *Siluae* 4.3, they present a constellation of jostling natural and artistic phenomena "like a flashy talent show in which natur , when beaten, is bested by having its artwork incorporated into the design of a human artist" (138).

28 Newlands 2002: 306–8. Martelli 2009: 158 notes, moreover, that while the Via Domitiana is open to hordes of public, in Statius' celebration of its construction it is "as yet quite literally untrodden."

29 Willis 2011: 38–55 explores, through her reading of Caesar in Lucan's *Bellum Ciuile*, how free and fast movement, particularly when enabled by new technology, can represent an assertion of totalitarian power and aggression against a well-spaced diversity of nature and cities. After he crosses the Rubicon,

"Caesar's occupation of Italy sets Rome in motion, scattering the people of Rome, reorganizing the material flows which constitute the Empire (53).

30 Newlands 2002: 306–9. Willis 2011: 45 draws attention to Lucan's assimilation of Caesar to Xerxes bridging the Hellespont in *Bellum Ciuile* 2.672–82; there, certainly, the identification is not a compliment

31 Smolenaars 2006: 230–3; Morgan 2010: 52–9; Coleman 1988: 103.

32 Reitz 2012: 340.

33 Newlands 2012: 24 offers some cautionary words on assuming that praise of Domitian lies at the heart of Statius' *Siluae*, noting that only seven of the twenty-seven poems published in Statius' lifetime were dedicated to the emperor. She acknowledges, though, that *Siluae* 4.3 is the third of three poems in a row that are devoted to imperial praise. In the letter to Marcellus that prefaces the fourth book of *Siluae*, Statius draws attention to this fact: *reor equidem aliter quam inuocato numine maximi imperatoris nullum opusculum meum coepisse; sed hic liber tres habet* ("To be sure, I do not believe that any one of my little works has opened without invoking the divinity of our great emperor; but this book has three," *Silu.* 4 *praef.*).

34 Purcell 1990: 23 (my italics).

35 Fantham 2009: 180, with Coleman 1988: 125 and Newlands 2002: 308–9.

36 On Domitian's adoption of the title *dominus et deus*, see Suet. *Dom.* 13.2 and Dio 67.4.7. In this context Ahl 1984: 78ff. offers an extended defence of Statius' praise poetry as double-speaking critique. The phrase is echoed in the Sibyl's salutation of Domitian as *dux hominum et parens deorum* (*Silu.* 4.3.139).

37 Purcell 2012: 380.

38 Morgan 2000: 117 discusses the strange lack of digression in Statius' Sibyl compared with Vergil's sibylline *ambages*. For the use of hexameters in real sibylline oracles, see Parke 1988: 6.

39 Newlands 2002: 312–13.

40 Smolenaars 2006: 236–44; Morgan 2010: 71–3, with a discussion of how Vergil's *ambages* are replaced by an absence of *ambitus* on the Via Domitiana.

41 Pillinger 2019: 157–65. In this volume see Barchiesi on Helenus' introduction of Avernus.

42 Unlike other collections of sibylline oracles, the Sibylline Books were kept out of public circulation. The collection was burned in the destruction of the Capitoline temple of Jupiter in 83 BCE, but another collection was promptly assembled for consultation by the *quindecimuiri*. The collection as a whole was copied out afresh and moved to the Palatine under Augustus. See Dio 54.17.2–3 and (with slightly confused chronology) Suet. *Aug.* 31.1, with Parke 1988: 149n11; Miller 2009: 240, esp. n118, and Pillinger 2019: 165–73.

43 Thanks to Micah Myers (personal correspondence) for pointing out the arboreal connection.

44 Morgan 2010: 67.

45 Coleman 1988: 128; Smolenaars 2006: 226; Morgan 2010: 52–3 all draw attention to an inscription found at Puteoli (later partially erased), giving thanks from the citizens of Puteoli to Domitian in remarkably similar terms: "by the indulgence of the greatest and divine leader brought close to his city" (*indulgentia maximi diuinique principis urbi eius admota*), *AE* 1973: 137 = 1941: 73.

46 On the centripetal pull of Rome and the resistance of diverse localities within its empire, see Newlands 2012: 137.

47 On Domitian's absence from public life, and his resistance to the reader's gaze in the *Siluae*, see McCullough 2007/8.

48 Coleman 1988: 131; Smolenaars 2006: 237, with Newlands 2002: 314 on the possible hint of Lucr. 5.8: *deus ille fuit, deus*. Smolenaars 2006: 240 identifies the links between Statius' Sibyl's speech at *Silu.* 4.3.145–63 with that of Anchises in Vergil's underworld at *Aen.* 6.791ff. and with *Ecl.* 4.

49 On the sexualization of this scene, see Norden 1957 *ad loc.*; Horsfall 2013a: 117; Horsfall 2006: 478, with Fowler 2002 in particular. The intertextuality of this Vergilian scene with Catullus 51 and Sappho fr. 31 emphasizes the eroticized dimension of the triangular relationship, in which Apollo and the Sibyl are teasing Aeneas and the viewer. See further Pillinger 2019: 180–1. So too in Statius' poem, the poet is left as a gooseberry while the Sibyl and Domitian become the main players in the poem.

50 Rosati 2002 addresses the useful political detachment created by Statius' deployment of Muses.

51 On the "heat" of inspiration elsewhere in Statius: *Pierius calor menti incidit* (*Theb.* 1.3), with Rosati 2002: 250.

52 Like Smolenaars 2006: 244 and Morgan 2010: 54, Reitz 2012: 337 explores how the speed of the objects Statius praises is implicitly a celebration of the speed of his poetic composition, and vice versa: his poetic construction mirrors the world outside the text.

53 Morgan 2010: 74–5.

54 The Sibylline Books were written in Greek, like the other sibylline oracles. Servius (ad *Aen.* 6.321) explains further that the Cumaean Sibyl settled at Cumae after leaving Erythrae.

55 Morgan 2000: 116.

56 For Nauta 2002 the anonymous traveller marks *Siluae* 4.3 as a benefaction to the general public, rather than to the poet alone. See also Nauta 2008: 149.

57 Coleman 1988: 111 identifies the tr veller's vehicle as a *cisium*.

58 Gowers 1993: 55.

59 Gowers 2012: 188.

60 On the speed of the Sibyl and Aeneas in the *Aeneid*, see Herrero in this volume.

61 Tissol 1993; Solodow 1988: 136–56; in this volume see Keith on Vergilian underworlds in Ovid.

62 *Pace* Smolenaars 2006: 237, who reads the white hair as a sign of Statius' Sibyl's advanced age. Indeed, Morgan 2010: 114n66 notes how often Statius uses old age as a closural motif in the *Siluae;* surely that is the last thing that the Sibyl is being identified with here in *Siluae* 4.3, as she looks forward to the eternal life of Domitian.

63 With thanks to Alison Keith for bringing this to my attention. Note too Statius on Domitian's restoration of moral order earlier in the poem: *reddit ... reponit* (16–17).

64 Coleman 1988: 134–5, Smolenaars 2006: 242–4.

65 Coleman 1988: 135, followed by Smolenaars 2006: 243; Shackleton Bailey 2003: 266n21.

66 Smolenaars 2006: 241, who retranslates the line as "longer than *our* sons and grandsons."

67 Morzadec 2004: 88.

68 Another Horatian reference, with Horace *Carm.* 3.25.1–2; see Morgan 2010: 71.

69 See Kilgour in this volume on the response of later writers to this central problem of prophecy and its uncertainty in the *Aeneid.*

70 Feeney 1986: esp. 7–8, and Rossi 2002: 245.

71 Barchiesi 2005 discusses Vergil's "discourse of mobility."

72 Newlands 2012 notes on *Siluae* 3.5, the closural poem of *Siluae* 1–3, which is designed to cajole the poet's wife into retiring with him to Naples, that "The *Siluae* ... re-calibrate the trajectory of Vergil's career which associated Naples with the fi st poetry, *Eclogues* and *Georgics,* and Rome with the masterpiece, the *Aeneid.* In *Silu.* 3.5 Naples and *Siluae* are a post-epic destination" (145).

73 On Statius' divided loyalties, see Newlands 2012: 136–59 and Rosati 2011.

74 Woolf 2003.

75 See Roman 2010 on the roughly contemporaneous and parallel case of Martial's retirement to Spain.

76 Purcell 2012: 377 discusses the explicit marking of this on the city's radial roads.

77 On the concept of "circulation, see Purcell 2012: 383–4.

78 This does not mean that there is no narrative to Statius' life; *au contraire,* Henderson 2007 shows the drama to his withdrawals into private life and out again.

79 For an entertaining example of this in a contemporary interaction on the Appian Way, see Kaster 2012: 56.

3

In the Sibyl's Cave: Vergilian Prophecy and Mary Shelley's *Last Man*

MAGGIE KILGOUR

unde iste per orbem
primus uenturi miseris animantibus aeger
creuit amor?

When did this worldwide, sick obsession/to know the future fi st infect sad mortals?" (Statius, *Thebaid* 3.551–3)[1]

This paper begins and ends at the Sibyl's cave in 1826 when, four years after the drowning of her husband Percy Bysshe Shelley off the coast of Italy at Livorno, Mary Shelley published her fi st new novel since his death, *The Last Man*. In the "Author's Introduction," a nameless narrator recalls a trip in 1818 to Cumae, which climaxed with a visit to a cave in which she discovered "piles of leaves, fragments of bark, and a white filmy substance" covered with characters in languages ancient and modern that "seemed to contain prophecies, detailed relations of events but lately passed."[2] Her companion excitedly exclaimed, "This *is* the Sibyl's cave; these are Sibylline leaves" (3). Gathering together and deciphering as many of the leaves as possible, the narrator gave "form and substance to the frail and attenuated Leaves of the Sibyl" (4), piecing together a narrative from the twenty-fi st century (2073–2100) in which the entire world, with the obvious exception of the titular last man, is destroyed by the plague.

As this opening scene suggests, educated fi st by her father, the radical author William Godwin, and then by her husband, Shelley had had a good classical education.[3] Like most Romantics, Percy Shelley had been passionate about Homer, who was idealized as the model for the Romantic original genius, the fi st of all poets. The Shelleys had been reading him in June 1822 just before Percy drowned.[4] But Mary Shelley singled out Vergil as "a great favourite of mine."[5] She loved the *Georgics*, which she read many times, including in winter 1819 when she was in Naples and wrote: "I have been reading also Virgil's *Georgics*, which is, in many respects, the most beautiful poem I ever read – He wrote it at Baiæ; and sitting at the window, looking almost at the same scene that he did – reading about manners little changed since his days, has made me enjoy his poem, more, I think, than I ever did any other."[6] She had reread it also just before Shelley died, at the same time that they were reading Homer, and returned to it after his death. In April 1825, reading Vergil's depiction of the approach of spring helped revive her spirits after a period of depression (*Letters* 1: 476):

> My Percy is quite well – & has exchanged his constant Winter occupation of drawing for playing in the fields (which are now useful as well as ornamental) flying kite – gardening, &c – I bask in the sun on the grass reading Virgil, that is, my beloved *Georgics* ... I begin to live again, & as the Maids of Greece sang joyous hymns on the revival of Adonis, does my Spirit lift itself in delightful thanksgiving on the awakening of Nature to geniality & the feeling of delight in my careful mind.

For Shelley, the *Georgics* suggest the possibility of renewal after her devastating loss, a promise that, like nature, her life will go on. At the same time, in *The Last Man*, Vergil's poem also gives her a haunting image of total destruction that leaves no hope of renewal, as her descriptions of the plague and its effects on the world look back to the bleak ending of *Georgics* 3.[7]

Tracing the birth of Rome from the destruction of Troy, the *Aeneid* is also a story of renewal. Shelley also frequently refers to and quotes from *Aeneid* 1–6, which she had read aloud to her husband from 6 to 9 January 1818, and which they had reread together in March–May 1820.[8] In a letter of August 1826 she quotes, or rather misquotes, the famous lines from Aeneas's descent to hell to describe her own sad life in which "to smile at ill luck & bear with unaltered brow hateful employments & care for tomorrow – *hic labor hoc opus est*."[9] She drew a further parallel between her experience and *Aeneid* 6 at the opening of *The Last Man*, in which she makes her narrator an Aeneas who descends into the Sibyl's cave to see the future.[10] Like many others, she associated Vergil with prophecy and knowledge of the future; in fact, she occasionally used the *sortes Vergilianae* that had developed out of the medieval tradition of reading the Vergil of the fourth *Eclogue* as a Christian prophet.[11] (She had tried it the spring before Shelley died.)[12] In this paper, I place Shelley's attraction to Vergil in a long tradition of adapting and interpreting Anchises' prophecy of the future of Rome in *Aeneid* 6. Like other writers, Shelley was drawn to Vergil's vision of history, and especially to the way his presentation of his own historical present and much of the Roman *past* as the *future* made time paradoxically both a teleological line marching to a grand climax and a process of endless renewal. Moreover, breaking off with the figure of Augustus's heir Marcellus, Vergilian history leads up to the repeated premature death of young men, a paradoxical cycle of radical rupture that for Mary Shelley foretells her husband's death.

Anchises's prophecy in *Aeneid* 6.756–886, reinforced by the images on Aeneas' shield in Book 8, gave Roman history a linear, teleological shape. Rome marched forward from Aeneas to Augustus, whose reign retrospectively gave Aeneas's journey its ultimate meaning and purpose. History thus has a goal, a sense of closure and fulfilment [13] For later Christian writers, Vergil's episode was useful as it constructed an essentially typological relation between past and present, Aeneas and Augustus, similar to that which Christians used to make the New Testament the fulfilment of events and characters, types, prefigured in the Old. Through a similar logic Aeneas became a type for Christ and Vergil himself a prophet pointing towards a revelation of providential history and the establishment of a Rome in which, as Dante says, *Cristo è romano* ("Christ is Roman").[14] All roads may lead to Rome, but for Christians they more importantly lead to Christ. In his unfi - ished epic, *Davideis*, a work explicitly modelled on "the *Pattern* of our Master *Virgil*," the seventeenth-century English poet Abraham Cowley shows how Vergilian prophecy can be mapped onto the biblical begat narratives.[15] In *Davideis* 2, Anchises's genealogy of Rome is grafted onto the tree of Jesse when Cowley's hero David has a dream vision of history from himself down to Christ, in whom Christian history is fulfilled Moreover, at the end of his dream, when he hears of the incarnation, David awakens, and the angel Gabriel appears to him to reassure him that his vision is no dream (304–5):

> Hail, *Man* belov'ed! from highest heav'en (said he)
> My mighty *Master* sends thee *health* by me.
> The things thou saw'est are full of *truth* and *light*,
> Shap'd in the *glass* of the divine *Foresight*.
> Ev'n now old *Time* is harnessing the years
> To go in order thus; hence empty fears;
> Thy Fate's all *white*; from thy blest seed shall spring
> The promis'd *Shilo*, the great *Mystick King*.
> Round the whole earth his dreaded name shall sound,
> And reach to *Worlds*, that must not yet be *found*.
> The *Southern Clime* him her sole *Lord* shall stile,
> Him all the *North*, ev'en *Albions stubborn Isle*.

My *Fellow-Servant*, credit what I tell.
Straight into shapeless air unseen he fell.

The description of Christ's dominion in the last six lines echoes *Aeneid* 6.794–7, in which Augustus *super et Garamantas et Indos | proferet imperium; iacet extra sidera tellus, | extra anni solisque uias* ("will advance his empire beyond the Garamants and Indians to a land which lies beyond our stars").[16] Like Vergil's Augustus, Cowley's Christ is an imperialist whose realm will expand to cover the earth. Or rather, from a Christian perspective, Augustus's earthly empire is a type of Christ's spiritual empire, which completes and ends what Augustus started.[17]

Cowley's insistent addition that this is no dream – Gabriel's assurance that what David has seen is "full of *truth* and *light*, | Shap'd in the *glass* of the divine *Foresight*" – moreover, reassuringly rewrites the troubling end of Vergil's episode in which Aeneas exits from the gate of ivory of false dreams. The end of *Aeneid* 6 calls the status of Vergil's story, and indeed Roman history, into question: is it just a false dream presented to delude Aeneas and the reader?[18] In contrast to Virgil's uncertain vision, biblical history is presented as unambiguously real. Cowley thus asserts the standard Christian belief that classical myths are merely shadowy types that have been superseded by Christian truths. For the seventeenth-century Cowley, the Christian story he is telling is far superior to its pagan models, showing also how modern, rational, and scientific truth surpasses primitive fiction .

This distinction between classical myth and Christian truth is central in Dante, whose entire *Commedia* is a revision of *Aeneid* 6, with Dante as both a new Aeneas and a new Vergil. Going beyond his pagan model, Dante descends to the underworld in order to rise higher; it is not in hell but in heaven that he gets his vision of the future, revealed to him by his ancestor Cacciaguida. Although Vergil the character has disappeared from the poem by this point, his work is still needed to make Cacciaguida visible to Dante: Cacciaguida appears mediated through a simile that immediately tells the reader the significance of this meeting in Dante's journey (*Paradiso* 15.25–7):

Sì pïa l'ombra d'Anchise si porse,
se fede merta nostra maggior musa,
quando in Eliso del figlio s'acco se.

With like affection did the shade of Anchises stretch forward (if our greatest Muse merits belief), when in Elysium he perceived his son.

The explicit parallel with *Aeneid* 6 makes Cacciaguida the Dantesque revision of Anchises and reinforces the conventional difference between the classical and Christian quests. At the very beginning of the *Commedia,* Dante had protested to Vergil, *Io non Enëa … sono* ("I am not Aeneas," *Inferno* 2.32) to suggest that he is no hero. At the end, however, he becomes a new and greater kind of hero, one whose quest takes him beyond that of his pagan precursor, who himself could only take the pilgrim as far as the Earthly Paradise before he had to return to eternal life in Limbo. As a Christian prophet, Dante sees more than Vergil could, and so realizes how his own quest replaces that of Aeneas.[19]

Vergil's history of Rome was therefore interpreted to make it compatible with Christian history and to create a typological and so teleological relation between classical and Christian. Roman history marched towards the coming of Christ that would ultimately bring history to an end with the last judgment. But Vergil's representation of Augustus as the culmination of Roman history was also imitated by writers with more secular interests. Authors of dynastic epic followed Vergil to praise their patrons as new Augusti. In *Orlando Furioso,* Ariosto recalls Vergil when he presents the history of Ferrara as the line of the d'Este family that is revealed through a prophecy to Bradamante, female founder of the family tree, which climaxes triumphantly with his own patron, Alfonso. Following Ariosto, Spenser used Vergil's model to tell the story of England as the genealogy leading from his heroine Britomart to Elizabeth. In Ariosto, the revelation of the future takes place not in the Sibyl's but in Merlin's cave, a locale even more appropriate for Spenser since the Tudors traced their line back to King Arthur. Spenser's Merlin tells Britomart the history of England, which leads to a grand finale in Elizabeth (3.3.49.6–9):

> Then shall a royall virgin raine, which shall
> Stretch her white rod ouer the *Belgicke* shore,
>   And the great Castle smite so sore with all,
>   That it shall make him shake, and shortly learne to fall.[20]

Elizabeth, like Augustus and Christ, conquers the world. As Augustus made clear the meaning of Aeneas's journey, Elizabeth validates Britomart's, offering it a larger goal.

Vergil's reversal of time thus suits not only Christian history but dynastic epic and political propaganda generally, as it makes the poet's present a future triumphant culmination of past promise. As Ariosto and Spenser both recognize, of course, the poet's prophetic vision has to stop short when the future literally becomes his own present. Even Vergil could not really see the future. Ariosto can get around this limitation by gesturing vaguely beyond his time to (3.59.3–8):

ogni tuo ramo, il cui
valor la stirpe sua tanto sublima,
bisognerà che si rischiari e abbui
più volte prima il ciel, ch'io te li esprima:
e sarà tempo ormai, quando ti piaccia,
ch'io dia licenza all'ombre, e ch'io mi taccia.

Many others worthy of renown,
The which to name might find one work to do
From Phoebus' rising to his going down.
Now therefore, if you will consent thereto,
I here will end and send the spirits down.[21]

In Spenser, however, Merlin tells of the reign of Elizabeth and then stops abruptly (3.3.50.1–4):

But yet the end is not. There *Merlin* stayd,
As ouercomen of the spirites powre,
Or other ghastly spectacle dismayd,
That secretly he saw, yet note discoure.

As many critics have noted, the sudden and ominous end of the narrative recalls the abrupt breaking off of Anchises's presentation with the figure of the young Marcellus, who, as Denis Feeney notes, represents a "future which is painted gloriously (872–81), and then taken away from us, unrealised."[22] When Vergil reaches his own present, the story of Rome comes to an untimely end with mourning for the premature death of Augustus's nephew and heir. While Augustus has fulfilled the past, he leaves an unimaginable future. The scene was resonant in England from the 1580s on when the succession and thus the future of England was uncertain. As John Watkins pointed out, moreover, "Like Vergil, Spenser found himself in the awkward position of composing a dynastic epic for a sovereign whose barrenness threatened to extinguish the dynasty."[23] The fact that Alfonso d'Este had five sons meant that Ariosto could point with some confidence towards a bright future; what was in store for England was much more uncertain.

Spenser's revision thus brings out one of the darker aspects of Vergilian history, undoing its appearance of typological closure and fulfilment by gesturing to the unknowability of what lies ahead. The grand climax of Merlin's prophecy, like Anchises's vision of the future, is not fulfilment but truncation and incompletion. In Vergil, moreover, this discontinuity, imagined as the death of a young man, will be replayed at the end of the *Aeneid* with the abrupt and violent death of another young man who represents a future that will never happen: Turnus. As the death of Marcellus ends the story of Rome, the death of Turnus brings the poem to a sudden, shocking halt. It suggests that, underneath its teleological thrust, Vergilian history is both circular and fragmented, as what it renews is paradoxically the breaking off of succession and promise.[24]

Other writers had noted and built on this unsettling contradiction. In the vision of history given to Adam at the end of *Paradise Lost*, Milton reasserts Vergilian closure in the workings of providential history only to show that such closure is itself a problem. Like Cowley, Milton shapes biblical history through Vergil, as the angel Michael displays to Adam the future of the world that will lead from himself to Christ. Critics debate over whether Milton means us to see his history as real progress – a *felix culpa* – or not. In the end, Adam sees it positively, but, newly made and now befuddled by the fall, his interpretive skills are not completely reliable. Moreover, Milton draws particular attention to what it means to be able to see the future. Presented with the story of the flood Adam fi st complains bitterly (11.770–6):

> Let no man seek
> Henceforth to be foretold what shall befall
> Him or his Children, evil he may be sure,
> Which neither his foreknowing can prevent,
> And hee the future evil shall no less
> In apprehension then in substance feel
> Grievous to bear.

Knowledge of the future is the worst kind of knowledge without power: it reveals the helplessness of humans that for Milton is the most distressing consequence of the fall and that is indeed one of his central preoccupations in his late works. The fact that the future can be seen by Adam means that it is already determined; Milton shows how the fall fixes history in a rigid and relentless pattern, in which humans re-enact Adam's and Eve's deadly original sin over and over again. As in Vergil, repetition seems to pull against the teleological thrust of typology.[25] Even worse, while – or in fact because – Christ brings salvation and ultimately the closure of the apocalypse, individual human actions seem useless: if Christ alone can defeat evil and redeem us, why should we try to achieve anything at all? Characteristically, Dante distanced his cosmos from the deterministic element of Vergilian history. In

Purgatorio 6, the prayers to speed up the souls' ascents to paradise prompts Dante to ask Vergil why in *Aeneid* 6.376 the Sibyl had told Palinurus: *desine fata deum flecti sperare precando* ("cease to hope that heaven's decrees may be bent by praying"). In Vergil's universe, ruled by irrevocable Fate, prayers have no efficacy in Dante's cosmos governed by a loving God, they do.[26] Again classical and Christian worlds separate. For Milton, however, they are part of a continuum: Vergilian history is the form that history takes after the fall when a free, growing, and open-ended world turns into a bound and closed one. The very closure of typology is a sign of the restriction of free will that is a consequence of Adam and Eve's sin. The modelling of the vision of the future at the end of *Paradise Lost* on *Aeneid* 6 shows that the fall is a fall into Vergilian history.[27]

For Mary Shelley also, history after the death of her husband takes a Vergilian shape. Adam's lament for his foreknowledge provides the epigraph for Shelley's novel, and in many ways introduces its main theme: what does it feel like and what does it mean to know the future?[28] As her experiments with the *sortes Vergilianae* suggest, Shelley was obsessed with trying to predict and control future events. Throughout her letters and journals she refers to constant forebodings and premonitions, seeing herself as a kind of Sibyl: "were not my prophesies of last year strange & true? – Now in vain would I exert my Sibylline propensities –."[29] In retrospect, she frequently read her own works as eerily prophetic. Looking back, she said that: "it seems to me that in what I have hitherto written I have done nothing but prophecy what has arrived to. Matilda [Shelley's very painful, chillingly autobiographical novel] fortells even many small circumstances most truly – & the whole of it is a monument of what now is –."[30] Another letter written after Percy Shelley's drowning suggests with staccato breathiness that her description of the drowning of the character of Euthanasia in her earlier novel *Valperga* anticipated it: "Is not the end of mine wondrous – the fate – the shore – how miserably foretold – it is very strang[e]."[31] She had written her own fate without knowing it.[32] But this hardly makes her the author of her own destiny; as she constantly complains, prophetic insight is not a source of power. On hearing of Byron's death, she wrote to his mistress: "How much you feared this voyage! every day I am more certain that God has endowed us with the power to foresee our misfortunes. But we are all Cassandras."[33] The theme of prophecy runs through her works: Beatrice in *Valperga* is a prophet, while in *The Last Man*, false prophets arise at the end of the world. While the opening epigraph warns us of the horrors of knowing what will come, the opening setting of the Sibyl's cave thrusts us into a world in which everyone is trying to piece together the future.[34] The internal narrator Lionel, who is in many ways a version of Shelley herself, is also prone to presentiments and frequently wishes, rather ironically, that he could see the future (310–11):

The coming time was as a mighty river, down which a charmed boat is driven, whose mortal steersman knows, that the obvious peril is not the one he needs fear, yet that danger is nigh; and who floats awe-struck under beetling precipices, through the dark and turbid waters – seeing in the distance yet stranger and ruder shapes, towards which he is irresistibly impelled. What would become of us? O for some Delphic oracle, or Pythian maid, to utter the secrets of futurity! O for some Œdipus to solve the riddle of the cruel Sphynx! Such Œdipus was I to be – not divining a word's juggle, but whose agonizing pangs, and sorrow-tainted life were to be the engines, wherewith to lay bare the secrets of destiny, and reveal the meaning of the enigma, whose explanation closed the history of the human race.[35]

As the world falls apart and Lionel tries to imagine the future, he goes to a performance of *Macbeth*, a play concerned with prophecy and succession, which he sees in horror as a prefiguration of his own situation (203–4)[36]

Shelley's novel was not well received – to put it mildly – and was then almost totally neglected for at least 150 years. Recent reappraisals of Shelley's works have wanted to reclaim it as part of the tradition of Romantic prophecy, praising its critique of imperialism especially as visionary. Timothy Ruppert claims moreover that "Shelley challenges the deterministic, even fatalistic perspective of history as the record of absolute necessity."[37] He argues that the loop of time created by presenting the narrative that comes from the future has a radically disruptive (i.e., good) effect:

This seemingly vertiginous narrative experiment allows Shelley to unsettle hierarchical, linear understandings of human temporality and so to present history as founded indecisively on disrupted time. Shelley thus assays various notions of literary and temporal continuity to show that humankind's fate, despite history's myriad nightmares, is never foreordained; accordingly, her *Last Man* is less a doomful prediction of imperial decay than a prophecy of hope justified by the regenerative power of the human imagination.[38]

But Ruppert's argument depends partly on a reading of the presentation of history in Milton that I find overly idealistic. Adam's outburst that the fall is fortunate is undermined by Milton's representation of history as a process of endless degeneration and misery for human beings that makes such optimism seem insensitive to the cold reality of human suffering. Recuperative readings of Shelley's work seem themselves to share an idealism that the novel recurrently shows to be impotent against the force of the plague. (I also think that if a novel is going to demonstrate "the regenerative power of the human imagination" it needs itself to be more imaginative or indeed just better written than *The Last Man*. Fascinating as it is in many ways, it is not Shelley's finest novel, nor likely to displace her husband's poetry from the canon.)[39] Far from breaking free from determinism, the novel embraces it passionately, insisting that history is, as Milton showed, locked in endless repetition. Shelley herself became increasingly fatalistic; as she wrote in a letter of 1827: "The power of Destiny I feel every day pressing more & more on me, & I yield myself a slave to it."[40] In the novel, her alter ego Lionel describes the reality of things (290–1):

> Thus from eternity, it was decreed: the steeds that bear Time onwards had this hour and fulfillment enchained to them, since the void brought forth its burthen. Would you read backwards the unchangeable laws of Necessity? Mother of the world! Servant of the Omnipotent! eternal, changeless Necessity! who with busy finge s sittest ever weaving the indissoluble chain of events! – I will not murmur at thy acts. If my human mind cannot acknowledge that all that is, is right; yet since what is, must be, I will sit amidst the ruins and smile. Truly we were not born to enjoy, but to submit, and to hope.

Humans are completely passive in the hands of greater forces; even the most dynamic, politically ambitious, and revolutionary character in the novel, Raymond (based on Byron), admits: "Did we form ourselves, choosing our dispositions, and our powers? I find myself, for one, as a stringed instrument with chords and stops – but I have no power to turn the pegs, or pitch my thoughts to a higher or lower key" (47).

Lionel's invocation of Necessity echoes Percy Shelley in *Queen Mab* 6.198–238, which celebrates "Necessity! thou mother of the world" (6.198), "all that the wide world contains | Are but thy passive instruments" (213–14), a passage itself influenced by Mary's father, William Godwin.[41] In her edition of her husband's *Poetical Works*, Mary had annotated these lines explaining that the universe is "only an immense and uninterrupted chain of causes and effects, no one of which could occupy any other place than it does occupy, or act in any other place than it does act," as "Every human being is irresistibly impelled to act precisely as he does act" (Shelley 1927: 800). As this suggests, moreover, Mary Shelley's universe is also an immense and uninterrupted chain of allusions to other literary works, whose presence exerts a determining force on her narrative. *The Last Man* is full of quotations, allusions, and references to a vast and eclectic range of authors including not only Vergil but also Homer, Dante, Ariosto, Milton (especially "Lycidas" of course), Shakespeare, Fénelon (whose popular *Télémaque* was a big influenc – they were reading it just before Shelley died), Caldéron, Burke, Keats, Marvell, and Sophocles. The range of references reflects the massive reading program Shelley had embarked on with her husband.[42] As in Vergil, however, intertextuality increases the sense of predetermination: the story has already been written, and is just replayed over and over.[43] All Western literature becomes the Sibylline leaves that are gathered together to tell the one story of the end of the world. Above them all, however, Percy Shelley's works, his life, and especially his death, hang over the novel as the typological fulfilment of everything that had been previously written: the dreadful truth that earlier writers had prophesied.[44] Though the world is destroyed by plague, the dominant pattern of imagery is that of water, boats, ships, and sea voyages. Three of the main characters drown (including the hero Adrian, who is an idealized portrait of Percy), and there are several flood , one of which almost washes England away entirely.[45] Percy's death is expanded into a cataclysmic cosmic disaster; the emotional truth that the death of the beloved is the apocalyptic end of the world becomes real.

Imagined as a *flood*, however, Shelley's end of the world is less apocalyptic than a throwback to the Old Testament, and to the very event that prompted the despair of Milton's Adam. As Vergil had foreseen, the future is simply a repetition of the past, the replaying of the untimely death of young men who for Shelley are all figures for her drowned husband. For Shelley, as for Vergil and Milton, the fact that the future can be seen shows it is fixed unchangeable, the same thing and, indeed, story, over and over. For her, however, this is a source of comfort, as it closes off the uncertainty that Vergil and Spenser feared. All history leads not to Rome or even to Christ, but to the coast of Livorno, where on 8 July 1822, Percy Shelley's boat capsized. Perhaps one reason why Mary Shelley loved Vergil, especially the *Georgics*, was that Vergil's vision of a fallen world of hard and endless labour appeared prophetic of her own sad and lonely fate.

NOTES

1 Text of *Thebaid*: Mozley 1967; trans. Ross 2004: 75.

2 Cited from *The Last Man* 1985: 2, 3. All further citations are from this edition.

3 In Godwin's essay "Of the Study of Classics" he praises classical, and particularly, Roman writers, for freeing us from superstition, bringing us closer to nature, and offering models of heroism not available in the commercialized modern world; see Godwin 1965: 36–55.

4 See Shelley 1987: 1: 410–11 (1–8 June 1822).

5 "Virgil is a great favourite of mine – his harmonious style his grace and majesty make interesting an otherwise dull account of war & diplomatics, but where his subject is worthy his style, he may claim rivalship with the greatest Poets"; letter to Hogg, 30 August 1824, in Shelley 1980–8, 1: 447). The English

Romantic preference for Greek literature, especially Homer, seen as more primitive and therefore authentic and truly poetic than the more refined but derivative Vergil, has perhaps been overemphasized in critical discussions. While Vergil had been a central model for eighteenth-century Augustan poets against whom the Romantics defined themselve , he was a continuing presence in the works of the next generation; see the essays in Heinzelman 1991. Because of the centrality of Latin in education, most writers had absorbed Vergil deeply; Keats, who never learned Greek but was inspired by Chapman's Homer, translated all of the *Aeneid* himself. Bush 1969: 62–4 notes Wordsworth's deeply Vergilian melancholy, and remarks the influence of *Aeneid* 6 on the *Laodamia*. On the cultural importance of Rome generally in this period, see also Sachs 2010.

6 Shelley 1980–8: 1:85. The influence of the *Georgics*, popular in the sixteenth through the eighteenth centuries, and continued through the nineteenth, can be seen also in Wordsworth; see especially Goodman 2004: 106–43, and Graver 1991: 137–59.

7 Other models have been noted as well, including Vergil's source, Lucretius. In the novel Shelley refers readers to more recent accounts in the works of Boccacio, DeFoe, and the American writer, Charles Brockden Browne (1985: 193). As I will discuss further, the intertextual layering, in which the Vergilian scene is recalled at the same time as its sources and later imitations, is part of Shelley's paradoxical vision of history as the eternal rewriting of a final rupturing disaster.

8 She read the books in this order: 1 and 6 fi st; followed by 2; then 3 and 4; see 1987: 1: 189, 267, 313–17. Her journals up until Shelley's death are fascinating records of her intense program of study – they are basically book lists with occasionally personal remarks, often in code. Her later journals become more self-absorbed and she stops listing the works she has been reading.

9 1980–1: 528 (to Leigh Hunt; 12 August 1826). Shelley worried that she misremembered the gender of *labor*, but her error is that of inversion: the original is of course *hoc opus, hic labor est*. On this famous phrase, see also Keith, Gladhill, and Stok in this volume.

10 Romantic descents to an underworld, like that in Keats' *Endymion*, have a general Vergilian atmosphere, recalling *Georgic* 4 as well as *Aeneid* 6. The description of the Sibyl's leaves in *The Last Man* comes from another prophetic part of the *Aeneid*, however: 3.441–52. Here Helenus tells Aeneas his future, in effect prophesying a further prophecy that will be given to Aeneas in a cave where he will meet a madwoman whose written prophecies are blown everywhere by the breeze and so impossible to read. As a result of this warning, when Aeneas enters the cave he cannily asks the Sibyl not to *write* but to *speak* the future (6.74–6); see Fowler 1997a: 268–9. On Helenus and the Sibyl, see also Barchiesi and Pillinger in this volume. The Sibyl only reveals Aeneas's

personal future (6.83–97), however, which he has in fact heard already; national history, the future of Rome, is told by his father in 6.756–886, and is then elaborated on his shield in 8.626–728.

11 See Shelley 1987: 2: 500 and 1980–8: 1: 148, 222, 495. On the practice and meaning of the *sortes*, see Parker in this volume.

12 1980–8: 1: 222 (7 March 1822); see also *Letters* 1:148 (18 June 1820).

13 As Kennedy 1997: 47 thus notes, the *Aeneid* is "the paradigm of teleological narrative."

14 *Purgatorio* 32.102. Cited from Singleton's translation of Dante's *Commedia* (1971–5); all further references will be from this edition. T.S. Eliot (1957: 128) is at the end of a long tradition when he interpreted Aeneas as "the prototype of a Christian hero"; see also Kennedy 1997: 49–50. On the treatment of the *Aeneid* as a sacred text compatible with a Christian view of history, see further Soranzo in this volume.

15 Cowley 1905: 11. Waller's edition, still the only one in print, frustratingly lacks line numbers so I am referring to pagination.

16 Text and translations of all of Vergil's works are from Fairclough 1999.

17 For the early Church Fathers, Augustus himself was part of providential history and treated as a kind of John the Baptist who prepared the way for Christ's coming. In 1768 Charles Rollin could still write (10: 317): "The vast extent of the Roman empire, in connecting together, by a free and constant commerce, all the parts of the then known world, opened all the ways for the preachers of the Gospel; to which the terrible calamities of the civil wars would have been a very great obstacle. The 'Prince of peace' must then be born in the bosom of peace; and thus God raised up Octavius to put an end to all dissensions, and establish a lasting tranquillity in the empire."

18 On the problems raised by this episode and the interesting attempts to resolve them by early commentators, see further Parker in this volume.

19 Hollander 1969, therefore, describes the relation between Dante and the classics as one of negative typology, a description, however, which does not do justice to the complexity of Dante's self-identification with and differentiation fro his "maestro." For a more nuanced reading, see Wetherbee 2008. For Dante's ambivalent relation to the classics more generally, see also Kilgour 2013.

20 Cited from Hamilton's 1977 edition of *The Faerie Queene*. All further references will be from this edition. Spenser is trying to encourage Elizabeth to stand up against Spain/Castille (Castle) and defend the Protestant Netherlands (the Belgicke shore).

21 Cited from Sanguineti's edition of Ariosto's *Orlando Furioso* (1974). I have used the delightful Elizabethan translation of Sir John Harrington (Ariosto 1963: 81).

22 Feeney 1986: 15.

23 Watkins 1995: 154.
24 The influential reading of the *Aeneid* by Quint 1993 argues that the poem starts off following a circular pattern of repetition, but takes a more teleological structure in the second half as it moves towards closure through a typological repetition with a difference. As other critics have noted, this simplifies the situation; see for example Hardie 1997: 142–51; Theodorakopoulos 1997: 155–65. As Theodorakopoulos notes especially, Vergil's use of intertextuality both creates a sense of progression (as the later author builds on an earlier writer to surpass him) and undermines it, as the poem keeps returning to its sources and replaying its own earlier moments. As I will argue later, Shelley's intertextuality similarly moves forwards to go backwards.
25 Regina Schwartz thus shows how in *Paradise Lost* 11–12 Milton uses typology, which traditionally creates closure, to undo it; see Schwartz 1988: 123–39, 127 especially.
26 On Dante's use of Vergil here, see especially Barolini 1984: 247–8; Schnapp 1991: 145–56; Hawkins 2003: 86–7. Hawkins 2003: 89–90, 92 also notes how Dante differentiates Cacciaguida's prophecy from that of Anchises, and points out the reimagining of the image of the Sibyl's leaves at the very end of *Paradiso* when Dante tries to recover his final vision *così al vento ne le foglie levi / si perdea la sentenza di Sibilla* ("thus in the wind, on the light leaves, the Sibyl's oracle was lost," 33.65–6).
27 On Vergil's influence generall , Gransden 1984: 95–116 is still valuable. For more recent accounts of Milton's engagement with Vergil, see Quint 2014, and more broadly, Kilgour 2016: 83–96.
28 Paley 1993: 114–15 notes how many Romantics saw Milton as a prophet. The relation of Shelley's text to the vision of the future in Milton's last books in particular is discussed by Ruppert 2009: 141–56.
29 Shelley 1980–8: 2: 15. See also 1: 340 in which she describes herself as "a dreamer" with a "kind of second sight."
30 Shelley 1980–8: 1: 336.
31 Shelley 1980–8: 1: 307.
32 Like Oscar Wilde, Shelley seems to believe that "Life imitates Art" (1989: 982). For Shelley, as for Vergil, moreover, fate is a text that has already been written; in *The Last Man* she presents a predetermined world in which "Genius, devotion, and courage; the adornments of his mind, and the energies of his soul, all exerted to their uttermost stretch, could not roll back one hair's breadth the wheel of time's chariot; that which had been was written with the adamantine pen of reality, on the everlasting volume of the past; nor could agony and tears suffice to wash out one iota from the act fulfille (87). The lines eerily anticipate one of the most famous passages in the fi st edition of Edward Fizgerald's 1859 translation of *The Rubaiyat* of *Omar Khayyam* (Khayyam

and Caldéron 1928: stanza LI, p. 18): The Moving Finger writes; and, having writ, | Moves on: nor all thy Piety nor Wit | Shall lure it back to cancel half a Line, | Nor all thy Tears wash out a Word of it.

33 Shelley 1980–8: 1: 421.

34 On the theme of prophecy in the text, see Paley 1993: 114–15.

35 On the subtext of the Oedipus story, see Anne McWhir's introduction to her edition of the text (Shelley 1996: xxxiv–xxxv).

36 The Vergilian elements in Shakespeare's play, which pay tribute to the ancestors of James I in a genealogical pageant modelled on *Aeneid* 6, have been noted; see Williams 2010; Wells 1997: 149–62.

37 Ruppert 2009: 145.

38 Ruppert 2009: 144.

39 I think Paley is therefore at least partly right when he argues that the book shows the failure of the imagination and of art, and is thus a repudiation of Percy's Shelley's ideals (Paley 1993: 114, 111 especially).

40 Shelley 1980–8: 1: 572.

41 See Mary's notes in *The Complete Poetical Works of Percy Bysshe Shelley* (1927: 800–3). All further references are to this edition.

42 Shelley 1987: 1: 406.

43 See above n8 and n27. I discuss the effects of intertextuality in the novel further in Kilgour 2005.

44 For Paley 1993: 115–16, Lionel's invocation of Necessity is an ironic rewriting of Shelley's *Prometheus Unbound*, which turns Percy's millennial optimism into a delusion at best, and at worst, a nightmare. See also Paley's discussion of the "failure of typology" in the novel (121).

45 See *The Last Man* 1985: 194; see also 268–9 and 295–6, where one of the many false prophets claims that God is going to flood the world again

4

Exploring the Forests of Antiquity: The Golden Bough and Early Modern Spirituality

MATTEO SORANZO

Of all the characters, themes, and elements found in Vergil's *Aeneid* 6, the golden bough Aeneas must find in order to descend into the underworld is among the most famous, and certainly the most mysterious. If one considers Erichtho's search for a corpse before Sextus' *katabasis* in Lucan's *Bellum Ciuile* (6.619–41) as not only an allusion, but also an attempt at grappling with the meaning of Aeneas' wondrous branch, one can say that Vergil's readers have been pondering over the *ramus aureus* since the fi st circulation of the *Aeneid* – a hermeneutic quest that continues to this day.[1] From the philosophical allegories of Fulgentius (fifth century CE) to the Christian Platonism of pseudo-Bernardus Silvestris (twelfth century), from the historical erudition of Servius to the historical positivism of Domenico Comparetti (1835–1927), the *ramus aureus* periodically returns in the history of Western hermeneutics, thus illustrating, more than its elusive meaning, the interpreters' changing methods, religious views, and philosophical assumptions.[2] The same branch that in 1890, in the age of positivism and colonialism, Sir James Frazer identified with a Druidic mistletoe rooted in Vergil's Celtic background and chose as the starting point of his monumental inquiry into the primitive mind, is now appreciated for its intentional ambiguity, which blends together references to ancient customs such as the use of golden leaves among pagan travellers with literary allusions to Homer's *Odyssey* and other ancient texts.[3]

While it would not be reasonable to look at past interpretations of the *ramus aureus* in search of the ultimate meaning of Vergil's mysterious talisman, this paper will focus on how Baptista Mantuanus (1447–1516) and

Giles of Viterbo (1469–1532), two Mendicant friars, Latin humanists, and Vergil enthusiasts from Renaissance Italy, interpreted the *ramus aureus* of Vergil's *Aeneid* 6 in their own works. Their interpretations not only constitute an episode in the millenarian history of Vergil's reception, but they also contribute to an understanding of the assumptions, anxieties, and hopes that characterized early modern readers. In line with Renaissance humanists, Mantuanus and Giles grounded their interpretations of the *ramus aureus* onto their personal take on Vergil's biography and their understanding of tradition. At the same time, however, they used their humanistic skills in conjunction with a tendency toward allegory, which is still grounded in the work of late ancient and medieval commentators. While illustrating how these friars' blend of allegory and historical erudition challenges enduring juxtapositions between medieval and humanistic reading practices, this essay sets out to demonstrate how their interpretive style is better understood as an act of cultural identity, which took place in the context of early modern religious pluralism. Rather than specimens of humanistic or medieval exegesis, Mantuanus and Giles' approach to *Aeneid* 6 will thus be interpreted as a case of how religious identities were negotiated against competing options offered by universities and the Church in early modern Europe.[4]

I. Mantuanus, Vergil, and Carmelite Observance

A Carmelite friar and a prolific writer of Latin poetry, Baptista Mantuanus became known among his contemporaries as a Christian Vergil. Indeed, his hagiographic poems in Latin, and more specifically his *Parthenice Mariana*, created an influential model of Christian poetry written in the language of ancient epic – a model destined to influence numerous poets including Jacopo Sannazaro (1458–1530), Marcus Girolamo Vida (1485–1566), and even John Milton.[5] In his early appreciation for Mantuanus' poetic talent, therefore, Erasmus of Rotterdam (1466–1536) made an insightful assessment not only of this poet's distinctive way of adapting Vergil's language to Christian themes, but also of the influence this experiment had upon sixteenth-century poetry in general.[6] Erasmus' generous assessment of Mantuanus' skills as a Latin poet, however, came at a cost as it contributed, among other things, to overshadowing other aspects of this author's compositions, such as his often neglected works as a philosopher and a theologian.[7] Also, Mantuanus' well-earned fame as the Christian Vergil ended up eclipsing his lifelong commitment to the reformation of his mendicant order, also known as Carmelite Observance.[8] Once placed in its original context, in my view, Mantuanus' peculiar take on Vergil is actually best appreciated as a facet of his theological and philosophical works, which are closely tied with the moment of spiritual fervour and scholarly renewal that characterized Observant Carmelites.

During the fifteenth century, the Carmelite Order was undergoing an authentic identity crisis. After the legendary times of its foundation on Mount Carmel and the distinctive hermitical vocation of its early members, late medieval Carmelites had lost – according to numerous members of this mendicant order – their distinctive monastic disposition and inclination for solitary meditation. In response to this general crisis, which was paralleled by analogous experiences among Augustinian Hermits, Dominicans, and other mendicant orders, some congregations of fifteenth-century Carmelites embarked on a project of internal reform known as Observance, which resulted in the foundation of independent communities of friars committed to enforcing their order's rule.[9] Among the characteristics of the Carmelite Observance, which almost brought this order to an internal schism, there was a renewed emphasis on solitude and seclusion as the necessary steps toward a personal encounter with God. Observant Carmelites, in this context, developed a form of spirituality centred on an individual experience of enlightenment, which set the stage for some of the greatest mystics of the seventeenth century, such as Teresa d'Avila and John of the Cross. In the numerous works written and published in the context of the Carmelite Observance, all these tendencies converged through a renewed interest and widespread identification with the prophet Elijah, whom Carmelites considered the founder of their order and a role model in their spiritual path toward perfection.[10]

Mantuanus played a central role in the Carmelite Observance, and yet literary critics tend to overlook what was arguably the central concern in this author's life. In fact, the constant presence of Observant themes throughout Mantuanus' works induce one to think that this author's impeccable knowledge of ancient literature and imitation of Vergil was part of a broader project to define a distinctive spirituality in line with the religious identity cultivated by his fellow brethren. In works such as a heartfelt autobiographical letter addressed to his father after becoming a Carmelite friar, for instance, Mantuanus reconsidered his own troubled biography and life-changing conversion to monastic life as a paradigm of a perfect spiritual life.[11] In his hagiographic poem on the conversion and martyrdom of Dionysius the Aeropagite, moreover, the poet himself identifies with this semi-legendary author. After listening to Paul's Sermon on the Aeropagus, Mantuanus' Dionysius ventures into a spiritual quest spanning from the depth of his soul to the furthest shores of the Mediterranean and the deepest recesses of Gaul. There, among rebellious people still devoted to pagan superstitions, Dionysius confronts the ancient gods of Greece and Rome in a conflict that mirrors, in fictional forms, the author's own attempt at mediating between ancient and Christian culture.[12] And similar themes, which are rooted in the often difficult adoption of humanistic learning among Observant Carmelites, can be found in Mantuanus' eclogues and other hagiographic poems, where unforgettable episodes such as the shepherd Pollux's mystical encounter with the Virgin Mary or Saint Paul's *raptus* should be read as fictional embodiments of the Carmelite emphasis on divine inspiration and the individual experience of enlightenment as prime sources of theological truth.[13] As he went on exploring spiritual themes in literary forms, I will show, Mantuanus approached Vergil as much more than a source of stylistic devices.

The rationale behind Mantuanus' original blend of Observant spirituality and ancient literary forms is best illustrated in his *Opusculum Aureum in Thomistas* – a short polemical treatise written before 1492 against theologians from the Dominican Order, their pedantic adherence to Thomas Aquinas, and their arid syllogistic style.[14] Although this text might be read as a humanistic attack against Thomism, it is my contention that Mantuanus' work was also in line with the agenda of Observant Carmelites, and an important document of this author's approach to Vergil. More precisely, this text was meant to give voice to a widespread frustration with a theological style modelled on the work of Thomas Aquinas, characterized by syllogistic reasoning and solely based on a limited canon of official authors. Against what he perceived as sterile academic pursuits, in his treatise Mantuanus outlined a form of poetic theology resulting from a personal encounter with God and rooted in an open canon of Old Testament and occasionally Graeco-Roman authorities. At the heart of his views, one finds a peculiar take on revelation as not limited in space and time, but actually manifesting itself intermittently throughout the centuries by means of special individuals considered as the recipients of divine inspiration (Mantuanus, *Opus Aureum*, quoted in Kristeller 1967: 150–1):

at spiritus dei multiplex et penetrabilior omni gladio habens homines pro instrumentis ab infinito fonte ueritatis nouos assidue riuolos profert, et sapientia quae pro delitiis habet esse cum hominibus omnibus quasdam ueritates tanquam commune pabulum communicat ut ea quae uulgo credenda proposuit. quaedam habet necessaria minus, danda non omnibus, sed his tantum qui per contemplationem se in digitos attollunt et caput animae, rationalem scilicet partem eleuant et fixa mentis acie uehementius intuentur. his quoque non aequaliter, sed pro captu, pro industria, pro studio, pro labore et, quod maximum est, pro arbitrio suo lumen infundit.

God's spirit, however, is multitudinous and more penetrating than a sword. With human beings as its instruments, it constantly brings forth new rivulets from the infinite spring of truth. Wisdom, which delights itself in being shared by everybody, as in a common meal distributes these truths in the form of arguments that she has established that people must believe. What it deems less necessary, it is not meant for everybody, but only for those who lift themselves on the tiptoes of their souls and raise their head through contemplation; those, I mean, who raise their rational faculty and with the sharp eye of intellect more vehemently see. To these individuals, God's spirit does not pour forth its light equally, but depending on their capacity, dedication, commitment, hard work and, above all, its own choice.

This view of divine inspiration, which can be traced back to early Christian writers such as Justin Martyr and Eusebius of Caesarea, is at the heart of Mantuanus' polemical view of theologians clinging solely to the authority of Thomas Aquinas. In line with other scholars of the time such as, most importantly, Marsilio Ficino (1433–1499), Mantuanus grounded his argument in the founding fathers of Christian inclusivism, thus implicitly endorsing the kind of perennialism that, in the complementary forms of *pia philosophia, prisca theologia,* and *philosophia perennis,* would have characterized the learned piety of Roman Catholic elites well into the Reformation.[15] Mantuanus, more specificall , followed the genealogy of *prisci theologi* outlined by Ficino himself in the *argumentum* appended to his *Poimander* (fi st printed in 1463), which includes not only Ficino's translation of this hermetic dialogue but also a large corpus of writings attributed to the legendary sage Hermes Trismegistus (Mantuanus, *Opus Aureum,* quoted in Kristeller 1967: 164):

ueterum autem hoc est gentilium theologorum primus fuit ille Aegyptius qui quod maximus et philosophus et sacerdos et rex fuerit Trismegistus appellatur, cui successit Orpheus Thracius Oeagri filiu , eius gratia profectus in Aegyptum, Orpheo Aglaophemus, Aglaophemo Pythagoras, Pythagorae Philolaus, Philolao Plato qui inuentam a Trismegisto theologiam summa ingenii ubertate prouexit et propterea theologus appellatur a nostris. sed de his alibi clarius copiosiusque disserendum.

Of the ancients, that is, gentile theologians the fi st was that Aegyptian Hermes, who since he was the most important philosopher, priest and king is called Trismegistus. After him came Orpheus the Thracian, son of Oeagrus, thanks to whom he arrived into Egypt. After Orpheus Aglaophemus, after Aglaophemus Pythagoras, after Pythagoras Philolaus, after Philolaus Plato, who with the utmost greatness of his genius brought with him the theology invented by Trismegistus and is thus called theologian by Christians. But we should discuss more clearly and extensively about these things in another work.[16]

In line with ancient theorists of *prisca theologia* and their Renaissance epigones, Mantuanus shrouded antiquity in a halo of sacredness. This theory, which – as Mantuanus declares in the *Opus Aureum* – the author himself planned to further explore in another work, has seldom been taken into consideration when discussing Mantuanus' imitation of Vergil. However, in what reads like an interpretation of Saint Paul's discussion of the spiritual gifts (1 Corinthians 12), Mantuanus' text presents the excellence of ancient writers in the liberal arts, including Vergil's poetic prominence, as part of a divinely ordained design, which implicitly legitimates his dedication to the Roman poet.[17] In light of an idea of divine inspiration as independent from ecclesiastical institutions, Mantuanus provided Vergil's poetic works with the status of biblical textuality and searched them for Christian themes wrapped up in poetic forms.

Mantuanus' take on Vergil is best illustrated by this poet's interpretation of the *ramus aureus* in the theological treatise entitled *De Patientia Aurei Libri Tres*. First published in Brescia in 1497 and dedicated to Francesco Fantuzzi – a prominent politician and patron of Carmelite convents – this treatise is organized into three sections, which deal respectively with 1) the physical and spiritual nature of humans; 2) the evils that afflict human souls, their causes and remedies, with a special discussion of the effects of prayers; and 3) physical and spiritual death, and cardinal and theological virtues, with a special emphasis on faith as a remedy against deadly spiritual affliction .[18] Consistent with the style of theological inquiry theorized in the *Opus Aureum*, Mantuanus addresses these issues in polished humanistic Latin and – consistent with the views outlined in his work against Thomism – in a dialogue with a canon of texts open not only to minor fathers of the Church but, most importantly, classical sources. In the third section, while discussing the soul's destiny after death, Mantuanus examines ancient and Christian accounts of heaven and hell. This line of argument brings Mantuanus to examine Vergil's *Aeneid* and to bring forth an allegorical, and rather curious, interpretation of the *ramus aureus* (*De Patientia Aurei Libri Tres* III.iii):

Quod fides per aureum Vergilii ramum figuratur et quedam de natura prophetiae enarrata. Fides est ille aureus Maronis nostri Ramus, qui ad Elysium pergentibus est necessarium. uidebat enim uir ille suopte ingenio seu divina magis inspiratione quam enthusiasmon graeci uocant, sicut et aduentum Christi ante peruiderat esse quoddam sapientiae genus sine quo futurae uitae non ualeat homini claritas apparere. et eam ramum aureum recte nuncupauit. est enim fides Ramus hoc est quidam delibatio diuinae sapientiae et aureus quidem quia et preciosissima et immarcessibilis ut auri substantia et recte etiam in magno nemore dixit inuenire, quo inter uarios et multiplices humanae sapientiae modos inter scilicet philosophantium sectas et traditiones hominum diuersas quasi arbor in amplissimo nemore fidei sapientia delitescit. quod Vergilius dixit *ipse uolens facilisque sequetur si te fata uocant aliter non uiribus ullis uincere nec duro poteris conuellere ferro.* quid aliud est quam quod dicitur a Christo *Nemo potest uenire ad me nisi pater meus traherit illum?*

That faith is figuratively represented through the golden bough and certain things told on the nature of prophecy. Faith is that golden bough found in our Vergil, which is necessary to those who are trying to reach *Elysium*. Because of his ingenuity, or rather because of some kind of divine inspiration, which Greeks call *enthusiasmos*, just like he had foretold the advent of Christ, Vergil could see that there is a kind of wisdom without which humans cannot see the light of eternal life, and rightly called it golden bough. Indeed, faith is a bough, that is, a certain kind of foretaste of divine wisdom, and it is made of gold, because it is precious and everlasting like the substance of this metal. And he rightly said that it is found in a large forest. Among the different and multiple methods of human wisdom, and among the different philosophical schools and traditions, faith hides like a tree in a large forest. When Vergil said: "[...] *for of itself will it follow you, freely and with ease, if Fate be calling you; else with no force will you avail to win it or rend it with hard steel*" [*Aen.* 6. 146–8], how is it different from what was said by Christ himself: "*No man can come to me, except the Father, who hath sent me, draw him*" John 6.44]?[19]

According to Mantuanus, Vergil's *ramus aureus* is to be interpreted as a prophetic foreshadowing of Christian *fides*. Precious, necessary for saving the soul from spiritual death, and, above all, freely given to men of worth – according to Mantuanus – Vergil's golden bough is a gift, which only by the help of the Sibyl – an allegory of *diuina sapientia* – Aeneas (an allegory of humankind) can obtain. Such a gift, however, is found only after a dangerous quest through a thick forest, along its misleading paths and shadowy groves, which for Mantuanus represents not only undetermined moral dangers but also the contrasting and often erroneous views and beliefs inherited from ancient culture. Mantuanus interprets Aeneas' *katabasis* as an allegory of the soul's destiny after death, and the golden bough as the virtue by which the soul can be saved from spiritual death, framing everything in a discussion of the destiny of human souls after death. In matching Vergil's hexameters with a passage from the Gospel of John, moreover, Mantuanus implicitly suggests that readers approach the *Aeneid* as a divinely inspired text. Now, was Mantuanus' interpretation original? And what does it teach us about the friar's take on Vergil's *ramus aureus*?

At fi st sight, Mantuanus' interpretation of Vergil's *Aeneid* is nothing other than another example of philosophical allegory tinged with Christian elements. Isolated from Mantuanus' theological works, this allegorical interpretation of the *ramus aureus* would thus confirm what scholars have often argued about fifteenth-century approaches to Vergil. Despite the renewed interest in philology brought about by the *studia humanitatis*, fifteenth-century commentaries did not mark a turning point in the reception of Vergil's *Aeneid*. Petrarch's letter to Federico d'Arezzo, for example, was ultimately in tune with medieval allegorical readings of Aeneas' life as a poetic representation of an individual's moral development. Cristoforo Landino's exercise in Vergilian exegesis found in the *Disputationes Camaldulenses*, moreover, further elaborated upon what, by then, was a traditional approach, without bringing forth any relevant innovation for what concerns the use of allegory as the prime tool for interpreting Vergil's masterpiece. In the footsteps of Petrarch's friend Coluccio Salutati, Landino's *Disputationes* ascribed a crucial significance to the *descensus ad inferos* as an allegory of the passage from an active to a contemplative life, and interpreted the *ramus aureus* as the fictional materialization of *sapientia* – that semi-practical virtue, often mentioned at the time of humanists, which Florentine philosophers such as Marsilio Ficino charged with new metaphysical nuances. And Ficino himself, whose works often give evidence of a vivid interest in Vergil's *Aeneid*, used the golden bough as an allegory of the *lumen mentis*, which, consistent with his Christian Platonism, Ficino believed would pour forth from God into the inspired minds of sages. Details aside, neither Petrarch, Salutati, Landino, nor Ficino – as Anthony Ossa-Richardson has recently argued – managed to write anything radically different from their twelfth-century predecessors based at Chartres, and they relied on allegory as much as the pseudo-Bernardus Silvestris and John of Salisbury did before them.[20]

And yet, at closer inspection, Mantuanus' emphasis on Aeneas' quest for the *ramus aureus* presents an original twist on an admittedly trite interpretation. While the *ramus aureus* as an allegory of faith is ultimately grafted onto the allegorical tradition of Mantuanus' predecessors from Chartres and Florence, his take on the forest where Aeneas finds it stems from a rather astute innovation rooted in the work of fifteenth-century humanists. In his commentary of Plato's *Timaeus*, widely available in Latin translation during the Middle Ages, late ancient commentator Calcidius had influentially used a verse from Hesiod's *Theogony* to explain the genealogy of the gods from the primordial *chaos*. Since this word was becoming quite foreign to his readers, Calcidius added a gloss that, in the Latin translation, interprets *chaos* as a synonym of *hylen* and *silua*, thus providing medieval readers with a rich source of metaphors of material imperfection or the bodily prison.[21] As MacPhail has recently argued, however, it was Angelo Poliziano who fi st provided *silua* with the textual turn this metaphor would take among European humanists including Erasmus of Rotterdam. During his lectures on Statius' *Siluae* at the Studio Fiorentino in 1480, more specificall , Poliziano not only listed a number of ancient authors who – like

Statius – described unpublished notes and fragmentary writing as *siluae*, but he also linked this term with formless matter (*hylen*) and *chaos* as Calcidius did.[22] While after Poliziano it became commonplace to describe one's own unfinished work as a *silua*, the Florentine humanist encouraged representing the work of the interpreter as a walk in the forest and implicitly – as Mantuanus realized – to reimagine Aeneas' quest for the *ramus aureus* as some kind of hermeneutic excursion.

In doing so, Mantuanus adapted the textual turn that the term *silua* had taken in the hands of fifteenth-century scholars such as Poliziano and, most importantly, Ficino, to Vergil's *Aeneid*.[23] He implicitly interpreted Aeneas not only as a medieval "everyman" but also as the allegorical personific - tion of the humanistically trained theologian, who ventured into the *silua* of antiquity in search of snippets of Christian truth. Differently from his Dominican opponents, who – following in the footsteps of Thomas Aquinas – dismissed poetry as *infima inter doctrinas* and grounded their theological arguments on a limited canon of texts, Mantuanus ventured into ancient poetry as Aeneas did into the forest found between Lake Avernus and Cuma.[24] Differently from his Chartrian predecessors and some of his Florentine contemporaries, moreover, Mantuanus was interested not only in what Vergil's *Aeneid* meant, but above all in how Vergil, despite his paganism, might have had access to such an arcane body of knowledge without knowing the Bible and the Gospel. Vergil, in this sense, became a test case for Mantuanus' polemical view of Thomism in tune with the optimistic view of divine inspiration cultivated among Carmelite Observants.

In pursuing a kind of poetic theology rooted in a personal encounter with God, Mantuanus' *De Patientia* described Vergil as the recipient of a kind of divine inspiration, platonically designated as *enthusiasmos*. In doing so, Mantuanus enriched his theological background with themes that, at the same time, Marsilio Ficino was exploring in his translations, exegetical summaries and commentaries of Plato's *Ion*, *Phaedrus*, and *Symposium*, which would constitute the cornerstone of Renaissance Platonism. More specifically, he explained that the presence of Christian doctrines in Vergil's text is a consequence of divine inspiration and a personal experience of revelation, which can occur regardless of a direct knowledge of traditional written sources. The kind of Vergil that emerges from Mantuanus' interpretation of *Aeneid* 6, to sum up, is the embodiment of the author's view of Christian tradition as multilinear, open to pagan and biblical sources, and, above all, centred on the individual's direct experience of God. Vergil's *ramus aureus*, in this perspective, becomes a prophecy of the divinely assigned gift, by which Observant Carmelites would have to find their way through the forests of antiquity to reach perfection and true salvation.

II. Giles of Viterbo and Augustinian Observance

Observant Carmelites like Mantuanus were not alone in exploring the forests of antiquity in search of the golden bough of Christian faith. *Prisca theologia, philosophia perennis,* and other forms of inclusivist approaches to pre-Christian culture such as those embraced by Ficino, Cristoforo Landino, Giovanni Pico, and many other early Renaissance writers had a tremendous impact also upon other mendicant friars, while deeply informing their ways of reading Vergil's *Aeneid*. One of them was Augustinian Hermit Giles of Viterbo (1469–1532), a restless reformer, influential cardinal, prolific poet, innovative theologian, and pioneer scholar of Cabala. Trained at the prestigious Augustinian Studio of the Eremitani in Padua and horrified by what he perceived as the moral depravity brought about by philosophers such as Pietro Pomponazzi, at a very young age Giles embarked on a lifelong crusade, which was largely inspired by the work of his friend and mentor Marsilio Ficino. Due to his exceptional knowledge of Greek and Latin literature, and most importantly of Plato and Vergil, wherever he went Giles was able to befriend prominent intellectuals.[25] While residing at the Augustinian convent of San Giovanni a Carbonara in Naples, for instance, Giles became a close friend of Giovanni Pontano and other members of his Neapolitan academy such as the poet Jacopo Sannazaro.[26] Much like it was for Mantuanus, Giles' lifelong devotion to Vergil is best understood as a tool by which the author tried to negotiate his identity against the options offered by the university and the Church of his time.

Similar to their fellow Carmelites, Augustinian Hermits were also undergoing a moment of crisis at the end of the fifteenth century. The hermitical vocation and commitment to perfection of their founding fathers from the forests of Malavalle and Lecceto, according to Giles and other Observant Augustinians, had been lost and their fellow brethren were too much involved in administrative tasks and secular commitments. Solitary meditation, along with a spirituality based on a personal encounter with God combined with a frequent reading of scripture, was the guideline of the project of reform pursued by Observant Augustinians.[27] As can be evinced from Giles' copious epistolary, moreover, this program of return to hermitical life brought about a sacralization of the Italian landscape, which offered – in Giles' view – remote retreats most apt for solitary meditation, such as Martana Island – a secluded island on Lake Bolsena – or the Cimini Hills in the vicinity of Viterbo.[28] In reviving the monastic vocation of their order, as the case of Giles amply demonstrates, Augustinian hermits, who placed a great emphasis on scholarship, were also inclined to revive and adapt esoteric practices such as Neoplatonic theurgy and Jewish Cabala to their spiritual needs.[29] In rediscovering Vergil, therefore, Giles not only emphasized this poet's compatibility with Christian faith, but he also inserted him into a fascinating, albeit largely invented, historical myth, which links together the ancient Roman poet and his immortal masterpiece with Arameans, Greek philosophers, and Etruscans, who Giles believed received the secret wisdom of Noah's religious teachings after the flood

Following in the footsteps of Augustine himself, whose lifelong frequentation of the *Aeneid* is discussed by Jacob Mackey in this volume, Augustinian Hermits were particularly inclined to look for snippets of Christian truth in the works of the Roman *uates*. While a novice, moreover, Giles was deeply influenced by the passion for ancient poetry and personal charisma of Mariano da Gennazzano (1412–89) – a preacher and a scholar committed to the Augustinian Observance and admired by Florentine humanists such as Angelo Poliziano.[30] Early evidence of Giles' distinctive interpretation of Vergil's *ramus aureus* can be found in his *Sententiae ad Mentem Platonis*, a lengthy commentary on Peter Lombard's *Sentences*, started in 1499 and left unfinished[31] Indeed, the composition of commentaries on Lombard's text was standard practice among young friars with scholarly aspirations. Giles' fulfilment of this otherwise common task, however, resulted in a fascinating attempt to demonstrate the perfect harmony between Plato, Christian theology, and another tradition traced back to the Etruscans. In a way that is comparable with Mantuanus' *Opus Aureum* and its polemical target (see above), the goal of Giles' *Sententiae* was the definition of a new religious wisdom (*diuina sapientia*) against, on the one hand, the dry disputations of Scholastic theologians, and, on the other hand, the narrow-mindedness of natural philosophers. Vergil, whom Giles considered both a Platonist and an Etruscan, was at the centre of this curious intellectual project.

Much like Landino, Ficino, and Mantuanus, in his commentary Giles interprets Aeneas as the embodiment of the *sapiens*, and the *silua* as the dangers he has to overcome to reach true wisdom. As he partakes in the textual turn this metaphor had taken among humanistically trained philosophers, including Mantuanus, the goal of Giles' Aeneas is to hunt (*uenare*) and track down (*uestigare*) the numerous traces of the Trinity, which are assumed to be scattered in the *silua* of ancient literature and religious confusion.[32] The *ramus aureus*, in this perspective, is interpreted as both the goal and the source of this search, which thanks to God's help – designated by the Sibyl – leads the *sapiens* to the knowledge of arcane doctrines, which Aeneas' *katabasis* is supposed to designate (Giles of Viterbo 2010: 121):

quod si uestigium atque umbra in mediam notitiam nos ducit, atque ita ad diuina cognoscenda per res humanas ductamur, necessaria ratione diuinum uestigium in rebus reperitur humanis. quod quidem si quis non conniuentibus oculis explorauerit, etiam in eo ipso diuina contemplabitur. quare *de Republica* libro secundo Plato ait, cum de uestigatione loqueretur acute cernentis ingenii esse opus, quod et Maro Latinum fecit, ait enim: "*ergo alte uestig[i]a oculis*" [*Aen*. 6. 145]. alte autem is uestigat, qui nec sola essentia nec humanis est uiribus contentus, sed amore ac diuina adiutus Venere per Sybillinae ducis oracula, aureum legit ramum.[33]

If footprints and shadows lead us in the middle of knowledge, and from there we are guided to the understanding of divine matters through the acquaintance with things human, then by necessity it follows that a divine imprint is found in things human. If someone will explore an object without distracted eyes, through contemplation he will recognize it has something divine within itself. That's why Plato, in the second book of the *Republic*, says that when *uestigatio* is discussed, a perspicacious nature is what is needed. Vergil turned this into Latin, by saying: "Search then with eyes aloft" [*Aen*. 6.145]. And "aloft" indeed "searches with the eyes" the man who is not content with his simple essence and human strengths, but with the help of Love and divine Venus finds the Golden Bough through the oracles of his sibylline guid .

Much like Mantuanus, Giles does not limit himself to assuming the presence of Christian motifs throughout Vergil's works. At the heart of these friars' scholarship, on the contrary, one finds a lifelong commitment to demonstrate how this apparent exception to the unfolding of Christian history was actually possible. Mantuanus contented himself to reviving, through Ficino's mediation, the ancient apologetic tool of *philosophia perennis* and other traditional themes of late second-century Christian inclusivism. Giles, on the other hand, ventured into this avenue of inquiry armed with a peculiar taste for genealogical myth-making and a terrific erudition, which brought him to insert Vergil himself into a fully formed, and to my knowledge unprecedented, historical myth. Using the useful taxonomy introduced by intellectual historian Moshe Idel, one can argue that while Mantuanus explained Vergil's foreknowledge of Christian mysteries within a multilinear view of tradition based on the Platonic concept of *enthusiasmos*, Giles outlined a unilinear theory of transmission, the purpose of which was demonstrating Vergil's knowledge of the Old Testament through a succession of masters and disciples.[34]

First sketched in the *Sententiae*, this genealogical myth is further explored in a speech Giles, then Prior General of his order, delivered in Saint Peter's Basilica on 12 Decembe 1507, in the presence of Pope Julius II.[35] At the heart of this discourse's grandiose message, one finds a prophetic interpretation of world history, which Giles – in an original blend of classical imagery and themes traceable to the works of Joachim of Fiore – organized into a succession of four Golden Ages, each linked with Lucifer, Adam, Janus and the Etruscans, and Christ.[36] While the Christian Golden Age, quite predictably, is said to be culminating in the papacy of Julius II, the long section on Janus and the Etruscans provides the context for Giles' discussion of Vergil. Based on the antiquarian forgeries and genealogical speculations of his compatriot Annio of Viterbo (1432–1502), Giles argued that after the Deluge Noah's religious teachings were transmitted to the Arameans, the Egyptians, and – most importantly – the Etruscans.[37] The people of Etruria, in Giles' view, not only inherited Noah's Semitic language, but they also lived according to the religious customs and beliefs of Israel, thus paving the way on the one hand to Pythagoras, who transmitted this tradition to Plato, and on the other hand to the Roman Catholic Church, which thus became the rightful recipient of this forgotten biblical legacy. Vergil's *Aeneid,* because of this view of tradition, could be used as a reliable prophecy and a tool of spiritual meditation, alongside David's Psalms and Plato's dialogues.[38] Based on these premises, *Aeneid* 6 is considered a sacred text, which hides a wisdom compatible with Christian doctrine:

easdem distinxit Platonicus Latinus, cum ad aurum et beatam uitam assequendam instituit; Sibyllae ducentis scientia prius, deinde numinis afflantis sapientia institui nos oportere significauit his uero Hetruscos dedisse operam sexto docet libro Diodorus, qui eos perscrutationi rerum naturalium et theologiae plurimum temporis impendisse dicit. cumque geminas docuisset intellectus notitias, geminos postea amores edocuit uoluntatis, cum subiecit, *geminae cum forte columbae* et *maternas agnoscit aues.*

The Latin Platonist [Vergil] also distinguished these virtues, when he taught the pursuit of gold and the blessed life; he wrote that we should be taught with the science of the guiding Sibyl and with the wisdom of divine inspiration. Diodorus Siculus argues that the Etruscans did so in Book 6, when he claims that they spent a lot of time investigating natural things and theology. For since the intellect imparts two kinds of knowledge, eventually, when it descends, it informs two kinds of love in the will: "when [...] twin doves, as it chanced" and "he knew them for his mother's birds." [*Aen.* 6.190, 193][39]

In his works, therefore, Giles approached *Aeneid* 6 as a sacred text, which not only bears the imprint of divine inspiration but, given Vergil's Etruscan origins, is part of a tradition directly linked with the Bible, Plato, and Pythagoras. Strange as it might sound to a modern reader, Giles' approach to Vergil ultimately expands on what Augustine, the founder of Giles' order, had to say about this poet in his *City of God*. Also, Giles' genealogical and historical myth-making were meant to demonstrate how biblical wisdom, via the

Etruscans, had made its way into Greek philosophy and Roman poetry; a trajectory that, in Giles' perspective, ends and culminates in Rome, at the same time the city of Vergil and the capital of Christendom.

III. Conclusion

Both Mantuanus and Giles, to conclude, did not use allegory only to come to terms with the otherness of the *ramus aureus* and the mysterious imagery of *Aeneid* 6. In a way that foreshadows the combination of textual hermeneutics, occultism, and modern spiritualism discussed by Grant Parker in this volume, these friars adapted their exegetical practice to the distinctive spirituality of their orders. In their effort to bring back the Carmelite and Augustinian Orders to their original vocation in the context of the Observance, these friars developed a theory concerning the sources of Vergil's knowledge of Christian doctrines rooted on the one hand in the Platonic theory of divine frenzy or *enthusiasmos* and on the other hand in a complex genealogical myth, which brings together Greek, Roman, and biblical traditions. Their polemical construction of a multilinear and a unilinear tradition, moreover, was closely tied to the spirituality of their respective orders, and their distinctive take on tradition. Bringing back to mind James Frazer, and his attempt at filtering the golden bough's foreignness through the lens of history, the interpretations of Baptista Mantuanus and Giles of Viterbo might surprise us as curious specimens of bigotry and methodological backwardness. As Jonathan Z. Smith has recently assessed, however, Frazer's interpretation of the *ramus aureus*, along with the underlying theory of his history of religion, was ultimately founded on wobbling methodological premises and unwillingly ended up using allegory, its methodological scapegoat, as an exegetical tool.[40] As Andrew Laird has recently contended, moreover, in the long run allegory and historical criticism are ultimately different expressions of the same need of filling the distance between texts and their historically situated readers, by making old texts useful or at least plausible.[41] Strange as they may seem at fi st sight, therefore, I believe that Mantuanus and Giles should be discussed for the motivations leading to, rather than the results of, their interpretations. This brings me to a last, and broader, point.

Recent scholarship in the history of religions has challenged the infl -ential narrative of Europe as a uniformly Christian continent moving toward modernity and secularization. Since the Middle Ages, Christians, at closer inspection, often cohabited with Jews and Muslims within the same European cities, while European Christian identities were themselves the result of a negotiation among theological doctrines, orally transmitted beliefs, folkloric legends, and esoteric traditions such as Hermeticism, Neoplatonism, and Cabala. Scholars such as, for instance, Kocku von Stuckrad, consequently are now prone to examine European identities in the context of a twofold pluralism, which resulted from interactions among different institutions of learning (e.g., universities, monastic or humanistic *Studios*, the Church, religious congregations, etc.) and competing claims to knowledge used in a field of options and possibilities.[42] Both Mantuanus and Giles proposed allegorical interpretations of the golden bough to make a claim to knowledge, which was part of the apologetic strategy of their religious orders at the time of the Observance. Whether they took Vergil's golden bough to be the unpredictable manifestation of divine inspiration before the coming of Christ, or rather the result of a forgotten Etruscan fringe of a biblical legacy, Mantuanus and Giles used Vergil as part of an act of cultural identity grounded in their respective views of tradition. Against the dry disputation of Scholastic theologians or the materialistic views of natural philosophers, both the Carmelite and the Augustinian friar brought forth individual experience and variety of sources as the roots of Christian truth. Rather than a choice with an end in itself, therefore, their allegorical readings of the golden bough, much like Frazer's historical rationalization or the recent preference for the symbolic openness of Vergil's symbol, is best understood as an act of cultural identity, taking place in a field remarkable for its internal variety.

NOTES

1 Some interesting points on Lucan's allusion to Vergil, which is noted in every commentary of *Bellum Ciuile*, can be found in Masters 2007: 189–92.

2 Literature on commentators of Vergil's *Aeneid* 6 is immense. Besides the useful companions published by Brill and Cambridge University Press, as far the early modern period is concerned two central works are Wilson-Okamura 2010 and Kallendorf 2007b. The ever-expanding bibliography on Vergil and his reception can be followed on www.vergil.org/bibliography/.

3 For a thorough review of the modern literature on the *ramus aureus* and a persuasive take on its intentionally ambiguous character, see Horsfall 2013a 2.157–64. Horsfall's commentary also points to the possible religious meanings of the *ramus* outside of a strictly literary context. On Frazer, see also Barchiesi in this volume.

4 On early modern pluralism and a discursive approach to the study of religion, see von Stuckrad 2005. I have attempted to adjust von Stuckrad's approach to Mantuanus, Giles, and other early modern poets in Soranzo, 2013: 229–62.

5 For biographical details on Mantuanus, see the introductions in Mantuanus and Piepho 1989 and Mantuanus and Severi 2010.
6 Piepho 1994: 46–54.
7 On Mantuanus' philosophical works, see Kristeller 1967: 80–104; Rosa 1976: 227–64.
8 To my knowledge, the only study on Mantuanus' contribution to the Carmelite Observance is Saggi 1954.
9 On the Carmelite Observance, see Andrews 2006: 49–68.
10 Andrews 2006: 54.
11 Soranzo 2013: 237–8.
12 On Mantuanus poem on Dionysius the Aeropagite, see Soranzo 2015: 185–209.
13 Soranzo 2015: 204–8.
14 For the date of this text, which was never published during the author's lifetime, see Kristeller 1967: 80.
15 For a recent reappraisal of this vast topic, see Hanegraaff 2012: 5–76. Among other things, Hanegraaff offers a useful distinction of *prisca theologia, philosophia perennis*, and *pia philosophia* as three complementary forms of Christian inclusivism.
16 On Ficino's genealogy, see Hanegraaff 2012: 46.
17 Mantuanus, *Opus Aureum* (quoted in Kristeller 1967: 167–8).
18 Valuable insights on this otherwise poorly known text are to be found in Bolisani 1958: 157–70.
19 Unless otherwise indicated, translations are mine. Excerpts in English from Vergil's *Aeneid* follow H.R. Fairclough's translation with G.P. Goold in the Loeb Classical Library (Fairclough 1999). When quoted in English, the *Vulgate* follows the Douay-Rheims translation.
20 Ossa-Richardson 2008: 351–3.
21 On Calcidius' discussion of matter as *silua*, see Winden 1959: 31.
22 MacPhail 2014: 10–11.
23 Quite interestingly, Landino adopted this philosophical take on *silua* in his interpretation of Dante's *selva oscura* in *Inferno* 1.
24 On the forests of *Aeneid* 6, see also Barchiesi in this volume.
25 O'Malley 1968: 1–18.
26 Soranzo 2014: 117–32.
27 Andrews 2006: 163–72.
28 Deramaix 1990: 173–276.
29 O'Malley 1968: 40–99.
30 Bausi 2001: 232–4.
31 Giles of Viterbo 2010: 1–23.
32 For Ficino, the metaphor of the intellectual inquiry as the exploration of a forest also entailed the juxtaposition of Platonists, designated as keen-scented hounds

(*sagaces canes*), and Scholastics, designated as rabid dogs. On Ficino's canine metaphor, see Robichaud 2006: 44–9.

33 Having checked Nodes' text against Ms. Vat. Lat. 6325, fol. 38^{v}, I have decided to substitute *uestigia* with the imperative *uestiga* found in the manuscript and in Vergil's *Aeneid.*

34 Idel 2002: 143–56. For a useful, mildly critical assessment of Idel's taxonomy, see Hanegraaff 2012: 58–9.

35 The Latin text is published in O'Malley 1969: 265–338.

36 Reeves 1969: 267–73.

37 Besides O'Malley's 1968 monograph, useful information on this topic can be found in Collins 2001: 107–37.

38 O'Malley 1969: 275.

39 Quoted in O'Malley 1969: 292–3. See also O'Malley 1968: 19–39.

40 Smith 2004: 8–9. Smith, who wrote his doctoral dissertation on Frazer, has further elaborated on his take on this author in a number of other works. The introduction to *Relating Religions,* however, constitutes a useful summary of his views. See also Smith 1973.

41 Laird 2007: 151–76.

42 Von Stuckrad 2010: 7–24. Among the numerous methodological essays authored by this scholar, see at least von Stuckrad 2005: 78–97.

5

Aeneas' Steps[1]

MIGUEL HERRERO DE JÁUREGUI

I. Roman Walking – in a Greek Underworld

A basic metaphor for a narrative is a path, and it requires little effort to envisage reading a text as walking along with the characters through the route traced by the author. This is not a privilege of modernity, not even that of written literature, and Pindar's fruitful usage of the *oimos* as the way his song advances should serve as a reminder. However, the image is as living today as in antiquity: to offer the closest possible example, Alessandro Barchiesi's walk into the Cumaean woods in this volume takes us "step by step" into his analysis of Vergil's poem. And, to remain within the pages of this book, Statius also conceives his *Thebaid* and *Siluae* 4.3 as a walk in Vergil's footsteps, as Emily Pillinger's chapter shows. Walking is, therefore, a ubiquitous literary image, both ancient and modern, that involves the characters, the author, and the public.[2] Yet in few contexts is it more meaningful than in the accounts of a journey into a territory in which treading is by definition impossible, i.e., the land of the dead: when Dante chose Vergil as his guide to his Hell, he was confirming the deep impact that *Aeneid* 6 had for generations of readers over the centuries, and it is not an accident that he follows in the footsteps of Vergil's Sibyl and Aeneas.

Curiosity about how Aeneas trod into Hades and walked through it should be natural – and yet it is seldom raised as an issue. It is perhaps due to the importance of vision and speech that walking has been downplayed. Most of Vergil's account of Aeneas' visit to the underworld consists of descriptions, either by the narrator, by the Sibyl, or by characters who dwell there, like Deiphobus or Anchises. Between these descriptive passages, some lines tell of Aeneas' progress following the Sibyl's lead. These short sections, built around verbs of motion, have received little attention in comparison to the huge amount of bibliography dedicated to each detail of the Vergilian underworld. In fact, they are usually undervalued because of the assumption that "Vergil rarely expends real effort in passages of narrative transition," in the recent words of one of the most authoritative commentators of *Aeneid* 6, Nicholas Horsfall.[3] This kind of dismissive judgment serves to justify a mere literal reading of these brief passages as a necessary burden, leaving them neglected in comparison to other descriptions and dialogues in *Aeneid* 6.

Precisely one of the most famous Vergilian verses, however, is marked by movement and hypallage: *ibant obscuri sola sub nocte per umbram* ("They walked a lonely road through the shadows, dark in the night," *Aen.* 6.268). This line alone should warn against the simple assumption that Vergil did not work on these "walking" lines as much as on those episodes of "speech" and "vision." An unprejudiced analysis of these passages should inquire into whether Vergil intended to load them with a deeper meaning than just transition between speeches, which in fact is the most logical a priori supposition.

Timothy O'Sullivan (2011) has discussed at length how significant the manner of walking was in Roman culture, where it was considered a feature that defined one's personality as much as the face: a Roman's gait accentuated in a performative way his inner moral and ethical qualities. Romans were extremely aware that their movements and motions were fundamental traits in delimiting their individual and collective identities. Aristocrats, slaves, philosophers, foreigners, they were all easily recognized by their tread. At the same time, one's gait is necessarily affected by the circumstances and the space through which one moves: walking along a transitional path requires a different kind of pace than the sort of ambulation one takes upon the arrival at a destination, and a conversational walk is not the same as a solitary one. This can be easily found in many, not to say all, human cultures, and is definitely the case in ancient Greece as well.[4] What is specifically Roman is the clear self-consciousness of walking as a fundamental descriptive trait. This is visible in many passages of the *Aeneid* where Vergil takes great care to depict Aeneas' walks meaningfully, particularly in his rushing out of Troy in Book 2, and in his walk with Evander around the future Roman sites in Book 8, in many aspects a reversal and inversion of the flight from Troy.[5] Therefore, it is fairly improbable, not to say impossible, that Vergil should have neglected this aspect in the most decisive and celebrated journey of his hero.

Furthermore, as Vergil emphasizes, Aeneas takes the same path to the underworld as Greek heroes like Hercules, Theseus, and Orpheus (6.119–23, 392–3). *Aeneid* 6 adapts to a Roman context a traditional theme of Greek literature, *katabasis*, where movement is a fundamental key of the tale. In effect, the journey to the land of the dead is a very ancient topic of epic poetry, which presented many variants and could be adapted to various contexts, all of which focus around the progress of the journey.[6] A particularly revealing instance is the eschatological derivation of this theme: the "Orphic" gold tablets, whose hexameters instruct the soul how to reach the abode of the blessed during its journey through Hades, use several verbs of movement and often describe the soul as walking.[7] The tablets are replete with fi st-person presentation ("I come"), second-person instruction ("you will go," "don't go," "you will walk"), and the third-person description ("she comes," "they travel").[8] Motion and movement during the rites of initiation could be viewed as oblique and imagistic reflections of the descent to Hades after death.[9] Ritual and poetic representations of *katabasis* had a long tradition of exploiting the nuances of walking and its meaning.

Therefore, given that the Roman audience is conditioned to notice the manner of walking as an essential feature of personality and the importance of gait in other passages of the *Aeneid* (not to mention the Greek katabatic precedents of *Aeneid* 6), it seems logical to examine the ambulatory episodes as potentially more meaningful than mere transitions between descriptive ones. As this chapter will show, the expressions chosen by Vergil to describe Aeneas' descent are not trivial, but situate it wholly in the tradition of *katabasis,* and the wording carefully achieves the desired connotations appropriate to this mythical theme. The journey to the underworld is defined as substantially different from any other trip because, among other things, visitors and inhabitants there walk and move in distinct and specific ways. Gods move differently from humans; the living walk differently from the dead, and among the dead those in Elysium experience motions and movements quite apart from the sorts experienced elsewhere in the underworld.[10] Steps and style of walking are subtle indications of essential differences, out-of-placeness, and even trespass, when it comes to the movement of different kinds of beings (gods, humans, souls) through different spaces (upper, under, and on ground). To this end, from lines 6.637–9, when Aeneas and the Sibyl finally enter Elysium, their mode of walking and that of the characters they encounter will be markedly different.[11]

For the sake of clarity, let me anticipate fi st a conclusion that will result from the analysis of these passages. The progress of the Sibyl and Aeneas has three features that mark their movement as different from that of the souls of the dead of pre-Elysium underworld: determination (i.e., goal-oriented movement), firmness (i.e., physical character of the movement), and urgency (i.e., swift movement). As we shall see, it is not by chance that these elements recede at the moment Aeneas and the Sibyl enter Elysium, since the status of the dead there is unique in terms of both time and space (and also kind and quality). Movement there will be accordingly described in a different way from how it was illustrated up until that point. The pregnant significance of Elysian motion will be made patent through a separate scrutiny of these three (obviously interconnected and overlapping) dimensions.

II. Purposeful Treading

During the visit to the underworld in *Aeneid* 6 one can perceive a fundamental difference between three types of walkers: the Sibyl and Aeneas, the souls of the dead that have not reached Elysium, and those in Elysium. Their way of walking portrays the status of each of these three groups, respectively, as occasional visitors, the dead in disgrace, or happy souls. In drawing this distinction, Vergil was most probably following the tradition of earlier katabatic accounts in which the type of movement in the underworld sharply separated those dwelling in Tartarus (or other dangerous places) and those in Elysium (or similarly blessed spots). Such a distinction can be clearly perceived in Plutarch's famous description of the katabatic experience undergone by mystic initiates (Fr. 167 Sandbach):[12]

οὕτω κατὰ τὴν εἰς τὸ ὅλον μεταβολὴν καὶ μετακόσμησιν ὀλωλέναι τὴν ψυχὴν λέγομεν ἐκεῖ γενομένην· ἐνταῦθα δ' ἀγνοεῖ, πλὴν ὅταν ἐν τῷ τελευτᾶν ἤδη γένηται· τότε δὲ πάσχει πάθος οἷον οἱ τελεταῖς μεγάλαις κατοργιαζόμενοι. διὸ καὶ τὸ ῥῆμα τῷ ῥήματι καὶ τὸ ἔργον τῷ ἔργῳ τοῦ τελευτᾶν καὶ τελεῖσθαι προσέοικε. *πλάναι τὰ πρῶτα καὶ περιδρομαὶ κοπώδεις καὶ διὰ σκότους τινὲς ὕποπτοι πορεῖαι καὶ ἀτέλεστοι*, εἶτα πρὸ τοῦ τέλους αὐτοῦ τὰ δεινὰ πάντα, φρίκη καὶ τρόμος καὶ ἱδρὼς καὶ θάμβος· ἐκ δὲ τούτου φῶς τι θαυμάσιον ἀπήντησεν καὶ τόποι καθαροὶ καὶ λειμῶνες ἐδέξαντο, φωνὰς καὶ *χορείας* καὶ σεμνότητας ἀκουσμάτων ἱερῶν καὶ φασμάτων ἁγίων ἔχοντες· ἐν αἷς ὁ παντελὴς ἤδη καὶ μεμυημένος *ἐλεύθερος γεγονὼς καὶ ἄφετος περιιὼν* ἐστεφανωμένος ὀργιάζει καὶ σύνεστιν ὁσίοις καὶ καθαροῖς ἀνδράσι, τὸν ἀμύητον ἐνταῦθα τῶν ζώντων καὶ ἀκάθαρτον ἐφορῶν ὄχλον ἐν βορβόρῳ πολλῷ καὶ *ὁμίχλῃ πατούμενον ὑφ' ἑαυτοῦ καὶ συνελαυνόμενον*, φόβῳ δὲ θανάτου τοῖς κακοῖς ἀπιστίᾳ τῶν ἐκεῖ ἀγαθῶν ἐμμένοντα.

Thus we say that the soul that has passed thither is dead (*olôlenai*), having regard to its complete (*eis to holon*) change and conversion. In this world it is without knowledge, except when it is already at the point of death; but when that time comes, it has an experience like that of men who are undergoing initiation into great mysteries; and so the verbs *teleutân* (die) and *teleisthai* (be initiated), and the actions they denote, have a similarity. *In the beginning there is straying and wandering, the weariness of running this way and that, and nervous journeys through darkness that reach no goal,* and then immediately before the consummation every possible terror, shivering and trembling and sweating and amazement. But after this a marvelous light meets the wanderer, and open country and meadow lands welcome him; and in that place there are voices and dancing and the solemn majesty of sacred music and holy visions. *And amidst these, he walks at large in new freedom,* now perfect and fully initiated, celebrating the sacred rites, a garland upon his head, and converses with pure and holy men; he surveys the uninitiated, unpurified mob here on earth, the mob of living men who, *herded together in mirk and deep mire, trample one another down* and in their fear of death cling to their ills, since they disbelieve in the blessings of the other world.

In Plutarch's analogy between the experience of mystic rituals and that of the soul upon death, a sharp contrast stands out between the walking of the souls before arriving to the abode of the blessed and afterwards. The former err in despair, while the latter stroll peacefully. Plutarch takes this for granted in a dialogue on a different topic (the soul's activity during sleep), so he is likely echoing an extended notion of how the dead move in the underworld. So does Vergil in *Aeneid* 6, where two opposed underworlds are characterized, among other things, by ambulation.

In effect, prior to Elysium the dead wander aimlessly in darkness. Those that have not received proper burial "for a hundred years flutter and wander about these banks" (*centum errant annos uolitantque haec litora circum,* 6.329) and Dido "roamed in the great wood" (*errabat silua in magna,* 6.451). Vergil plays with the double meaning of the verb *errare,* linking it to Dido's elegiac *error,* highlighted by her presence in the *lugentes campi* (see Myers in the present volume), while aligning it also to the wandering/roaming of the dead. Also the verb *uolitare,* with the frequentative suffix suggesting disorderly flutterin , is subtly different from the more serious *volant* of 706, employed for the souls awaiting reincarnation in Elysium: Vergil compares the latter with bees flying from flower to flower (708–9) and forming a great column (*tanto agmine,* 6.712). Unlike the wandering souls of the pre-Elysian underworld, this orderly formation has, among other things, a clear goal in sight, their insertion into new bodies, and Aeneas stresses their desire to return (*tam dira cupido,* 721). *Volitare* suggests precisely the contrary; those flitting souls lack order and mission.[13] Effectively, *uolitare* is another word for *errare.*

In stark contrast to the fluttering dead surrounding them, Aeneas and the Sibyl walk with a clear goal in the fi st part of their journey. Under the Sibyl's guidance, Aeneas does not get lost in the dark and follows the predetermined path, a point that Vergil repeats several times in narrative descriptions such as: "they continued on the journey they had begun and drew near to the river" (*iter inceptum peragunt fluuioque propinquant*, 6.384); or "then they continued on their assigned path, and they were already in the furthest fields (*inde datum molitur iter, iamque arua tenebant* | *ultima*, 6.477–8). In these two sentences, the river and the fields acquire a sense of place on a linear route. This is also patent in the emphatic word *uia*, which constitutes the core of the imperative instructions of the Sibyl to Aeneas, both in the initial "enter upon your path" (*inuade uiam*, 6.260) and the final "come and make your path and accomplish the task you have undertaken" (*carpe uiam et susceptum perfice munus*, 6.629).[14]

Following a *uia* marks a meaningful contrast between the living visitors and the dead.[15] The dead wander in a bounded space, while the living are free to continue their journey. This opposition is clearly marked in Deiphobus' farewell to Aeneas (6.545–7): "I shall be restored to the darkness (*reddarque tenebris*). Go, great glory of Troy, go (*i, decus, i, nostrum*) and enjoy a better destiny. Thus much he spoke and upon that word turned his steps (*in uerbo uestigia torsit*)." Deiphobus can only *reddere* and *torsere*, Aeneas can *ire*. Of course, there is an emphatic interpretation of this contrast in terms of Trojan past vs. Roman future, but this conceptual opposition is grounded in a more basic image, the difference between the aimless walking of the dead and of the goal-oriented path of the living.[16]

Once Aeneas arrives in Elysium, the movement changes dramatically. There, as Musaeus says, "no one has a settled habitation" (*nulli certa domus*, 6.673). Aeneas and the Sibyl have now only an "easy route" that Musaeus shows them (*facili iam tramite sistam*, 6.676), not towards a specific fixed place but towards a person who moves freely, Anchises. Aeneas' father will lead them everywhere while "they range widely over the whole region" (*sic tota passim regione uagantur*, 6.886) until he has shown "every single thing to his son" (*natum per singula duxit*, 6.888).[17] Lack of a fixed stable place has nothing to do with being lost, but with being free to stroll everywhere, similar to Plutarch's blessed initiate. The dead in the former part of the underworld have assigned places (*datae sedes*, 431) that bond them to a place of unhappiness. The distinction *errare*/*uagare* with which Vergil opposes the movement of the unhappy and blessed dead is framed between non-purposeful and purposeful movement. Aeneas and the Sibyl too are contrasted with the pre-Elysian souls through their teleological walking, while being assimilated to the souls in Elysium by joining in their walks and movements.

There is in both parts of the underworld, however, one common trait: nowhere can Aeneas reach his goal without being guided along the path, be it the Sibyl, Musaeus (*sistam*, 6.676; *ostendit*, 6.678), or Anchises (*trahit*, 6.753; *emittit*, 6.898). It is a world in which only the privileged (just like

Plutarch's initiates) can reach their goal without becoming *errantes*. This clear contrast with the upper world, where Aeneas (outside of *Aeneid* 3) is always able to find his own way, is highlighted immediately after exiting through the Gates of Dreams. Aeneas "cuts his way through to the ships" (*ille uiam secat ad nauis*, 6.899). This sort of expression is impossible in the underworld. The emphatic *ille* and the verb *secare* express that Aeneas has regained all his power to walk autonomously through his own itineraries in the world of the living.

Yet Aeneas' docility in Hades does not mean passivity. The teleological orientation of Aeneas' walking entails a specific emotional dimension in the description of his movement in the fi st part of the journey. As Plutarch shows above, a route through Hades not only needs to be oriented towards a goal, but must also overcome and bypass the fears and terrors of the journey that might obviate one's reaching the goal. Courage is necessary. This mandate is expressed at the moment Aeneas enters the underworld: asked by the Sibyl to enter with courage and with a stout heart (*nunc animis opus, Aenea, nunc pectore firmo*, 261) he follows her with *haud timidis passibus* (6.263).[18] This lack of timidity in Aeneas' steps shows confidence that he will arrive at his intended goal, Elysium and Anchises. His gait expresses determination towards a goal that needs steps that are both steady and fast. Firmness and swiftness, the two other features of Aeneas' movement in the underworld, are necessary consequences of his teleological pace.

III. Firmness

The second aspect of Aeneas' gait that contrasts with the fluttering of the dead is its solid physicality. A well-known touch of delicate humour, Aeneas' unbalancing of Charon's boat with his weight (6.413), profits from this contrast between the corporality of the living and the evanescence of the souls. Aeneas' embodied walk is reflected in the verbs chosen to express his progress, which markedly suggest marching in and filling a space. The Sibyl tells him upon starting their trip to "enter upon your path and draw your sword from its sheath" (*inuade uiam uaginaque eripe ferrum*, 6.260). Even if, as she herself will tell the Trojan hero only thirty lines later, the sword is useless against "insubstantial bodiless beings" (*tenuis sine corpore uitas*, 6.292), her fi st order shows Vergil's concern to depict his journey as a physical trip, in which walking is real and corporeal, unlike the fluttering movement of the dead. Likewise, Aeneas, upon crossing the river Acheron and arriving at Elysium's gates, is said twice to "seize the entrance" (*occupat aditum*, 6.424 and 635).[19] Like the *inuadere* of 260, the verb *occupare* suggests filling the space with one's body.[20] *Occupare* is not a casual way of saying "entering," but is the appropriate verb to show Aeneas' physical movement in space. In fact, Charon immediately recognizes Aeneas and the Sibyl as passengers of a different kind, as he sees them "passing through the silent forest and drawing their feet near to the bank" (*per tacitum nemus ire pedemque aduertere ripae*, 6.386). The line contrasts the silence of the lifeless forest with the physicality of the feet that makes them awkward to Charon. And he says (6.388–91):

> Whoever you are, who are making your way to my river under arms (*armatus qui nostra ad flumina tendis*), say why you are coming (*quid uenias iam istinc*) and halt your step (*comprime gressum*). This is the place of ghosts (*umbrarum*), of sleep and of drowsy night; it is wrong to ship living bodies in the barque of Styx (*corpora uiua nefas Stygia uectare carina*).

Along with his weapons, it is Aeneas' walk, physical and purposeful, that clearly marks him as a living body that, Charon thinks, is not fit for the sort of incorporeal motion appropriate beyond the Styx.

In contrast to this emphasis on steps, which transmit an impression of orderly and firm walking, the descriptions of the movements of the dwellers of this fi st part of the underworld express disorder and levity: *uolitare* (6.293 and 329); *turba effusa ruebat* (6.305). The unhappy dead are compared to falling leaves and to fluttering birds (*quam multa ... lapsa cadunt folia ... multae glomerantur aues*, 6.309–11). There is a clear echo of the bird-like and bat-like gibbering and flying about of the souls in Hades in the *Odyssey*, where they can also fly like a dream.[21] Palinurus, when approaching them, just moves along (*sese agebat*, 6.337), just as Dido pulls herself (*corripuit sese*, 6.472), suggesting sudden ghost-like starts. Deiphobus, in the aforementioned farewell scene, "turns round his foot-traces" (*uestigia torsit*, 6.547): as a spirit, walking on foot-traces is more appropriate for Deiphobus than bodily steps are. By contrast, the expression *uestigia pressit* of 6.331, referring to Aeneas standing while watching the souls, means "to halt." *Premere* marks the physical pressure that imprints *uestigia*, while *torsere* expresses an airy turning round with no bodily weight.[22]

Treading belongs to the living, and it is therefore logical that the dead want to talk to Aeneas and walk along with him (*conferre gradum*, 6.488), as if siding their steps with the living hero might give the souls a moment of recovered life and goal-oriented movement. This image recalls the passage in the Odyssean *Nekyia* where Achilles enjoys a brief moment of happiness upon hearing good news about his son and, as a consequence, starts walking with long steps (φοίτα μακρὰ βιβᾶσα, 11.532).[23] For a moment, contact with Odysseus has given Achilles a hint of his characteristically swift feet.

Besides notable exceptions like Ajax in the *Odyssey* or Dido in the *Aeneid*, the dead want to engage in conversation with the living visitors. And when this visitor is Aeneas, this conversation should take place, in typically Roman fashion, while walking side by side with him.[24] That is why in 6.485, "to left and right the ghosts thronged thickly about Aeneas" (*circumstant animae dextra laeuaque frequentes*), Vergil has turned the Homeric model of the orderly visions in the *Nekyia* into an ephemerally lively Roman group stroll.

Instead, once Aeneas and the Sibyl reach Elysium, Vergil makes no mention of the manner of their walking. It ceases to be relevant. Rather, it is now Musaeus who takes a decided step in front of them (*ante tulit gressum*, 677). Also, the firm standing on feet of the dwellers of Elysium is shown in lines that recall how they practice sports and dancing (6.642–5):

pars in gramineis exercent membra palaestris
contendunt ludo et fulua luctantur harena
pars pedibus plaudunt choreas et carmina dicunt.

Some of them exercise their limbs in grassy rings, struggle in play and wrestle in the dark yellow sand. Some stamp out dances with their feet and call out the song.

This singing and dancing in Elysium clearly echoes traditional images of the eschatological *thiasoi* of initiates, as in Plutarch's aforementioned passage, whose initiate "celebrates the festival together with the other sacred and pure people."[25] The firmness of their step is all the more relevant given that it is not identical to the physicality of their bodies, as shown patently by the fact that Anchises is unembraceable (6.700–2, like Patroclus in *Iliad* 23.100 and Anticleia in *Odyssey* 11.204–8). In spite of their airy quality as souls, the marked firmness of the footsteps of the dead that have attained a state of blessedness contrasts with the levity of those inhabitants of the pre-Elysian underworld. It seems clear, then, that walking steadily on one's feet is a sign of stability, of "health," that corresponds either to the living or to those already in Elysium, who act very much like the living.

This contrast echoes a well-known motif in Greek accounts about the characteristic features of those who are close to death: a common sign of being half dead is to limp (or to be partially barefoot) or to be unable to stand firmly on both feet. Carlo Ginzburg has described with parallels from multiple European traditions how limping or losing one's equilibrium is often a sign of death approaching, and Alex Purves has shown the specific importance of this image in early Greek poetry.[26] In the fi st part of the netherworld, Aeneas' markedly decided steps contrast with the footless movements of the dead. His steady walking is a sign of real life and a guarantee that he will not remain fluttering in the netherworld. Once he has arrived at Elysium, this contrast is no longer necessary, and all he needs is to follow the ethereal but equally firm steps of the blessed

IV. Urgency

In addition to determination and firmnes , Aeneas' hasty walking shows his urgency to complete his journey.[27] Every verb of movement suggests briskness: the Sibyl enters the cave in a frenzied state (*furens antro se inmisit*, 6.263) and Aeneas moves at the same pace as her (*passibus aequat*, 6.264). When exiting Charon's skiff he "quickly departs from the bank" (*euaditque celer ripam*, 6.425). Swiftness is emphasized as fundamental by the Sibyl herself, who tells him: "come now, take the way, complete the task, let us hurry up" (*sed iam age, carpe uiam et susceptum perfice munus; | acceleremus*, 6.629–30). And upon these words "they went together through a dark stretch of the way. They make quick work of the distance before them and draw near the doors" (*et pariter gressi per opaca uiarum | corripiunt spatium medium foribusque propinquant*, 6.633–4). This haste is again in contrast to the lack of temporal pressure on the dead, whose wandering has no apparent end. And again, this hurriedness lasts only until they arrive at Elysium. The Sibyl interrupts Deiphobus, alleging they are pressed for time, but nobody thinks of interrupting Anchises, who has all the time in the underworld to relay to his son everything in detail.

This rushing belongs to the tradition of *katabasis*, and it is one of the main differences between an arrival in a strange land (e.g., Scheria) and descent into the underworld. In the former, as it is to be expected, one normally advances slowly, measuring every movement. In the underworld swift movement seems compulsory, as if some danger always threatens. In the tales of *katabasis* there is often a narrative tension between such hurriedness and the poetic wish to recount completely and with rich details the topography of the underworld (the theme of the "round trip" through Hades studied by Jan Bremmer 2009). The Sibyl embodies this tension, as she both makes and allows for long digressions, while also rushing Aeneas along in alternate moments. Curiosity is limited by fear, and the exploratory pace must be accelerated after every description or extended dialogue. Likewise, Odysseus stops his νεκυομαντεία for fear that a Gorgon, or even Persephone herself, might appear (*Od.* 11.633–5); Pirithous and Theseus stopped walking to sit down and remained forever in Hades; and in Aristophanes' *Frogs* Dionysus asks Hercules "the swiftest way to get down to Hades" (φράζε τῶν ὁδῶν | ὅπῃ τάχιστ' ἀφιξόμεθ' εἰς Ἅιδου κάτω, 117–18). In the *Aeneid* fear of traps or dangers (like Cerberus waking up or the appearance of some other monster) is not mentioned, but it looms large over the whole episode: the unshakeable haunting of death's dread compels the living to make their way as quickly as possible until they reach the very place where the souls blend with a form of physicality. A living being is out of place in the world of the dead, and as such, is in constant danger.

This sense of urgency in *katabasis* resembles the narrative counterpart of the ritual need to quickly bury the dead. Patroclus asks Achilles in the *Iliad* to complete his funerary rites as quickly as possible in order to get to Hades (θάπτέ με ὅττι τάχιστα πύλας Ἀΐδαο περήσω, 23.71). Several gold tablets, depicting a soul in transit to the underworld, also emphasize the imminent pressure of time. In the longest tablet (from Hipponion), the soul is dying of thirst and is in a hurry to be given water "quickly" (δίψαι δ' εἰμ' αὖος καὶ ἀπόλλυμαι· ἀλλὰ δότ' ὦκα), a line that is found in another long tablet (from Petelia) with the variant αἶψα instead of ὦκα.[28] It is symptomatic that another tablet (from Pelinna) has as ritual utterance: "quickly you fell into milk" (αἶψα εἰς γάλα ἔθορες).[29] This tablet and an almost identical one also from Pelinna have another important temporal element: they seem to take for granted that the transition between death and rebirth (in Hades) is accomplished on the same day: "you have died and you have been born on this very day" (ἤματι τῶιδε). In one day, the entire voyage of the soul from death to everlasting bliss is accomplished.[30]

With these parallels in mind, there is a hint in *Aeneid* 6 that Aeneas' steps are hurried not only because of the traditional vague fear of underworldly threats, but also as an echo of the ritual urgency to accomplish quickly the transition to the realm of the dead. When Aeneas enters the underworld, it is dawn (6.255), and when speaking to Deiphobus, it is midday (6.535–6). Conversation goes on and "perhaps they would have spent in such talk all the given time" (*et fors omne datum traherent per talia tempus*, 6.537). To put it in Roman terms, Aeneas and Deiphobus were immersed in a private *ambulatio* between friends in which nobody cares about time as is typical of those pleasant moments of *otium*.[31] But the Sibyl gets impatient and advises that "night is rushing, Aeneas, and we pass the hours in weeping" (*nox ruit, Aenea; nos flendo ducimus horas*, 6.539). It is this precise temporal limitation that clarifies the sense of *datum tempus* at 6.537. Servius suggested that the ritualized descent into the underworld should be accomplished in one day (*ad Aen.* 6.535). Commentators tend to think that this is an ad hoc explanation that aims to explain a posteriori a difficult line.[32] Yet, given the lack of any other satisfactory explanation for the passage, and the formula of the two Pelinna tablets, one can surmise that Servius points to the correct interpretation of the text. It is not so much a mathematical counting of hours by the Sibyl, as it is the intuitive knowledge that any delay is contrary to *katabasis*, which requires swift walking until the final goal is reached.[33] The ritual alluded to by Servius is most likely not the direct reference behind the Sibyl's words, but it is a good parallel for the urgency that surrounds both katabatic myths and rites, since the journey to Hades must be accomplished in a single, exceptional day, and this apportioned time cannot be exceeded.

Thus Aeneas' haste in the pre-Elysian underworld reminds us that the time of the living is different from that of the dead. Those that wander aimlessly in the murky netherworld have no sense of time: no pressure, but no leisure either. Only walking beside Aeneas and talking to him give them a hint of a temporally contingent experience, and therefore "it is not enough to see him once" (*nec uidisse semel satis est*, 6.487). Instead, in Elysium, the mortal time of Aeneas and the Sibyl is subsumed within the superior eternity of the blessed. Past and future can be observed from the serene present, whose sublime timelessness is not under the constraints of human time, but is far above it. Thus, Aeneas' urgency in the fi st part of his trip disappears completely in the second, where he only needs to follow the stroll of the blessed.

VI. Conclusion

Resolution, firmnes , urgency. These features of Aeneas' walking are repeatedly emphasized by Vergil. As the previous paragraphs have demonstrated, there are enough parallels in accounts of *katabasis* to show that the manner of walking can be essential for success (or failure, in the case of Theseus and Pirithous).[34] The most eloquent instance is a gold tablet from Thurii, which contains a *symbolon* uttered by the soul upon its arrival at the land of the blessed, and highlights empathically the connection between swift feet and the goal of motion: "I reached the desired crown with swift feet" (ἱμερτοῦ δ' ἐπέβαν στεφάνου ποσὶ καρπαλίμοισι).[35] The last clause is an epic formula used here in an eschatological sense, which characterizes the resolute, firm and swift steps of the Greek epic heroes: Achilles pursues Hector with swift feet (καρπαλίμοισι πόδεσσι, *Il.* 22.166); Odysseus enters Arete's palace swiftly (καρπαλίμως ὑπὲρ οὐδὸν ἐβήσετο δώματος εἴσω, "he walked swiftly over the threshold into the house," *Od.* 7.135), walking alone in this verse at the same pace as Athena who had led him swiftly into the city while he followed behind her divine traces (ἡγήσατο Παλλὰς Ἀθήνη | καρπαλίμως· ὁ δ' ἔπειτα μετ' ἴχνια βαῖνε θεοῖο, "Pallas Athena led swiftly and he followed the footsteps of the goddess," *Od.* 7.37–8). Undoubtedly a good translation of the Greek καρπαλίμως, which suggests decisiveness and briskness, would be the Vergilian *haud timidis passibus* at *Aeneid* 6.264. Indeed, one can well imagine Hercules walking καρπαλίμως when he travelled through Hades in the poem that Vergil used, among several others, as a source for his own version of the theme. Aeneas, in this sense, walks over the footsteps of Hercules and previous protagonists of the descent to Hades whose steps would have also been determined, firm and swift.[36]

However, the poetic and ritual traditions of *katabasis* are not the only background against which Aeneas' manner of walking though Hades can be judged to be an important feature. In the Roman culture to which Vergil's most immediate audience belonged, there were several other possible resonances that we must take into account when evaluating the (intended) impact of the poem in the audience. For instance, the military triumph and the *pompa funebris* famously resonate in the procession of the souls of Roman future heroes, both as a collective (*tanto agmine,* 6.712) and as individuals (*insignis spoliis Marcellus opimis ingreditur,* 6.855). Concerning Aeneas' treading into Hades, we may perhaps recall a male ritual of initiation, comparable to the female wedding, namely, the *deductio in forum,* in which walking was fundamental to the introduction of a young citizen to the places and people that would mark his future *cursus honorum*. Aeneas' walking tour of Hades – his reception by his old Trojan friends who want to accompany him, his being told about the different people he sees – constitutes an experience with some affinity to such introductory walks for those who come for the fi st time into the forum.[37] Aeneas undergoes in Book 6 an experience that could resonate in the minds of the Roman audience as an initiatory walk through his past and future, and many may have read Vergil's depiction of his descent as a literary version of this Roman custom, which makes it distinct from its acknowledged Greek models.

Through all these various clusters of poetic resonances, in the lines that link the different speeches that constitute the most famous parts of the episode (and in several cases, of the whole poem), Vergil accomplished a portrait of Aeneas' gait that identified him as a visitor to the underworld who walks through the land of the dead, through the history of the Roman people, and through the destiny of human beings. The poet took great care in depicting the steps of Aeneas, the Sibyl, and the other characters, and did so in a way that the connoisseurs of Greek katabatic traditions, his Roman audience, and still further, future readers could walk easily along with them through this extraordinary route.

NOTES

1 At the last moment I was regrettably unable to attend the Cumaean conference, but I am very grateful to Bill Gladhill and Micah Myers for including my paper in the volume springing from it. To them, and also to Alex Purves, Marco

Antonio Santamaría, and Jan Bremmer, I am indebted for several helpful suggestions and comments on previous drafts of this paper – the errors remain of course mine alone.

2 On walking as the metaphor for telling and reading in literature, cf. Solnit 2000: 64–78.

3 Horsfall 2013a: 2.436 (*ad* 635). The transitional passages of Book 6 that will be analysed are the following: 260–4, 268–9, 331–2, 384–91, 424–5, 477, 628–38, 677–8, 752–5, 886–9, 897–900. English translations are taken from Horsfall, with slight modification . In his commentary, Norden 1957 pays only slight attention to some of the "walking" lines as echoes of Ennian verses (cf. his comments *ad* 384, 488 and his Anhang I).

4 There is much recent literature about the various cultural meanings of walking: cf., e.g., the collection of studies in Ingold and Vergunst 2008. On the notions associated with ways of walking in ancient Greece, cf. Bremmer 1991: many of the features that characterize the walking of the epic hero can be found in the specific case of the katabatic tr veller.

5 O'Sullivan 2011: 11–12, 150–2. That Vergil was aware of the characterizing nuances of the different kinds of walking is well shown in many passages of the *Aeneid*: 1.405: *uera incessu patuit dea*; 1.690: *gressu gaudens incedit Iuli*; 2.724: *implicuit sequiturque patrem non passibus aequis*; 5.649: *diuina signi decoris … uocisque sonus uel gressus eunti*; 10.640: *dat sine mente sonum gressusque effingit euntis*. Whole scenes, like Evander and Aeneas' stroll (8.306–12) and Nisus and Euryalus' frustrated flight (9.380–92) focus on walking; on the significant monosandalism of the Ernians in 7.688 cf. Firpo 2002.

6 Among Vergil's sources in *Aeneid* 6 one can count *Odyssey* 11, Plato's eschatological myths, a *katabasis* of Hercules and another of Orpheus (cf. Horsfall 2013a). According to Bremmer 2009 (reprinted with some updates in Bremmer 2014), apart from these sources Jewish apocalyptic tradition is also perceivable in the topic of a "tour of Hell." It is difficult to discern in many cases which sources are directly alluded in the *Aeneid* and which others just share elements of the katabatic tradition (cf. Herrero 2015a).

7 On the tablets (quoted with Bernabé's numbering in his edition of *Orphicorum Fragmenta*), cf. Bernabé-Jiménez 2008; Graf-Johnston 2013. Cf. Herrero 2015a for the particular case of the "Orphic" gold tablets and other ritual evidence as a key to interpret some passages of *Aeneid* 6.

8 *Orph. Fragm.* 488–91: ἔρχομαι … ἥκω…; *Orph. Fragm.* 474.2: εἶς; 5: μηδὲ ἔλθῃς; 15: ἔρχεαι. Cf. similar expressions in *Orph. Fragm.* 475: ἐ‹μ›πέλασ‹ασ›θαι; 485: εἶς; 487: ὁδοιπόρ‹ει›; 491: ἴθι; 493: εἴσιθ‹ι›. *Orph. Fragm.* 474: στείχουσι; 491: ἔρχεται.

9 Cuche 2014 studies the religious importance of running in Greek rituals. See Herrero 2015a on the katabatic experiences in Greek cults (also reflected in the *Aeneid* 6), and 2015b on the conceptions of inner movement that are reflected in ritual gestures.

10 For the special walking of the gods, cf., e.g., *Il.* 19.91–4 (Ate's swift walking with soft feet over men's heads), *Il.* 14.285 (Hypnos and Hera standing over a tree).

11 Line 6.637 is a "definite break a sharp dividing line": Solmsen 1990: 215, reacting against other divisions that overlook this fundamental one.

12 Translation from Burkert 1987: 91–3, whose comment on the passage unpacks the many layers of Plutarch's analogy of initiation and death. For *choreia* in Vergil's underworld, cf. also Curtis in this volume.

13 The verb *uolito* has venerable resonances that may have been also present here: Ennius' *uolito uiuos per ora uirum* (fr. 46 Courtney) was famously echoed by Vergil in *Georg.* 3.9: *uictorque uirum uolitare per ora*. As Lennartz 1999 suggests, Ennius possibly in had mind Sappho's fr. 55 V (φοιτάσῃς πεδ' ἀμαύρων νεκύων ἐκπεποταμένα) as a "contrastive model." Vergil restricts the fateful *uolitare* of the souls to one hundred years, and one of those wandering souls, Palinurus, finds consolation in the fame of his name (6.378–83) as if aiming for an equilibrium between the negative *uolitare* of the souls and the positive *uolitare* of the celebrity among mortals.

14 Note also how Statius' *uia Domitiana* reads like an extension of Vergil's underworld road, as discussed by Emily Pillinger earlier in this volume.

15 Charon will note in 6.384–90, discussed below, the purposeful walking of the newcomers (*ad flumina tendis*), and will question them about it (*quid uenias*).

16 On this passage as marking the transition between past and future, cf. Williams 1990: 198.

17 There is a delicate distinction between 6.888 and the previous expression in 6.565 (*perque omnia duxit*), which the Sibyl uses to explain how Hecate told her what there is in Tartarus. This general overview (rather than a physical tour, cf. Horsfall 2013a *ad* 888) seems akin to the view from above (ἐφορῶν) that the blessed in Plutarch's fragment have of the uninitiated who dwell in disgrace. While the souls that reincarnate have to ascend into the upper world (719: *ad caelum*), in other expressions (887: *aëris in campis latis*) Elysium seems to be in a celestial setting, consistent with Plutarch's Platonic conception of the realm of the blessed souls.

18 This seems to be Vergil's translation of the imperative θάρσει, which is frequently used in epic tales, including *katabaseis*, and in mystic rituals often compared (e.g., by Plutarch) to the experience of death: cf. Herrero 2016.

19 The repetition of this expression, criticized by Horsfall as lack of attention (cf. p. 95 above), may purposefully echo the narrative doublets of arrival scenes to a dangerous land, which often have preliminary and definitive arrival , as well

as the ritual entrances into complex sanctuaries with several stages. E.g., upon arriving at Scheria Odysseus supplicates three times (*Od.* 5.445–50, 6.149–85, 7.146–53) and twice receives instructions (6.255–315, 747–77); the Orphic tablets present the soul supplicating the guardians of the underworld and also Persephone (in Riedweg's 2011 reconstruction of a prototypical poem, these would be doublet scenes). In *Aeneid* 6, the passing of Cerberus and the gates to Elysium in 6.424 and 635 are both assimilated to entrances into *adyta;* a similar explanation can be supposed for *inuade uiam* (6.260) and *carpe uiam* (6.629).

20 In spite of Horsfall's interpretation of *occupat* at lines 6.424 and 6.635 as "moving swiftly" (2013a: 317, 436 *ad loc*), the context of both passages supports the emphasis on spatial embodiment; in 6.424 Aeneas' body is exceptionally free of danger because Cerberus is asleep and in 6.635 he purifies his body (*corpusque recenti spargit aqua* are the words following *aditum*).

21 *Od.* 11.222, 11.605, 24.7.

22 Therefore *torsit* is to be preferred to the variant *pressit* at 5.547 in some manuscripts. Cf. Horsfall 2013a *ad* 331, with comments also on 159 and 197, where some other passages are mentioned that seem to indicate "slow movement."

23 Cf. Santamaría 2014 on *Od.* 11.532, pointing out a parallel image in the choir of initiates in Aristophanes' *Frogs* 345, who recover strength in their knees: γόνυ πάλλεται γερόντων. Another parallel is *Orph. Fragm.* 488.5–6, commented on at pp. 105–6.

24 O'Sullivan 2011: 6. The meeting with Dido offers (purposefully) the inverse situation; it is Aeneas who tells Dido to halt her step (*siste gradum*, 465), which she refuses.

25 On the dancing and paean-singing of this choir, cf. Curtis in this volume. Cf. also Edmonds 2011, who, along with a controversial interpretation of the last line in the Hipponion tablet (*Orph. Fragm.* 474.12) as "you will celebrate rites with the other blessed ones," gives some further parallels for ritual ceremonies as a vision of the afterlife bliss (e.g., Aristophanes *Frogs*).

26 Ginzburg 1989: 213–31; Purves 2006 (independently of Ginzburg). Some clear instances: *Il.* 15.269, 21.302; Aristoph. *Ran.* 345.

27 I draw freely in this section from my account of underworld time in Herrero 2015a: 338–40. Cf. Pillinger in this volume.

28 *Orph. Fragm.* 474.11–12 (Hipponion); 476.8 (Petelia).

29 Although probably the original word was αἶζα (goat), in correspondence with the bull and the ram of the previous and following lines (cf. Méndez Dosuna 2009), the scribal mistake introducing a new word, αἶψα, suggests again the swiftness typical of the funerary / initiatory rites alluded to by the tablet.

30 Since *katabasis* is a climactic and unique moment, the parallel with tragedy, which according to Aristotle must depict all crucial events in one turn of the sun

(*Poet.* 1449b13), is relevant as indicative of the urgency of finishing the action (ritual or mythical) in one day. One-day duration may have become a *topos* of *katabasis*: for instance, in Lucian's portrait of the inverse journey, Protesilaus is given just one day to go back to the living (*Dial. Mort.* 28). Cf. Herrero 2013 on the notion of the single day and 2015a on its application to the katabatic experience.

31 O'Sullivan 2011: 83–4.

32 Horsfall 2013a: 2.383.

33 The Sibyl sees any delay as deviating from the purpose of the trip (cf. O'Sullivan 2011: 104, where *perambulare* with too many stops has a negative connotation). For other elements of time and chronology in the underworld of *Aeneid* 6, see Gowers in this volume.

34 Pirithous' hat in the images showing him sitting in the underworld is a sign of an unfinished journe , since he sat before having concluded it (cf. *LIMC s. v.*, and Bremmer 2015).

35 On the formula in the Thurii tablet, cf. Santamaría 2011. As in many other mystic *symbola* (e.g., the Eleusinian *kykeona epion, ekernophoresa*, etc.), it is expressed with a ritual aorist; also in the previous hexameter: "I flew out (*exeptan*) from the grievous circle of heavy suffering." Cf. Graf and Johnston 2013: 125–9.

36 Cf. O' Sullivan 2011: 104, quoting Cic. *Fin.* 5.5. (*historia uestigium ponimus*) as an instance of those who walk on Roman history.

37 O'Sullivan 2011: 55–8. Cf. Bettini 1991: 145–7, on the watching of the *imagines* of the Roman heroes as echoing an explanation of the statutes in the Forum.

6

Vergil's Underworld and the Afterlife of Lovers and Love Poets[1]

MICAH YOUNG MYERS

This paper explores how Vergil's representation of the afterlives of lovers in the *lugentes campi* of *Aeneid* 6 engages with depictions of the underworld in contemporary Latin love elegy, while also affecting subsequent elegiac treatments of the afterlife. I start by analysing the epigram ascribed to Domitius Marsus on the death of Tibullus as evidence for contemporary awareness of the poetic links between Vergil and Tibullus on the topic of the afterlife (Part I). After reviewing the *lugentes campi* passage (Part II) and the underworld scenes in Tibullus 1.3 (Part III), in the fourth and longest section of the paper I discuss the relationship between the two. Tibullus 1.3 and Vergil's *lugentes campi* have long been seen as drawing on the same literary traditions. I argue for specific correspondences that to this point have not been fully appreciated. Although it is impossible to answer definitivel whether Tibullus 1.3 is responding to *Aeneid* 6 or vice versa, I follow the traditional chronology that places the publication of Tibullus 1.3 prior to *Aeneid* 6 reaching its final form.[2] Part V turns to *Amores* 3.9, Ovid's *epicedion* for Tibullus, a well-known site for allusions to Tibullus' poetry, especially 1.3. I argue that Ovid alludes to *Aeneid* 6 as well as to Tibullus, with Vergil's vision of the afterlife functioning as a lens and a refraction point that contributes to the reshaping of the afterlife of love poets in *Amores* 3.9.[3] The paper concludes by briefly surveying other elegiac representations of the afterlife in order to show that the elegies discussed here are a testament to a larger series of interactions between elegy and *Aeneid* 6.

I. Domitius Marsus Fr. 7 Courtney

I begin at the end of the lives of Vergil and Tibullus, and at the end of the Tibullan corpus, with the epigram ascribed to Domitius Marsus that concludes Tibullus Book 3. Marsus' epigram is replete with allusions to the poetry of both Vergil and Tibullus, and signals that the two poets are linked through their representations of the afterlife:

> Te quoque Vergilio comitem non aequa, Tibulle,
>   mors iuuenem campos misit ad Elysios
> ne foret aut elegis molles qui fleret amore
>   aut caneret forti regia bella pede.

You too, Tibullus, unfair death sent as a young man to the Elysian fields to be a companion to Vergil, so that there would not be anyone to mourn soft loves in elegiacs or to sing the wars of kings in heroic meter.[4]

The poem presents Tibullus, who died shortly after Vergil, likely in late 19 or 18 BCE, as the latter's companion in the Elysian Fields.[5] Marsus claims with conventional hyperbole that the demise of Tibullus and Vergil brings an end to the elegiac and epic genres.[6] The epigram presents Tibullus' poetry as the mourning of "soft loves," with *molles* suggestive of elegiac aesthetics and *fleret* gesturing to elegy's putative origins as a genre of lament.[7] Vergil is connected with epic, the singing of the wars of kings, *fortis* in meter and content where elegy is soft. Yet, in a flourish that points to the entanglements of the two genres, elegy is described in a hexameter line and epic in a pentameter. Marsus drives home this tension between content and meter by dividing the two-word description of epic (*forti ... pede*, 4) between the ends of each hemiepes, that is, at the very points that his pentameter is distinguished from a hexameter.

The epigram also alludes to the poetry of both Tibullus and Vergil. First, let us consider the allusions to Vergil. Marsus' verses about the end of two poets' lives point to the middle of the *Eclogues*, of the *Georgics*, and of the *Aeneid*. Marsus' phrase, *ne ... | aut caneret forti regia bella pede* (3–4), is reminiscent of Vergil's Callimachean claim of an unsuccessful attempt at epic at *Eclogues* 6.3–4: *cum canerem reges et proelia, Cynthius aurem | uellit, et admonuit...* ("When I was trying to sing of kings and battles, Apollo grabbed my ear and warned...").[8] Yet in Marsus' poem, *Mors* takes the epic-preventing role that Apollo plays in *Eclogues* 6. In addition, Marsus' diction recalls the *Aeneid*'s second invocation at 7.41–2: *dicam horrida bella, | dicam acies actosque animis in funera reges* ("I will tell of savage wars, I will tell of battle lines and of kings driven by their own courage to their deaths"), where Vergil himself returns to the language of *Eclogue* 6.3–4.[9] The allusions to Vergil in the final verse of Marsus' epigram also reinforce the Vergilian echoes in the opening phrase, *te quoque ... Tibulle*. This wording recalls *Georgics* 3.1 (*te quoque, magna Pales*) and that passage's programmatic centrality. This allusion, moreover, like the allusions to *Eclogue* 6 and *Aeneid* 7 in Marsus' fourth verse, brings us once again to the middle of a Vergilian poem.[10]

Even more relevant for Marsus' phrase *te quoque ... Tibulle* are the opening four lines of *Aeneid* 7, which commemorate the death of Aeneas' nurse, Caieta, beginning: *tu quoque litoribus nostris, Aeneia nutrix, | aeternam moriens famam, Caieta, dedisti* ("You too, Caieta, nurse of Aeneas, in death gave eternal fame to our shores," 1–2). Vergil's *tu quoque* in *Aeneid* 7.1 is in dialogue with *Georgics* 3.1, while both poems are in turn activated in Marsus' use of the phrase.[11] Since, moreover, the opening four lines of *Aeneid* 7 have epigrammatic characteristics, they are particularly well suited for Marsus' allusion. Marsus' reference to Vergil's description of Caieta's death is also fitting since Caieta is the figure whose story bridges the close of Book 6 (900–1) and opening of Book 7, putting her single appearance in the *Aeneid* directly after Aeneas' exit from the underworld and the Elysian Fields, the very place where Marsus' epigram places Vergil and Tibullus.[12]

Along with the allusions to Vergil in the epigram, Marsus' phrase *campos ... Elysios* in the second verse recalls the appearance of those same words in Tibullus 1.3, the elegist's most extensive meditation on the afterlife: *ipsa Venus campos ducet in Elysios* ("Venus herself will escort [me] into the Elysian Fields," 58). *Campos ... Elysios* appears in the same metrical *sedes* in both poems, with Marsus' *Mors ... misit* answering Tibullus' *Venus ... ducet* as well as recalling the Tibullan poet-lover's fear in 1.3 that *Mors* will come for him (1.3.4–5, 55–6, 65). Marsus even preserves Tibullus' polysyllabic line ending *Elysios*, although by the time of Tibullus' death such endings had become unfashionable (Hollis 2007: 311). Marsus' reference to Tibullus as a *iuuenis* (2) likewise has an echo in 1.3.63, where Tibullus describes Elysian Fields populated by *iuuenum series*. Thus, in this epigram about the deaths of Tibullus and Vergil, Marsus intertwines allusions to the epic and elegiac genres and to the representations of death and the afterlife in the works of each poet. In addition, Marsus' epigram signals something that I will explore further: namely, that Vergil and Tibullus were linked not only through the chronological proximity of their deaths, but also through their representations of the afterlife, particularly the afterlife of lovers and poets.[13]

II. Vergil's *Lugentes Campi*

The *lugentes campi* (*Aen.* 6.440–76) are the famous penultimate region in the section of the *Aeneid*'s underworld inhabited by various types of untimely dead (the ἄωροι and βιαιοθάνατοι).[14] Vergil presents these "mourning fields as the place for the souls of those destroyed by *durus amor*. They also are the setting for the final interaction in the *Aeneid* between Aeneas and Dido. In this and subsequent sections of the paper, I build on an observation that goes back at least to Eduard Norden (1957: 247–54): that alongside the epic, especially Odyssean, allusions in this passage there are features that point to other genres, including Hellenistic and Roman amatory poetry. Norden sees the disparate generic elements in the *lugentes campi* passage as Vergil combining epic with the "psychological refinement of Hellenistic poetry to create a passage with the effect and intensity of tragedy (1957: 247). More recently, Andrew Feldherr has emphasized the polyphony of sense and meaning signalled by the simultaneous presence of features from epic and amatory poetry in this section of Book 6 (1999: esp. 104–5). I quote the *lugentes campi* passage at length, omitting Aeneas' address to Dido save for one verse (440–55, 460, 472–6):

nec procul hinc partem fusi monstrantur in omnem
lugentes campi; sic illos nomine dicunt.
hic quos durus amor crudeli tabe peredit
secreti celant calles et myrtea circum
silua tegit; curae non ipsa in morte relinquunt.
his Phaedram Procrinque locis maestamque Eriphylen
crudelis nati monstrantem uulnera cernit,
Euadnenque et Pasiphaen; his Laodamia
it comes et iuuenis quondam, nunc femina, Caenus
rursus et in ueterem fato reuoluta figuram
inter quas Phoenissa recens a uulnere Dido
errabat silua in magna; quam Troius heros
ut primum iuxta stetit agnouitque per umbras
obscuram, qualem primo qui surgere mense
aut uidet aut uidisse putat per nubila lunam,
demisit lacrimas dulcique adfatus amore est ...

inuitus, regina, tuo de litore cessi ...

tandem corripuit sese atque inimica refugit
in nemus umbriferum, coniunx ubi pristinus illi
respondet curis aequatque Sychaeus amorem.

nec minus Aeneas casu percussus iniquo
prosequitur lacrimis longe et miseratur euntem.

Not far from here, spreading out in all directions, are shown the mourning fields they call them by that name. Here are those whom hard love consumed with cruel wasting. Hidden paths conceal them and a myrtle forest offers cover; even in death love's cares do not depart. In these fields Aeneas sees Phaedra, Procris, and sad Eriphyle displaying the wounds from her cruel son, and Evadne, and Pasiphae. Along with these women Laodamia goes as companion, and Caeneus, once a boy and now a woman and then turned again into her former form by fate. Among these women Phoenician Dido, freshly wounded, was roaming in the great wood. As soon as the Trojan hero was near and recognized her dim outline through the shadows – like one who sees or thinks he sees the moon rise amid the clouds at the beginning of the month – he shed tears and spoke to her with sweet love … [Aeneas said:] "… unwillingly, Queen, did I depart your shores …" At last Dido pulled herself away and filled with hate she fled back into the shady grove where her fi st husband Sychaeus greeted her with his affections and matched her love. Aeneas was no less stricken by cruel fate, trailing her with his tears and pitying her as she departed.

The amatory and elegiac elements in the *lugentes campi* include (1) the description of love as a wasting disease (*durus amor crudeli tabe peredit*, 442), a concept familiar from amatory poetry;[15] (2) the unrelenting amatory *curae* (444, 474);[16] (3) myrtle, whose association with Venus as well as funerals makes it particularly appropriate for dead lovers (443); (4) Dido wandering (*errabat*) in a manner evocative of a distracted *amator* (450–1);[17] and (5) Aeneas addressing Dido with *dulcis amor* (455), in a speech that at 460 alludes to the words of the *coma Berenices* in Catullus 66.39 (*inuita, o regina, tuo de uertice cessi*). The latter allusion imbues Aeneas' explanation of what caused him to leave Carthage with a Catullan elegiac aspect – as well as a Callimachean one (fr. 110 Pf.).[18] These amatory and elegiac elements are, in addition, foreshadowed by Vergil's description of the nearby Styx as *inamabilis* in 438–9, directly before the *lugentes campi* passage. Although there are various proposed explanations for this epithet, *inamabilis* on one level anticipates the unhappy lovers to follow.[19]

Feldherr sees another reflection of the *campi*'s elegiac aspect in Vergil's presentation of their topography. He notes that the description of the landscape emphasizes what is difficult to see or entirely indiscernible, and that the region "frustrates and contradicts efforts to produce an objective description of it within the context of Aeneas' epic itinerary."[20] The fields have no clear shape or boundary. Instead they spread out in every direction (440). Nor is it only their boundaries that are difficult to discern. When Aeneas stands near Dido, he still must strain to see her through the shadows (452–3). She is described as *obscura* and, in a famous simile, like a new moon covered by clouds (453–4), a state of obscurity that echoes the *campi* themselves.[21] In addition to their undefined boundaries, the heart of the *campi* is presented as filled with secret paths and shrouded by myrtle trees (443–4), topographical elements that emphasize once again the obscuring nature of the field , and, I note, even seem to complicate the label *campi*, a word typically associated with open expanses.[22]

Similar to the topographical description of the *lugentes campi*, the diverse list of figures who inhabit the field (445–51) evoke amatory themes, but complicate rather than clarify the interpretation of the passage. The catalogue recalls the Homeric precedent of the heroines that Odysseus sees in his *nekyia* (*Od.* 11.225–339), as well as other catalogues of women and of victims of love in Hades.[23] The list of inhabitants, however, also comprises a diverse group that, as many scholars note, resists the very categorization offered at 6.442–4 that they were victims of love.[24] For instance, Eriphyle's display of the fatal wounds that she received from her "cruel" son at 6.445–6 indicates that "cruel wasting" and "hard love" were not responsible for her death.[25] Rather than attempting a new answer about the catalogue of inhabitants of the *lugentes campi*, I shall turn to a broader question: why are all these amatory and elegiac features present in the *lugentes campi*? Conversely, why does Vergil link only dead lovers with the *lugentes campi* when the name's mourning implications seemingly could also apply to the souls in adjacent parts of the "untimely dead" section of the underworld, who are also depicted as mourning (e.g., *animae flentes*, 427; *tenent maesti*, 434).

One answer is that Vergil may offer a further reference to elegy by attaching the phrase *sic illos nomine dicunt* to the title *lugentes campi* (441). Norden takes *nomine dicunt* as implying that the passage is indebted to an earlier text, hypothesizing that it was likely a lost Hellenistic source (1957: 249). James O'Hara suggests that the phrase *nomine dicunt*, like other "naming" words in Vergil, is a signpost for etymological word play. As O'Hara notes, Servius is also interested in the etymology of *lugentes campi*, glossing the phrase as *lucis egentes* ("lacking light," *ad Aen.* 6.441), an etymology for *lugentes* that is also offered by Isidorus (*Diff.* 1.227).[26] O'Hara suggests another possibility: that the "mourning" of the *lugentes campi* specifically points to elegy by playing on its putative derivation from the lament *e e legein* ("to say woe woe") or *eleos* ("pity").[27] If so, the *lugentes campi* are not just the "Mourning Fields," but perhaps the "Elegiac Fields" as well.

Why might Vergil embed a wordplay on elegy in the phrase *lugentes campi*? The period during which Vergil composed the *Aeneid* coincided with much of the poetic output of Tibullus as well as Propertius. Vergil's interest in Roman elegists' representations of *amor*, moreover, extends back to Gallus, as the *Eclogues* testify. If through etymological worldplay Vergil references elegy, it imbues the entire *lugentes campi* passage with a deeper elegiac significance and encourages readers to consider these dead lovers alongside the dead lovers and love poets of Latin love elegy. Yet Vergil is not simply recreating an elegiac underworld here, as the diverse catalogue of inhabitants of the *lugentes campi* demonstrates. For, while Propertius (1.19, 2.28) and Tibullus (1.3) describe underworlds that include groups of women, the women in these elegiac underworlds are not the same as those in the *lugentes campi*. Indeed, the women in the *lugentes campi* are not significant figures in Latin love elegy. This discrepancy, however, may be Vergil's point: the picture of *amor* in the *lugentes campi* recalls elegy and other amatory poetry, but it is definitively not the presentation of love and the afterlife of lovers that the elegiac poet-lovers imagine for themselves. This contrast comes to the fore through comparison with Tibullus 1.3, to which I now turn.

III. The Afterlife of Lovers in Tibullus 1.3

In Tibullus 1.3 the poet-lover attempts to accompany Messalla on a journey, only to fall ill. Too sick to continue travelling, he is left behind on Corcyra, called Phaeacia in the third verse, a place name that begins a series of references to the *Odyssey* and Odyssean themes throughout the poem.[28] Due to his illness, the poet-lover fears that his death may be near. Should death come, he imagines that in the afterlife he will gain entrance to Elysium. Given the Odyssean allusions in 1.3, Tibullus' description of the underworld recalls on one level Odysseus' *nekyia* and Homeric traditions about the afterlife. Yet, the Elysium Tibullus depicts differs from the traditional picture of a paradise populated by heroes.[29] Instead, Tibullus combines conventional elements with amatory and elegiac themes to create Elysian Fields tailored to rustic lovers and love poets (57–66):

sed me, quod facilis tenero sum semper Amori,
   ipsa Venus campos ducet in Elysios.
hic choreae cantusque uigent, passimque uagantes
   dulce sonant tenui gutture carmen aues;
fert casiam non culta seges, totosque per agros
   floret odoratis terra benigna rosis
ac iuuenum series teneris inmixta puellis
   ludit, et adsidue proelia miscet Amor.

illic est, cuicumque rapax mors uenit amanti,
et gerit insigni myrtea serta coma.

But me, for I am always open to tender Love, Venus herself will escort to the Elysian Fields. There dances and songs thrive. Birds flit about chirping sweet song from slender throats. Unworked the ground bears cassia, and through all the fields the pleasant earth blooms with fragrant roses. Troops of young men, mixed with tender girls, play, and Love constantly entangles them in battles. In that place is every lover snatched away by death, and a myrtle garland crowns their hair for all to see.

Tibullus' description of Elysium begins and ends with claims that it is for lovers, both the poet-lover in particular (*quod facilis tenero sum semper Amori*, 57) and lovers in general (*cuicumque … amanti*, 65). Venus, adopting Mercury's role as *psychopompos*, will lead the soul of the poet-lover to an Elysium featuring choruses, song, and birds singing amid fields that spontaneously produce a Golden Age-like bounty.[30] Young men "play" (*ludit*, 64) with *tenerae puellae*, evoking the sexual valence of *ludere* in other elegy and amatory poetry (e.g., Cat. 17.17 and 61.204, Prop. 1.10.9). *Amor* mingles the Elysian youth in "battles" (64), transferring *militia amoris* to Elysium (Houghton 2007: 156). Furthermore, the agricultural imagery of 61–2 combines a rustic setting with amatory activities in a manner that mirrors the rural agricultural fantasy central to Tibullan elegy.

At verse 60, birds sing *tenui gutture carmen*. The phrase evokes the Alexandrian aesthetic of "slender song" prized by elegists (cf. Prop. 3.1.8, Ov. *Trist.* 2.327), signalling that this is not just a lovers' Elysium, but a programmatically elegiac one (Houghton 2007: 156–7). The Tibullan poet-lover's opening explanation of why he will gain entrance to Elysium (*quod facilis tenero sum semper Amori*, 57) may also be a programmatic reference to his status as an elegiac poet as well as an *amator*. After all, *amor*, like the plural *amores*, may represent love elegy, especially when personified (Harrison 2007: 65). Moreover, David Wray demonstrates that in love elegy, and especially in Tibullus, *facilis* has a poetological connotation as well as an erotic one. Wray exposes the poetological connotation by demonstrating that *facilis* through its etymological association with *facere* can function as a calque on *poiētikos*, a word linked to poetic production by virtue of its connection with *poiein*. Wray uses this point to interpret Tibullus' description of his poet-lover as a *rusticus* tending plants with a *facilis manus* in 1.1.7–8 as a metaphor for Tibullus' poetic production (2003: 232–3). Later in 1.1 Tibullus uses a form of *facere* + *manus* again, this time in a manner that resonates with poem 1.3, when the poet-lover imagines his death (*te teneam moriens deficiente manu*, 60). Michael Putnam, building on Wray, notes that in this phrase the death of the elegiac lover is associated with hands that are no longer capable of making poetry (2005: 127–9). In this context Tibullus' phrase in 1.3.57, *facilis tenero sum semper Amori*, may be seen as encoding a reference to the poetological valence of *facilis*, with the wording indicating that the Tibullan poet-lover will gain entrance to Elysium not just because he is "open to tender love," but also because he is a "producer of love elegy."[31]

The elegiac emphasis of Tibullus 1.3's underworld continues in the depiction of Tartarus in verses 67–82. Tibullus' Tartarus, like his Elysium, includes traditional elements, but emphasizes amatory themes, in this case violations of love.[32] Tibullus' description of Tartarus culminates with *illic sit quicumque meos uiolauit amores, | optauit lentas et mihi militias* ("Let him be in that place, whoever violated my loves, whoever wished that my campaigns be long," 81–2). This use of *quicumque* recalls the earlier use of the word in the same metrical *sedes* surrounded by similar diction to refer to dead lovers who gain entrance to Elysium (*illic est, cuicumque rapax mors uenit amanti*, 65). These parallels further signal the thematic continuity in 1.3's elegiac underworld. In short, Tibullus 1.3 reconfigures underworld traditions around the principle of rewarding lovers and love poets, while punishing amatory transgressors.

IV. Tibullus' Elysium and Vergil's *lugentes campi*

Tibullus' elegiac Elysium and Vergil's *lugentes campi* are often mentioned together as both engaging with similar traditions about the underworld.[33] This section, however, will argue that, while the two poets engage with a broader tradition, the links between the two poems are more direct than previously appreciated. In my view *Aeneid* 6 offers a rebuttal of Tibullus' elegiac vision of an amatory death and afterlife. Vergil's rebuttal, moreover, affects subsequent representations of the afterlife in Latin love elegy.

Just prior to the description of an elegiac Elysium, the Tibullan poet-lover imagines an epitaph for himself that attributes his death to his attempt to accompany Messalla abroad (55–6):

> HIC IACET INMITI CONSUMPTUS MORTE TIBULLUS,
> MESSALLAM TERRA DUM SEQUITURQUE MARI.

Here lies Tibullus, consumed by savage death while following Messalla on land and sea.

Tibullus' phrase *terra … sequiturque mari* does not simply describe where the poet-lover travelled. Rather it is a variant of *terra marique*, a marked phrase linked to imperial conquest and worldwide empire.[34] Its appearance here recalls Tibullus' fi st mention of Messalla in 1.1, where the same phrase describes the latter as an imperial conqueror, everything the poet-lover is not (53, 55): *te bellare decet terra, Messalla, marique | ... me retinent uinctum formosae uincla puellae* ("It's right that you, Messalla, campaign on land and sea ... the chains of a beautiful girl hold me captive"). By using *terra marique* again in 1.3, the Tibullan poet-lover claims as his cause of death the attempt to participate in Messalla's realm of imperial activity. His assertion of "death by imperial activity," with salvation in the afterlife thanks to love, stands in contrast to Vergil's *lugentes campi*, where lovers killed by love's cruel wasting spend a mournful afterlife. In both poems, moreover, it is the imperial agents, Messalla and Aeneas, who survive and continue on their journeys. Dido is in the *lugentes campi* because Aeneas, in order to fulfil his role in Rome's fated *imperium*, left her lovesick, sailing from Carthage in a manner not unlike how Messalla on his imperial mission left behind the ill poet-lover in Tibullus 1.3. Furthermore, Aeneas' travels on the way to Latium are described at the opening of the *Aeneid* with phrasing that contains an echo of *terra marique* within an allusion to the Homeric adventures of Odysseus: *multum ille et terris iactatus et alto* ("That man much tossed on land and sea," *Aen.* 1.3). Thus a parallel emerges between the oppositional pairs of Tibullus-Messalla and Dido-Aeneas.[35]

If *terra marique* is the cause, *inmitis Mors* is the agent of death in Tibullus' imagined epitaph, a role that Vergil gives to *durus amor.* Yet this difference between the two texts again signals engagement between Vergil and Tibullus, since the latter's *Mors* and former's *amor* are both described with modifie s that deny their softness (*inmitis, durus*). In addition, Vergil's wasting imagery (*durus amor crudeli tabe peredit,* 6.442) parallels Tibullus' (*consumptus Morte*) in that the semantic ranges of both *consumo* and *peredo* encompass wasting, consuming, and eating.[36]

Another point of contact between the two poems relates to the presence of myrtle. The final element of Tibullus' Elysium is that dead lovers wear myrtle garlands upon their heads as a "conspicuous" marker of their status as lovers (*insignis,* 1.3.66).[37] In Vergil's *lugentes campi* myrtle has the opposite function, obscuring dead lovers as they continue to suffer from amatory *curae* (443–4) rather than marking them as rewarded for living their lives as *amatores.* Commentators on both passages note that myrtle's amatory as well as funerary associations are evoked by its presence each text.[38] Yet Vergil's *myrtea circum | silua tegit* (6.443–4) also pointedly reverses the role of myrtle in Tibullus' phrase *gerit insigni myrtea serta coma* (1.3.66).

The most programmatic contrast between the two texts, however, relates to love. Tibullus' *Amor,* the saviour that will win him entrance into Elysium, is *tener*. Vergil's description of *amor* as *durus* not only fits the mournful context of the *lugentes campi*, but also creates an intertextual and intergeneric polarity with Tibullus' *tener*. The contrast between *durus* and *tener* is similar to elegy's oppositional pairing of *durus* and *mollis*, the latter a polarity with well-established generic and gendered dimensions: epic versus elegy; masculine versus feminine and effeminate.[39] When *tener* is directly juxtaposed with *durus*, the former often describes what makes something desirable, while *durus* indicates what is cruel and unattainable. Ovid's Narcissus, who in the *Metamorphoses* embodies both qualities, provides an apt example: his *tener* beauty attracts many admirers; *durus* pride causes him to reject them all (3.353–5). Nor can Narcissus be read outside of the tension between *tener* and *durus* in Tibullus' and Vergil's representations of the afterlives of lovers: in the *Metamorphoses* Narcissus also becomes a dead lover eventually, spending his afterlife staring at his own reflection in the Styx (3.504–5), a river that, in addition to being the most famous body of water in the underworld, is also the one that Vergil mentions – and to which he gives the epithet *inamabilis* – directly before the *lugentes campi* (see above).[40]

To illustrate the polarity between *durus amor* and *tener amor* that Vergil engages in the *lugentes campi*, I will review several instances where *durus* and *tener* are opposed elsewhere in Latin poetry. Then I will look specifically at other occurrences of the phrases *durus amor* and *tener amor.* Although the instances of *tener* and *durus* discussed include examples that post-date Tibullus 1.3 and *Aeneid* 6, I posit that the *tener-durus* polarity was established by the time of Tibullus Book 1, and likely preceded it given the apparent association between Gallus and *durus*.[41]

Tibullus, who uses *tener* at a more frequent rate than the other Augustan elegists, prominently displays his interest in the *durus-tener* opposition.[42] For instance, in 1.1 Delia is associated with *duritas* when the excluded poet-lover sits before her "hard doors" (*duras ... fores*, 56). Yet a few verses later the poet-lover discloses that he is certain that Delia will reveal herself ultimately to be *tenera*. In a death fantasy akin to 1.3, he imagines that Delia will cry at his death because there is not *durus* iron around her breast nor flint in her *tener* heart (63–4): *flebis: non tua sunt duro praecordia ferro | uincta, neque in tenero stat tibi corde silex* ("You will weep: your breast is not encased in hard iron, nor does flint stand in your tender heart"). The generic valence of the *durus-tener* opposition is at play here, since Tibullus' description of Delia's iron-free *praecordia* and *tener* heart suitable for elegiac poetry recalls the metallic hearts that epic poets from Homer onwards claim would be needed to recite difficul topics.[43] Vergil may allude to this fi st Tibullan death fantasy in *Aeneid*

6's *lugentes campi* passage. When he presents Dido standing like hard flint (*quam si dura silex ... stet*, 6.471), it recalls the Tibullan poet-lover's assertion that flint does not stand in Delia's heart (*neque in tenero stat tibi corde silex*). If Vergil recalls Tibullus 1.1.63–4 in the description of Dido at 6.471, it is all the more reasonable to posit that he was aware of Tibullus' oppositional use of *tener* and *durus.*

Vergil already addresses elegy's *tener-durus* opposition in *Eclogue* 10.47–9. In verses that are closely linked to Gallus' elegies (Serv. *ad Ecl.* 10.46; cf. Prop. 1.8.6–7), Lycoris is called *dura* for accompanying another man to the Rhine frontier, but Vergil's Gallus worries that she may hurt her *tener* feet in the frozen landscape, a metapoetic phrase that reflects how *tener* is linked generically and metrically to elegy. As these examples illustrate, elegy and other poetry with amatory themes associate *durus* with epic and with whatever makes love unhappy, while *tener* is linked to elegy and whatever is desirable. As I shall explore next, when these adjectives are combined with *amor* in Latin poetry, they signal even more intensely different visions of love. In my view Vergil's phrase *durus amor* responds to Tibullus' *tener amor* and exemplifies the difference between the latter's elegiac Elysian Fields and the former's epic *lugentes campi.*

First, I shall contextualize the term *durus amor* within Vergil's own poetry and within elegy. In the *lugentes campi* passage, *durus amor* offers an intratextual contrast to the description of Aeneas addressing Dido with *dulcis amor* at 455 and with Sychaeus equalling Dido's love at 474 (*aequat ... amorem*). It also presents a contrast with the love for Rome's future glory that Anchises incites in Aeneas during the Parade of Heroes (*incenditque animum famae uenientis amore,* 6.889).[44] The different presentations of *amor* within Book 6 epitomize the ambivalent representations of love in the *Aeneid* as a whole.[45] The phrase *durus amor* at *Aeneid* 6.442 is also a reference to Vergil's earlier use of the same phrase at *Georgics* 3.258 in a passage depicting the power of love over animals and humans alike. Here *durus amor* describes the lethal love that drove Leander to swim the Hellespont, ultimately leading to his death as well as Hero's. In his discussion of this passage, Mynors finds comparisons to Vergil's phrase in Apollonius' rebuke of σχέτλιος Ἔρως, the fatal "merciless Desire" that drives Medea to kill her brother (*Argon.* 4.445), and in the phrase δεινὸς Ἔρως ("dreadful Desire") in, e.g., Meleager (Gow-Page *HE* 4022).[46]

Aside from these occurrences in Vergil, *durus amor* is a rare phrase in Latin poetry. In love elegy, although obstacles to love, such as an unwilling *puella* and locked doors, are often *durae,* love itself is described with this adjective only twice: Propertius 1.3.14 and 2.34.49. In neither instance does *durus* carry the "deadly" connotation that it possesses in Vergil. The fi st time that *Amor* is described as *durus* in elegy – indeed in all of Latin literature – is in Propertius 1.3 when the inebriated poet-lover is at the bedside of the sleeping Cynthia (13–16):

> et quamuis duplici correptum ardore iuberent
> hac Amor hac Liber, durus uterque deus
> subiecto leuiter positam temptare lacerto
> osculaque admota sumere arma manu,

And though I was seized with a twofold passion, for on this side Love, on that Bacchus – each a hard god – were urging me to slide my arm gently beneath and to make an attack as she lay and to take kisses with my hand placed on my weapons.

These verses present *Amor*, together with Bacchus, as *durus*. Yet Propertius' *Amor ... durus* differs from Vergil's uses of the term. Here *durus* appears as part of a description of the poet-lover's sexual excitement (*ardore*), where he is tempted to force himself on Cynthia in her sleep (*positam temptare*) and to take in hand what he euphemistically calls his *arma*. Given this context, Leo Curran proposes that *durus* in Propertius 1.3 signals the poet-lover's sexual arousal.[47] The presentation of Love and Bacchus as *duri*, moreover, plays on the trope of Love becoming more powerful when he combines forces with other gods, especially the god of wine.[48]

Propertius again uses the phrase *durus amor* in 2.34, an elegy famously linked to Vergil through its allusions to the latter's poetry. In this poem *duri amores* are connected to the elegy's addressee Lynceus, whom the Propertian poet-lover counsels about changing from writing philosophical epic to elegy. At 49–50 he warns: *nec tu iam duros per te patieris amores: | trux tamen a nobis ante domandus eris* ("Nor will you endure hard loves by yourself: though you are wild, you must fi st be tamed by me"). Propertius' presentation of *amores* as *duri* here, however, hinges on the description of Lynceus as an epic *durus poeta* a few verses earlier (44), a quality that is perhaps also echoed when Lynceus is called *trux* in verse 50. Within this context, what makes love *durus* is Lynceus' resistance to love and his association with *durus* epic. Stephen Heyworth explains that in this couplet "The taming will consist in replacing the hard subject-matter of natural philosophy, which comes naturally to Lynceus, with the *mollitia* of the life of love: the paradox is signalled by the epithet *duros* in 49" (2007: 273). Thus, reflecting upon Lynceus' troubled transformation into an elegiac lover and love poet, Propertius deploys the image of love as *durus* precisely because it does not fit the elegiac presentation of *amor*, but rather *durus* Lynceus' connections to epic.

While in elegy *amor* and *durus* are only linked in the two exceptional instances above, when the term *tener amor* occurs it is often programmatic. The phrase appears fi st in Tibullus. It is also found in Ovid, but never in Propertius. The phrase frequently refers to elegiac poetry, contrasting the amatory life with the military one, and distinguishing elegy from other poetic genres, especially epic. Ovid uses the phrase several times in poems connected with Tibullus, suggesting that for the younger elegist the term may have had a Tibullan ring. The following survey traces the phrase *tener amor* through Ovid *Tristia* 2, *Tristia* 3.3, *Tristia* 4.10, *Amores* 2.18, and *Ars Amatoria* 1 before turning back to Tibullus.

At *Tristia* 2.361–2, prior to embarking on a review of the literary canon that emphasizes the pervasiveness of amatory themes, Ovid laments that, while he is not the only one to have composed *teneri amores,* he is the only one to have been punished for it. Though in *Tristia* 2, *tener amor* includes elegy as well as amatory themes in poetry more generally, elsewhere in the *Tristia* Ovid uses *teneri amores* specifically to refer to his elegiac output, twice defining himself as an elegist by using the term *tenerorum lusor amorum*. The fi st instance is on his imagined epitaph in *Tristia* 3.3.73–4:

HIC EGO QUI IACEO TENERORUM LUSOR AMORUM
INGENIO PERII NASO POETA MEO.

Here I lie, the player of tender loves, who died because of my own talent, the poet Naso.

In these lines Ovid closely links *tenerorum lusor amorum* with his status as a poet, signalling that the phrase is a metaphor for love elegy. Ovid repeats the phrase in the opening verse of *Tristia* 4.10 (*ille ego qui fuerim, tenerorum lusor amorum*), his elegiac autobiography, a poem that is in a sense an expanded version of the epitaph in 3.3. In addition, Ovid may well have Tibullus' use of *tener amor* in 1.3 in mind when he uses this phrase, since he models *Tristia* 3.3 after Tibullus 1.3 and his imagined epitaph recalls Tibullus' in 1.3.55–6. Although the content of each epitaph is different – Tibullus' lacks any explicit reference to his status as a poet, while Ovid focuses only on poetry – Ovid's use of *tener amor* engages with Tibullus' phrasing in the verse immediately following his epitaph that has been central to this paper (1.3.57): *facilis tenero sum semper Amori.*[49] In addition, Ovid's allusion to 1.3.57 in his description of himself as an elegist lends further support to the argument advanced above that Tibullus' phrasing encodes a reference to poetic output.

Ovid also uses the phrase *tener amor* two times in an earlier autobiographic elegy, *Amores* 2.18. At the opening of the poem the term distinguishes Ovid's elegiac poet-lover from the epicist Macer (1–4):

> Carmen ad iratum dum tu perducis Achillen
> primaque iuratis induis arma uiris,
> nos, Macer, ignaua Veneris cessamus in umbra,
> et tener ausuros grandia frangit Amor.

While you are prolonging your poem to include Achilles' wrath and clothing the conspiring heroes in the fi st arms of war, Macer, I tarry in the idle shadow of Venus, and tender Love is dashing the grand ventures that I would attempt.

Poem 2.18 opens in a manner reminiscent of the beginning of Propertius 1.7 and of Cupid's metrical intervention in *Amores* 1.1 by contrasting Macer composing his Trojan War epic with the Ovidian poet-lover yielding to Venus and having his own epic (*grandia*) ambitions dashed by *tener Amor*. In the succeeding lines his *puella* aligns with the amatory gods to change his poetry from *arma* to *militia amoris* (5–12). After complaining that Love and his *puella* drew him away from writing tragedy too (13–18), he uses the phrase *tener Amor* a second time in a couplet that presents him as an elegiac poet-lover (19–20): *artes teneri profitemur Amoris* – | *ei mihi, praeceptis urgeor ipse meis!* ("I profess the arts of tender Love – But alas! I am subjugated by my own teachings"). Uncertainties surrounding the chronology of Ovid's amatory works and the second edition of the *Amores* leave it unclear whether Ovid refers to the *Amores* or the *Ars Amatoria* in 2.18.19–20.[50] Whichever work Ovid refers to here, he also employs the phrase *tener amor* programmatically in the opening of the *Ars* to describe love elegy (1.7): *me Venus artificem tenero praefecit Amori* ("Venus appointed me as a craftsman for tender Love"). This verse presents the *Ars*' narrator as a *praeceptor amoris*, while also pointing to his role as a "craftsman" of elegiac poetry. In this verse Ovid in addition uses derivatives of *facere* – *artificem* and *praefecit* – like Tibullus does at 1.3.57.

There is another vexed issue in *Amores* 2.18, one with an additional possible link to Tibullus: namely, who is the Macer addressed in the opening?[51] I will not attempt a new solution to that problem, except to note, given the Tibullan connection in Ovid's use of *tener amor* elsewhere, that it is all the more plausible that Ovid's Macer is the same as the one addressed by Tibullus in elegy 2.6. This final poem of Tibullus' second book is the only instance other than 1.3 where Tibullus uses the phrase *tener amor*. It occurs in the opening verse: *castra Macer sequitur: tenero quid fiet Amori?*

("Macer marches for camp. What will become of tender Love?"). The propemptic qualities of 2.6.1, which present Macer as a departing addressee, recall the address to Messalla at the opening of 1.3.[52] Furthermore, *tenero … Amori* appears in the same form and metrical *sedes* as at 1.3.57. Both instances also contain derivatives of *facere*: *fiet* in 2.6 and *facilis* in 1.3. One interpretation of 2.6.1, as well as the following lines where Tibullus considers going to camp too (*castra peto*, 9) only to have his own foot bring him back (*pes … ipse redit*, 14), is to read it as a referring to genre: Macer is turning from love poetry to epic by heading for camp and leaving *tener Amor*;[53] Tibullus' desire to follow Macer suggests epic pretensions, but his *pes*, in both a metrical and corporeal sense, will not allow it (Keith 1999: 51). Thus, in Tibullus 2.6 *tener Amor* again refers to elegiac love and perhaps to elegiac poetry.

Taken together these examples show *tener amor* as a marker of (particularly Tibullan) elegiac love and of elegy itself, similar to *molles amores* in the description of Tibullus' poetry in Marsus' epigram discussed at the beginning of the paper. It is, therefore, fitting that in 1.3 Tibullus imagines that his openness to *tener amor* will gain him entrance to an afterlife in Elysian Fields where the traditions associated with Elysium have been transformed into a space uniquely appropriate for lovers and love poets. Yet Tibullus' Elysian fantasy elides the disappointments and disasters of love that precede 1.3 and which are to follow in his subsequent elegies. Vergil's *lugentes campi* offer a corrective: elegy as lament, love as *durus*, as leading to death and to an afterlife in fields that are not Elysian. Further, love's cares endure in the *lugentes campi*, while in Tibullus' amatory afterlife *iuuenes* and *puellae* mix (63–4), but beloveds from their previous lives, including Delia, go unmentioned. As for the poetic and choral aspects of the Elysium tradition in Tibullus 1.3, choruses and poets appear in Vergil's Elysian fields as well, but not among the dead lovers.

V. *Amores* 3.9: Dead Lovers and Love Poets after *Aeneid* 6

Vergil's *lugentes campi* do not just rebut Tibullus 1.3. They also change elegy's subsequent discourse about the afterlife of lovers and love poets. By way of example, I shall consider briefly *Amores* 3.9, Ovid's *epicedion* for Tibullus. *Amores* 3.9 is a well-established site for the reception of Tibullus' poetry, especially 1.3.[54] Allusions to Tibullus 1.3 include Delia's worship of Isis (3.9.33–4; cf. Tib. 1.3.23–6), references to death on Phaeacia (3.9.47–8; cf. Tib. 1.3.3–4), and the mourning of Tibullus by his sister, mother, and Delia (3.9.49–54; cf. Tib. 1.3.5–9). In my reading, *Amores* 3.9 also responds to depictions of the afterlife in *Aeneid* 6. A link to the *Aeneid* is established in *Amores* 3.9.7–15, when Ovid describes Venus and Love's distress at Tibullus' funeral as equal to their sadness at the death of Aeneas, a death that, although not depicted in the *Aeneid,* is established early in the epic during Jupiter's prophecy (1.259–66). In addition, at 3.9.14 Ovid describes Iulus with the epithet *pulcher,* a descriptor for Iulus that appears elsewhere only in the *Aeneid* and related texts.[55] Yet most salient for the present paper are Ovid's hints at engagement with the Elysium of *Aeneid* 6, to which I now turn.

In the final verses of *Amores* 3.9 Ovid depicts Tibullus' afterlife. What he describes for Tibullus is fundamentally different than what Tibullus imagines for his poet-lover in 1.3 (*Am.* 3.9.59–66):

Si tamen e nobis aliquid nisi nomen et umbra
restat, in Elysia ualle Tibullus erit.
obuius huic uenias hedera iuuenalia cinctus
tempora cum Caluo, docte Catulle, tuo;
tu quoque, si falsum est temerati crimen amici,
sanguinis atque animae prodige Galle tuae.
his comes umbra tua est; siqua est modo corporis umbra,
auxisti numeros, culte Tibulle, pios.

If, however, anything survives of us aside from name and shade, Tibullus will be in the Elysian valley. May you come to meet him along with Calvus, learned Catullus, your young temples crowned with ivy; and you too, if the charge that you dishonoured a friend is false, Gallus, wasteful of your blood and soul. To these poets your shade is a companion; if indeed there is any shade that survives the body, you have increased the number of the blessed, refined Tibullus.

The Elysium that Ovid presents here is not the amatory paradise of Tibullus 1.3. Nor is it the *lugentes campi* of *Aeneid* 6. Ovid places Tibullus in Elysium, but it is an Elysium whose only named inhabitants are poets. In addition, in 3.9 Ovid three times describes Tibullus as a *uates,* twice with the modifie *sacer.*[56] Ovid employs *uates* five times in 3.9 overall, more often than in any of his other love elegies. In verse 66, Tibullus increases the ranks of the *pius* when he joins Catullus, Calvus, and Gallus in an Elysium that is populated by composers of erotic verse, but lacks the erotic characteristics of Tibullus 1.3. This image of the afterlife, along with Ovid's repeated use of *uates* and *sacer,* recalls the scene in *Aeneid* 6 when Aeneas and the Sibyl reach the Elysian Fields – the only *campi* in Book 6 aside from the *lugentes campi* – and meet a group of *sacerdotes casti* and *pii uates* headed by Musaeus (6.661–8). Moreover, Ovid's placement of Tibullus and the other love poets *in Elysia ualle* (60) recalls from *Aeneid* 6 the Elysian souls *in ualle reducta* (6.703) that feature in the Parade of Heroes. Vergil and Ovid each engage with larger traditions about dead poets and the underworld in these passages.[57] Yet Ovid indicates that the *Aeneid* is particularly significant for *Amores* 3.9 through the references to Aeneas, *pulcher* Iulus, Elysian valleys, and *uates*. *Vates* is especially marked because of the critical role Vergil played in resuscitating the term for Roman poetry.[58]

Thus, through allusion to *Aeneid* 6 Ovid creates a new elegiac Elysium for Tibullus that diverges from the one the poet-lover imagines for himself in 1.3. But Ovid's afterlife for lovers and love poets is decidedly not Vergil's *lugentes campi*. Instead Ovid offers a vision of Tibullus' death that draws from the latter's poetry, while depicting an afterlife that uses traditions about poets in the underworld that had recently been presented in Vergil. As I stated at the opening of the paper, *Aeneid* 6 functions as a lens for Ovid, a refraction point that contributes to the reshaping of the afterlife of love poets in *Amores* 3.9's commemoration of Tibullus.

VI. Conclusion

The poetic conversations between Tibullus 1.3, *Aeneid* 6, and *Amores* 3.9 are one piece of the engagement between Vergil and the elegists on the topic of the afterlife of lovers and love poets. I will only mention in passing here how some other elegiac representations of the underworld may fit into this exchange between love poetry and *Aeneid* 6. For instance, in Propertius 1.19 the underworld features a chorus of Trojan women (13–14) and *Amor* is *magnus*, with the ability to return from the underworld (12).[59] In Propertius 3.5.1 the modifier attached to *Amor* is neither *magnus*, *tener*, nor *durus*, but *deus pacis*. Propertius 3.5 presents the underworld in a manner that is drastically different from *Aeneid* 6: it is an undifferentiated place for conquerors and conquered, rich and poor alike (13–18). If we can trust the emendation to 3.5.18 – a vexed line – it appears that the poem professes that the best option is to live a peaceful life focused on amatory pursuits.[60] Therefore, in contrast to *Aeneid* 6, both Propertius 1.19 and 3.5 assert that the greatest type of spirit to be is a dead lover. While the Propertian poet-lover is more ambivalent about the spirits of dead lovers in 4.7 when the ghost of Cynthia appears to him, her report of separate places for good and evil lovers may have points of contact with Tibullus 1.3 as well as *Aeneid* 6. Finally – and most speculatively – if, as some have suggested, Vergil's depiction of Orpheus' *katabasis* in *Georgics* 4 is indebted to Gallus' own poetry, then it is another instance of engagement between Vergil and the elegists on the topic of the underworld.[61]

These interactions between Vergil and the elegists, as well as the ones discussed previously in this chapter, are all the more significant because elegy and epic repeatedly distinguish themselves from one another, and not just on the topic of the afterlife. Yet they do so in a manner that often reveals the extensive intertwining of the two genres. By engaging on the theme of the underworld, Vergil and the elegists push the connection between elegy and epic beyond the boundaries of death, while also anticipating the importance of *Aeneid* 6 to future representations of the afterlife of poets. This paper has in addition endeavoured to expose further some of the generic implications within *Aeneid* 6. Vergil situates elegy in the underworld, but he does so in a manner that indicates that elegy cannot continue to Elysium. Elegy is occluded from the higher generic sphere of epic, and yet Vergilian epic itself cannot continue without moving through the elegiac *lugentes campi.*

NOTES

1 I am grateful to Bill Gladhill, James O'Hara, and audiences at the 2013 Symposium Cumanum, the 2014 Classical Association of Canada Annual Meeting, and the 2016 Midwest Classical Literature Association for their comments, questions, and advice on earlier versions of this paper.

2 Tibullus Book 1 is typically dated to 26/5 BCE (e.g., Lyne 1998a: 520–3; cf. Knox 2005). Vergil's *epicedion* for Marcellus (6.860–86) dates at least elements of Book 6 to after Augustus' nephew's death in late 23 BCE (e.g., Horsfall 2013a: 1.xiv).

3 On Ovid's engagement with *Aeneid* 6 see also Keith in this volume.

4 All translations are my own.

5 For the date of Tibullus' death: McGann 1970; Maltby 2002: 39–40. Hollis 2007: 304–5 places Marsus' poetic output from the 30s to after 20 BCE, although firm dates are lacking.

6 Courtney 1993: 303; Hollis 2007: 311. For the convention of associating the death of a poet with the end of a genre in lament poetry see: [Mosch.] *Ep. Bion.* 11–12 (see Reed 1997: 268); Sextilius Ena fr. 1 Courtney; Cornelius Severus fr. 13.11 Courtney. Nor is Marsus a disinterested party when it comes to epic and love elegy, as he may have written in these two genres: Fogazza 1981: 17–25; Courtney 1993: 300; Cameron 1995: 312; Hollis 2007: 305.

7 On *mollis* and elegy see esp. Fedeli 1985: 69–70 and below. On elegy and lament see now O'Hara 2017: xxin3, xxiin4, and discussion below. For *flere* and elegy cf. Ov. *Am.* 3.9.3–4; *Tr.* 5.1.5; [Ov.] *Ep.* 15.7. Marsus may also recall Tibullus' use of *flere* in funerary contexts, especially the poet-lover's prediction that Delia

will cry (*flebis*) at his funeral at 1.61–3 (see discussion of this passage below); cf. 1.3.7–9; 2.4.46.

8 Hollis 2007: 311.

9 For the relationship between *Ecl.* 6.3–4 and *Aen.* 7.41–2, see esp. Thomas 1999 [1985].

10 As Bill Gladhill (*per litteras*) notes, Pales is an aptly rustic god for Marsus to connect with Tibullus, all the more so in light of the image in *Ecl.* 5.35 of Pales along with Apollo mourning the dead Daphnis.

11 On *Aen.* 7.1 and *G.* 3.1: Fraenkel 1945: 1n2, cited by Thomas 1999 [1985]: 110. The phrase "you also" appears several other poems in reference to death. Especially relevant is the use of *tu quoque* in reference to Icarus' death at *Aen.* 6.30. On this passage, see the introduction to the volume. Other instances include Cic. fr. 2 Courtney; Caes. fr. 1 Courtney; *AP* 7.263; Ov. *Am.* 3.9.63. Also perhaps important is Call. *Hec.* Fr. 253.3 Pf, although the context there is not death. See Mariotti 1963: 610; Merkelbach 1971; Courtney 1993: 304; Kyriakidis 1998: 79–82; Horsfall 2000: 46, 2013a: 2.24; Dinter 2011.

12 On the epigrammatic characteristics of the opening of *Aeneid* 7 see: Barchiesi 1979; Dinter 2005: 159–60. Bill Gladhill (*per litteras*) makes the interesting suggestion that by linking his epigram for Tibullus and Vergil to Vergil's for the *nutrix* Caieta, Marsus equates Tibullus and Vergil to "poetic *nutrices.*"

13 Cf. Horsfall 2013b, 2014, 2015 on poets in *Aeneid* 6's Elysium and on the possibility that Vergil implies that in the afterlife he will join the Elysian Poets' Corner.

14 For these terms, see esp. Norden 1957: 11–13; Horsfall 2013a: 2.320–22.

15 Norden 1957: 249–50 lists several parallels, in particular the use of τήκεσθαι to describe "wasting away" in amatory contexts in Theoc. 1.66 and 2.29 and *tabescere* in in Prop. 1.15.20. The following list of amatory and elegiac elements is based on Feldherr 1999: 96, 98, 104–13.

16 Prop. 1.15.29–31 offers an apt comparison for the *cura* as *amor* trope.

17 Cf. Milanion wandering in Prop. 1.1.11. On movement in *Aeneid* 6, see Herrero in this volume.

18 See Feldherr 1999: 107–11; Horsfall 2013a: 2.345 for references and discussion of the much-debated allusion to Catul. 66.

19 See also Keith in this volume on *inamabilis* in Vergil and Ovid.

20 Feldherr 1999: 87; see further 96–8, 101–2. I would add that the emphasis on topography in the description of the *lugentes campi* distinguishes the *campi* from the previous parts of the ἄωροι section of the underworld, which lack any topographical characterization, save for their being separated from the world above by the Styx (424–5, 438–9). The final area inhabited by the *bello clari,* is described simply as *arua … ultima* (477–8). In this volume see also Stok's

discussion of Serv. *ad* 6.596, which connects Vergil's description of the *lugentes campi* to Tityos' libido "open far and wide."

21 Feldherr 1999: 96–8, 101–2. On Vergil's moon simile and the allusion to Apollonius 4.1477–80, see esp. Tatum 1984: 438–40 with further references.

22 *OLD s.v.*; *TLL* 3.212–16.

23 For the Odyssean links in *Aen.* 6.445–9, see esp. Serv. *ad Aen.* 6.445; Knauer 1964: 112–14. For other influences in Vergil's catalogue of inhabitants of the *lugentes campi*, see esp. Robertson 1980: 287–8; Horsfall 2013a: 2.331, who concludes that Lucian *Cataplus* 5–6 provides definitive evidence of a pre Vergilian tradition for a distinct space in the underworld for victims of love.

24 On the catalogue of inhabitants, see esp. Perret 1964; Kraggerud 1965; West 1980a, 1980b; Tatum 1984; further bibliography at Horsfall 2013a: 2.332.

25 Garcia 2008 reviews various attempted explanations for Eriphyle's presence.

26 O'Hara 2017: 78–9, 171–2. O'Hara also notes that De la Cerda presents a different etymology, explaining the fields' name as coming from their proximity to Cocytus River, whose name derives from *kōkuō* ("mourn").

27 O'Hara 2017: xvii. While O'Hara is correct that this word play does not refer only to Latin love elegy but to erotic poetry more broadly, below I offer some specific engagements with Tibullus 1.3.

28 On the Homeric elements in Tib. 1.3 see esp. Eisenberger 1960: 191–6; Bright 1971, 1978: 17–37; Mills 1974; Ball 1983: 50–65.

29 Lee-Stecum 1998: 119–21. *Od.* 4.561–69 and Hes. *Op.* 168–73 provide prominent examples of Elysium populated by heroes. See Smith 1913: 253; Nisbet and Hubbard 1978: 203–5; Brazouski 1990.

30 Venus as *psychopompos*: Houghton 2007: 154. For choruses and flora similar to Tib. 1.3, cf. Pind. *Ol.* 2.62–80 and fr. 129; Aristoph. *Ran.* 154–7; [Plat.] *Axioch.* 371c; Verg. *Aen.* 6.657–8; Lucian *Ver. Hist.* 2.5. See Curtis in this volume on choruses in *Aeneid* 6's Elysium and Horace's *Carmen Saeculare.*

31 Houghton 2007: 156n19; Hanslik 1970: 139.

32 Houghton 2007: 158–65. See also Cairns 1979: 54–7; Murgatroyd 1980: 120; Masaracchia 1982.

33 Smith 1913: 254; Cairns 1979: 51–2; Murgatroyd 1980: 118; Maltby 2002: 202. See also Keith in this volume.

34 Lee-Stecum 1998: 118. See Momigliano 1942 for *terra marique* and its associations with worldwide empire, as well as its Hellenistic antecedents.

35 I thank an anonymous reviewer for pointing out the connection between *Aen.* 1.3 and *terra marique.* On this verse, see also Barchiesi in this volume.

36 *OLD s.v.*; *TLL* 4.606.5 ff. For *inmitis* as parallel to *durus* see *TLL* 7.3.467.7–8.

37 Maltby 2002: 205; *TLL* 7.1.1902; *OLD s.v.* 1.

38 Maltby 2002: 205; Horsfall 2013a: 2.334 are representative.

39 On *durus* and *mollis*, see esp. Pichon 1902: 136, 204–6; Fedeli 1980: 198; Keith 1994: 34 and 1999: 53; Wyke 2002: 168–9, 174–6. Debrohun 1994: 48n36 discusses the *durus-mollis* opposition; at 51 she notes Propertius' use of *tener* along with *mollis* in contrast with *durus*. On the use of *tener* in relation to elegy: *OLD s.v. tener* 6b; *TLL s.v. durus* 5.1.2308.76 ff.; Catul. 35.1; Ov. *Am.* 3.8.2 and *Rem.* 757. See also Pichon 1902: 277–8; Henkel 2014: 456.

40 In a play on the theme of echoes and echoing, Ovid imbues the entire Narcissus and Echo episode with many allusions. See Hinds 1998: 5–8.

41 See below on *Ecl.* 10 and Cairns 2006: 89, 115 on links between Gallus and *durus* and *tener*.

42 Henkel 2014: 456n19 calculates that Tibullus uses *tener* 28 times (2.26/100 lines); Ovid 22 times in the *Amores* (.89/100 lines); Propertius 11 times (.27/100 lines).

43 Esp. *Il.* 2.489–90; Enn. *Ann.* 469–70 Skutsch. See Henkel 2014: 471–2.

44 I am thankful to an anonymous reviewer for this point.

45 Ovid (*Tr.* 2.529–39) confirms that early reade s were aware of the *Aeneid*'s complex representation of *amor* through his comments on Vergil's intertwining of heroic themes and *amor* in his epic. See Barchiesi 1997: 27–8; Thomas 2001: 75–8.

46 Mynors 1990: 223. Shackleton Bailey 1967: 55 proposes that δεινὸς Ἔρως also underlies Propertius' *magnus Amor* that is able to come back from the underworld at 1.19.12. If Shackleton Bailey is correct, Vergil's *durus amor*, in addition to engaging with Tibullus' *tener amor*, may also offer a correction for Propertius' *magnus* by exploiting the negative side of the semantic range of δεινός in Greek. See also the discussion of Propertius 1.19 in the conclusion of this paper.

47 1966: 198–9. Curran acknowledges that *rigidus* is the more common descriptor, but cites as parallels Ov. *Fast.* 2.346 and possibly Cat. 16.11. See also Fedeli 1980: 122, who notes that the sexual interpretation of *arma* is already proposed by Beroaldo.

48 Fedeli 1980: 120–1; cf. Callim. *AP* 12.118; Rufin *AP* 5.93; Ach. Tat. 2.2.3; Plaut. *Aul.* 745; Ov. *Am.* 1.6.59–60.

49 On the relationship between *Tr.* 3.3, 4.10, and Tib. 1.3, see Huskey 2005: 378–9.

50 McKeown 1989: 74–89, esp. 86–8 and 1998: 384–5.

51 See esp. McKeown 1998: 382–3; Hollis 2007: 424–5.

52 Cairns 1979: 181–3; Maltby 2002: 466.

53 O'Neil 1967; Bright 1978: 217–19; *contra* Murgatroyd 1994: 239–40.

54 Reed 1997: 261n1 and Huskey 2005: 367n3 catalogue important studies. I follow Boyd 1997: 179–80 in reading *Am.* 3.9 as an expression of "sentiment and cleverness" towards Tibullus rather than parody. Perkins 1993 presents an argument for parody.

55 Based on a PHI Latin search, the other instances that Iulus is called *pulcher* are: *Aen.* 5.570, 7.107, 7.477–8, 9.293, 9.310, Serv. ad *Aen.* 9.291, and *Argumenta Aeneidis Decasticha* 9.7. See also Boyd 1997: 182.

56 Ov. *Am.* 3.9.5: *uates … Tibullus*; 3.9.17: *sacri uates … uocamur*; 3.9.41: *sacer uates.*

57 On Ovid's sources: Reed 1997. For Vergil Orphism is especially prominent here: Habinek 1989: 231–3; Horsfall 2013a: 2.455–6 with further references. See also Herrero in this volume on Orphic elements in other parts of Vergil's underworld. On *Aeneid* 6's Poet's Corner, see also Gowers in this volume.

58 Clausen 1994: 277–8 on *E.* 9.33–4. *Am.* 3.9 also engages with Ovid's *epicedion* for Corinna's parrot, *Am.* 2.6 (Cahoon 1984; McKeown 1998: 110), where Ovid's Elysian aviary likewise has points of contacts with *Aen.* 6: McKeown 1998: 137–8 notes that *Am.* 2.6.49 describes a hill in Elysium, a rare feature in the Elysium tradition, but also found at *Aen.* 6.676–9. In addition, the birds that inhabit the region are *piae uolucres* (51), a phrase that recalls Vergil's *pii uates.*

59 See discussion in Lyne 1980: 101 and 1998b. For *magnus amor,* see Weber 2008 and n46 above.

60 On 3.5.18: Goold 1967: 80–1; Fedeli 1985: 185–6.

61 I am grateful to Damien Nelis for this point. As Delvigo 1995: 24 notes, the theory that Orpheus' *katabasis* in *Georgics* 4 is indebted to Gallus is already proposed by Thilo 1886: xxiv. See also Coleman 1962: 68–71; Boucher 1965: 65n10. Erycius' epigram (*AP* 7.377) imagining Parthenius' torture in the underworld for his supposed criticism of Homer offers an example of broader traditions about the afterlife of (love) poets.

7

Vergilian Underworlds in Ovid

ALISON KEITH

I. Lingering on the Threshold

Ovid's familiarity with Vergil's poetry is apparent in every line of his oeuvre, starting with *Amores* 1.1: *arma graui numero uiolentaque bella parabam* | *edere* ("I was preparing to bring forth 'arms' in epic measure and violent wars"), whose fi st hemistich echoes the incipit of the *Aeneid* in both form and content (*Aen.* 1.1: *arma uirumque cano,* "arms and a man I celebrate").[1] An interest in *Aeneid* 6 more particularly, and in Vergil's mysterious underworld, emerges as early as Corinna's epiphany in *Amores* 1.5 (3–6):

pars adaperta fuit, pars altera clausa fenestrae,
quale fere siluae lumen habere solent,
qualia sublucent fugiente crepuscula Phoebo
aut ubi nox abiit nec tamen orta dies.

Part of the window was open, the other part closed –
such is nearly the light the woods are accustomed to have,
so dully does twilight glow, when Phoebus flee ,
or when night has gone but day not yet risen.

In his commentary on these lines, J.C. McKeown notes that the triple comparison (*quale … qualia … aut*) is far from otiose, for Ovid enhances his description of light effects "suggestive of the numinous atmosphere conducive to divine epiphany"[2] with an allusion to Vergil's description of the dim light of the underworld as his hero Aeneas embarks on a *katabasis* under the guidance of the Sibyl (*Aen.* 6.268–72):[3]

ibant obscuri sola sub nocte per umbram

perque domos Ditis uacuas et inania regna:
quale per incertam lunam sub luce maligna
est iter in siluis, ubi caelum condidit umbra
Iuppiter, et rebus nox abstulit atra colorem.

They went dimly beneath the lonely night, through the shade
and empty halls of Dis, through his phantom kingdom:
such as a journey in the woods beneath an ill light by a
fitful moon when Jupiter conceals heave with shadows
and black night has stolen colour from things.

Sustained interest in *Aeneid* 6, however, comes into focus somewhat later, perhaps most notably (still in a ludic, and erotic, vein), in the *Ars Amatoria* (1.453–4): *hoc opus, hic labor est, primo sine munere iungi: | ne dederit gratis quae dedit, usque dabit.* ("This is the work, this is the labour': to get laid without paying fi st: lest she have given for free what she gave, she'll keep on giving"). Of the notorious line *Ars* 1.453, Adrian Hollis (1977) observes that "one can hardly believe that the echo of *Aeneid* 6.129 is unconscious" (*Aen.* 6.126–9):

Tros Anchisiade, facilis descensus Auerno:
noctes atque dies patet atri ianua Ditis;
sed reuocare gradum superasque euadere ad auras,
hoc opus, hic labor est.

Trojan son of Anchises, the descent to Avernus is easy:
night and day the door of black Dis stands open;
but to retrace your steps and walk out to the upper air –
this is the toil, this is the task.

Indeed, Ovid's cheeky statement of his didactic project (and every lover's amatory project) is particularly outrageous in its adaptation of the Vergilian Sibyl's portentous words to Aeneas.[4] No wonder the *princeps* was not pleased with Ovid, subverting the heroic mission of Vergil's august Aeneas to the salacious, newly criminalized project of amatory seduction.

But the reminiscences of *Aeneid* 6 may not end here. For a few lines later, the poet-*praeceptor* urges his students to immerse themselves in the *bonas artes* of liberal studies, in order to develop their rhetorical talents to the fullest, and thereby win a girlfriend (*AA* 1.459–62):

disce bonas artes, moneo, Romana iuuentus,
non tantum trepidos ut tueare reos:

quam populus iudexque grauis lectusque senatus,
tam dabit eloquio uicta puella manus.

Roman youth, I advise you, learn the liberal arts, not only to
protect fearful defendants in the lawcourts: as the populace,
serious judge, and chosen Senate will hold out their hands
in submission, conquered by your eloquence, so will your girl.

Ovid here appropriates a characteristically Ennian hexameter clausula, *Romana iuuentus* (*Ann.* 499, 550, 563 Sk), for his own "grandiloquent" line that Hollis (1977: 112) suggests recalls *Georgics* 2.35–36: *quare agite o proprios generatim discite cultus, | agricolae* ("Therefore come, farmers, and learn the arboriculture appropriate to each kind of tree"). Yet there may also be more than a touch of continuing parodic engagement with *Aeneid* 6, in the line's resemblance to another famous passage in the sixth book of the *Aeneid* (6.851–3):

tu regere imperio populos, Romane, memento
(hae tibi erunt artes), pacique imponere morem,
parcere subiectis et debellare superbos.

Remember, Roman man, to rule peoples with your power,
(these will be your arts), to impose custom on peace,
to spare the conquered and battle down the proud.

In this, one of the most explicitly didactic passages in the whole of the *Aeneid*, Vergil interpellates his Roman male audience as military masters of the Mediterranean. This is "poetry that trains men, by inculcating the values, examples of behavior, [and] cultural models" by which Rome won her empire.[5] Ovid's *Ars* too ostensibly aimed to "train men," though in nothing so lofty as winning an empire; rather, as Ovid expresses it here, the immediate goal is the use of the "good" (or "liberal") arts necessary to win a compliant girlfriend.

Ovid's interest in *Aeneid* 6 continues in *Ars* 2, where the poet-*praeceptor* relates the myth of Daedalus, ostensibly in order to demonstrate the difficulty of reining in the winged god *Amor* (*AA* 2.21–97). Alison Sharrock has well discussed the manifold literary tensions addressed in Ovid's didactic elegiac treatment of the very *artificer-cum*-architect with whom Vergil opens the sixth book of the *Aeneid* (6.14–33):[6]

Daedalus, ut fama est, fugiens Minoïa regna
praepetibus pennis ausus se credere caelo
insuetum per iter gelidas enauit ad Arctos,

Chalcidicaque leuis tandem super astitit arce.
redditus his primum terris tibi, Phoebe, sacrauit
remigium alarum posuitque immania templa.
in foribus letum Androgeo; tum pendere poenas
Cecropidae iussi (miserum!) septena quotannis
corpora natorum; stat ductis sortibus urna.
contra elata mari respondet Cnosia tellus:
hic crudelis amor tauri suppostaque furto
Pasiphae mixtumque genus prolesque biformis
Minotaurus inest, Veneris monimenta nefandae,
hic labor ille domus et inextricabilis error;
magnum reginae sed enim miseratus amorem
Daedalus ipse dolos tecti ambagesque resoluit,
caeca regens filo uestigia tu quoque magnam
partem opere in tanto, sineret dolor, Icare, haberes.
bis conatus erat casus effingere in aur ,
bis patriae cecidere manus …

Daedalus, so the story goes, fled the kingdom of Minos an
dared to entrust himself to heaven on swift pinions; he floate
on an unaccustomed route to the cold North and at last
he stood lightly poised above the Chalcidian citadel.
Restored to earth fi st here, Phoebus, he offered to you
his oarage of wings, and he laid a huge temple.
On the doors was the death of Androgeos; then (alas!) the
Athenians, ordered to pay the annual penalty of seven living
sons; the urn stands there, the lots now drawn.
Opposite, rising from the sea, the Cretan land faces this:
here is the cruel love of the bull, Pasiphae mated
through deception, the mixed race of the biform offspring,
the Minotaur, memorial of unspeakable lust; there is
that house of toil and its unfathomable winding;
but Daedalus, pitying the princess' great love, himself
unwound the deceptive tangle of the palace, guiding blind
feet with the thread. You too, Icarus, would have received
a large share in so great a work, were grief to allow;
twice he had made the attempt to fashion your fate in gold,
twice his father's hands fell …

Sharrock observes that the Vergilian Daedalus has Callimachean resonances, as an inventor and artist whose work is cut short, while further literary symbolism can be seen in Vergil's decision to present the myth in an ecphrasis, a literary form that has affinities with the Hellenistic epyllion. Ovid's adaptation in the *Ars* of the Vergilian set piece emphasizes Daedalus' Callimachean daring and innovation, both metaphors for his consummate artistry, and sets Daedalus' Callimachean values into ironic relationship with his son Icarus' epic pretensions, as someone who flies too high, with the whole myth presented at greater length than in the *Aeneid* (perhaps an allusion to its epic provenance), and in a self-consciously didactic manner.

II. Into the Labyrinth

Ovid makes more sustained, and perhaps more lofty (though often still parodic), use of Vergil's underworld machinery at several points in the *Metamorphoses*. In Book 8, for example, he returns to the myth of Daedalus and Icarus, and exploits the wider context of its setting there in the war between Athens and Crete to engage more closely with the Cretan myths inscribed by Daedalus on the temple of Apollo at *Aeneid* 6.24–30.[7] Thus Ovid elaborates Vergil's allusions to the unhappy passions of Pasiphae and Ariadne, along with Daedalus' construction of a labyrinth in which to conceal the biform Minotaur (*Met.* 8.152–82), before redoubling his treatment of the myth of Daedalus and Icarus (*Met.* 8.183–235), and concluding, by way of a coda, with the death and metamorphosis of Daedalus' nephew Perdix (*Met.* 8.236–59). The lexical texture of Ovid's account of the sordid history of the Minotaur is heavily indebted to Vergil's in *Aeneid* 6 (and through him to that of Catullus in poem 64): thus Minos' sacrifice of "one hundred bodies of bulls" (*Met.* 8.152) seems to look to Vergil's resuscitation of an Ennian periphrasis (*Ann.* 88–9 Sk: *ter quattuor corpora sancta | auium*, "thrice four holy bodies of birds") in his reference to the Athenian youths destined for the Minotaur (*Aen.* 6.21–2). Certainly, Ovid is working very closely with Vergil's diction in the lines that follow. Hollis (1970: 54) even identifies *Met.* 8.158 (*multiplicique domo caecisque includere tectis*, "to shut [*sc.* the Minotaur] in a labyrinthine dwelling with blind halls") as "one of the few Ovidian hexameters which could have been written by Vergil." For Ovid's line showcases the amplification of the fi st half of the line in the second, so characteristic of the master's style.

Ovid's reworking of the labyrinth brings us, at least symbolically, into the underworld itself, and in the middle of his account of the tragic love story of Ceyx and Alcyone in *Metamorphoses* 11, he ventures further into the Vergilian underworld, to include an extended meditation on the relationship between Sleep and Death in a celebrated ecphrastic description of the house of Sleep. Unaware that her husband Ceyx has drowned, Alcyone offers daily prayers to Juno to bring her husband home safely, until the goddess, aghast that the widow's hands pollute her altars, decides to communicate the truth of her husband's fate to Alcyone (*Met.* 11.578–88):

> ante tamen cunctos Iunonis templa colebat
> proque uiro, qui nullus erat, ueniebat ad aras
> utque foret sospes coniunx suus utque rediret,
> optabat, nullamque sibi praeferret; at illi
> hoc de tot uotis poterat contingere solum.
> At dea non ultra pro functo morte rogari
> sustinet utque manus funestas arceat aris
> "Iri, meae" dixit "fidissima nuntia uoci ,
> uise soporiferam Somni uelociter aulam
> exstinctique iube Ceycis imagine mittat
> somnia ad Alcyonen ueros narrantia casus."

> But most of all she worships Juno's shrine, praying for
> the man who is no more, that her husband may be kept
> safe from harm, that he may return once more,
> loving no other woman more than her. And only this prayer
> of all her prayers could be granted her. But the goddess
> could no longer endure these entreaties for the dead. And that
> she might free her altar from the hands of mourning,
> she said: "Iris, most faithful messenger of mine,
> go quickly to the drowsy house of Sleep,
> and bid him send to Alcyone a dream-vision
> in dead Ceyx's form to tell her the truth about his fate."

Throughout the allegorical description of *Somnus*, "Sleep," and his court (*Met.* 11.592–673), Ovid engages Vergil (*Aen.* 6.273–81, 703–5), and through him Homer (*Od.* 16.562–9, 11.14–19) and Hesiod (*Theog.* 758–60), in intensely intertextual dialogue and literary competition.[8] As befits characters in a metamorphic world, moreover, the Ovidian *Somnus* and his courtiers (especially the "Dreams," *Somnia*) are experts in shape-shifting, skilled in "equalling true forms by imitation" (*Met.* 11.626), as Ovid notes through his self-reflexive emphasis on "imitation" in the passage.

Already in Juno's commission of Iris, Ovid self-consciously sounds the theme of imitation, in the goddess' characterization of her messenger as *fidissima nuntia uocis*, "a most faithful reporter of her words" (11.585), a phrase that raises issues of verbal authority and imitation. In her request that Iris solicit dreams to inform Alcyone of the true fate of her husband by means of his likeness (*Ceycis imagine*, 11.587), Ovid implicitly sets into play the problematic of epic emulation in his use of the word *imagine* in conjunction with truth-telling dreams.[9] For one of the most famous passages in Homeric epic dealt with the emanation from the Gates of Sleep of both true and false dreams (*Od.* 19.560–9):[10]

ξεῖν', ἦ τοι μὲν ὄνειροι ἀμήχανοι ἀκριτόμυθοι
γίγνοντ', οὐδέ τι πάντα τελείεται ἀνθρώποισι.
δοιαὶ γάρ τε πύλαι ἀμενηνῶν εἰσὶν ὀνείρων:
αἱ μὲν γὰρ κεράεσσι τετεύχαται, αἱ δ' ἐλέφαντι:
τῶν οἳ μέν κ' ἔλθωσι διὰ πριστοῦ ἐλέφαντος,
οἵ ῥ' ἐλεφαίρονται, ἔπε' ἀκράαντα φέροντες:
οἱ δὲ διὰ ξεστῶν κεράων ἔλθωσι θύραζε,
οἵ ῥ' ἔτυμα κραίνουσι, βροτῶν ὅτε κέν τις ἴδηται.

My friend, dreams are things hard to interpret, hopeless
to puzzle out, and people find that not all of them en
in anything. There are two gates through which the
insubstantial dreams issue. One pair of gates is made of
horn, and one of ivory. Those of the dreams which issue
through the gate of sawn ivory are deceptive dreams,
their message is never accomplished. But those that come
into the open through the gates of the polished horn
accomplish the truth for any mortal who sees them.

Ovid is clearly alluding to the Homeric passage in Juno's reference to the veracity of Iris' report of her words and in her request for a truthful report from the dream vision sent to Alcyone (11.587–8): *mittat | somnia ad Alcyonen ueros narrantia casus* ("Let him send dreams to Alcyone that tell the true events"). But Ovid also refers here to Vergil's reworking of the Homeric passage at the end of *Aeneid* 6 (lines 893–6):

Sunt geminae Somni portae, quarum altera fertur
cornea, qua ueris facilis datur exitus umbris,
altera candenti perfecta nitens elephanto,
sed falsa ad caelum mittunt insomnia Manes.

There are twin gates of Sleep, one of which is said to be
of horn, from which easy exit is given to true shades,
while the other was constructed from white ivory
and gleams, but the dead send false dreams to heaven.

Ovid's debt to the Vergilian passage is evident not only in his introduction of *Somnus* in the genitive case (11.586) but also in his transformation of Vergil's "false dreams" (*falsa … insomnia, Aen.* 6.896) into "dreams that tell the truth" (*somnia … ueros narrantia casus,* 11.588). He thus indulges in two of his favourite compositional strategies in Juno's instructions to Iris, alluding to his Homeric model both directly and indirectly through the Vergilian intermediary. Ovid's play with fictionality is still further complicated in this passage, when Somnus dispatches Morpheus, one of his courtiers, to convey a true event to Alcyone (the death of her husband Ceyx) but in the guise of a false (dream) Ceyx.[11]

Ovid also follows epic convention by making the abode of Sleep contiguous with that of Death, i.e., setting it in the underworld (*Met.* 11.602–4): *saxo tamen exit ab imo | riuus aquae Lethes, per quem cum murmure labens | inuitat somnos crepitantibus unda lapillis* ("But from the bottom of the cave there flows the stream of Lethe, whose waves, gently murmuring over the gravelly bed, invite to slumber"). Lethe, particularized as a river, belongs to the geography of the underworld from Vergil onwards (*Aen.* 6.703–5): *Interea uidet Aeneas in ualle reducta | seclusum nemus et uirgulta sonantia siluae, | Lethaeumque domos placidas qui praenatat amnem* ("Meanwhile, Aeneas in a secret valley can see a sheltered grove and sounding forests and thickets and the stream of Lethe flowing past tranquil dwellings"). In this juxtaposition of Sleep and Lethe, Ovid looks closely at the model of Vergil, who pointedly locates the brothers Sleep and Death at the entrance to his underworld (*Aen.* 6.273–8):

uestibulum ante ipsum primisque in faucibus Orci
Luctus et ultrices posuere cubilia Curae,
pallentesque habitant Morbi tristisque Senectus,
et Metus et malesuada Fames ac turpis Egestas,
terribiles uisu formae, Letumque Labosque;
tum consanguineus Leti Sopor.

Before the entrance, at the jaws of Orcus,
both Grief and goading Cares have set their couches;
there pale Diseases dwell, and sad Old Age,
and Fear and Hunger, that worst counsellor, and ugly Poverty
– shapes terrible to see – and Death and Trials
Death's brother, Sleep.

In the opening of the ecphrasis, therefore, Ovid outdoes Vergil (as well as Homer and Hesiod) by composing a description of the cave of Sleep (and of the god himself) that is skilfully woven from elements of the epic tradition but both newly comprehensive and comprehensively innovative.[12] The complexities multiply, moreover, as the cave of Sleep is a place where, in a sense, the shade of Ceyx resides, as if in an underworld, and a place that perhaps comments on the dreamlike quality of Aeneas' *katabasis* in *Aeneid* 6.[13]

Ovid even draws attention to his emulative achievement in the new emphasis he gives to Sleep's imitative and metamorphic courtiers: *hunc circa passim uarias imitantia formas | somnia uana iacent totidem, quot messis aristas, | silua gerit fronds, eiectas litus harenas* ("Around him on all sides lie empty dream-shapes, mimicking many forms, many as ears of grain in harvest-time, as leaves upon the trees, as sands cast on the shore," *Met.* 11.613–15). As is entirely appropriate in a poem about transformation, the dream-shapes that dwell in the court of the Ovidian Sleep are themselves metamorphic, inasmuch as they can assume a variety of forms. The word choice and arrangement of 11.613 are particularly telling in this context (*uarias imitantia formas*) since they hint at Ovid's programmatic self-consciousness here in their echo of the opening line of the poem: *in noua fert animus, mutatas dicere formas | corpora* ("My mind is bent to tell of bodies changed into new forms," *Met.* 1.1–2).[14] But in addition to this intratextual literary dynamic, cued by the internal echo of *mutatas ... formas* in the phrase *uarias ... formas,* the word *imitantia* also seems to function as a signal to Ovid's readers that "the whole scene in which it is placed is an Ovidian *imitatio,* which at once renovates and questioningly transforms" the whole of the prior epic tradition concerning Sleep.[15] Ovid draws attention to the imitative quality of dreams precisely because he invokes them in a passage that imitates epic tradition – a nice example of what Stephen Hinds has called "allusive self-annotation."[16] The phrase is thus doubly self-reflexive in that it offers implicit comment not only on Ovid's own metamorphic project in the *Metamorphoses,* but also on the nature of his emulative engagement with the epic tradition here (and indeed throughout the poem).

It is in Book 4, however, that Ovid offers his most sustained distillation of the elaborate geography of the Vergilian underworld, when Juno herself undertakes a *katabasis* – against all epic convention, which traditionally restricts the gods of the upper air to heaven and earth (*Met.* 4.432–45):

est uia decliuis, funesta nubila taxo;
ducit ad infernas per muta silentia sedes.
Styx nebulas exhalat iners, umbraeque recentes
descendunt illac simulacraque functa sepulcris;
pallor hiemsque tenent late loca senta, nouique,
qua sit iter, manes, Stygiam quod ducat ad urbem
ignorant, ubi sit nigri fera regia Ditis.

mille capax aditus et apertas undique portas
urbs habet, utque fretum de tota flumina terra
sic omnes animas locus accipit ille nec ulli
exiguus populo est turbamue accedere sentit.
errant exsangues sine corpore et ossibus umbrae,
parsque forum celebrant, pars imi tecta tyranni,
pars aliquas artes, antiquae imitamina uitae.

There is a downward-sloping path, dark with funereal yew; it leads to the seat of the underworld through muted silence. The idle Styx breaths out mist, and there descend recent shades and the likenesses of those that have obtained funerals; paleness and cold hold the rough places far and wide; new ghosts don't know where the route is that leads to the Stygian city, where the wild palace of black Dis is. The capacious city has a thousand entrances and open gates on every side; just as the ocean receives rivers from the whole world, so that place receives all the souls, nor is it too small for any number of people, and perceives a crowd approaching. Bloodless shades wander, without body and bones; some throng the forum, others the halls of the underworld tyrant, others pursue their erstwhile occupations, imitations of the old life.

Ovid here pointedly reverses the opening of his description in *Metamorphoses* 1 of the road to the gods' abode in heaven (*est uia sublimis, Met.* 1.168), and throughout his underworld *topographia* he emphasizes the pale and silent darkness of the underworld, familiar already from Homer (*Od.* 11.14–19) and Roman republican tragedy (perhaps from Ennius *apud* Cic. *Tusc.* 1.48),[17] but emphasized most recently by Vergil (*Aen.* 6.264–312). Ovid retains the outline of Vergil's underworld geography, highlighting by allusion various notable features of his predecessor's netherworld, such as the silence (*Aen.* 6.264–5: *umbrae silentes | … loca nocte tacentia late,* "silent shadows … places hushed in the night abroad"); wooded aspect (*Aen.* 6.271: *iter in siluis,* "a journey into the woods"; cf. *Aen.* 6.386: *per tacitum nemus,* "through the silent grove"); pale, dull light, from which "black night has leached colour from the world" (*rebus nox abstulit atra colorem, Aen.* 6.272), reflected in the pallor of the diseases that live there (*Aen.* 6.275, *pallentesque habitant Morbi*); and rugged terrain, emphasized in an echo of the Vergilian phrase *loca senta* (*Aen.* 6.462 ~ *Met.* 4.436). Ovid also underscores the prominence of the river Styx, Aeneas' fi st port of call in Vergil's underworld narrative (*Aen.* 6.295: *hinc uia Tartarei quae fert Acherontis ad undas,* "thence runs the road which leads to the waters of Tartarean Acheron"; 323–4: *Cocyti stagna alta uides Stygiamque paludem | di cuius iurare timent et fallere numen,* "you see the deep pools of Cocytus and the Stygian swamp, by whose divinity the gods fear to swear and to forswear their oaths"; 385: *nauita quos iam inde ut Stygia prospexit ab unda,* "the ferryman had already caught sight of them from the Stygian stream"). Ovid maintains, as he reverses, Vergil's distinction between buried and unburied corpses (*Aen.* 6.325–6, 305–8, esp. 306: de*functaque corpora uita,* "bodies *defunct* of life"; cf. *Geo.* 4.475, Hom. *Od.* 11.36–41), in his reference to "properly buried shades" (*simulacraque* functa *sepulcris, Met.* 4.435). He varies Vergil's *atri ianua Ditis* ("doors of black Dis," *Aen.* 6.127) in *nigri fera regia Ditis* ("savage halls of black Dis," *Met.* 4.438) even as he respects the Vergilian underworld's capacity to add ever more numbers of dead (*Aen.* 6.127 ~ *Met.* 4.439–42). Ovid also retains the Vergilian continuity between the habitual pursuits of life and death in the *Sedes Beatae* (6.653–5), in his picture of the dead imitating their former life (*Met.* 4.443–5); though his lines may also remind us of Aeneas' encounters with the figures of his past – Palinurus, Dido, and Deiphobus – who remain trapped in their mortal pursuits even in death (especially Dido, relegated to the *lugentes campi,* where she continues to play out the disastrous love with Aeneas in which Venus, and Vergil, enmesh her). Moreover, as Colin Burrow has observed, this picture also evokes, on a metaliterary level, the Vergilian traces in Ovid's underworld (*la traccia del modello*), literary imitations of their former (Vergilian) life.[18]

Ovid does not hesitate, however, to ring changes on the Vergilian picture, for example by transforming the fortified walls of Tartarus (*moenia lata uidet triplici circumdata muro, Aen.* 6.549) into an underworld city (*Stygiam … urbem, Met.* 4.437), and relocating Cerberus' station from the banks of the Cocytus-Styx to the threshold of Dis' city (*Met.* 4.450), thereby further domesticating the household plan of Vergil's underworld *domus* (*Aen.* 6.273). More notable still, however, are the changes Ovid rings on the identity of the underworld traveller and the context of her *katabasis* (*Met.* 4.447–63):

sustinet ire illuc caelesti sede relicta
(tantum odiis iraeque dabat) Saturnia Iuno.
quo simul intrauit sacroque a corpore pressum
ingemuit limen, tria Cerberus extulit ora
et tres latratus semel edidit. illa sorores
nocte uocat genitas, graue et implacabile numen;
carceris ante fores clausas adamante sedebant
deque suis atros pectebant crinibus angues.
quam simul agnorunt inter caliginis umbras,

surrexere deae. sedes Scelerata uocatur:
uiscera praebebat Tityos lanianda nouemque
iugeribus distractus erat; tibi, Tantale, nullae
deprenduntur aquae, quaeque imminet, effugit arbor;
aut petis aut urges rediturum, Sisyphe, saxum;
uoluitur Ixion et se sequiturque fugitque;
molirique suis letum patruelibus ausae
adsiduae repetunt, quas perdant, Belides undas.

Saturnian Juno continued her journey there, having left the heavenly
abode behind (so much she granted to hatred and anger).
As soon as she entered the underworld and pressed its threshold
with her sacrosanct person, it groaned and Cerberus raised his
three mouths and uttered three barks at once. She summoned
the sisters born of Night, a grim and implacable goddess;
they were sitting before the altars of the prison which were
shut with adamantine bolts, and combing the black snakes from
their hair. As soon as they recognized her amid the mist's
shadows, the goddesses rose. The place is called Wicked:
Tityos offered his vitals for plucking and had been stretched
over nine acres; for you, Tantalus, there were no waters to be
caught, and the tree that hangs over them flees way;
you either seek or push a rock, Sisyphus, that will return;
Ixion is rolled on his wheel, following and fleeing himself and,
Belus' granddaughters, the Danaids who dared to plot the death
of their paternal cousins, constantly seek the water which they lose.

Ovid has reduced the Vergilian Aeneas' lofty purpose of braving the perils of the underworld to meet with his dead father and learn the glorious destiny of the Roman people, to just another sordid project arising from Juno's jealousy, as she determines to avenge herself on a sexual rival and destroy not a nation but, in this case, the last of Dionysus' aunts. Of course this is consistent with Vergil's characterization of Juno in the *Aeneid,* as Ovid wittily underscores with his parenthetical observation *tantum odiis iraeque dabat* (*Met.* 4.448), which recalls, as it responds to, Vergil's question in the proem to the *Aeneid* 1.11, *tantaene animis caelestibus irae*? ("Does such great anger animate celestial beings?"). But Ovid's Juno outdoes her Vergilian counterpart by descending all the way to the underworld, where Vergil's Juno had merely summoned Allecto up from hell: *flectere si nequeo superos, Acheronta mouebo* ("If I cannot bend the gods above, I shall rouse Acheron," *Aen.* 7.312).[19]

These transformations at the level of plot emerge particularly clearly by contrast with Ovid's continuing close, albeit condensed, fidelity to the machinery of the Vergilian underworld. The groaning of Dis' threshold under Juno's weight conforms to the epic convention, emphasized by both Vergil and Ovid, of the insubstantiality of the underworld shades, and recalls in particular the groan emitted by Charon's skiff when the corporeal Aeneas and his guide the Sibyl embark for the opposite shore (*Aen.* 6.413–14: *gemuit sub pondere cumba | sutilis et multam accepit rimosa paludem*). Cerberus' three heads and three barks likewise conform to classical epic convention, and closely rework Vergil's description in *Aeneid* 6 (417–22):

> Cerberus haec ingens latratu regna trifauci
> personat aduerso recubans immanis in antro
> … ille fame rabida tria guttura pandens
> corripit obiectam.

> Huge Cerberus, reclining expansively in the cave, makes the
> kingdom resound with his three-throated barking …
> Opening his three throats with ravenous hunger, he snatched at
> the offering.

It is, in fact, precisely upon his arrival at the triple-walled abode of Tartarus, with its adamantine gate (*Aen.* 6.552: *porta aduersa ingens solidoque adamante columnae*, "opposite was a huge gate and columns of solid adamant"; cf. *Il.* 8.15), that Aeneas sees Tisiphone, standing guard night and day over the sinners in the underworld (*Aen.* 6.555–6): *Tisiphoneque sedens palla succincta cruenta | uestibulum exsomnis seruat noctesque diesque* ("And Tisiphone in her seat, girt with bloody cloak, guards the vestibule unsleeping, day and night"). It is for this reason that the Ovidian Juno summons the Furies, the "sisters born of Night," from their post before the bolted doors of the infernal prison (*Met.* 4.451–3). The Furies' careful styling of their snaky tresses is also indebted to a Vergilian model, though this time not of the Furies themselves but of their hellish sister *Discordia,* who shares a line with them in the entrance to the underworld (*Aen.* 6.280–1): *ferreique Eumenidum thalami et Discordia demens | uipereum crinem uittis innexa cruentis* ("and the Eumenides' iron bedchamber and impassioned *Discordia,* binding her snaky hair with bloody fillets") The Furies' location in the *sedes Scelerata* here in Ovid recalls the Vergilian Sibyl's exclusion of *pius* Aeneas from the *sceleratum limen* (6.562–3: *dux inclute Teucrum | nulli fas casto sceleratum insistere limen,* "renowned leader of the Teucrians, it is right for no pure man to set foot on the wicked threshold") and Tibullus' use of the very phrase (Tib.1.3.67–8:

at scelerata iacet sedes in nocte profunda | abdita, "but the abode of crime lies hidden in deep night");[20] and the Sibyl likewise emphasizes Tisiphone's role in punishing the sinners of Tartarus (*Aen.* 6.570–2):[21] *continuo sontis ultrix accincta flagello | Tisiphone quatit insultans, toruosque sinistra | intentans anguis uocat agmina saeua sororum* ("Constantly punishing the guilty, Tisiphone, girt with her whip, exults in striking them, and with her left hand straining the twisting snakes, she summons the savage ranks of her sisters").[22] The list of sinners reflects not only Homero-Vergilian, but especially Tibullan, precedent: Tityos (*Od.* 11.577, *Aen.* 6.595–600); Tantalus (*Od.* 11.582–92, Tib. 1.3.77–8); Sisyphus (*Od.* 11.593–600; not mentioned by Vergil); Ixion (unknown to Homer, fi st in Pindar, *Pyth.* 2.21; cf. Tib. 1.3.73–4, *Aen.* 6.601); and the Danaids (Tib. 1.3.79–80).[23]

Tisiphone's prominence in the Vergilian underworld explains her preeminence in Ovid's narrative, where Juno commissions her (rather than Allecto) to conduct her petty revenge on Ino, the last of Dionysus' aunts, and overthrow her husband Athamas' household (*Met.* 4.481–8):

> nec mora, Tisiphone madefactam sanguine sumit
> importuna facem fluidoque cruore rubente
> induitur pallam tortoque incingitur angue
> egrediturque domo; Luctus comitatur euntem
> et Pauor et Terror trepidoque Insania uultu.
> limine constiterant; postes tremuisse feruntur
> Aeolii pallorque fores infecit acernas
> solque locum fugit.

> Without delay, Tisiphone takes up her torch, dripping
> with unlucky blood and puts on her cloak flowing re
> herself with gore, and girding with twisted snake she goes forth
> from the house of Hades; Grief accompanies her as she goes,
> and Fear and Terror and Madness with her fearful face. They
> stopped on the threshold; the doorposts of Aeolus' son are
> reported to have trembled and pallor infected his maple doors
> while the sun fled the plac .

Tisiphone's accoutrements are heavily indebted to her Vergilian model, from her cloak dripping with gore to the snakes with which she is girt (*Aen.* 6.570–2, 555). Of particular interest is the company she keeps in Ovid's narrative – *Luctus, Pauor, Terror,* and *Insania* (*Met.* 4.484–5). For these personifications recall those that crowd the vestibule of Vergil's underworld (*Aen.* 6.273–81). *Luctus* stands at the head of both catalogues (*Met.* 4.484

~ *Aen.* 6.274), and his Ovidian companions *Pauor* and *Terror* recall Vergil's *Metus* (6.276) and the other *terribiles uisu formae* (6.277), which Aeneas sees at the entry to the underworld. Moreover, Tisiphone's arrival infects the maple doors of Athamas' palace with the pallor (*Met.* 4.487) characteristic of Vergil's ill-lit underworld (cf. *Met.* 4.436; and the *pallentes Morbi* of *Aen.* 6.275). No wonder the sun flees a palace (*Met.* 4.488) that has been contaminated by the infernal powers.

Ovid's conjuncture in *Metamorphoses* 4 of supernatural *katabasis* and chthonic infection of a household condenses in a brilliant miniature the expansive movement of *Aeneid* 6 and 7, from Aeneas' descent to the underworld to Juno's summons of Allecto to overthrow Latinus' compact with the Trojan strangers. Through quotation, condensation, and close narrative recapitulation, Ovid reveals his deep understanding of Vergilian thematics and atmospherics. His tone, however, may still be felt to leave something to be desired. Juno's derisive laughter at her victims' misapprehension of the identity of the vengeful god persecuting them invites our own complicit mirth in Ovid's Vergilian parody (*Met.* 4.523–4): *"euhoe Bacche!" sonat; Bacchi sub nomine Iuno | risit et "hos usus praestet tibi" dixit "alumnus"* ("He cries 'Euhoe, Bacchus!' At Bacchus' name, Juno laughed and said 'May your nurseling supply you with these experiences'")!

A similarly mischievous undertone can be heard in *Metamorphoses* 14, where Ovid's rehearsal of the myth of Aeneas engages most directly with Vergil's underworld narrative of *Aeneid* 6. There Ovid recapitulates *in nuce* the elaborate rituals that attend Aeneas' encounter with the Sibyl on the threshold to the underworld – his entrance into her cave (*antra Sibullae | intrat, Met.* 14.104–5), her impassioned prophecy (*deo furibunda recepto, Met.* 14.107), and her command that he pluck the Golden Bough (*Met.* 14.113–15).[24] But the brevity of his summary of his model's solemn ceremonial activities undermines the sublimity with which Vergil had invested the proceedings and reduces the heroic stature of the Vergilian Aeneas' visit to the mysterious underworld to just another fleeting encounter on an abbreviated tour of the Mediterranean (*Met.* 14.116–19):

paruit Aeneas et formidabilis Orci
uidit opes atauosque suos umbramque senilem
magnanimi Anchisae. didicit quoque iura locorum,
quaeque nouis essent adeunda pericula bellis.

Aeneas obeyed: he saw the wealth of terrifying Orcus, his
descendants, and the aged shade of great-hearted

> Anchises. He also learned the laws of the place,
> and the dangers he would have to broach in new wars.

Especially indecorous is Ovid's reversal of Vergil's emphases in *Aeneid* 6: where Vergil draws out the machinery of Aeneas' initiation by the Sibyl, Ovid condenses it; and where Vergil expatiates on the geography of the underworld and the stories recounted by the ghosts of Aeneas' past, Ovid reduces them to bald summary. Worst of all, where Vergil is brief, Ovid offers unseemly expansion (*Met.* 14.120–1): *inde ferens lassos aduerso tramite passus | cum duce Cumaea mollit sermone laborem* ("From there, bearing his weary paces on the return journey, he lightens the task in conversation with his Cumaean guide"). Ovid here alludes once again to the Vergilian Sibyl's portentous lines (*Aen.* 6.128–9): *sed reuocare gradum superasque euadere ad auras | hoc opus hic labor est* ("But to retrace your steps and walk out to the upper air – this is the work, this is the labour"). As Sara Myers explains, "Ovid exploits in his typically humorous literal manner the Sibyl's claim ... that Aeneas' greatest task will be to win his way back out of the Underworld"; as she also notes, however, "Vergil's Aeneas had found it in fact much easier to get out of the Underworld than to descend into it."[25] With this quip, moreover, Ovid introduces the story of Apollo's attempted seduction of the Sibyl along with his gift to her of prophetic power and an extended old age, subjects beneath the epic dignity of the poet of the *Aeneid* though undoubtedly consistent with Ovid's earlier composition of amatory elegy.

III. *De Profundis*

The last laugh, however, belonged to the *princeps,* who in relegating Ovid gave him the opportunity to experience the torments of the underworld fi st hand. It is in the exile poetry that Ovid's evocations of the Vergilian underworld align portentous atmospherics with an appropriately sombre tone. As is well known, Ovid depicts Tomis and the region of his exile in terms suggestive of the underworld.[26] Thus he represents the night of his departure from Rome as that of his death, with his household in mourning as if at his funeral (*Tr.* 1.3.1–2, 21–4):

> Cum subit illius tristissima noctis imago,
> qua mihi supremum tempus in urbe fuit ...
> quocumque aspiceres, luctus gemitusque sonabant,
> formaque non taciti funeris intus erat.

femina uirque meo, pueri quoque funere maerent,
inque domo lacrimas angulus omnis habet.

When the image of that exceedingly sad night recurs to me,
which was my final occasion in the city
Wherever you looked mourning and lamentation re-
sounded, and there was the sense of a noisy funeral within.
Women and men, children and slaves grieve at my
funeral, and in the house, every corner had tears.

Throughout the exile poetry, moreover, Ovid repeatedly likens relegation to death as, for example, in *Tr.* 3.3.53–4: *cum patriam amisi, tunc me periise putato:* | *et prior et grauior mors fuit illa mihi* ("Believe that I died then, when I lost my native land; and that death of mine was earlier and more grievous").[27]

More portentous still, however, is his characterization of the inhospitable region of Tomis as a *locus inamabilis* (*Tr.* 5.7.43–4): *siue locum specto, locus est* inamabilis, *et quo* | *esse nihil toto tristius orbe potest* ("Or if I look at the place, the *unlovely* place, than which there can be none sadder in the whole world"). For this is the same adjective as that with which the Ovidian Tisiphone describes the underworld in the fourth book of the *Metamorphoses* (4.477–8): *inamabile regnum* | *desere* ("leave the unlovely kingdom") and as Venus describes it again in *Metamorphoses* 14 (*Met.* 14.590–1): *satis est inamabile regnum* | *aspexisse semel, Stygios semel isse per amnes* ("it's enough to have seen the unlovely kingdom once, to have traversed the Stygian stream once"). In both passages, the Ovidian speakers borrow a Vergilian coinage describing the waters of the underworld (*Geo.* 4.479): *Cocyti tardaque palus inamabilis unda* ("the sluggish pool of Cocytus, an unlovely stream"; cf. *Aen.* 6.438: … *tristisque palus inamabilis undae*). Here at last, in the poetry of his relegation, Ovid matches his predecessor's portentous theme to his own newly funereal tone in a final evocation of the Vergilian underworld.

NOTES

1 I cite Ovid's *Amores* and *Ars amatoria* from the edition of Kenney 1994; the *Metamorphoses* from Tarrant 2004; the *Tristia* from Owen 1915; and Vergil's *Aeneid* from Mynors 1969. Translations are my own unless otherwise indicated.

2 McKeown 1998: 107.

3 The otherworldly context of Corinna's epiphany is further enhanced by a possible reminiscence of *Aen.* 6.451–4, where Aeneas spies Dido's shade,

recognizing her "through the shadows, darkly, like a man who sees, or thinks he sees, the moon rising through the clouds at the beginning of the month" (*quam Troius heros | ut primum iuxta stetit agnouitque per umbras | obscuram, qualem primo qui surgere mense | aut uidet aut uidisse putat per nubile lunam*). See Hardie 2002: 44–5. On the *selva oscura* motif in *Aeneid* 6, see also Barchiesi in this volume.

4 On the reception of this passage in Senecan tragedy, Servian commentary, and in a letter by Mary Shelley, see Gladhill, Stok, and Kilgour, respectively, in this volume. On the intertextual importance of Ovid's *Ars amatoria*, and his Cretan tales there and in *Metamorphoses* 8, in Seneca's *Phaedra*, see also Gladhill in this volume, with further bibliography.

5 Conte 1994: 83, discussing the epic poetry of Ennius and Livius Adronicus.

6 Sharrock 1994: 87–195.

7 On Seneca's reception of this passage in the *Phaedra*, see Gladhill in this volume.

8 Bill Gladhill observes (*per litteras*) that Ovid's competition here with the most prominent members of the classical epic tradition is set within "a sort of Dream Theatre in which all the elements of dreaming reflect stagecraft and actin , mimesis."

9 *OLD s.v. imago* 1, 3, and 7, esp. 7(b).

10 I quote from Allen 1917.

11 My thanks to one of the referees for this formulation of Ovid's play with fictions at this point in his "Ceyx and Alcyone."

12 I am grateful to Bill Gladhill for the phrasing here.

13 I am grateful to one of the referees for drawing out these paradoxes in Ovid's meditation on fictionality at this point in the passag . Vergil seems to comment on the dreamlike quality of his underworld, in his notice of Aeneas' departure from it through the gates of ivory *his ibi tum natum Anchises unaque Sibyllam | prosequitur dictis portaque emittit eburna* ("Then after his disquisition there, Anchises accompanies his son together with the Sibyl and sends them forth from the ivory gate," *Aen.* 6.897–8).

14 Cf. Anderson 1963.

15 Quotation from Burrow 1999: 275.

16 Hinds 1998: 1–10.

17 Cicero cites the Ennian lines as part of an argument against the Epicurean analysis of religious superstition: *quae est anus tam delira, quae timeat ista, quae uos uidelicet, si physica non didicissetis, timeretis, "Acherunsia templa alta Orci, pallida | leti, nubile tenebris loca"? non pudet philosophum in eo gloriari, quod haec non timeat et quod falsa esse cognouerit?* ("What superstitious old woman is so weak as to fear these 'deep Acherousian regions of Hell, pale with death, places cloudy with shadows,' which you would clearly fear if you hadn't

learned physics? Isn't a philosopher ashamed to boast of the fact that he doesn't fear these things and that he recognizes them to be false?").

18 Burrow 1999: 276. On the *lugentes campi*, see Myers in this volume.

19 Bill Gladhill reminds me (*per litteras*) that Vergil's sensitivity to epic decorum requires that his Olympian gods respect the integrity of the underworld from which they are shut off. "In the *Metamorphoses*, the cosmology is more permeable," with the Olympian gods reaching a quasi-Roman Tartarus and men like Caesar and Augustus making their way to Olympus.

20 I quote Tibullus from Lee, rev. Maltby 1990.

21 Cf. Tib. 1.3.69–70.

22 On Servius' discussion of the punishment of sinners in Vergil's underworld, see Stok in this volume.

23 On Tibullus 1.3 and *Aeneid* 6, see also Myers in this volume.

24 On Ovid's close attention to Vergil's diction in this section of the *Metamorphoses*, see Myers 2009: *ad loc.*

25 Myers 2009: 81–2.

26 Nagle 1980: 22–32; Evans 1983: 34–8, 54–6, 59, 65–7, 71–3, 134–7; Doblhofer 1978 and 1987: 169–73; Videau-Delibes 1991: 333–64; Williams 1994: 12–13; and Grebe 2010, with extensive bibliography.

27 Cf., e.g., *Tr.* 5.9.19, *P.* 1.8.27, 4.9.74.

8

Mortem aliquid ultra est: Vergil's Underworld in Senecan Tragedy

BILL GLADHILL

In discussing the "disturbed emotional states" of Senecan tragedy, Richard Tarrant states that "[I]t is as if Seneca had taken up residence in the darkest corner of the Virgilian imagination," a sentiment which channels Charles Segal's powerful analysis of Seneca twelve years earlier: "[T]he powerful symbol of the underworld, corresponding to the darker hell of the soul, finds a place in nearly every Senecan Tragedy."[1] It is difficult not to read Segal into Tarrant, and to suggest that the "darker hell of the soul" and the "darkest corner of the Virgilian imagination" waft from the gloom of Vergil's *Aeneid* 6. No other text influenced Seneca more as a tragedian; he returns to it again and again and again.[2] Heroes (Hercules and Theseus) and demons (Tantalus and Thyestes) tumble onto stage from a Vergilian underworld.[3] Horrific topographies – like the infernal groves in the *Oedipus* and the *Thyestes* – are cut from *selva oscura* of *Aeneid* 6, emphasizing the deep infl - ence of Vergil's groves, as Alessandro Barchiesi discusses in chapter 1.[4] So, too, the sounds of Vergil's hell rebound against and echo throughout Seneca's tragic phonosphere, whether the three throats of Cerberus, the doleful groans of mourning woods, or the bellowing of underworld shades. Thebes in the fi st choral ode of the *Oedipus* is literarily enveloped by Vergil's poetic hell, where the "fi st city" becomes the site of necromantic revelation, as the tragic dead vertically ascend to the dramatic space of a Romanized Thebes.[5] In the *Thyestes*, at the behest of a Fury, Tantalus impregnates the tragic stage with the dark pollution of Tartarean satiation. The entire episode is Allectine. More emphatically, the messenger's speech reveals the deep and secret recesses of the House of Atreus, where we move through a pastiche of images culled from *Aeneid* 6, from hellish woods, to Stygian swamps, *manes*, Cerberan barks, and a gloomy, Sibylline *sacerdos* in the form of Atreus (*Th.* 614–716).[6] *Aeneid* 6 lurks in every corner, like a "shadow text."[7]

Senecan Tragedy represents one of the more vital instances of Vergilian reception in the Latin literary tradition.[8] But it is a reception in parts and flashe , incorporating discrete episodes of *Aeneid* 6 into each tragedy. *En masse*, Seneca's utilization of *Aeneid* 6 is totalizing, but in isolation, each tragedy responds to (primarily) a single scene. Yet, they all reflect the ways Senecan Tragedy embodied Vergilian epic and built it into its dramatic system.[9] I am not interested in giving a complete impression of Seneca's use of *Aeneid* 6 in all of his tragedies. Rather, the present analysis focuses on three tragedies, the *Hercules Furens*, *Phaedra*, and *Oedipus*. These tragedies offer succinct and critical reflections of Seneca's employment of Vergilian allusion in Julio-Claudian drama.

Outside of Lucan's *Bellum Ciuile* and Statius' *Thebaid*, Seneca's *Hercules Furens* represents the longest and most sustained engagement with the *Aeneid* – and *Aeneid* 6, in particular – in Roman literature.[10] Juno's opening monologue is broadly modelled on the goddess' speeches in *Aeneid* 1 and 10.[11] The relationship between *uirtus* and *furor* in *Hercules Furens* is largely a reflection and refraction of the roles of *pietas* and *furor* in the *Aeneid*. Hercules and Aeneas become dramatically linked (as they are in *Aeneid* 8), as one hero, marked by *uirtus*, and the other, by *pietas*, both undergo apotheosis after succumbing to the destructive potential of *furor*. Structurally, each text is split nearly in half by their mutual underworld descents. The *katabaseis* of Aeneas and Hercules become palimpsestic journeys, where beneath the hellish topography of the *Hercules Furens* are the poetic contours of Vergil's underworld and its own literary antecedents, including Hercules' own prior descents in Greek literature.[12]

The cluster of allusions between the two texts is particularly dense. For example, like the woods around Avernus (*tenent media omnia siluae*, "the woods take hold of the middle in its entirety," *Aen.* 6.131), Taenarus presses upon the sea with its dense woods (*densis ubi aequor Taenarus siluis premit*, *HF* 663). Taenarus does not now, and most likely did not then, have anything like a forest pressing upon the sea. The woods' description in *Hercules Furens* is a result of the geopoetic affiliation with Vergil's Cumae.[13] Seneca's *hic ora soluit Ditis inuisi domus | hiatque rupes alta et immenso specu | ingens uorago faucibus uastis patet* ("Here the house of hated Dis opens its mouth and the rock gapes deep and in an immense cave a huge chasm opens with its vast maw," *HF* 664–6) and *nocte sic mixta solet | praebere lumen primus aut serus dies* ("[I]n such a way with night mingled is dawn or dusk accustomed to offer light," 671–2) reconceptualize Vergil's *noctes atque dies patet atri ianua Ditis* ("the door of dark Dis lies open night and day," *Aen.*

6.127) and *hinc uia Tartarei quae fert Acherontis ad undas | turbidus hic caeno uastaque uoragine gurges | aestuat atque omnem Cocyto eructat harenam* ("From here this road leads to Tartarean Acheron's waters. Here thick with mire and a vast abyss the whirlpool seethes and into Cocytus belches all of its sand," *Aen.* 6.295–7). Both underworlds conflate the imagery of a house, open night and day, along with devouring jaws and a swirling whirlpool. Vergil's famous formulation, *sed reuocare gradum superasque euadere ad auras, | hoc opus, hic labor est* ("but to recall one's step and to pass out into the air above, this is the work, this is the labour," 6.128–9) is reworked by Seneca as (*HF* 675–9):

nec ire labor est; ipsa deducit uia
ut saepe puppes aestus inuitas rapit,
sic pronus aer urguet atque auidum chaos,
gradumque retro flectere haut umquam sinun
umbrae tenaces.

And the labour is not in going; the very path leads down just as a storm often seizes hold of unwilling ships, in the same way the sinking air and greedy chaos urge on, and in no way at all ever do the gripping shades allow anyone to bend back their step.

Seneca adds a simile that analogizes the tenacious pull of the shades – and the pressing influence of the *aer* and *chaos* – to the rapacity of a storm upon ships. The force of winds upon ships comes to represent the unseen grip of the dead. In effect, Seneca unpacks the precise cosmological causes that make an underworld return an *opus* and *labor*, as the *aer*, *chaos*, and the hellish shades have the same force as a tempest upon ships. The gravitational pull of death is as much a law of nature as the wind.[14]

Likewise, Theseus' description of Charon (*HF* 764–72) clearly draws on Vergil's ferryman (*Aen.* 6.298–304). While Vergil states *canities inculta iacet* ("his white hair lies unkempt," 300), Seneca uses *impexa pendet barba* ("a tangled beard hangs down," 766), a phrase that alludes to *impexis … barbis* at *Georgics* 3.366, in a description of northern tribes that is wholly connected to traditions related to the Cimmerians.[15] In place of Vergil's *stant lumina flamma* ("his eyes are set in flam ," *Aen.* 6.300), Seneca stresses *concauae lucent genae* ("his hollow cheeks glimmer," *HF* 767). The luminosity of the Senecan Charon's sunken cheeks reflects the fiery eyes of Vergil's Charon. Each Charon guides his skiff in similar ways: *ipse ratem conto subigit uelisque ministrat* ("he himself with a pole propels the boat and with sails guides it," 6.302) in Vergil and *regit ipse longo portitor conto ratem* ("the ferryman himself directs the boat with a long pole," *HF* 768) in Seneca.

Seneca's Charon (*cultu et aspectu horridus … squalidus … deformem sinum nodus coercet,* "in style and appearance horrid … squalid … a knot ties his unsightly garment's fold," 764–7) borrows his clothing from Vergil (*sordidus ex umeris nodo dependet amictus,* "a foul cloak hangs down from his shoulders by a knot," 6.301). The two texts construct a coherent and consistent description of Charon, with each focusing on a slightly different, but related, element. This reverberation is emblematic of the relationship between *Hercules Furens* and the *Aeneid,* more generally. *Aeneid* 6 is the master text behind Theseus' description of Hercules' descent. This is beyond doubt. Yet, both narratives exist in a sort of ponderous simultaneity. Allusion constructs a static textual space. One underworld is focalized through Aeneas, the other through Theseus, and their descriptions cohere. Allusion confirms and reifie . *Hercules Furens* cements Vergil's *Aeneid* 6 as The Underworld.

Hercules Furens also shows marked divergences from *Aeneid* 6. When Aeneas fi st meets Charon, he asks the Sibyl about the *turba* crowded along the confluence of a number of underworld rivers (*uia … fert Acherontis ad undas,* 6.295; *omnem Cocyto eructat harenam,* 6.297; *Cocyti stagna alta … Stygiamque paludem,* 6.323; *Stygias undas* 6.376), until he sees Palinurus, who then gives an extended retelling of the end of *Aeneid* 5. The same narrative dilation is repeated with Dido, Deiphobus, and Anchises, where movement through the underworld slows to a stop as Aeneas talks to ghosts. Seneca's Hercules does not "endure any delays" (*non passus ullas natus Alcemena moras, HF* 773). Hercules says nothing and then beats up Charon with his oar: *ipso coactum nauitam conto domat* ("the ferry man compelled by his very pole Hercules subdues," 774). Hercules and Aeneas board the same boat. While the boat groans under Aeneas' weight as it takes in water from the marshy Styx: *simul accipit alueo | ingentem Aenean. gemuit sub pondere cumba | sutilis et multam accepit rimosa paludem* ("at the same time he accepts huge Aeneas onto the boat. Under his weight the fitted skiff groaned and through its fissures took in much water," *Aen.* 6.412–14), Hercules' ship drinks in the river Lethe from each of its sides, which Seneca marks with the cluster of *t* and *b* sounds imitating the sound of the Lethe's trickling into the skiff: *sidit et grauior ratis | utrimque Lethen latere titubanti bibit* ("he sits down and the boat made heavier on each side drinks up the river Lethe over its tottering side," *HF* 776–7). While Vergil stresses the hugeness of Aeneas with the elided *ingentAenean,* Seneca ironically states that a boat, which could take on nations, succumbs only *uni,* "to one" (*cumba populorum capax | succubuit uni,* "the skiff capacious of nations succumbed to one," 775–6). The ponderous rhythm of huge Aeneas is humorously replaced by the slight "one."

The divergences continue when, after crossing the river Lethe, Hercules sees numerous monsters he has conquered (*HF* 778–81):

tunc uicta trepidant monstra, Centauri truces
Lapithaeque multo in bella succensi mero;
Stygiae paludis ultimos quaerens sinus
fecunda mergit capita Lernaeus labor.

Then the conquered monsters shook, the savage Centaurs and the Lapiths inflamed to wars in their great drunkenness; while searching for the last secrets of the Stygian bog, the Lernaean labour sinks its abundant heads.

The passage joins Aeneas' encounter with imaginary monsters at the entrance to the underworld to his encounter with the Argive dead shaking with great fear (*ingenti trepidare metu, Aen.* 6.491). The mass of intertextuality magnifies the inconsistency of the underworld topography through which each hero travels. This inconsistent geopoetic space between *Hercules Furens* and *Aeneid* 6 is part of a broader theme discussed by Alessandro Barchiesi and Emily Pillinger in the present volume. Seneca has contracted the boundaries of Vergil's underworld in *Hercules Furens,* as though it were a space to be expanded by future heroes, whose deeds and journeys become part of an expanding, imperial *katabasis,* even if these descents of future heroes come earlier in the literary tradition. So, Hercules' monsters become "stabled" (*stabulant*) near the entryway of Vergil's underworld (*Aen.* 6.285–9), as Charon's embarkation point is moved from the river Lethe to the Styx, and various *campi* (6.441, 6.640, 6.887) are set between the Styx and Lethe. Essentially, Seneca imagines an underworld prior to the imperial expansion of Aeneas' *katabasis*. Seneca's underworld exhibits an awareness of the urban reorganization of Avernus and Cumae already built into *Aeneid* 6, as Barchiesi discusses above, and is continued in Statius' own reinvention of the Cumaean Sibyl on the Via Domitiana, as Pillinger has addressed. Seneca's underworld in *Hercules Furens* is markedly pre-urban from this perspective. To this end, Hercules' return takes a single line – in a *postquam* clause nonetheless – while the *Aeneid* deliberates on the nature of return itself after a long tour throughout the rest of the expansive underworld.[16] Vergil's underworld is an urban park; Seneca's is a stream with a bog and some monsters.

Seneca's allusions to *Aeneid* 6 occur at such a high frequency that an aural effect is achieved. *Aeneid* 6 can be heard in the background of Theseus' underworld ecphrasis, as though he has culled his own telling from lines of the *Aeneid*. What do we make of this marked and consistent allusive strategy? Outside of the topographical changes to Vergil's underworld, the allusions are relatively innocuous. They capture the mood and atmosphere of *Aeneid* 6, which then becomes the authorized, master text of Seneca's katabatic narrative. The aural resonances between the two texts are so pronounced that they are part of the auditory experience of Seneca's *Hercules Furens*. Seneca's ultimate aim here may simply be for pleasure and entertainment. We ought to imagine Seneca's audience hearing the vast array of literary allusions to a text that held the central position of sublime poetry in Roman literature.[17] The allusions are not recherché. They do not promote notions of correction nor is their recognition requisite for deeper levels of analysis. In fact, one could cut the entire *katabasis* from *Hercules Furens* without any real violation of textual or dramatic integrity (the same is true of *Aeneid* 6). The recognition of the allusions and their subtle interactions offer a window into what brought literary pleasure to Seneca's audience, the sublime poetry of *katabasis* replete with continual (and sometimes humorous) references to Vergil. So Aeneas delays around the Stygian waters in conversation. Hercules hurries without saying a word. Charon's flicke - ing eyes in Vergil cast shadows over his cheeks in Seneca. Huge Aeneas is replaced by *unus*. The monsters Aeneas fears shudder in fear of Hercules. Hercules' descent ends with the capture of Cerberus and his quick exit, while Aeneas plods through post-Herculean mythic and historic time, dragging Allecto after him in the following book, like a ghoulish anti-Eurydice. Charon's skiff is filled with the water of two different rivers, one of which is the liquid form of forgetfulness. Seneca's Lethe results in the topography forgetting itself, as a few lines later in *Hercules Furens* the Hydra hides in the *palus Stygia* (780). The entire topography of the river Lethe in the Elysium fields in *Aeneid* 6, too, is effaced. The Lethe, famous in Vergil for spiritual oblivion in the process of reincarnation, sloshes about the feet of Seneca's Hercules. The underworld has yet to expand its frontiers, to be Vergilianized, while alluding wholly to Vergil. The underworld is inchoate and progressive. The interplay between the two texts ought to be read in terms of the aural reception of Senecan recitation and performance.[18]

We might even imagine it in the context of recitation pieces of Neronian underworlds in which *Aeneid* 6, *Bellum Ciuile* 6, Petronius' *Cena Trimalchionis*, and *Hercules Furens* could be performed, read, and appreciated in light of one another as adaptive responses to poetic underworlds. *Aeneid* 6 was an instant classic, and a particularly fruitful text for poetic exploitation, if we follow the lead of Ovid's Sibyl, who referentially calls it *regna nouissima mundi* (14.111) in clear reference to Vergil's *regna* in *Aeneid* 6 (*regna inuia uiuis*, 6.154; *inania regna*, 6.269; *haec … regna*, 6.417; *durissima regna* of Tartarus, 6.566). These *regna* can be incorporated into narratives, immediately heightening the intensity and deepening the meaning of texts. It is impossible not to read Lucan *Bellum Ciuile* 6 without recognizing that he is in complete dialogue with *Aeneid* 6 on multiple levels.[19] Petronius' *cena Trimalchionis* clearly orbits *Aeneid* 6, but Petronius works within another tradition as well.[20] He was more than aware that *katabasis* has a particularly Platonic flar , which extends beyond just the allegory of the cave and the myth of Er in the *Republic* to include the *Symposium* and *Phaedo,* in particular.[21] Petronius maps the *Symposium* upon the katabatic *cena,* while his Trimalchio becomes anti-Platonic through a continual critique of Plato's *Phaedo* and through wholly obliterating the notion of Platonic forms as outlined in the Republic. In Trimalchio's life and afterlife there is no guiding Sibyl or Platonic Anchises (see Gowers in this volume), and there can certainly be no Platonic forms; just food within food within more food. There is no Sun to illuminate truth. And so reality hides realities within realities within realities. Trimalchio's underworld is merely shadow and shade, where even the Sibyl wishes only to die (*Sat.* 48). Trimalchio's epitaph says it all: *nec unquam philosophum audiuit* ("he never listened to a philosopher," *Sat.* 71). But he read Vergil. The audience of Seneca's *HF* was certainly engaging in a much broader reorientation and assessment of *Aeneid* 6.

Scholarship on the influences on Senecan drama has drawn a complicated picture of literary tragedy.[22] It is likely the case that Seneca's engagement with tragedy occurred both as a reader (and listener) of Graeco-Roman tragedy and as a spectator of theatrical tragedy. He understood tragedy extremely well. But Seneca has also overlaid his tragic design with, at times, a mind-boggling array of allusions to Augustan poets. Part of the scenery and stagecraft of Senecan tragedy is this powerful engagement with Augustan literature.[23] In many ways, his allusive interaction with models functions like a literary *skene*. Much of the tension of his dramas is built into the idea that his characters are walking onto a stage that has already been shaped by the performance of prior tragedies and texts over the centuries. In addition, there is a sense that an active and miasmatic underworld seethes underneath the stage. It is understood that the vertical force of hell flows into and blends with the horizontal space of the tragic stage. As *Hercules Furens* shows, this space is almost entirely formed and shaped by Vergil.

Seneca's *Phaedra* also has an underworld built into its theatrics. Early in the tragedy Phaedra states that illicit marriage beds have driven Theseus to the underworld (*stupra et illicitos toros | Acheronte in imo quaerit Hippolyti pater,* "the father of Hippolytus searches for debaucheries and illicit marriage beds in deep Acheron," *Ph.* 97–8). Later in the drama, Theseus comes on stage directly from Tartarus, where he had been wandering for four years (*iam quarta Eleusin dona Triptolemi secat,* "already for the fourth time does Eleusis divide the gifts of Triptolemus," 838).[24] Theseus in Euripides' *Hippolytus* enters the dramatic space from Delphi, Seneca's Theseus from hell. The shift is vital; the erotic thrust of the drama between Phaedra and Hippolytus is conterminous with Theseus' escape from the underworld. Seneca emphatically builds the underworld into the architecture and meaning of his tragedy. In this regard, Theseus' fi st words on stage are suggestive (840–9):

ambiguus ut me sortis ignotae labor
detinuit inter mortis et uitae mala ...
heu, labor quantus fuit
Phlegethonte ab imo petere longinquum aethera
pariterque mortem fugere et Alciden sequi.

When an ambiguous labor of an unknown fate detained me between the evils of death and life ... alas, how great a labour it was to search for the distant upper air from deep Phlegethon and equally to flee death and follow Alcides.

While these lines clearly gesture to Vergil's *sed reuocare gradum superasque euadere ad auras, | hoc opus, hic labor est* (*Aen.* 6.128–9; see discussion above), they likewise share verbal echoes with another passage in *Aeneid* 6, the ecphrasis on the doors of the temple of Apollo (*Aen.* 6.23–30):

contra elata mari respondet Cnosia tellus:
hic crudelis amor tauri, suppostaque furto
Pasiphaë, mixtumque genus prolesque biformis
Minotaurus inest, Veneris monimenta nefandae;
hic labor ille domus et inextricabilis error;
magnum reginae sed enim miseratus amorem
Daedalus ipse dolos tecti ambagesque resoluit,
caeca regens filo uestigia

In contrast, upraised from the sea responds the Cnosian land: here the cruel love of the bull, and Pasiphaë furtively falsified and the mixed species and the biform offspring is there, the Minotaur, the monuments of unholy Venus; here is that labour and that inextricable wandering of the house; but indeed, having taken pity on the great passion of the queen, Daedalus himself resolved the tricks of the abode and its twisted turnings, guiding blind footsteps with a string.

Among the many complex engagements of Seneca's *Phaedra* with its literary models – including the two *Hippolyti* of Euripides as well as the foundational elegiac systems in Ovid's works (Seneca's Phaedra surely read Ovid's *Ars Amatoria*) – the opening ecphrasis of *Aeneid* 6 is manifestly influentia .[25] Seneca embeds many of the themes found in the ecphrasis and encodes them in his tragic design. In the passage above Seneca imitates the narrative connection between Aeneas' underworld descent and the myth of Pasiphae, the Minotaur, and Daedalus. From Pasiphae's insertion into the bovine simulacrum, to the Minotaur's imprisonment in the *error inextricabilis*, the threading of the labyrinth, and finally to the fall of Icarus, Vergil's ecphrasis is replete with allusions to Theseus in Catullus 64.[26] Vergil's language applies simultaneously to Daedalus and Theseus, aligning the creator of the labyrinth with the only hero to have escaped its ambiguities with Ariadne's thread. Seneca's Theseus gestures to his own literary tradition through Vergil to Catullus upon his arrival on stage from the underworld.

Seneca's *Phaedra* draws further correspondences between Theseus and Daedalus. Theseus describes his ascent from the underworld as *patuit ad caelum uia* ("The road opened to the sky," *Ph.* 1213), recalling the flight of Daedalus, filtered through *Met* 8.186: *et caelum certe patet; ibimus illac* ("certainly the sky is open, we will go there"). In addition, Theseus' prayer to Neptune results in the creation of a bullish (*taurus*, *Ph.* 1036), biform sea monster: *tum pone tergus ultima in monstrum coit | facies et ingens belua immensam trahit | squamosa partem* ("then behind the back its hindmost shape comes together into a monster and the massive, coiling leviathan drags its immense tail," 1046–8), overtly recalling the Minotaur as Hippolytus emphatically states: *haud frangit animum uanus hic terror meum: | nam mihi paternus uincere est tauros labor* ("this empty terror shatters my resolve not at all: for it is my paternal labour to conquer bulls," 1066–7).[27] Both the ecphrasis and the tragedy end with fathers mourning their sons. Underworlds, bulls, mazes, illicit sex, and dead sons encourage a more sustained analysis of Seneca's strategy in alluding to *Aeneid* 6.

Daedalus, Pasiphae, the Minotaur, the labyrinth, and Icarus in *Aeneid* 6 are fundamental to the tragic architecture of Seneca's *Phaedra*. In order to understand Seneca's engagement with *Aeneid* 6, it is necessary to discuss briefly some of the key themes of the ecphrasis. Servius *ad Aen.* 6.14 highlights a complex system of human-bovine reproduction that draws a number of important correspondences worth assessing:

igitur Pasiphae, Solis filia Minois regis Cretae uxor, tauri amore flagrauit et arte Daedali inclusa intra uaccam ligneam, saeptam corio iuuencae pulcherrimae, cum tauro concubuit, unde natus est Minotaurus, qui intra labyrinthum inclusus humanis carnibus uescebatur.

Moreover, Pasiphae, the daughter of the Sun, the wife of Minos, the king of Crete, burned with passion for a bull and through the art of Daedalus was confined within a wooden cow, which was covered in the hide of a most beautiful heifer. She had sex with a bull and from this was produced the Minotaur, who having been confined within the labyrinth feasted on human flesh

Servius *ad Aen.* 6.14 describes a cascading series of inclusions and incorporations, which eventually culminates in his rationalizing account of the Minotaur where Vergil's *mixtum genus* points to Pasiphae's giving birth (*peperit, enixa*) to twins (*geminos*), one belonging to Minos and the other to a certain Taurus, a *notarius* of Minos, hence the name Minotaurus. Pasiphae is confined (*inclusa*) within a cow simulacrum and is then impregnated by a bull (*concubuit*). A bull-monster (or twins) then gestates within her womb, until she gives birth and her offspring is confined (*inclusus*) in the winding dungeon of Daedalus' labyrinth, where it consumes human flesh [28] Pasiphae is incorporated into a wooden bull and within her becomes incorporated the Minotaur. At the moment the Minotaur is born, it is again enclosed for a second time into the vertiginous labyrinth. Pasiphae is to the wooden cow as the Minotaur is to the labyrinth while the movement of bull semen through Pasiphae's womb is analogized to the movement of children through the labyrinth until they reach the Minotaur's mouth. In this series of correspondences and analogies, Pasiphae's womb and the labyrinth are linked.[29] The labyrinth becomes a metaphorical emblem of the womb. In fact, the noun *uolua/uulua* ("turning-rolling around") could mean womb, which itself was thought "to wander" in Plato's (among others') view.[30] The twisted internalizations from Pasiphae's inclusion in the heifer, to her enclosing the bull's semen in her womb, are recapitulated upon the birth of the Minotaur, as it becomes enclosed within a womb-like work of Daedalus. The only exit from the labyrinth is through the jaws of the Minotaur itself (that is, until Theseus). Daedalus' heifer catalyzes internality after internality to the point where birth and death merge with the semiotics of labyrinthine error. Aeneas' underworld descent in *Aeneid* 6 opens with a myth on the dark origins of life and birth. Whereas Pasiphae's inclusion results in birth, the Minotaur's inclusion results in death, within a mythic system that aligns each along a similarly marked ontological aporia; the origins of life and the afterlife are equal conundra.[31] Alberto Pérez-Gómez states that "[T]he labyrinth is a metaphor of human existence: ever-changing, full of surprise, uncertain, conveying the impression of disorder, a *gap*, (chaos understood in the etymological sense) between the only two certain points that it possesses birth (entrance) and death (its centre)."[32] This is certainly right, but labyrinths are also a function of texts and contexts, and in the case of *Aeneid* 6 the origins of life and the nature of the afterlife are powerfully aligned.

It has been noticed that Seneca's bull engages in detail with Vergil's *Georgics* and particularly martial epic moments of the *Aeneid*.[33] But its precise relationship with Vergil's ecphrasis on Cumae is less clear, especially given the semiotic distortions and potentialities of Daedalus' labyrinth. In place of confounding internalizations – from Pasiphae's inclusion in a wooden heifer to the Minotaur's growth inside the womb and then subsequent imprisonment – Hippolytus himself becomes the node upon which labyrinthine externalization and internalization coincide. In fact, the entire narrative sequence of the ecphrasis collapses upon him at once. Theseus' prayer to Neptune replicates Minos' prayer in the mythic tradition; the sea-bull itself becomes a conflation of Minos' bull (see below), Daedalus' bull, and the Minotaur (see above); Hippolytus' death runs parallel to the death of Icarus; Daedalus and Theseus become mourning fathers. Seneca, however, effectively blurs and blends the sea-bull with nature itself. The natural landscape – which Hippolytus had encompassed and conquered at the beginning of the tragedy (*Ph.* 1–84), into which he himself had entered (*uocor in siluas,* "I am called to the woods," *Ph.* 82) – now tears him apart.[34] The *taurus* in the *Phaedra* becomes quickly conflated with the natural landscape of the poem. First, the earth shakes (*terrae tremuere,* "the earth trembled," *Ph.* 1050), which causes Hippolytus' horses to deviate from their course in language that is reminiscent of Icarus' (and Phaethon's) descent (*iamque derrantes uia,* "now wandering off course," *Ph.* 1069). The monster continues to rush Hippolytus (*nam toto obuius | incurrit ore corniger ponti horridus,* "for against him with full boldness did the horrid horn-bearer of the sea rush," *Ph.* 1080–1), until he is tossed from the chariot (*praeceps in ora fusus implicuit cadens | laqueo tenaci corpus,* "poured headlong onto his face, falling he entwined his body in his fast-holding rein," *Ph.* 1085–6). The natural landscape then obliterates Hippolytus as fields (*arua, Ph.* 1093) become bloodied with his head (*inlisum caput, Ph.* 1093) rebounding against the rocks (*scopulis*). His hairs (*comas, Ph.* 1094) are pulled out by the brambles (*dumi, Ph.* 1094), and his face (*ora, Ph.* 1095) is battered by a rock (*lapis, Ph.* 1095), until a long stake impales his groin (*tandemque raptum truncus ambusta sude | medium per inguen stipite ingesto tenet,* "at last a tree trunk with a burnt stake holds him seized in the middle as a branch was thrust through his groin," 1098–9). He explodes (*pariter moram | dominumque rumpunt,* "they burst their delay and their master at the same time," *Ph.* 1101–2) with the "butcher's broom" (*omnis ruscus*) bearing part of his body (*corporis partem tulit, Ph.* 1104).[35] The landscape and Hippolytus' body merge into a unified whole with little distinction between the places through which the slaves wander and where they find Hippolytus' body parts (*errant per agros funebris famuli manus, | per illa qua distractus Hippolytus loca | longum cruenta tramitem signat nota,* "bands of slaves wander through the funereal field , where Hippolytus, having been ripped to pieces through those places, signs a long tract with a gory mark," *Ph.* 1105–7). The physical union between Pasiphae and the bull has undergone a radical shift that still finds its *telos* with an act of penetration (*per inguen, Ph.* 1099).

Nature penetrates Hippolytus to the point of annihilation. In the process, he becomes a sort of inverted Pasiphae.[36] A bull penetrates Pasiphae *in siluis,* who gives birth to the Minotaur, which is then imprisoned in a labyrinth. The landscape itself in the *Phaedra* penetrates Hippolytus, whose body then undergoes a marked semiotic expansion as it becomes both a sign of Daedalus' labyrinth and an underworld maze. This blurring between labyrinthine error and death (*errant per agros funebris, Ph.* 1105) recalls the relationship between the opening ecphrasis of *Aeneid* 6 and the subsequent descent into the underworld. In fact, when Theseus recognizes his crime, he curses himself to Vergil's Tartarus: *grauiora uidi, quae pati clausos iubet | Phlegethon nocentes igneo cingens uado. | quae poena memet maneat et sedes, scio* ("I saw very serious things, which Phlegethon orders the prisoners to endure, encircling the guilty with a flaming stream. I know what penalty, what *seats* awaits me myself," *Ph.* 1226–8). The noun *sedes* in the mouth of Theseus is particularly marked given its Vergilian connection. The *Phaedra* affirms Vergil's *sedet aeternumque sedebit | infelix Theseus* ("unhappy Theseus sits and will sit for eternity," *Aen.* 6.617–18). Theseus knows what penalty and seat await him; he has experienced *sedes* already and he will experience them again (see Stok in this volume).

In fact, it is difficult not to read the final episode of the tragedy in Tartaran terms, as though Theseus has re-entered the underworld through the labyrinthine viscera of Hippolytus' flesh which he attempts to mould into the body of his son (*Ph.* 1256–60):

> disiecta, genitor, membra laceri corporis
> in ordinem dispone et errantes loco
> restitue partes: fortis hic dextrae locus,
> hic laeua frenis docta moderandis manus
> ponenda: laeui lateris agnosco notas.

Father, set in order the scattered limbs of a mangled body, and restore the parts straying from their place: this is the place for the brave right hand, here must be set the left hand, an expert in keeping the reins in due course: I recognize the familiar bits of his left side.

Hippolytus is atomized. He becomes a displaced system of bits and pieces, replicating Daedalus' labyrinth: right, then left, then left, from hand, to hand, to ribs. The language recalls Miguel Herrero's discussion above of Aeneas' ambulatory journey through the underworld, behind which stand the Orphic gold tablets and the underworld directions inscribed on them. All that remains of Hippolytus is the abject, becoming just gap and void. While Theseus attempts to recompose his son, he becomes lost in the wandering parts. As Theseus picks up the right and left hands of his son, he again moves through Vergil's description of the master craftsman Daedalus, whose successful *anabasis* is accompanied by the death of his son. Daedalus' hands drop in pantomimic performance of his plummeting son. Theseus too cannot recompose his son's body as he grips his son's hands.

The *Phaedra* and Daedalus' doors in *Aeneid* 6 converge at the end with the hands of Daedalus and Theseus: two fathers incapable of recomposing their sons in the contexts of labyrinths, monstrous births, underworld descents, and death. The maze of both narratives ends with absence. The ecphrasis ends with the ultimate labyrinth – total and complete darkness, a maze without a path, no twists, no turns, no markers, which might act as sightlines and directionality for the soul's movement through the death-scape. As Theseus attempts to solve the riddle of Hippolytus' obliterated body, he is faced with the reality that there is no solution, no escape.[37]

Seneca's *Hercules Furens* engaged with *Aeneid* 6 directly. The *Phaedra* moved in and around the book's opening ecphrasis to constellate a diverse set of issues related to death and birth, underworlds, labyrinths, and bodies. Seneca's *Oedipus* also moves through mazes, underworld descents, birth, and death, in which Seneca has situated a political rendering of *Aeneid* 6.[38] We see this constellation of features in the representation of the Sphinx herself. The Sphinx's riddles are labyrinthine: *nec Sphinga caecis uerba nectentem modis | fugi … nodosa sortis uerba et implexos dolos | ac triste carmen alitis solui ferae* ("nor did I flee the Sphinx, binding her words in unseen ways … I solved the knotted language of fate and the interwoven tricks and the gloomy song of the winged beast," *Oed*. 92–3, 101–2). Its monstrous physicality (and its consumption of humans in the manner of lions), along with the mazelike language of her riddles, links the Sphinx to the semantics of the underworld.[39] The riddle itself is concerned with the human life cycle, absenting from it the precise ontological conundrum of birth and death. The monstrous Sphinx is an embodied underworld, replete with labyrinths, jaws, death, and a riddle that spans the life of a human from birth to old age.

The Oedipus myth too is concerned with the confounding of the generational cycle.[40] The transition from infancy to adulthood into old age includes both an individual's life cycle as well normative generational cycles, in which the elderly give way to adults who have themselves produced a new generation of infants. The movement from 4 to 2 to 3 inscribes a broad generational system of continuity and order based upon normative reproduction and social order. Oedipus stands outside of this progression. At birth he is clipped. Rather than succeeding his father, he meets him at a crossroads. The meeting point of the three paths reflects the moment when infancy, adulthood, and old age converge. Linear, generational time rewinds into itself. The adult son kills his aged father, then retraces his father's footsteps to Thebes, re-entering his mother and her womb, catalyzing a series of doublets in which sons become brothers, daughters sisters, and mothers wives. Familial relationships become intertwined and labyrinthine. Oedipus replicates the Sphinx's riddle. The crippled and zigzagging Labdacid moves through – and unmasks – the riddling, labyrinthine tricks of the enigmatic Sphinx. The myth of the Sphinx had always moved through narratives of *katabasis* and the labyrinthine, as the narrative focuses on the double conundra: the origins of life and the moment of death in the context of generational order and progression. In ancient consciousness birth and death were fundamentally linked, a feature of thought we see in the similar representations of birth (*ad oras luminis*) and death (*ad fauces Orci*).[41]

So, Seneca's *Oedipus* includes an inbuilt, katabatic impregnation that allows for a seamless exploitation of underworld elements of *Aeneid* 6. For example, Seneca grafts onto his Oedipal groves (*Oed.* 153–79) the sylvan spaces of *Aeneid* 6, building into the framework of his tragedy Vergil's hellish environment (*Oed.* 530–47). When Creon returns from Delphi to relate the Pythia's prophecy, the prophetess emphatically gestures to the Sibyl: *incipit Letoa uates spargere horrentes comas | et pati commota Phoebum; contigit nondum specum, | emicat uasto fragore maior humano sonus* ("The Letoan prophet begins to spread her shaking hairs and moved to endure Phoebus; not yet has she reached the cave, a sound greater than something human breaks forth in a vast din," *Oed.* 230–2). The portrayal is a marked condensing of Vergil's expansive description of the Sibyl's ecstatic, prophetic state. Seneca's *commota* stands in place of *subito non uultus, non color unus* ("suddenly, her face was not uniform, nor her colour"). *Spargere horrentes comas* gestures to *non comptae mansere comae; sed pectus anhelum* ("her hair did not stay composed; her chest panted"). Likewise, the sound of Seneca's Pythia reimagines the impressive sonic crescendo of Vergil's Sibyl (*Aen.* 6.42–51):

excisum Euboicae latus ingens rupis in antrum
quo lati ducunt aditus centum, ostia centum,
unde ruunt totidem uoces, responsa Sibyllae …
et rabie fera corda tument, maiorque uideri

nec mortale sonans, adflata est numine quand
iam propiore dei.

A huge side of the Euboean rock is cut out into a cave where one hundred broad entry ways lead, one hundred mouths, from where rush as many voices, the responses of the Sibyl … and her heart swells with savage madness, and greater she resounds something that seems in no way mortal, when inspired by the divine power of the god, already so near.

Furthermore, *pati … Phoebum* (*Oed.* 230) responds to lines 77–82 where Vergil describes Apollo's overpowering influence over the Sibyl. Even their respective prophetic utterances show allusion: *ambage flexa Delphico mos est deo | arcana tegere* ("it is the custom for the God of Delphi to keep covered his arcane secrets bent with ambiguity," *Oed.* 214–15) and *talibus ex adyto dictis Cumaea Sibylla | horrendas canit ambages antroque remugit, | obscuris uera inuoluens* ("with such things spoken from the sanctuary the Cumaean Sibyl sings horrendous ambiguities and turning truth into obscurity she bellows in the cave," *Aen.* 6.98–100). Seneca succinctly filte s the Pythia through Vergil's iconoclastic Sibyl, who in turn becomes the model for Apollo's traditional prophetess.[42]

This alignment then opens literary space for Seneca's Teiresias to become something wholly new (a similar shift from a Sibylline Pythia to Erichtho is found in Lucan). Seneca's Teiresias takes on Charonic features.[43] Teiresias (*sacerdos intulit senior gradum, Oed.* 548) and Charon (*iam senior, Aen.* 6.304) are both "old." Teiresias is dressed nearly in the same costume as Charon (*Oed.* 551–5):

ipse funesto integit
uates amictu corpus et frondem quatit;
squalente cultu maestus ingreditur senex,
lugubris imos palla perfundit pedes,
mortifera canam taxus adstringit comam.

The prophet himself covers his body with a funereal cloak and shakes his garland; gloomy in his squalid appearance the old man approaches, the lugubrious robe pours down to the bottoms of his feet, a death-bearing yew branch keeps his white hair bound.

Compare *Aeneid* 6.298–301:

portitor has horrendus aquas et flumina serua
terribili squalore Charon, cui plurima mento

canities inculta iacet, stant lumina flamma
sordidus ex umeris nodo dependet amictus.

The horrendous ferryman keeps watch over these waters and rivers, Charon in his terrible squalour, on whose chin a mass of unkempt white hair lies, his eyes stand in flam , a sordid cloak hangs down from his shoulders by a knot.

Both characters are marked by their squalour with Charon's sordid *amictus* hanging from his shoulders by a knot, and Teiresias' *palla* hanging down to his feet, his *amictus funestus* covering his body. While Vergil's Sibyl in part gestures to Teiresias (and Circe) in the *Odyssey*, Seneca's Teiresias alludes to Vergil's Charon. Charon transports the souls across the Styx; Teiresias brings them back. Thebes itself becomes a katabatic space, a second destination for the dead, a place worse than Tartarus.

The explicit connection to Vergil's Charon, likewise, functions as a marked introduction to one of the most powerful responses to Vergil's underworld in the Latin literary tradition. The parallels are beyond doubt.[44] Seneca links his text to Vergil through an accumulation of similes describing the throng of souls. Seneca compares souls to clouds, leaves, bees, waves, and birds while Vergil compares them to falling leaves, birds, and bees. However, Seneca's bee simile (*Oed.* 601–2) is based on actual (and prophetic) bees in *Aeneid* 7.64–7.[45] Seneca too models the various abstractions of death, disease, and old age (*Oed.* 589–95) on the entities Aeneas encounters in the underworld's *uestibulum* (*Aen.* 6.273–7). While Vergil's abstractions are more expansive, Seneca's are closely connected to the dramatic context of the *Oedipus* and the programmatic plague. Likewise, the parade of tragic Thebans responds to the *pompa* of heroes in *Aeneid* 6.756–892. The long line of great Romans in the *Aeneid* gives way to the tragic imperial house of Thebes in the *Oedipus*, acting almost as an addendum to Vergil's parade. The centripetal force of Vergil's passage – from Silvius (*Italo commixtus sanguine*, 6.762) to Romulus (*Assaraci quem sanguinis Ilia mater | educet*, 6.778–9) – swirls around the central clan: *Caesar et omnis Iuli | progenies magnum caeli uentura axem* (6.789–90). The passage then praises Augustus for the next seventeen lines, at which point Anchises enumerates a number of Romans, until drawing Aeneas' attention to Marcellus. Roman history orbits the imperial *gens* of Augustus. While in Vergil the Roman souls are a function of a proleptic and prophetic, unrealized future, in Seneca the spirits are emphatically present: Zethus, Amphion, Niobe, Agave, Pentheus tumble onto stage, followed then by Laius, who reveals the foul criminality of Oedipus (more of a monster than the Sphinx, *Oed.* 641). Even Niobe becomes a sort of macabre Anchises as she counts her dead children (*numerat umbras, Oed.*

615) recalling *recensebat numerum* (*Aen.* 6.682).[46] The *Oedipus* reads like a pastiche of Vergilian reminiscences culled from *Aeneid* 6, culminating in a succinct re-performance of the Roman parade.

Why has Seneca so profoundly engaged with perhaps the most politically poignant moment of the *Aeneid* in which the republican past slips imperceptibly into the imperial present? The expansive and imperialistic frame of Vergil's underworld, with its emphatic Augustanism, has been replaced by the horror of crime within a single imperial house. Rome's seven hills are enclosed by seven-gated Thebes. The epic cadence of Vergil's parade ends with the tragic rhythms of a criminal family. Thebes comes to represent not an anti-Rome, but the Thebes within Rome (or the Rome within Thebes).[47] The profound and expansive view of Roman history from the point of view of the underworld – with its teleological imperialism – is obliterated, and is then replaced with the consequences of this teleology: generational disease, crime, and incest, for which the only cure is the expulsion of the imperial family itself. By charging his *Oedipus* with the heavy beats of *Aeneid* 6 and the broad consequences of its implications on Roman history, Seneca creates a highly topical and allegorical tragedy that unmasks the underlying consequences of an Imperial Rome under the influence of the Julio-Claudian *gens*.

Aeneid 6 is wholly interwoven with Senecan tragedy. Vergil provided a profoundly elaborate and sophisticated vision of the underworld that Seneca could activate at every register of language and narrative. At times the allusions could simply constellate characters and texts for humorous recognition. At other times they operated like a sort of literary *skene* through which the tragedy moved. At other times his references engaged with the deep psychosocial structures of underworld descents and their broader connections to birth, life, and death. *Aeneid* 6 impregnated Senecan tragedy with a profound dramatic experience, which absorbed the dark and haunting milieu of Vergil's hell. *Aeneid* 6 functions almost like a character within the tragedy, something that has an active role in filtering and distilling the content of the drama, acting as a living, breathing space within Seneca's tragic dimension.

NOTES

1 Tarrant 1995: 229; Segal 1983: 179. On Seneca and his literary tradition, see Maguinness 1956; Tarrant 1978; Putnam 1992; Schiesaro 1994; Goldberg 1996; Staley 2010: 97–120; Ker 2015; Trinacty 2016.

2 Putnam 1992 and Staley 2010 are essential here and throughout much of the paper.

3 Schiesaro 2003: 32–6.

4 Cf. Trinacty 2014: 216.
5 Hardie 1990; Braund 2006; McNelis 2007.
6 Smolenaars 1998.
7 Zissos 2009: 193.
8 All tragedy after the publication of the *Aeneid* most likely engaged Vergil, if Seneca the Elder's statement on Ovid's *Medea* can be generalized (*Suas.* 3.7). See Goldberg 1996: 275n14.
9 See Busch 2007: 265; Zissos 2009; Trinacty 2014: 28–9, who stress the dialogic nature between Seneca and his source material that creates (29), "differing points of view for literary material being employed. In each case the voice remains Seneca's but the ramifications for interpretation chang ."
10 See Shelton 1978: 50–7; Boyle 1997: 230n48; Trinacty 2014: 36–7. On Statius, see also Pillinger in this volume.
11 Fitch 1987; Putnam 1992; Boyle 1997: 107; Trinacty 2014: 131–8.
12 See Robertson 1980 on Hercules' and other Greek myths of descent.
13 See Barchiesi in this volume.
14 See also Keith, Kilgour, and Stok in this volume on reworkings of *Aen.* 6.128–9 in Ovid, Mary Shelley, and Servius, respectively. On underworld returns, see Herrero in this volume.
15 Thomas 1988 *ad loc.*, 3.357–9. On Cimmerians and *Aeneid* 6, see Barchiesi in this volume.
16 See Herrero in this volume on the need for speed in the underworld.
17 It is marked that Porter 2016 does not address sublimity and *katabasis* although such content surely adheres to his working definition of the sublime (see p . 5–7).
18 This is not the context to rehearse the debate on the precise performance moments of Senecan tragedy. While my heart wants Seneca to have directed his tragedies on stage, my mind and gut suggest that these were recitations.
19 See Feeney 1986: 16–19.
20 Courtney 1987; Bodel 1994.
21 See Holmes 2008; Repath 2010.
22 See Tarrant 1995.
23 Trinacty 2014 is fundamental here.
24 Note that Theseus frames his four-year absence in terms of Eleusis. The irony is significant The slow return of Theseus may imply a lack of initiation into the mysteries. See Herrero in this volume. There is no sense of a redemptive underworld in Senecan tragedy.
25 See Boyle 1997: 86–9 on Ovidian and particularly Euripidean allusion.
26 Cf. 64.112–15. See Barchiesi 1994: 443n22, on Callimachus' influence in these lines. On the labyrinth in literature more generally, see Doob 1990.
27 The sea-bull also recalls Minos' prayer to Neptune to give him a bull to sacrific , which was then produced from the sea and subsequently inseminated

Pasiphae (see Apollodorus 3.1.3). The description of the monster is marked. In particular, *immensam … partem*, while generally construed as a Scylla-like tail, may have a phallic impression. See *pars*, *OLD* 6. Given the cluster of erotica and sexual penetration with its implied bestiality along with the myth of Pasiphae in the background, the impression should not be categorically dismissed.

28 Phaedra at 120–3 prays for a Daedalus to replicate this precise deed for her.

29 For the labyrinth as a ritualized rite of passage as death and rebirth/grave and womb (and much else), see Borgeaud 1974: 5.

30 See Krell 1975; Faraone 2011.

31 On the "womb/tomb" in Joyce's *Ulysses*, which is deeply engaged with the present discussion, see Garvey 1995.

32 Pérez-Gómez 1985: 51.

33 See Segal 1984; Trinacty 2014: 181–5.

34 Boyle 1985: 1302–3.

35 It is notable that butcher's broom berries are bright red with fleshy seeds inside (almost testicular in character).

36 On the relationship between the Cretan Bull and Hippolytus, see Boyle 1985: 1316–20; Paschalis 1994: 121–3. In fact, Seneca has assimilated Hippolytus to both the Cretan Bull and the wooden bull of Daedalus.

37 See Horace *Sat* 1.4.62 (*inuenias etiam disiecti membra poetae*, "you would discover even the limbs of a dismembered poet"). Seneca may be alluding to Horace's dismembered poet here as well, gesturing to the influence of *Aeneid* 6 (among other texts) in his *Phaedra*. I thank Micah Myers for this reference.

38 On *Aeneid* 6 and the *Oedipus*, see Trinacty 2014: 37–9 (who also links the material to *Hercules Furens*).

39 See *Oed.* 93–8.

40 Much of this analysis is culled from Vernant 1982. But see Bremmer 1988 for a critique of this approach.

41 See Corbeill 2004: 67–106.

42 Cf. in this volume Pillinger's discussion of Statius' reception of the Sibyl in *Silu.* 4.3.

43 Trinacty 2014: 220, who emphasizes his Sibylline qualities as well.

44 Trinacty 2014: 215–31.

45 See Boyle 2011; Trinacty 2014: 222.

46 Boyle 1997: 91 makes a similar point on Seneca's *Troades* engagement with Vergil's Trojan-Augustan ancestry.

47 On Thebes and Rome, see Hardie 1990; Braund 2006.

9

Servius on Sinners and Punishments in Vergil's Underworld

FABIO STOK

In *Aeneid* 6.548 Aeneas, seeing the walls of Tartarus, asks the Sibyl about the damned whose wails he hears. The Sibyl expounds on the structure of Tartarus and then lists a series of sinners (580–607), sins (608–14), and punishments (614–17). The series of the sinners echoes that of *Odyssey* 11.568–631, with some names in common: after the judge Radamanthus she mentions the Titans (580–1), the Aloadae (582–4), Salmoneus (585–94), Tityos (595–600), and the Lapiths, Ixion, and Pirithous (601–7).[1] The double punishment inflicted on the Lapiths, that is the hanging boulder (602–3) and the prohibition to eat (603–7), is usually associated with Tantalus,[2] not the two heroes mentioned by Vergil (this oddity has occasioned several textual adjustments aiming at restoring the usual version).[3] The punishments mentioned after the series of sins are the rolling stone (attributed by the mythological tradition to Sisyphus) and the wheel, to which Ixion is usually condemned (616–17).[4] Then Theseus (617–18) and Phlegyas, who warns the sinners (618–20), are mentioned.[5]

Vergil's treatment of sinners was debated in late antiquity by several authors, because of the relevance of this topic for religion and the ideas about the afterlife. Servius' comment on these lines is particularly important, considering its widespread diffusion in the fifth century.[6] His interpretation presents similarities with the Neoplatonic one proposed some years later by Macrobius, but Servius is less interested than Macrobius in philosophical allegorism and, unlike him, mainly used Lucretius's rationalistic criticism of the mythological figures of the underworld. This approach allows Servius to present Vergil's scene as a literary fable, an interpretation that presents similarities to that of Augustine and other Christian writers, and was thus more suitable for the Christian users of his commentary.

In Vergil's narration the Sibyl specifie , in these terms, the punishment to which Tityos is condemned (595–600): his huge body, stretched over nine full acres, is attacked by a vulture, which gnaws at his liver.[7] Servius, commenting on 6.596, begins by endorsing the interpretation of it given by Lucretius:

per tota nouem cui iugera corpus porrigitur: quantum ad publicam faciem, magnitudinem ostendit corporis, sed illud significat quia de amatore loquitur, libidinem late patere, ut ait supra: nec procul hinc partem fusi monstrantur in omnem Lugentes Campi [6.440–1]. sane de his omnibus rebus mire reddit rationem Lucretius et confirmat in nostra uita esse omnia quae finguntur de infer .

Over nine full acres his body is stretched: with respect to the common appearance, he shows the size of the body; but since he speaks about love, it signifies that libido stands open far and wide, as he says above, "not far from here, outspread on every side, are shown the Mourning Fields." Indeed, Lucretius marvelously gives a principle for all these matters and asserts that everything portrayed about those below are in our life. (trans. Irvine 1994)

Servius refers to *De rerum natura* 3.978–1010, where Lucretius presents a list of sinners and punishments that echoes, like Vergil's list, the abovementioned episode of the *Odyssey*: it includes Tantalus, Tityos, Sisyphus, and the Danaids. Lucretius proposes a "psychological" interpretation of the punishments suffered by these characters: *ea nimirum quaecumque Acherunte profundo | prodita sunt esse, in uita sunt omnia nobis* ("Yes, we may be sure, all those things, of which stories tell us in the depth of Acheron, are in our life," *DRN* 3.978–9).[8] The punishment of Tityos, whose body is devoured by the birds, represents for Lucretius human erotic passion: *Tityos nobis hic est, in amore iacentem | quem uolucres lacerant atque exest anxius angor | aut alia quauis scindunt cuppedine curae* ("This is our Tityos, whom as he lies smitten with love, the birds mangle, yea, aching anguish devours him, or care cuts him deep through some other passions," *DRN* 3.992–4).

Servius' attribution of *libido* to Tityos is connected with the rape attributed to him by tradition; Servius *ad Aen.* 6.595 describes it in chaste terms: *amauit Latonam* ("he loved Leto"). Servius Danielis is more explicit (probably like its source Aelius Donatus): *confisus uiribus, Latonam uiolare temptauit* ("relying on his own strength he attempted to rape Leto"). Servius gives the Lucretian interpretation of the wide body of Tityos, observing that his libido "stands open far and wide," and also interprets a detail of the myth omitted by Lucretius (but present in Vergil), that the vulture gnaws at the liver of Tityos. The explanation is "scientific" founded on the localization of the passions in the different parts of the body. Servius continues in his comment *ad Aen.* 6.595:

Dicit enim Tityon amorem esse, hoc est libidinem, quae secundum physicos et medicos in iecore est, sicut risus in splene, iracundia in felle; unde etiam exesum a uulture dicimus in poenam renasci, et enim libidini non satis fit re semel peracta, sed recrudescit semper, unde ait Horatius incontinentis aut Tityi iecur [Carm. 3.4.77].

For he says that Tityos is love, that is, libido, which according to natural philosophers and physicians is in the liver, as laughter is in the spleen and anger in the gallbladder. Whence he is said to be reborn in his punishment, devoured by a vulture, for it is not enough for libido to happen only in a completed circumstance, but always becomes raw again, whence Horace's line, the liver of lawless Tityos. (trans. Irvine 1994)

The localization of the passions in the body is consistent with the idea that the underworld represents human life. Servius seems, in this regard, to generalize Lucretius's statement that these punishments "are all in our life" (3.379: *in uita sunt omnia nobis*): Servius generalizes this statement to the whole underworld and therefore presents it as fiction *finguntur*).

Servius also applies Lucretius's interpretation of the punishment of Tityos to the other punishments described by Vergil (*de his omnibus rebus*). In the following scholium he adopts the Lucretian interpretations of the punishments of Tantalus and Sisyphus and adds that of Ixion, not considered by Lucretius (*ad* 6.595):[9]

ipse etiam Lucretius dicit per eos super quos iam iam casurus imminet lapis superstitiosos significari qui inaniter semper uerentur et de diis et caelo superioribus male opinantur; nam religiosi sunt qui per reuerentia timent. Per eos autem qui saxum uoluunt ambitum uult et repulsam significari quia semel repulsi petitores ambire non desinunt. Per rotam autem ostendit negotiatores, qui semper tempestatibus turbinibusque uoluuntur.

Lucretius himself says that the superstitious are signified by those whom a rock about to fall from above threatens at any moment. They are always uselessly afraid and maliciously inclined toward the gods and heaven above. But the religious are those who fear by reverence. By those who roll the stone he intends to signify bribery and political defeat, since once political candidates are defeated they do not give up soliciting favours. By the wheel he shows businessmen, who are always turning affairs by the right times and fortune's wheel. (trans. Irvine 1994)

Servius, in discussing the cases of Tityos/Tantalus/Sisyphus/Ixion, superimposes Lucretius's series on top of Vergil's and removes from the latter the anomalies we have reported above. Particularly puzzling to Servius was the attribution to Ixion and Pirithous of the punishments inflicted on Tantalus, according to tradition. In the scholium to 6.603 he comments on the punishment stating *aliud est* ("it is another thing") and then recounts the story of Tantalus.[10] Conversely, commenting on 6.601 he remembers the traditional punishments of Ixion: *ad inferos trusus est et illic religatus ad rotam circumfusam serpentibus* ("he was thrown in hell and bound to a wheel encircled by serpents"). This attribution is confirmed in the scholium to 6.616, where Vergil describes the punishment of the wheel (without the name of the sinner): Servius specifies that it was the punishment of Ixion and quotes *Georgics* 4.484 noting the incongruence between this passage and the previous statement of the *Aeneid*: *licet supra dixerit "quos super atra silex"* ("although he said before 'over whom hangs a black crag'").[11] The incongruence is explained by Servius with an argument he uses often in the presence of mythographical variants: *nam de his fabulis uariae sunt in ipsis auctoribus opiniones* ("the same authors indeed have different opinions about these fables").

The same argument is adopted by Servius for another of the Vergilian anomalies of this episode, the presence of Theseus among the sinners; surprising because the same Theseus is mentioned by Aeneas in 6.122 as visiting the underworld, while alive, together with Hercules (and also by Charon in 6.393, with Pirithous). The incongruence had already been noted by Hyginus (fr. 8 Fun.), who affirmed that Vergil, if he had had time to revise the *Aeneid*, would have corrected it. Servius *ad Aen.* 6.617 indicates the anomalous presence of Theseus among the sinners: *contra opinionem, nam fertur ab Hercule esse liberatus* ("in contrast to the current opinion, it is indeed told that he was freed by Hercules"). But also in this case he concludes that *frequenter enim uariant fabulas poetae* ("the fables of the poets are frequently different").

Servius, like Lucretius, interprets the punishments of hell allegorically. In the case of Tityos, as we have seen, he confirms the Lucretian interpretation, but not in the case of Tantalus, for whom Lucretius had proposed an "atheistic" interpretation: the character suffers because he fears the gods (3.982–3): *in uita diuum metus urget inanis | mortalis casumque timent quem cuique ferat fors* ("rather 'tis in life that the vain fear of the gods threatens mortals; they fear the fall of the blow which chance may deal to each"). Servius *ad* 6.595 prefers to interpret the punishment with reference to the *superstitiosi*, guilty of bad religion, *qui inaniter semper uerentur et de diis et caelo superioribus male opinantur* ("who have groundless fears and mistaken beliefs about the gods and the celestial entities"); he sets against the latter those who are *religiosi* and *reuerentia timent* ("have awe").

The other punishment of Tantalus, the prohibition of eating and drinking (not considered by Lucretius), is interpreted by Servius *ad.* 6.603 as an allegory of *auaritia* ("greed"), validated by a quotation from Horace (*Serm.*

1.1.69–70): *quid rides? Mutato nomine de te | fabula narratur* ("Why do you laugh? Change the name, and the joke's on you"). In the Vergilian picture the approach to food is prevented by the *Furiarum maxima* (6.605), identifiable with Allecto or Maegera (the third, Tisiphone, Vergil seats in the vestibule of Tartarus). Servius *ad* 6.605 prefers to identify her with *Fames* ("Hunger"), probably through his reading of *Aeneid* 3.252, where the Harpy Celaeno is called *Furiarum maxima.*

Lucretius interprets the punishment of Sisyphus as an allegory of political careerism (3.995–7): *Sisyphus in uita quoque nobis ante oculos est, | qui petere a populo fasces saeuasque secures | imbibit et semper uictus tristisque recedit.* ("The Sisyphus in our life too is clear to see, he who open-mouthed seeks from the people the rods and cruel axes, and evermore comes back conquered and dispirited.") Servius *ad* 6.596 paraphrases quite literally *petitores* ("candidates"). Also for the punishment of Ixion, that of the wheel, ignored by Lucretius, Servius refers to Roman society and identifies the sinners as businessmen (*negotiatores*), always subject to the wheel of fortune.[12]

What is the function of the Lucretian interpretation in the context of Servius' exegesis of *Aeneid* 6? An answer to this question is given by the scholium to 6.127, on the words pronounced by the Sibyl when she and Aeneas arrive at the entrance to the underworld:

"noctes atque dies patet atra ianua Ditis": id est omni tempore homines in fata concedunt. Et hoc poetice: nam Lucretius ex maiore parte et alii integre docent inferorum regna nec esse quidem posse.[13] nam locus ipsorum quem possumus dicere, cum sub terris esse dicantur antipodes? In media uero terra eos esse nec soliditas patitur, nec κέντρον terrae: quae si in medio mundi est, tanta eius profunditas esse non potest, ut medio sui habeat inferos, in quibus esse dicitur Tartarus, de quo legitur "bis patet in praeceps tantum tenditque sub umbras, | quantus ad aetherium caeli suspectus Olympus" [578–9]. ergo hanc Terram in qua uiuimus inferos esse uoluerunt, quia est omnium circulorum infima planetarum scilicet septem, Saturni, Iouis, Martis, Solis, Veneris, Mercurii, Lunae, et duorum magnorum. Hinc est quod habemus "et nouies Styx interfusa coercet" [439]: nam nouem cingulis cingitur terra. ergo omnia quae de inferis finguntu, suis locis hic esse comprobauimus. quod autem dicit "patet atri ianua Ditis | sed reuocare gradum superasque euadere ad auras | hoc opus hic labor est" [127–9] aut poetice dictum est aut secundum philosophorum altam scientiam, qui deprehenderunt bene uiuentium animas ad superiores circulos, id est ad originem suam redire, quod dat Lucanus Pompeio "ut uidit quanta sub nocte iaceret nostra dies" [9.13]: male uiuentium uero diutius in his permorari corporibus permutatione diuersa et esse apud inferos semper.

"Night and day the door of the gloomy Dis stands open." That is, men have always to obey the fate. That is said poetically: Lucretius indeed in a large part and others entirely teach that the kingdom of hell cannot be. Indeed where can we put it under the Earth, if those who we call Antipodes exist? It cannot exist in the middle of the Earth: that is not allowed by its solidity and by its being the centre. Enough depth does not exist for Tartarus, of which it is written that "it is stretching into the gloom twice as far as is the upward view of the sky toward heavenly Olympus." They wanted therefore that hell is the Earth where we live, because it is in the lowest of all the circles, that is of seven planets, Saturn, Jupiter, Mars, Sun, Venus, Mercurius and Moon, and the two greatest. It is for this reason that we read that "the Styx imprisons with his nine-fold circles": there are indeed nine circles from which the Earth is surrounded. We have therefore demonstrated that all that is told about hell occurs here, in this place. For this reason Vergil says, "the doorways of gloomy Dis are open but to recall steps and pass out to the upper air, this is the task, this is the hardship," which is said poetically or according to the deep science of philosophers, who take this to mean that the souls of those living well return to the upper circles, that is to their origin. Lucan grants this to Pompey: "he saw how much our day lies below the night." But the souls of those living badly die for a very long time in their bodies in a different permutation and are ever among those below.

In this scholium Servius refers to *DRN* 3.978–9, deducing from it the same conclusion we have read in the commentary to 6.596, that the underworld cannot exist. To validate this statement Servius challenges the traditional locations of the underworld. Scientific reasons are marshalled against locating it within the Earth: the Earth's massiveness (*soliditas*), dependent upon its being at the centre of the universe, does not permit the existence of a subterranean world. The use of the Greek term κέντρον underlines its scientific meaning: Cicero also uses it in *Tusc.* 1.40 when referring to the scientific theory of the four elements, according to which the terrestrial elements are carried by their own weight toward the centre of the Earth. Servius also adds a second argument, given by the *Aeneid* itself: the depth of Tartarus, says the Sibyl, is equal to twice the distance between the top of Olympus and the sky (6.578–9).[14] Such a great depth, notes Servius, is impossible, because it is not possible that the underworld could be situated in a cavity of the Earth.

Servius also criticizes the location of the underworld in the lower hemisphere of the Earth.[15] This solution took into account the sphericity of the Earth, but raised the problem of the illumination of the underworld, which was traditionally characterized by darkness. Servius treats this problem in the scholium to *Georgics* 1.243, where he presents opposite opinions about the illumination of the other side of the Earth: *alii dicunt a nobis ascendentem solem ire ad antipodas, alii negant et uolunt illis tenebras esse perpetuas* ("some people affirm that the sun which rises in our regions goes to the antipodes, others deny this opinion and say that in those regions there is always darkness"). Commenting on *Aeneid* 6.127 (and also 6.532), Servius affirms the existence of inhabitants of the antipodes, and therefore denies this collocation of the underworld.

Having rejected the traditional locations, Servius affirms that the underworld is to be identified with the Earth itself, taking into account its astronomical position at the centre of the circles formed by the planets and the stars. This identification is justified by the common etymology of the words *inferi* and *infima*, the Earth being the last and lowest of the planets (Cicero's *Dream of Scipio* 17 also qualifies the Earth as *infima*). Different from the *Dream of Scipio*, in which the Earth is counted among the nine circles, Servius adopts a version in which the Earth is surrounded by nine circles, that is, by the seven planets (including the Sun and the Moon) and by two other great circles that Servius does not identify. One of them is certainly that of the fixed stars, the other is perhaps the crystal sphere whose introduction in the astronomical system is fi st recorded by Ptolemy.[16] According to Servius, Vergil allegorically alludes to these nine circles when he refers to the nine circles formed by the river Styx in *Aeneid* 6.439.

In the final part of the scholium Servius correlates the astronomical system with the Platonic theory of metempsychosis, according to which souls become incarnate on Earth and after death and, if they have behaved well, return to their astral home (as an example of this, Servius cites the apotheosis of Pompey in Lucan's poem).[17] Also in the second part of the scholium Servius defines the Vergilian underworld as fiction (*poetice dictum*), but in identifying it with the Earth he modifies the Lucretian statement that the underworld is "in our life," that is, in our mind or imagination. In the Porphyrian approach adopted by Servius, "in our life" becomes "on the Earth," that is, in the bodily life of the soul. This conclusion highlights Servius's exploitative utilization of Lucretius, adapted to a Neoplatonic theory of the soul. This juxtaposition is also detectable if we analyse the possible sources used by Servius.

The Neoplatonic framework of the Servian exegesis is similar to that detectable in the interpretation of the Vergilian episode proposed by Macrobius in his commentary on Cicero's *Dream of Scipio*. The identification of hell with human life is connected, as in the Servian scholium, with the Platonic theory of metempsychosis (1.10.10):

hoc animae sepulcrum, hoc Ditis concaua, hoc inferos uocauerunt et omnia, quae illic esse credidit fabulosa persuasio, in nobismet ipsis et in ipsis humanis corporibus adsignare conati sunt: obliuionis fluuium aliud non esse adserentes quam errorem animae obliuiscentis maiestatem uitae prioris, qua antequam in corpus truderetur potita est, solamque esse in corpore uitam putantis.

They called the body the tomb of the soul, the vaults of Pluto, and the infernal regions; everything that fable taught us to believe was in the lower regions they tried to assign to us ourselves and to our mortal bodies. The river Lethe was to them nothing more than the error committed by the soul in forgetting its former high estate before it was thrust into a body and thinking that its sole existence was in a body. (trans. Stahl 1990)

Macrobius also considers the infernal punishments as poetical fiction (*fabulosa persuasio*), really regarding human earthly life, when the soul incarnates. He does not mention the name of Vergil, but the episode of the *Aeneid* is clearly echoed (1.10.12–15):

ipsam quoque poenarum descriptionem de ipso usu conuersationis humanae sumptam crediderunt, uulturem iecur inmortale tondentem (598) nihil aliud intellegi uolentes quam tormenta conscientiae obnoxia flagitio uiscera interiora rimantis (599), et ipsa uitalia indefessa admissi sceleris admonitione laniantis, semperque curas, si requiescere forte temptauerint, excitantis tamquam fibris renascentibus (600) inhaerendo, nec ulla sibi miseratione parcentis lege hac qua "se iudice nemo nocens absoluitur" (Juv. 13.2–3) nec de se suam potest uitare sententiam. Illos aiunt epulis ante ora positis (604) excruciari fame et inedia tabescere, quos magis magisque adquirendi desiderium cogit praesentem copiam non uidere et in affluentia inopes egestatis mala in ubertate patiuntur nescientes parta respicere, dum egent habendis. Illos radiis rotarum pendere districtos (616–17) qui nihil consilio praeuidentes, nihil ratione moderantes, nihil uirtutibus explicantes, seque et actus omnes suos fortunae permittentes, casibus et fortuitis semper rotantur. Saxum ingens uoluere (616) inefficacibus laboriosisque conatibus uitam terentes. Atram silicem lapsuram semper et cadenti similem (602–3) illorum capitibus imminere qui arduas potestates et infaustam ambiunt tyrannidem numquam sine timore uicturi, et cogentes subiectum uulgus "odisse dum metuat" (Cic. *Off.* 1.97), semper sibi uidentur exitium quod merentur excipere.

The description of the punishments, they believe, originated in human experience, and the vulture gnawing at the deathless liver, they would have us understand is nothing more than the pangs of a conscience prying into our insides as though they were guilty of offense, and incessantly tearing at our very vitals with the chastisement of a sense of guilt, and like the vulture clinging to the "liver that grows anew," always stirring up cares that are ready to subside, never relenting with a feeling of

> pity. This is the rule, that "no guilty man is acquitted who has himself for judge"; one cannot escape his own decision in regard to himself. Those who have food set before them and yet are tortured with hunger and wasting away from starvation are really, they say, the men whom a longing to acquire more and more compels to overlook their present wealth, men affluent yet needy, suffering the evils of poverty amidst their plenty, not knowing how to take stock of their possessions because of a lust for possessing. They "hang out stretched on spokes of wheel" who are reckless about the future, who never govern their actions by reason nor solve their problems by recourse to the virtues. They entrust themselves and all their business to fortune, and so are always whirled about by chance and accidents. Those who "roll a huge stone up a hill," they are consuming their lives in futile and tedious efforts. Those who find themselves with "the dark stone ever wavering which seems ready to fall back on their heads" strive for the arduous places of power and the accused sovereignty of an autocrat, destined never to reach their goal without fear, and compelling their subjects "to hate them at the same time as they fear them." These men always seem to obtain the end they merited. (trans. Stahl 1990)

Macrobius does not mention the names of the sinners, but the punishments are those described by Vergil: Tityos, the fi st punishment of Tantalus, Ixion, Sisyphus, and the second punishment of Tantalus (omitting the names, Macrobius avoids the problems of attribution given by the Vergilian text). The allegoric interpretations of the punishments are different from those given by Lucretius.[18] Macrobius does not highlight sins, but modalities of conscience and behaviour: the punishment of Tityos is interpreted as an allegory of guilt (Lucretius and Servius: *libido*); that of Ixion of impulsiveness (Servius: *negotiatores*); that of Sisyphus represents those who are spending their life in impossible enterprises (Lucretius and Servius: *petitores*). Considerably different is the interpretation of the rock overhanging Tantalus, which, for Macrobius, represents those who are aspiring to power and tyranny (Lucretius: fear of the gods; Servius: *superstitio*). For the other punishment of Tantalus, the prohibition of eating, not considered by Lucretius, Macrobius and Servius agree and interpret this punishment as an allegory of greed. It seems likely that in this case Servius used a source near to that of Macrobius. For the other punishments, instead, he adopted the interpretation of Lucretius.

The common features of Macrobius and Servius probably derive from a Neoplatonic exegesis of the *Aeneid*, perhaps the work (or the works) mentioned by Servius in the preface to Book 6 of his commentary.[19] Servius superimposed the Lucretian interpretation on to the Neoplatonic exegesis of this source (not without discrepancies, as we have seen).[20]

This presence of Lucretius in Servian exegesis has been considered surprising[21] or insignificant[22] but for several aspects it is connected with the exegetical approach of Servius. In fact, it is noteworthy that the Lucretian interpretation is adopted by Servius not only for the infernal punishments, but for the whole underworld: "the kingdom of hell cannot be" (*ad* 6.127). This statement is affirmed also in other parts of the commentary: in the scholium to *Aeneid* 5.725 commenting the words of Anchises's ghost: *nate, mihi uita quondam, dum uita manebat, | care magis* ("Son, dearer to me than life, in days when life was mine," 5.724–5), Servius writes: *bene addidit "dum uita manebat": nulla enim est uita post mortem* ("he did well to add 'in days when life was mine': for there is no life after death"). Also the debated comment to *Aeneid* 6.893, on the exit of Aeneas from the ivory gate, seems linked with the Lucretian interpretation: *poetice apertus est sensus: uult autem intelligi falsa esse omnia quae dixit* ("the poetical meaning is clear: he wants to be understood that all that he said is untrue").[23]

One of the reasons for Servius's adoption of the Lucretian interpretation was probably his closeness to his own conception of *fabula* ("fable"). Also Macrobius, as we have seen, defines Tartarus and the infernal punishments as *fabulosa persuasio*, but the latter is not a simple fable, but a fi st step to the philosophical knowledge, set "before the zeal of philosophers for the study of natural science grew to such vigorous proportions" (*antequam studium philosophiae circa naturae inquisitionem ad tantum uigoris adolesceret*, 1.10.9). This statement presupposes Macrobius's differentiation between the *fabulosa narratio*, that is, the poetry containing elements of truth, and the simple *fabula*, insignificant for philosophical truth (1.2.6–11). Macrobius identifie these different types of fables in his clash with the Epicureans, who had criticized the fable-like nature of the Platonic Myth of Er in the final part of the *Republic*. At variance with the Epicureans Macrobius favours the fable told by Cicero in his *Dream of Scipio*: *haec ipsa ueritas per quaedam composita et ficta profertur, et hoc iam uocatur narratio fabulosa, non fabula* ("it rests on a solid foundation of truth, which is treated in a fictitious style. This is called the fabulous narrative, to distinguish it from the ordinary fable," 1.2.9).

Servius ignores Macrobius's classification of the types of fables and instead uses a different tradition, which distinguished between *fabula, argumentum*, and *historia*,[24] *fabula* being a topic or narrative opposing the natural laws: *dicta res contra naturam* (*ad Aen.* 1.235). The Lucretian interpretations undoubtedly fit well into this definition That Servius considered the Vergilian underworld a fable is confirmed by the scholium at *Aeneid* 6.127, where he says that the Vergilian narrative of the underworld should be interpreted "poetically" (*poetice*). Adapting the Lucretian interpretation to the Neoplatonic framework, Servius also, like Macrobius, introduces a correlation between the fable and the philosophical truth (he affirms that the Vergilian narrative should be understood poetically or according to the deep science of philosophers). But this correlation is less stringent than that of Macrobius, and does not imply a detailed allegorization of the Vergilian narrative.

Servius's approach also concerns the image of Vergil, who in the Neoplatonic exegesis was considered to be entirely Platonic. Augustine, influenced by that exegesis, says that Vergil wrote *Aeneid* 6.750–1 "presumably under Platonic influence (*Ciu.* 10.30).[25] For Servius, Vergil does not follow a single philosophical school and is also influenced by Epicureanism (*ad Aen.* 6.254): *sciens ergo de deorum imperio uarias esse opiniones, prudentissime tenuit generalitatem. Ex maiore autem parte Sironem id est magistrum suum Epicureum sequitur* ("knowing that on the power of the gods there are different opinions, he speaks in general terms. But for the greatest part he follows Siro, his Epicurean teacher").[26] In the exegetical tradition, Vergil's Epicureism was mainly removed: Aelius Donatus (and probably like Suetonius before him) in his *Life of Vergil* does not mention Vergil's scholarship at the school of Siro.[27] The recovery of this biographic topic was functional not only for the interpretation of the underworld, but also for Servius's frequent use of Lucretius, and for lexical, stylistic, and scientific problem .[28]

Furthermore, the Lucretian interpretation allows Servius to propose a judgment on the Vergilian underworld, which presents analogies also offered by the Christian writers of his age. Augustine speaks of *poetica fabulosaque figmenta* for the boat of Charon (*Cur. Mort.* 2.1), and for the episode of Cacus he uses a definition similar to that of Macrobius, *poetica et fabulosa narratio* (*Ciu.* 19.12), but with a meaning that ignores the Macrobian philosophical *fabulosa narratio* and is instead similar to that of the Servian concept of *fabula.* In *De bono mortis* Ambrose considers the pagan infernal punishments as *fabulae poetarum* frightening mindless people (8.33):

mortem insipientes uerentur (...) quod poenas reformident, poetarum uidelicet fabulis territi, latratus Cerberi (*Aen.* 6.417) et Cocyti fluminis tristem uoraginem (296–7), Charontem tristiorem (299), Furiarum agmina (572) aut praerupta Tartara (577–8), in quibus Hydra saeuior sedem habeat (576–7), Tityi quoque uiscera reparandis fecunda suppliciis, quae uultur immanis sine ullo fine depascitur (595–600), Ixionii quoque orbis perpetuam sub poenae atrocitate uertiginem, tum saxi desuper imminentis super capita adcubantium inter epulas inpendentem ruinam (601–4).

The mindless are afraid of death ... fearing the punishments, frightened by the fables of the poets: the barks of Cerberus, the gloomy chasm of the river Cocytus, gloomier Charon, the array of the Furies or deep Tartarus, within which dwells the still fie cer

Hydra and the fruitful bowels of Tityos, restored by torture, which the monstrous vulture devours continuously, and also the wheel of Ixion, to whom the harsh punishment puts dizziness eternal, and the impending crash of the unsafe boulder hanging above the heads of those who are sitting before a feast.

Ambrose seems aware of the exegetical difficulty set by the punishments of Ixion: he reproduces the Vergilian attribution of Tantalus's punishments to Ixion, but also adds Ixion's traditional punishment, that of the wheel. Afterwards Ambrose confirms that *haec plena sunt fabularum* ("these arguments are full of fables") but also adds: *nec tamen negauerim poenas esse post mortem* ("but I would not deny, however, that there are some punishments after death," 8.33), referring to the Christian afterlife.

A similar judgment on the pagan underworld is given by Paulinus of Nola in *Carmina* 31.475–82. He proposes a series of sinners that takes into account not only Vergil, but also Ovid's *Metamorphoses* 4.447–63 (Tityos, Tantalus, Ixion, Sisyphus, and the Danaides are mentioned).[29] Paulinus also denotes the falsity of the fables of the poets, to which he opposes the Christian truth: *haec inopes ueri uanis cecinere poetae, | qui Christum ueri non tenuere caput* ("the poets, ignoring the truth, sang those things for the silly men, and do not know the Christ, source of the truth," 483–4).

Servius, in presenting Vergil's underworld as *fabula* and denying the existence of the infernal punishments, was probably considering the Christian and Christianized readers of his commentary.[30] The convergence is limited to the criticism of the pagan underworld: differently from Ambrose and Paulinus, who contrast it with the Christian afterlife, Servius uses the Lucretian interpretation to promote the Neoplatonic conception of the soul and its afterlife. However, in using Lucretius, he was in a difficult position, because the Epicurean refusal of any afterlife was obviously unacceptable for Christians. Lactantius criticizes Epicurus for his refusal of the afterlife and contrasts his point of view with that of the Stoic Zeno, considering it similar to the visions of the biblical prophets (*Diu. Inst.* 7.7.13):

esse inferos Zenus stoicis docuit et sedes piorum ab impiis esse discretas et illos quidem quietas ac delectabiles incolere regiones, hos uero luere poenas in tenebrosis locis atque in caeni uoraginibus horrendis: idem nobis prophetae palam dicunt. Ergo Epicurus errat, qui poetarum id esse figmentum putauit et illas inferorum poenas quae feruntur in hac esse uita interpretatus est.

The existence of a world below was the teaching of the Stoic Zeno, with different abodes in it for the pious and the impious, the pious dwelling in areas of peace and delight and the impious paying their penalties in areas of darkness and ghastly pools of mud; the prophets put the same picture to us. Epicurus was therefore wrong in thinking it a figment of the poets and in interpreting the well-rehearsed punishments of the world below as events of this life. (trans. Bowen and Garnsey 2003)[31]

The scholium to 5.725 quoted above, where Servius writes that "there is no life after death," could arouse perplexities from a Christian perspective: the compiler of the Servius Danielis, probably a monk of the seventh century, omitted this ambiguous statement replacing it with a simple paraphrase of the Vergilian line: *ut ostendat uita fuisse cariorem* ("to show that life was dearer to him").[32]

Another consequence of the Servian idea of *fabula* concerns the relationship of Vergil with his own work. The author of a fable does not believe in what he recounts. By presenting the underworld as *fabula* Servius protects Vergil from the criticisms of his work, saving his image of omniscient expert (in the preface to *Aeneid* 6 he presents Vergil as *totus scientia plenus*, "overflowing with knowledge")

Augustine in the *De utilitate credendi* 10[33] proposes a similar disjunction between the author and the content of his work: in fact, he distinguishes between works containing falsities of which the authors are aware (*id quod falsum est uerum putatur, cum aliud qui scripsit putauerit*, "that which is false is thought true, when the author thought otherwise"), and works containing falsities that are considered true by their authors (*id quod falsum est uerum putatur, id tamen putatur quod etiam ille qui scripsit putauit*, "that which is false is thought true, but the thought is also that of the author"). Augustine mentions as examples of these two types of work Vergil and Lucretius. The *iudex mortuorum* Rhadamanthus is a character of the *Aeneid* (6.566–9), but Vergil knows that he never existed. Lucretius presents an untrue theory of the soul believing that it is true. Augustine's judgment on Vergil is confirmed by Servian exegesis, for which the Vergilian underworld is fictitiou . The reader who believes in Vergil's Rhadamanthus, continues Augustine, makes a double mistake: he takes the false for the true, and believes in what the author did not believe in. He who reads and agrees with Lucretius makes only one mistake, but he is not less guilty (*non minus miser est*). We can deduce that the person who reads Vergil and is aware of his falsity does not make mistakes. Servius's exegesis is not very far from the warning of Augustine.

NOTES

1 Odysseus in the Homeric underworld sees, after the judge Minos (11.568–71), Orion (572–5), Tityos (576–81), Tantalus (582–92), Sisyphus (593–600), Theseus, and Pirithous (631).

2 In the *Odyssey* 11.582–92 Tantalus cannot drink or eat despite standing in the water and having fruits around him. In the Greek lyric and tragedy he is commonly standing under a hanging boulder. Both punishments were depicted in a painting by Polygnotus described by Pausanias 10.31.12.

3 *Aen.* 6.601–2: *quid memorem Lapithas, Ixiona Pirithoumque | quos super atra silex*, etc. ("Why tell of the Lapiths Ixion and Pirithous, over whom a black crag, etc."). Adjustments: lacuna after l. 601 and variant *quo* instead of *quos* at l. 602 (Courtney 1981: 19; Conte 2009: 183); correction to *Pirithoumque* <et> / *quo* (Fairclough 1999: 574); transposition of 6.602–7 to after 6.615 (Perret 1984); 6.601 interrogative and *quo* at 6.602 (Öberg 1987: 106–7). The Vergilian anomaly is explained by Putnam 1990.

4 Also in *Georg.* 3.37–9 (together with Sisyphus, as in the *Aeneid*) and 4.484.

5 In Pindar *Pyth.* 2.24 a similar warning is given by Ixion, who moreover is Phlegyas's son (see Zetzel 1989: 270–1).

6 See Kaufmann 2010.

7 Cf. the *Odyssey*, where there are two vultures (11.578).

8 Trans. Bailey 1947. Although this Lucretian treatment of the underworld does not appear in the extant writings of Epicurus, it is not necessary to assume a different source (like Cumont 1920, who conjectured that Lucretius used a Neo-Pythagorean tradition): Seneca *Epist.* 24.18 considers *Epicurea cantilena* ("Epicurean refrain") the idea that the fear of punishments in the underworld is without foundation.

9 The Servian scholium has suggested that Ixion was originally present in the Lucretian series, but was subsequently lost because of a lacuna in the text; however, this hypothesis does not seem necessary (cf. Kenney 1981: 229). The idea that infernal punishments are illusory is also asserted by Cicero in *Tusc.* 1.10 (he mentions the examples of Tantalus and Sisyphus).

10 This observation should be attributed to Servius, and not to his source; instead of it the Servius Danielis has *sicut supra diximus* ("as we said before"), referring to the scholium on Tantalus *ad Georg.* 3.7 (Servius removed this and other similar references because in his commentary, unlike those of Servius Danielis and Aelius Donatus, the *Georgics* are commented on after the *Aeneid*, not before).

11 Another commentator, the Pseudo-Probus *ad Georg.* 3.37, had more faith in the Vergilian version and used it in interpreting *Georgics* 3.39, *immanemque rotam et non exuperabile saxum* ("the massive wheel and the remorseless stone"): he attributes to Ixion the double punishment of the wheel and the stone, instead of attributing the stone to Tantalus.

12 More references to sins in the context of the Roman world are pointed out by Servius: see Berry 1992; Powell 1998.

13 This text is published by Jeunet-Mancy 2012: 48. The text edited by Thilo, *ne posse quidem esse*, is likely that of the Servius Danielis.

14 Vergil doubles the distance given by Homer *Iliad* 8.16.
15 See Cumont 1949: 191–6.
16 Setaioli 1995: 74–5.
17 Servius adopts the theory of metempsychosis in the version given by Porphyry: see Stok 2013.
18 Flamant 1977: 579n.
19 That Macrobius used a Neoplatonic commentary on Vergil is admitted by Armisen-Marchetti 2003: lx–lxi, who also resumes the attribution of this commentary to Marius Victorinus, proposed by Courcelle 1955a: 66–9 and others (Setaioli 1995: 240 is sceptical about this attribution). In the past the source of Macrobius' passage was identified by Cou celle 1943: 28–9 as Porphyry, and by Dodds 1960: 9 as Numenius. In the opinion of De Ley 1967, Macrobius freely reworked several sources.
20 We can leave aside the problem of the source used by Servius, the same *De rerum natura* or an exegetical source. In the scholium to 6.127 the words Lucretius *et alii* suggest the use of a source, where Lucretius was mentioned, but the aim of Servius seems to be to distinguish the more moderate position of Lucretius (*ex maiore parte*) from a more radical (*integre*), perhaps more consistently Epicurean.
21 Wallace 1938: 141.
22 Courcelle 1955b: 103–4 considers the interpretation based on Lucretius a variant of the Neoplatonic exegesis; Setaioli 1995: 189 attributes the use of Lucretius to Servius's aversion to mystical attitudes.
23 Murgia 2004: 191. See also Parker, ch. 14 in this volume.
24 See Lazzarini 1984: 119–21; Dietz 1995: 70–1; Stok 2016.
25 See Mackey in this volume.
26 Vergil's Epicurean scholarship is remembered by Servius also in the commentary to the sixth *Eclogue*, in which he considers Silenus as the allegorical personification of Siro *ad ecl.* 6.13).
27 Stok 2010: 116.
28 See Deschamps 1999.
29 See Bordone 2007–8: 287. On the Ovidian passage, see Keith in this volume.
30 Servius was commonly set in the milieu of the fourth-century's pagan revival (e.g., Jones 1986: 113), but a revision of this collocation has been proposed by Murgia 2004: 190–1 and Cameron 2011: 176–7. For later exegetical adjustments of Vergil's underworld to the Christian vision, see Soranzo, ch. 12 in this volume.
31 Lactantius quotes Epicurus, but he is probably referring to Lucretius.
32 Murgia 2004: 192.
33 See Stock 1996: 164–9; Lim 2004: 119–23.

10

Paradise and Performance in Vergil's Underworld and Horace's *Carmen Saeculare*[1]

LAUREN CURTIS

Amid the ghosts and shadows of Vergil's underworld, this essay is about a vibrant living image: the singing, dancing body. It re-examines how one of the *Aeneid*'s earliest Roman reception texts, Horace's *Carmen Saeculare*, engages with Vergil's underworld a mere two years after Vergil's death.[2] The *Carmen Saeculare* (henceforth *CS*) has enjoyed increased scholarly attention in the past two decades, and its relationship with the *Aeneid* has prompted discussion.[3] But few readers have considered what connections between these texts are opened up when another plane of reference is brought into the picture: their shared allusions to Greek performance culture. By examining how Vergil's underworld and Horace's hymn incorporate performance, both real and imagined, I hope to shed light on how *Aeneid* 6 offers a rather surprising model against which Horace redefines the nature and role of lyric song in Augustan Rome.

In Vergil's Elysium, Aeneas and the Sibyl witness hymns for Apollo (specifically paeans) being performed by choruses of ancient heroes (*Aen.* 6.642–62). The *CS*, conversely, presents itself as an innovative Roman version of a Greek choral hymn, and in particular a paean, sung by Rome's children. I argue that the chorus' – and especially the paean's – traditional Greek associations with social harmony and civic foundation in the realm of Apollo inform both Vergil's Elysium and, as Horace rewrites Vergil's underworld just two years later, the new Rome that the *CS* imagines. Both texts, one might say, make an association between paradise and performance. The result is a dynamic interplay of reception and reimagination in which, fi stly,

Greek performance culture is used as a basis for generating a new set of ideas about Rome's political and cultural ascendancy. Second, this performance culture, as assimilated by Roman texts, becomes a point of contestation between Horace and Vergil for the appropriate literary expression of such ideals. Horace's lyric *carmen* proclaims itself to be a choral hymn; I propose, moreover, that its very choral form rereads and restages Vergil's Elysian paeans. Through his reading of Vergil, Horace creates his own distinctive vision of how Rome's foundation narrative can be expressed through communal performance. In so doing, he appropriates the Roman reception of ancient Greek song culture from epic back to the lyric domain of the public choral voice.

In making such an argument, this essay grapples with the very question of what it means for Vergil's underworld to have an "afterlife." For the chronological process of intertextuality between these two Roman texts, so close in time and context, is full of slippage. Horace's *CS* clearly alludes to Vergil's underworld, but the festival of which the *CS* was part – Augustus' *ludi saeculares* – already has a place within *Aeneid* 6 as well. In the cultural Zeitgeist of the Augustan *saeculum*, the question of what image or idea has priority becomes chronologically hazy. Horace's *CS*, then, is not just reading Vergil's underworld; it also reappropriates into the domain of public ritual Vergil's recently mythologized version of itself. In putting the chorus on stage at Rome, Horace takes Vergil's model for Greek performance culture being pressed into the service of the Roman state and reclaims its pragmatic possibilities.

I. Vergil's Choral Elysium

I begin with the connections between choral performance and narratives of foundation and social harmony in *Aeneid* 6.[4] After hearing Deiphobus' harrowing account of Troy's final night, Aeneas and the Sibyl move on to the happier scene of Elysium (*Aen.* 6.642–62). There, they witness the heroes of old enjoying the activities they took part in during life: athletics, feasting, song, and dance: "another group is beating out choral dances with their feet, and singing songs" (*pars pedibus plaudunt choreas et carmina dicunt*, 644). As the internal audience of this performance, Aeneas and the Sibyl presumably hear and enjoy its content; the reader simply learns its form.[5] By drawing attention both to the heroes' choreography (*choreas*) and their song (*carmina*), Vergil conjures up the Greek concept of χορεία, the combined performance of dance and song.[6] Emphasizing the musical element of the experience, Orpheus accompanies them on his seven-stringed lyre (645).

Also present in Elysium are the founders and early kings of Troy (*Aen.* 6.648–50):

> hic genus antiquum Teucri, pulcherrima proles,
> magnanimi heroes nati melioribus annis,
> Ilusque Assaracusque et Troiae Dardanus auctor.

Here is the ancient race of Teucer, most noble race, great-hearted heroes born in happier years: Ilus and Assaracus and Dardanus, founder of Troy.

These Trojan figures are surrounded by yet more choral singing and dancing: around them, heroes "are singing a happy paean in a chorus throughout the grove fragrant with laurel" (*laetumque choro paeana canentis inter odoratum lauris nemus, Aen.* 6.657).[7] Their performance is also marked as choral (*choro,* cf. *choreas,* 644), but now the form of the song is further characterized as a particular kind of lyric hymn, a paean (*paeana*). As Servius notes in his lemma on these lines, paeans were especially associated with the worship of Apollo, and Vergil further emphasizes this Apolline context by locating the scene within a grove of laurels and by juxtaposing it with another set of performers, poets who "speak words worthy of Apollo" (*Phoebo digna locuti,* 662).[8] As in lines 648–50, this second group of choral performers is paired with a soloist. Instead of Orpheus, it is the *uates* Musaeus (6.666–78), who then directs Aeneas and the Sibyl out of Elysium towards a *uates* of a different kind, Anchises, who will unroll the future history of Rome.[9]

Why do choral song and dance, and especially the lyric genre of the paean, play such a prominent role in Vergil's Elysium? They have no parallel in Vergil's closest underworld model, the *katabasis* of *Odyssey* 11. They have more in common with Orphic underworld traditions, where *choreia* – always associated with joy and festivity in the ancient world – is part of a happy afterlife just as it was part of a happy life.[10] Closer to Vergil's Roman context, the tradition of joyful underworld *choreia* seems to have appealed to other early Augustan poets. The more lusciously erotic and beautiful underworlds of Propertius and Tibullus contain scenes of choral song and dance, possibly in response to a (now lost) Hellenistic intermediary.[11]

Beyond simple joy, Vergil responds to and incorporates into his scene the cultural values associated with *choreia* in the archaic and classical Greek world, especially those of Apollo's paean. For the Vergilian heroes' choral dance in honour of Apollo carries significance within the context of *Aeneid* 6's geopolitical narrative of the founding of two great cities, Troy and Rome. In archaic and classical Greece, choral performance was a communal activity, a rite whose harmony of voices and bodies represented and enacted the concord of the community's wider social order.[12] Moreover, the performance of paeans for Apollo tended to bear this association particularly strongly because of the god's connection with the founding of cities and the continued maintenance of civic order throughout the Greek world.

As the god of city foundations and the pre-eminently musical god, Apollo's worship often involved choral celebration that looked back to the founding of the community celebrating the rites.[13] The *locus classicus* for the expression of this idea in Greek poetry is Callimachus' *Hymn to Apollo,* a text well known to Vergil. Callimachus' hymn opens with the speaker urging a group of young men to perform a choral hymn for Apollo, whose epiphany is imminent ("young men, get ready for song and for the chorus," οἱ δὲ νέοι μολπήν τε καὶ ἐς χορὸν ἐντύνασθε, 8). As the hymn continues, its refrain (ἰὴ παιῆον) reveals that its form is, more particularly, a paean.[14] Within the hymn, Apollo is praised as the founder of cities (55–9):

> Φοίβῳ δ' ἑσπόμενοι πόλιας διεμετρήσαντο
> ἄνθρωποι· Φοῖβος γὰρ ἀεὶ πολίεσσι φιληδεῖ
> κτιζομένῃσ', αὐτὸς δὲ θεμείλια Φοῖβος ὑφαίνει.
> τετραέτης τὰ πρῶτα θεμείλια Φοῖβος ἔπηξε
> καλῇ ἐν Ὀρτυγίῃ περιηγέος ἐγγύθι λίμνης.

Following Apollo, men have measured out cities. For Phoebus always takes delight in founding cities, and Phoebus himself weaves the foundations. At four years old, Phoebus himself wove the fi st foundations in beautiful Ortygia, near the circular lake.

Immediately after this passage, Callimachus narrates Apollo's involvement in the founding of the author's own city, Cyrene, which Battus built after consulting with the god's oracle (65–8).

The rites to Apollo enacted in Callimachus' hymn serve to remember Apollo's foundational activities on a regular basis, and indeed the chorus conceptually unites the act of founding the city with the act of remembering it in song. They apply the language of foundation to their conception of themselves as singers: at lines 12–15 they present their song and dance as an action that will ensure that the city's "ancient foundations" (ἀρχαίοισι θεμέθλοις, 15) will remain firm The chorus refounds the city each time the hymn is performed, since the musical harmony of its members represents, in the ritual present, the human embodiment of its continued good order.

To see how the Apolline hymns of Vergil's Elysium contain similar resonances of city foundation, it is important to consider with which community Vergil associates his underworld *choreia.* As we saw, it takes place in the vicinity of "Ilus and Assaracus and Dardanus, founder of Troy" (*Ilusque Assaracusque et Troiae Dardanus auctor, Aen.* 6.650). These Elysian performances are thus associated with Troy's founding and earliest history. As we saw, the Trojan heroes are associated with Apollo's worship through physical proximity. Moreover, Vergil's language closely correlates them with Apollo's role as founder of cities. The epithet that emphasizes Dardanus' role as founder of Troy, *Troiae Dardanus auctor* (650), recalls the description of Apollo himself in the ecphrasis of his temple in the prologue of *Georgics* 3 (34–6):

> stabunt et Parii lapides, spirantia signa,
> Assaraci proles demissaeque ab Ioue gentis
> nomina, Trosque parens et *Troiae Cynthius auctor.*

Parian marbles will stand there too, living statues: the sons of Assaracus, the names of the race descended from Jupiter, and father Tros and the *Cynthian founder of Troy.*

In the *Georgics* passage, Apollo, called *Troiae Cynthius auctor,* completes the list of Trojan founders who will have statues in the temple. In *Aeneid* 6, Apollo's epithet is transferred to Troy's human founder, Dardanus, in a scene closely tied to worship of the city's divine founder, Apollo. The scene of joyful, Elysian *choreia,* then, specifically conjures before Aeneas' eyes the community that existed during the earliest days of Troy, emphasizing both its happy beginnings and its deep relationship with Apollo.

Vergil's Elysian paeans are unusual in Roman poetry insofar as they create the impression of a peaceful, harmonious world. Elsewhere in Augustan poetry, embedded paeans tend to pick up on another traditional aspect of the paean: its associations with military celebration on the battlefield Three other imagined Augustan paeans (Prop. 3.15.41–2, Arbonius Silo fr. 1 (Morel), and *Aen.* 10.738) all engage with the paean as it is represented in the battlefield context of Hom. *Il.* 22.391–2, when Achilles urges the Myrmidons to sing a paean after the death of Hector. In contrast, the effect created in Vergil's Elysium comes close to representing a golden age in its style and tone. These Trojan heroes lived during "better years" (*melioribus annis, Aen.* 6.649), a phrase that retrojects their happiness into a mythical past time far removed from the present.[15]

The image of these Trojan heroes being born in "better years" contains resonances of golden age imagery in earlier Latin epic. Towards the beginning of Catullus 64, as Catullus recounts the figures who attended the wedding of Peleus and Thetis, he addresses the mythical age of heroes: *o nimis optato saeclorum tempore nati | heroes, saluete, deum genus!* ("oh heroes, born in the greatly longed-for time of the ages, greetings, offspring of the gods!" Catull. 64.21–2). In Catullus, this enthusiastic apostrophe contrasts with the poem's end, where he decries humanity's present condition, "after the earth has been stained with unspeakable evil" (*postquam tellus scelerest imbuta nefando*, 397). In both Vergil and Catullus, these heroes represent an age, far removed from the present, that was in every sense better.

Vergil's image of an Elysian golden age, celebrated by Apolline song and linked to Troy's founding, contrasts powerfully with other scenes of Trojan choral celebration in the *Aeneid*. Elysium recalls the joyful singing and dancing with which the children of Troy welcomed the fatal horse at *Aen.* 2.238–9: *pueri circum innuptaeque puellae | sacra canunt funemque manu contingere gaudent* ("Boys and unwed girls sang sacred songs around it, and rejoiced to touch the rope with their hand"). The children's joyful singing and dancing usher in the final fall of Troy.[16] Ritual song and dance, usually a medium of joyful civic celebration, shows the city – including its youth, a future that will never come to pass – unknowingly acting out its own destruction.

The tendency in the *Aeneid* for communal, religious rites, and specifically choral performance, to become implicated in the narrative of Troy's downfall is picked up elsewhere in Vergil's underworld. In Deiphobus' tale of Troy's final night, Helen is depicted as a maenadic chorus leader who arouses the Trojan women to dance (*Aen.* 6.517–19):

illa chorum simulans euhantis orgia circum
ducebat Phrygias; flammam media ipsa teneba
ingentem et summa Danaos ex arce uocabat.

That woman, feigning a choral dance, was leading around the Phrygian women, shrieking like bacchants in their rites; in the middle she herself was holding a great flame and was calling the Greeks from the top of the citadel

In the case of both the children and the women of Troy, *choreia* – an activity usually enjoyed by and intended to celebrate the community – is turned inwards against the Trojans. In Elysium, these unsettling valences are reversed, so that choral song and dance regain a joyful, harmonious status as Aeneas is led to remember Troy's earlier, happier past.[17]

So far I have focused on the connection of Apollo's hymns to Troy, but Vergil's Elysian *choreia* also points forward to the founding of the epic's other major city, Rome. For the scene in Elysium, which recalled the "better years" of the ancient Trojan past, foreshadows and leads up to Anchises' forthcoming prophecy, which will proclaim the coming of a Roman golden age (*aurea saecula, Aen.* 6.792–3) that Augustus will found.[18]

As Friedrich Solmsen noted, there is considerable continuity between the scene in Elysium and Aeneas' encounter with Anchises. The community of souls that Anchises tends has much in common with the heroes in Elysium, and the verdant valley in which they are located looks much like the underworld's former paradise.[19] More importantly for our purposes, the transition from Elysium to Anchises' Parade of Heroes is carried out through the imagery of music, song, and poetry. Among the crowd of *pii uates* in Elysium Musaeus, characterized as *optimus uates* (669), stands out and directs them to Anchises and his waiting prophecy. There is, then, an unbroken chain of *carmina* from the Apolline paeans in Elysium, to Musaeus, to the prophetic hexameter speech of Anchises himself. The presence of Apollo, god of foundation, prophecy, and song, binds them together.

The transition from Elysium to Anchises' prophecy reveals, ultimately, the geopolitical shift from Troy to Rome. In Elysium, Aeneas witnesses a choral scene whose music, song, and dance are tied to the memory of the golden age of the Trojan past. But its nostalgic bliss soon gives way to the coming paradise whose exposition forms the culmination of *Aeneid* 6: the founding of a new race of Romans. Vergil fills Elysium with his deep knowledge of Apolline *choreia*, especially the paean, and its traditional associations in Graeco-Roman literature and culture. But they are eventually left behind. Their traditional Greek connotations of city foundation and social cohesion serve to prepare for Aeneas' encounter with his father's vatic authority and the knowledge that he holds about the future of Rome.

II. Horace's *Carmen Saeculare*: A Chorus at Rome

I now ascend from Vergil's underworld to consider, in the second half of this essay, the afterlife of Vergil's choral Elysium in Horace's closely contemporary *CS*. Vergil did not live to see the performance of Horace's hymn, which concluded Augustus' *ludi saeculares* in 17 BCE.[20] If he had, he would have witnessed a highly unusual event in Roman religious and literary history: the staging of a choral lyric hymn of thanksgiving by twenty-seven Roman boys and the same number of girls, sung in procession fi st on the Palatine and then on the Capitoline, in celebration of a new age.[21]

The notion of a restored *saeculum* had been in the air long before Augustus would claim and celebrate the phenomenon in 17 BCE. Vergil's fourth *Eclogue* contains saecular elements even before Augustus' assumption of power, and Tibullus 2.5, presumably in circulation before the poet's death in 19 BCE, treats in detail many of the features that would be prominent in Augustus' civic celebration.[22] But the connections between the *CS* and *Aeneid* 6, to which I now turn, are particularly close and complex.[23] The relationship between these two texts shows the processes of literary reception at their most elastic. The *CS* is a reception text of the *Aeneid,* yet its context and even its very form as a choral hymn are already anticipated by the text it receives.

The network of Apolline imagery in Vergil's underworld, of which his choral Elysium is part, foreshadows in many places the upcoming *ludi saeculares.* As Aeneas descends to the underworld, he makes the following promise (*Aen.* 6.69–74):

> tum Phoebo et Triuiae solido de marmore templum
> instituam festosque dies de nomine Phoebi.
> te quoque magna manent regnis penetralia nostris:
> hic ego namque tuas sortis arcanaque fata
> dicta meae genti ponam, lectosque sacrabo,
> alma, uiros.

Then I will dedicate a temple to Apollo and Diana, made of solid marble, and sacred days in Apollo's name. In our kingdom, a great inner shrine awaits you too: for here, kindly one, I will place your oracles and your secret prophecies spoken to my people, and will consecrate chosen men.

Aeneas alludes here to the transferal of the Sibylline books from the temple of Jupiter on the Capitoline to the temple of Apollo on the Palatine by Augustus himself in the 20s BCE. Moreover, his reference to Apollo's games (*festosque dies,* 70) probably calls to mind the *ludi saeculares* that were stipulated in the Sibylline oracle's pages.[24] Aeneas' own preparatory sacrifices are also very similar to the sacrifices that Augustus performed during the Saecular Games: both include sacrifices to Proserpina, to Dis, and to Earth (*Aen.* 6.250–1).[25] Finally, and strikingly, Anchises' famous exhortation to Aeneas to remember the Roman code of values, "remember, Roman" (*Romane memento, Aen.* 6.851), is a Latin version of the Sibylline oracle's mandate to celebrate the *ludi saeculares*: μεμνῆσθαι, Ῥωμαῖε.[26] The chronology of the two texts is uncertain: it is possible that the Sibylline oracle alludes to the *Aeneid* and not the other way around if, as seems likely, it was composed shortly before Augustus' games. But when all the evidence is taken together, it seems clear that in *Aeneid* 6 Vergil has in mind several aspects of the upcoming Games.

Embedded in Vergil's underworld, these foreshadowings of Rome's celebration of a new Augustan *saeculum* contribute to how the *Aeneid* itself represents the new age.[27] Vergil's references to these upcoming events thus exhibit an unusual mode of allusion, looking not backwards but rather forwards to the Games and their new *saeculum* in a voice that could be described as prophetic or visionary.[28] Indeed, Pierre Grimal has characterized this effect as a "mythic guarantee," arguing that by embedding the performance of the *ludi* in the *Aeneid*'s mythical narrative, Vergil lends Augustus' saecular celebration the weight and authority of tradition.[29]

In light of these connections, John Miller has suggested that *Aeneid* 6 prefigures the *ludi saeculares* in a further way. He briefly and intriguingly proposes that the paean sung by the heroes in Vergil's Elysium looks forward to the performance of the *CS* itself.[30] Such a reading seems eminently likely. As part of its ritual instructions for the Saecular Games, the Sibylline oracle instructed "Latin paeans" (Λατῖνοι παιᾶνες) to be performed by one chorus of girls and another separate chorus of boys (Phlegon of Tralles 149–50), an injunction that would ultimately be fulfilled by Horace's *CS*. Paeans for Apollo, then, are fi st imagined in Vergil's underworld and then actualized by Horace.

I would like to expand Miller's suggestion, and as I do so, read it in the other direction. That is to say, the "Latin paeans" of *Aeneid* 6 can also be seen as an intertext for the *CS* itself. If Vergil already offers a hint, in *Aeneid* 6, of what the performances surrounding a new Roman *saeculum* might look like, we can see Horace responding to Vergil when he instantiates the possibilities for Roman paeans in the performance of the *CS*. In Elysium, Vergil offers one possible vision for the execution of the Sibyl's mandate for "Latin paeans." What Horace comes up with in the event is quite different, actively reading and rewriting Vergil when his lyric hymn is produced at Rome.

As the final event of the multi-day celebration of *ludi saeculares*, the *CS* both contributes to and comments on the entire festival's celebration of a new age.[31] Performed by young girls and boys, who refer often to themselves as the youth of Rome and the guardians of its future, the hymn is a prayer for the continuation of Rome's peace, fertility, and prosperity.[32] The language of its prayer and promise is at times overtly political: the children make mention of Augustus' recent marriage legislation as the safeguard of this societal happiness (17–20). While *Aeneid* 6 showed Aeneas witnessing the Parade of Heroes and learning of the greatness and prosperity of Rome that was to come, the performers of the *CS* embody what such prosperity can look like in reality. At the end of the hymn, when they claim that they will go home to spread the news that their prayer has been answered (*spem bonam certamque domum reporto*, 74), they ensure that individual Roman households will be occupied by citizens who keep faith with Augustan values and (it is implied) will grow up to produce future generations who will preserve these values.[33]

The above summary of the hymn's religious and social intent suggests broad affinities with *Aeneid* 6 and, indeed, the presence of Vergil's underworld book is deeply felt in the *CS*. The hymn's opening invocation develops into a narrative of Aeneas' journey from Troy to Italy, which strongly recalls the *Aeneid*'s recently published version of the myth (37–53). Most strikingly, Aeneas is called *castus* (42) in a nod to Vergil's frequent characterization of the hero as *pius*. At the conclusion of the *CS'* embedded mythic narrative, the language of *Aeneid* 6 in particular comes to the fore (49–52):

quaeque uos bobus ueneratur albis
clarus Anchisae Venerisque sanguis,
impetret, *bellante prior, iacentem*
   lenis in hostem.

What the glorious descendant of Anchises and Venus asks of you with white oxen, may he obtain, *foremost in battle and gentle towards the enemy who has been laid low.*

The formulation of Roman values italicized above echoes the language of Vergil's Anchises, who told Aeneas that the task of the Romans will be to "spare the submissive and war down the proud" (*parcere subiectis et debellare superbos, Aen.* 6.853). The performing voice of the *CS* – and by extension, the voice of their poet Horace – takes on the prophetic mythical voice of Anchises (who is, in fact, recalled by name at line 50, *Anchisae Venerisque sanguis*). While the Vergilian Anchises' prophecy for the future of Rome derived potency from its mythical setting, the voice of the *CS* has a different power: it harnesses the voice of choral prayer to the gods in the here-and-now of the ritual present.[34]

Anchises' prophetic voice is not the only voice from *Aeneid* 6 that the chorus of the *CS* appropriates. Given the multiple resonances of the *Aeneid* and especially of Vergil's underworld in the hymn, I see the chorus of the *CS* also taking on the performative identity of Vergil's Elysian choruses and transforming it in a new context. The chorus of the *CS* can therefore be understood as drawing on multiple voices from within the *Aeneid*, recombining them to invest the chorus – and their poet – with multiple sources of authority as they are transformed from an epic to a public lyric setting.

The *CS*, as well as the paratexts surrounding it, take to heart and frequently allude to its identity as a choral song and specifically as a paean, like the song of Vergil's Elysian heroes. As I mentioned earlier, the Sibylline oracle mandated the performance of "Latin paeans" and "choruses" of boys and girls. In addition, the inscriptional *Acta* that recorded the Games after the event describe how "double choruses" were performed (*bi]ni chori*, 3), and again, more expansively, that there were "boys and maidens with both parents still alive, gathered to sing a song and hold choruses" (*pueri uirginesque patrimos matrim[osque] | [ad carmen can]endum chorosque habendos frequentes*, 20–1). At the opening of the hymn itself, its young performers refer to their singing as a fulfilment of the Sibylline oracle (*CS* 5–8):

> quo Sibyllini monuere uersus
> uirgines lectas puerosque castos
> dis, quibus septem placuere colles,
>   dicere carmen.

when the Sibyl's verses have advised that chosen young girls and pure young men should sing a hymn to the gods who look favourably on the seven hills.

In a closing self-referential sphragis, they finally refer to themselves as a "chorus taught to utter the praise of Phoebus and Diana" (*doctus et Phoebi chorus et Dianae | dicere laudes*, 75–6). The self-referential voice of Horace's chorus draws on and transforms a complex network of song traditions, from ancient Roman *carmina* to Greek choral models.[35] As Barchiesi has demonstrated, the *CS'* opening address to the Delian twins, Apollo and Diana, marks it out as a Roman version of a Greek paean, just as the Sibyl had asked for.[36] In typically Horatian fashion, however, the *CS* transforms the paean tradition even as it draws on it. For instance, Horace avoids the apotropaic elements traditionally belonging to the paean, in favour of a more radiantly optimistic vision of Rome's future.[37] He also combines the paean's traditionally all-male chorus with a chorus of young women (*uirgines lectae*, 6).[38] It is this combination of boys and girls that, as we saw earlier, represents Rome's future fertility, wealth, and happiness.[39]

As a paean to Apollo, albeit a rather unusual Roman one, the lyric form of the *CS* recalls the song and dance of the heroes in Vergil's Elysium. The confluence of allusion surrounding the paean in Vergil's underworld and Horace's *CS* is part of an ongoing creative and scholarly debate in the early Augustan period surrounding the role of Greek hymnic and choral culture in celebrating Rome. The instinct for this is very old, going back to moments in Rome's history of conquest in Greece such as the establishment of a cult and paeanic celebration of the Roman general Titus Flamininus and the inscription of a Greek paean and prosodion at Delphi in 128 BCE, which closes with a reference to Roman prosperity.[40] But Augustus' interest in Apollo, and the god's central place in the new regime's iconography, suggest new ways for the god's hymnic genre to be incorporated into literary texts that deal with Rome's new age.[41]

One domain in which these texts' differing valences can be appreciated is in their shared language surrounding a golden age. As we have seen, Vergil's choruses were performed amidst ancient Trojan heroes who stood as a bridge between Aeneas' former, now destroyed, community of Troy and Anchises' future promise of Rome. In contrast, Horace's "Latin paeans" are performed by Roman children whose frequent self-referential allusions to their status as adolescents show how they represent the fertility of Rome that they pray for. The golden age that the children's language conjures is not part of a mythical afterlife. Rather, their blessed *saeculum* exists in the present and will continue into the future. This idea is expressed most emphatically at lines 65–8:

si Palatinas uidet aequos aras,
remque Romanam Latiumque felix
alterum in lustrum meliusque semper
   prorogat aeuum.

if [Apollo] looks with favour on the Palatine altars and extends Roman power and blessed Latium into another cycle and into an age that is always better.

The children's language refers explicitly to the new age that their prayer ushers in (*lustrum, aeuum*). Their saecular vision explicitly recalls the golden age of Vergil's Trojan heroes. Vergil's heroes lived during "better years" (*melioribus annis, Aen.* 6.649). Horace's children herald a golden age that will be "always better" (*meliusque semper*). As they quote Vergil's heroes, they take the *Aeneid*'s claims much further, promising happiness that is eternal (*semper*) in its increase.

As the above discussion suggests, Horace's refiguring of Vergil's Elysian paean is ritually and spatially pointed. A hymn performed in the underworld (although Vergil's Elysian Fields are imagined as being blessed and happy) is relocated to the upper air, where it is associated explicitly with Olympian, rather than chthonic, deities, and filled with the imagery of light, day, and brightness.[42] The *CS'* resistance to chthonic or katabatic aspects should be viewed as part of the wider ritual innovation of Augustus' *ludi saeculares,* which, in Denis Feeney's words, "transformed the atmosphere and purpose of the *ludi,* orienting them away from infernal expiation towards future fecundity."[43] The identity of the *CS'* performers give them a particular role in this ritual recalibration: as children, they represent the current and future life of Rome, in contrast to Vergil's heroes who perished long ago.[44]

Part of the reason, I think, that Horace's hymn is so interested in recreating the paeanic voice of Vergil's heroes is to draw attention to its status as lyric poetry, in contrast to Vergil's epic. Its self-definition against Roman epic goes beyond Vergil, as Horace's singers also incorporate other markers of Latin epic into their own voice. As we saw, Vergil's Elysium incorporated language from the Latin epic tradition to represent its Trojan golden age, alluding to the apostrophe to the heroic age in Catullus 64. The *CS* itself folds the language of Catullus' epyllion into its construction of its own authoritative speech. At line 25, Horace's children address "you Parcae, who are truthful in song" (*uosque, ueraces cecinisse Parcae*). Their phrase echoes the second half of Catullus 64, which contains the song of the Parcae (306–83). Catullus' Parcae are called *ueredici* (306), and singers of a *ueridicum oraculum* (326). Horace's allusion is multilayered: Catullus' Fates form part of the inspiration for Horace's Parcae, but they are merged with the prophetic figure of the Sibyl, to whose books (as we have seen) the children also make reference.[45]

The singers of Horace's hymn, then, take on songs and voices that were embedded in epic. They do not simply allude to them; rather, they fold them into their own authoritative voice. The prophetic voice of Anchises, the religious voice of the Vergilian heroes' Elysian worship, and the song of the Fates are all channelled in the children's prayer. In Horace's creation of a song for a chorus of *pueri* and *uirgines*, one might also see a subtle allusion to – and inversion of – Vergil's Trojan children in *Aeneid* 2, who thought they were celebrating Troy's prosperity but were in fact ushering in its destruction.[46]

Horace's generic transformation of Vergil's embedded hymns is tied to one of the central concerns in the *Odes* and *CS*, of reclaiming for his new Roman setting the pragmatic authority of the Greek lyric tradition.[47] Horace's children take the imagined performance of Vergil's Elysian *choreia* and reinterpret it in a lyric setting where form and function are now aligned. Not only does their Greek-style hymn act as a "real" prayer for the Roman state; it is also, unusually in the hymnic tradition, certain that its prayer will be effective. At the end of the hymn, the singers announce, *spem bonam certamque domum reporto* ("I bring home a fine and sure hop ," 74). They do not just pray for a good *saeculum*. In part because they represent the city's future as a group of Roman children, they also guarantee its success.[48]

At the dawn of the new *saeculum*, each event of the *ludi* plays a part in Augustus' refoundation of Rome. The *CS* participates in this act of civic refoundation by means of its ritual prayer, and as the closing ceremony it also reflects upon the whole event. This process has been sensitively discussed by several scholars. Michèle Lowrie interprets the *CS* as a hymn that performs, displays, and transmits the foundational power expressed over the course of the *ludi*.[49] Michael Putnam speaks in similar terms of the *CS'* participation in the games' "ritual renovation" of Rome.[50]

By harnessing the pragmatic potential of lyric song, then, in the context of Rome's ritual renovation, the children's choral voice in the *CS* can be described as "foundational" in a way that is very different from, but closely in dialogue with, the paeans of Vergil's underworld. Horace's reclaiming of the paeanic form for his public lyric performance reworks the traditional associations of Apollo's paean with city foundation and social order. As we saw, the performance of Vergil's Elysian heroes provided a bridge between the Trojan past and the future foundation of Rome as they worshipped the founder-god Apollo at a pivotal moment of *Aeneid* 6. The choral voice of Horace's children, in the here and now of their ritual performance, deepens further the relationship between choral song and the foundation of Rome.

Moreover, the children's choral voice, singing Latin paeans to Apollo as part of Augustus' festival of civic renewal, does not simply hint at or depict the foundational power of song, as in Vergil's underworld – it actually creates it. The *CS*, we might say, transforms once again into ritual the choral voice that the *Aeneid* had encoded into myth. In this extraordinary event, the pragmatic power of Vergil's choral voice is made real.

NOTES

1 I would like to express my thanks to Bill Gladhill for his organization of the 2013 *Symposium Cumanum*, and to Bill and Micah Myers for their invitation to contribute to the resulting volume as well as their editorial feedback and suggestions.

2 For Vergil, I use the Oxford Classical Text of Mynors 1969; for Horace, the Teubner of Shackleton Bailey 1995 (3rd ed.). All translations are my own.

3 The *CS* was defended by Fraenkel as a significant part of Horace s *oeuvre* (1957: 364–832) but did not receive a full-scale monograph in English until Putnam 2000. See also Feeney 1998: 32–8; Barchiesi 2002; Lowrie 2009: 123–41; Miller 2009: 253–97; Thomas 2011. On the *CS'* relationship with the *Aeneid*, see Ableitinger 1972; Feeney 1998: 36; Putnam 2000: 122–4; Barchiesi 2002: 109–10; Lowrie 2009: 130 with n22.

4 The choral elements of Vergil's Elysium are discussed at greater length, and in relation to Deiphobus' narrative, at Curtis 2017: 209–19.

5 On vision in Vergil's underworld and Aeneas as witness to an unfolding series of spectacles, see Smith 2005: 82–90.

6 Plato defines χορεία as "the combination of dance and song" (χορεία γε μὴν ὄρχησίς τε καὶ ᾠδὴ τὸ σύνολόν ἐστιν, *Leg.* 654b). The English term "dance-song" has been used to translate Greek *choreia* in an attempt to express its multiple components. See Henrichs 1994–5: 56, who harks back (94n23) to Wilamowitz's earlier characterization of dithyrambs, hyporchemata and dramatic choruses as "Tanzlieder" (1895: 1.77). Compare Steiner's similar term "song-dance" (2011: 300). Ladianou 2005: 47–8 addresses the audience's combined sensory experience of χορεία. For a different approach to movement and gesture in this scene, cf. Herrero's contribution to this volume.

7 The Trojan founders are not explicitly said to engage in the choral performances – they appear to stand nearby with their armour – but there is a sense of closeness and overlap between the groups of heroes (Miller 2009: 147).

8 Serv. ad *Aen.* 6.657: PAEANA *proprie Apollinis laudes, quod nunc congruit propter "lauri nemus"* ("PAEAN is properly praise of Apollo, which is suitable here because of the 'grove of laurel'"). See further Horsfall 1993 on the "programmatic and poetical" associations of Vergil's laurel grove. While paeans could be addressed to many gods, including Dionysus, Ares, and Athena (and also sometimes to people), they were most often addressed to Apollo. Käppel 1992: 341–9 collects testimony for the paean's divine and human addressees (those to Apollo are at 341–3). See also Rutherford 2001: 23–36 on Apollo's centrality to the paean genre.

9 See further Gowers in this volume on the poets whom Aeneas encounters here and on Anchises' relationship with them.

10 Plato's false but telling etymology of χορός from χαρά ("joy") attests to this thoroughgoing connection (Pl. *Leg.* 654a). See Henrichs 1996: 17–18 on *choreia*'s joyful, festive connotations, in contrast to songs of lament. Norden 1957 *ad loc.* suggests that Vergil's *laetum* at *Aen.* 6.657 translates Greek εὔφρων, a word associated with paeans, and thus responds to their traditionally joyful character. On the apocalyptic and Orphic backgrounds of Vergil's Elysium, see Norden 1957: 295–6; Bremmer 2009: 25–30; Horsfall 2013a: 437, 444–5. Song appears in Apollo's grove at *Orph. Fragm.* 717.103 f. Bernabé. As noted above, Orpheus himself accompanies one of the Vergilian choruses (*Aen.* 6.645–7). See also Ar. *Ran.*, where the chorus of initiates performs ghostly song and dance (e.g., 449–53: "Let us go to the rose-filled flowery meadow , playing in our usual mode of lovely choruses (καλλιχορώτατον) which the blessed Fates join together"). The connection between *choreia* and underworld joy is also present in texts that are not specifically "Orphic"; see, e.g., Pind. fr. 129 S-M (from a *threnos*), which has many points of connection with Vergil's scene, including the enjoyment of feasting, music, and athletics (ἵπποις γυμνασίοισι

<τε> …| | τοὶ δὲ πεσσοῖς | τοὶ δὲ φορμίγγεσσι τέρπονται, 6–8) in the setting of a fertile, fragrant meadow.

11 See Papanghelis 1987: 176, and Myers in this volume on further correspondences between *Aeneid* 6 and elegy. Tibullus, who imagines inhabiting the underworld after his own death in Tib. 1.3, paints a luxurious picture of an erotic underworld to which he is guided by Venus. Choral song and dance contribute to this eroticized scene (*hic choreae cantusque uigent*, 59), since unlike the heroic *choreia* of the Vergilian underworld, it brings together boys and girls ("And a row of young men, intermingled with tender girls, plays around, and Love stirs up battles continuously," *ac iuuenum series teneris inmixta puellis | ludit, et adsidue proelia miscet Amor*, 63–4). Propertius develops this Tibullan image in Prop. 4.7 (Cynthia's description of the underworld), emphasizing the female performers: his underworld is teeming with women worshipping Cybele ("The Lydian plectrums sound for turbaned choruses," *mitratisque sonant Lydia plectra choris*, 63–4). On the contrast between Tibullus' and Propertius' underworld performances, see Warden 1980: 39, 44 and Papanghelis 1987: 176, 184. Also relevant is Horace's underworld scene at *Carm*. 2.13, in which the narrator meets Alcaeus and Sappho. Although monodic rather than choral, Horace's poetic underworld is likewise full of song.

12 Plato, for instance, says that the gods caused humans to sing and dance together, and thereby "joined them to each other" (ἀλλήλοις συνείροντας, Pl. *Leg*. 654a). *Choreia* is intimately connected with the creation and maintenance of good community in Plato's *Laws*; see Folch 2015; Prauscello 2015; and the contributions in Peponi 2013. On the chorus as a representation and embodiment of social order, see Bacon 1994–5: 11–20; Wilson 2003; Kurke 2012.

13 Dougherty 1993: 8 and 18–24 discusses the prominent place of Apollo in Greek foundation narratives, especially the role of his oracle at Delphi. Apollo was often known by the epithet ἀρχαγέτης ("fi st leader"), which was used by his worshippers in cities that he had helped to found. Statius alludes to this epithet when he mentions Apollo's role in the founding of Cumae: "You, Apollo, leader of people migrating far" (*tu, ductor populi longe migrantis, Apollo, Silu.* 4.8.47)." On Apollo's role in the *Aeneid*'s foundation story, see Miller 2009: 95–184.

14 The paean refrain begins at 21 (ὁππόθ' ἰὴ παιῆον ἰὴ παιῆον ἀκούσῃ, "whenever she [i.e., Thetis] hears ie paean, ie paean") and is repeated at 25 (ἰὴ ἰὴ φθέγγεσθε, "cry ie, ie"), 97, and 103.

15 Horsfall 2013a: 2.448 notes that the image goes back to Hesiod's ages of man in the *Works and Days*.

16 Although Vergil does not explicitly call the children a "chorus" or their celebration "*choreia*," the combination of their children's "singing" (*canunt*, 239) and their movement with the rope suggests a choral situation analogous to

the Elysian heroes' simultaneous performance of song and dance. Indeed, when explaining a reference to another rope dance at Ter. *Ad.* 752 (Wessner), Donatus assumes that the Vergilian passage refers to a choral dance (*lusus est natus ab eo fune, quo introductus equus durius in Troiam est, cum conexis manibus fune chorum ducunt saltantes,* "the game [in Terence] originates from the rope by which the horse was led with difficulty into Troy, when they led a chorus, dancing with a rope with hands joined").

17 On the disturbing choral resonances of this passage, see further Curtis 2017: 209–15.

18 Anchises himself makes a specific connection between the Trojan heroes in Elysium and the future ages of Rome. When he claims to foretell the glories of the "Dardanian race" (*Dardaniam prolem,* 756), his language recalls Aeneas' earlier meeting with Dardanus himself in Elysium (650).

19 Solmsen 1982: 424–5. Horsfall 2013a: 2.437–8 notes many of the linguistic and thematic markers in Elysium that prepare the ground for the Parade of Heroes.

20 On the context of the *CS* as part of the *ludi,* see Feeney 1998: 28–38; Thomas 2011: 53–61. Miller 2009: 247–52 discusses the song's relationship with the space of the Palatine temple complex. The text of the *CS* itself can be read alongside the Sibylline oracle that mandated the games (Phlegon of Tralles, *FrGrH* 257 F 37.132–69) and the monumental *Acta* that recorded the events of the multi-day celebration (*CIL* 6.32323 = *ILS* 5050, on which see Pighi 1965; Schnegg-Köhler 2002). See also Thomas 2011: 271–8 for a summary of the events of the *ludi,* as well as a text and translation of the oracle and the *Acta.*

21 As Barchiesi 2002: 108 notes, the song is unique because it is "the only surviving poem in Latin of which we know time and place of a choral performance, and independent evidence confirms that this definitely happene " See also White 1993: 123; Feeney 1998: 38; Putnam 2000: 1.

22 See Cairns 1979: 84–6. Saecular Games were held in republican Rome, although the number of times they were celebrated is difficult to establish with certaint . On the relationship of Augustus' games with the republican tradition, see Beard, North, and Price 1998: 201–6.

23 On the relationship between *Aeneid* 6 and Augustus' celebration of the *ludi saeculares,* see Merkelbach 1961; Zetzel 1989; Miller 2009: 139–49. Grimal 1954 attempts to date the composition of *Aeneid* 6 precisely in relation to the transfer of the Sibylline books to the temple of Palatine Apollo.

24 Grimal 1954: 53; Merkelbach 1961: 83; Zetzel 1989: 279; Miller 2009: 139–40.

25 Especially the black lamb that is sacrificed to Night and Earth and the sacrifice to Dis. See Zetzel 1989: 280–1.

26 Norden 1957 *ad loc.*

27 Zetzel 1989: 278–9 acknowledges the chronological uncertainties involved but concludes that "it would be surprising if Augustus had not had the *ludi* in mind for some time before the ritual was actually performed."

28 Miller 2009: 139: "Virgil himself was literally prophesying a momentous occurrence in Augustus' public program."

29 Grimal 1954: 58. Cf. Merkelbach 1961, who interprets *Aeneid* 6 as an aetiological account of the *ludi saeculares.*

30 Miller 2009: 148.

31 The hymn refers often to the performance context of the *ludi* (*tempore sacro,* 4; *ludos,* 22, where it refers to the future) and of saecular celebration (*alterum in lustrum,* 67); it even incorporates language about Augustus' sacrifices earlier in the festival (49–52). It also makes frequent reference to its setting within Rome's urban space (*urbe Roma,* 11; *urbem,* 39, *septem ... colles,* 57) and specifically within the alatine complex (*Palatinas aras,* 65).

32 See especially lines 29–32 and 59–60.

33 When Horace returns to a recollection of the *CS* in *Odes* 4.6, this implied promise of the children's future fertility is realized. The ode imagines that one of the female performers has grown up and is now a bride (*nupta iam,* 41) who remembers her performance of the *CS* as a child.

34 Cf. Putnam 2000: 122, who observes that Horace "turns Virgil's future into Rome's present."

35 Putnam 2000 passim offers a detailed examination of the different Greek and Roman backgrounds of Horace's hymn.

36 Barchiesi 2002: 112–23. See also Barchiesi 2000: 181–2. Horace will later return to the *CS'* identity as a paean, using Pindar's sixth paean as a significant site of allusion in *Odes* 4.6, his most detailed reflection on the *CS*. On the paeanic aspects of *Odes* 4.6, and its relationship with the *CS*, see Hardie 1998.

37 On the traditionally apotropaic nature of the Greek paean, see Rutherford 2001: 7–8, 15–16, 36–45.

38 On the paean as a choral genre typically performed by (young, military-age) men, see Rutherford 2001: 6.

39 Barchiesi 2002: 117–18.

40 The hymn to Flamininus is recorded at Plut. *Flam.* 16.3 = *CA* 173. For Limenius' paean, see Furley and Bremer 2001: 1.137 (translation) and 2.92 (Greek text and commentary).

41 On Augustus' identification with Apollo, see Zanker 1988; Miller 2009.

42 The principal gods addressed in the hymn are Apollo (1, 36, 62, 75) and Diana (1, 70, 75), who are figured also as *Sol* (8) and *Luna* (36); also addressed are Ilithyia (14), the Fates (25), and Earth (29), as well as the deities *Fides* (57), *Pax* (57), *Honos* (57), *Pudor* (57), *Virtus* (58), and *Copia* (60). References to brightness, light, and day are a prominent aspect of the *CS'* verbal imagery: *lucidum caeli decus,* 2; *alme Sol, curru nitido,* 9; *die claro,* 23; *fulgente arcu,* 61.

43 Feeney 1998: 29. As the *Acta* for the Augustan *ludi* make clear, Augustus added daytime rites for the Olympian gods to the chthonic cult that had been

typical of earlier republican *ludi*, and in addition to continuing worship at the traditional site of the underworld gods, the Tarentum in the Campus Martius, added rites (including the *CS*) carried out in the temple of Jupiter on the Capitoline and his new temple of Apollo on the Palatine.

44 Moreover, they are stipulated to be children with "both parents still alive" (*pueros uirginesque patrimos matrim[osque]*, *CIL* 6.32323.20), another detail that shows how important is flourishing life to the hymn s conception of its performers' identity.

45 Since the Sibylline oracle was also written in (Greek) hexameter, there may also be a tripartite transformation of epic poetry in the *CS* (Vergil's underworld, Catullus 64, and the Sibylline verses).

46 The identity and self-characterization of the singers of the *CS* as *pueri* and *uirgines* has several predecessors, from Catullus' hymn to Diana in the voice of boys and girls (34) to Horace's own earlier *Odes* 1.21 (the hymn to Diana and Apollo performed by boys and girls). In *Odes* 4.6, Horace will create a more explicit through-line of performance language between the Trojans' final doomed night of choral celebration (*laetam Priami choreis | falleret aulam*, 15–16) to the bright new Augustan age (*rite … canentes*, 37; *reddidi carmen*, 43).

47 Much has been written on this topic; Feeney 1993 and Barchiesi 2000 are fundamental.

48 In this regard, the happy, hopeful children of the *CS* may be seen to rewrite the *Aeneid*'s sombre poetics surrounding the death of youthful figure . While in the *Aeneid* Iulus is the only adolescent protagonist who survives to see the end of the poem, the *CS* reclaims the voice of children to suggest hope for the future rather than the pathos of loss.

49 Lowrie 2010: 42, an expansion and reformulation of Lowrie 2009: 123–4.

50 Putnam 2000: 149.

11

Why Isn't Homer in Vergil's Underworld? – and Other Notable Absences[1]

EMILY GOWERS

Vergil's underworld guards its secrets closely; it probably always will. We may never know why Aeneas emerges through the Gate of False Dreams or fathom why the Golden Bough initially resists before ultimately yielding to him.[2] There are two crucial frameworks that enhance the disorienting atmosphere of the subterranean episode. The fi st is that of the mystery religions, long associated with both the imagery and the process of *katabasis*, especially where Aeneas' predecessors among underworld survivors, Hercules and Orpheus, are concerned.[3] When the Sibyl sweeps the majority of observers away from her sacred space – 258 *procul, o procul este, profani* – she turns the underworld into an allegory for the limitations of all human knowledge.[4] Doors open and shut, revelations are filtered lips are sealed and unsealed.[5] Some things cannot be imparted to Aeneas because there is not enough time, while some zones are out of bounds even for such privileged visitors: Tartarus, for example, the supreme Chamber of Horrors, about which Aeneas hears only second-hand from the Sibyl, after her tour with Hecate.[6] Correspondingly, Vergil himself plays partial initiate at 266–7: *sit mihi fas audita loqui; sit numina uestro | pandere res alta terra et caligine mersas* ("May it be right for me to utter what I have heard; may it be with your [the gods'] approval to reveal matters plunged in darkness deep beneath the earth").

The second framework was originally proposed by Agnes Michels: the entire book is a dream sequence. This would be a scenario set up at the end of *Aeneid* 5, where Palinurus is purposely lulled to sleep by Somnus while the other sailors on Aeneas' boat drift along in alcohol-induced slumber.[7] Just as the helmsman tips imperceptibly overboard, so we never quite notice when upper world becomes underworld, so similar are the murky wooded landscapes above and below.[8] Aeneas' experience down there is choppy – what dream experts call "episodic": the Sibyl fades in and out, characters are interchanged. As in a dream, Aeneas' powers of cognition are strangely distorted. His father Anchises eludes his grasp, "like a shadow or like a dream"; once plucked, the Golden Bough mysteriously grows back again. The crowd of monsters that swarm around the tree of false dreams (285–9) – centaurs, chimaeras, harpies – are not just the stuff of Lucretian nightmares but also mental re-assemblages from Aeneas' recent experience: carnival float , sea monsters, and rapacious island dwellers.[9] Tempted to hack at them with his sword, he is told that it will go right through their bodiless forms (290–4). As for the underworld landscape, with its darkness and thickets, it produces further symbolic confusions. As the Sibyl and Aeneas make their way, it is "like a journey through the woods under the meagre light of a half-seen moon" (*quale per incertam lunam sub luce maligna* | *est iter in siluis*, 270–1).[10] Why is this Sibyl called, uniquely by Vergil, Deiphobe (36)?[11] Is she meant to blur into Priam's mutilated son, Deiphobus, and, if so, why? And why, when Aeneas swims up to the surface again, does this seem so startlingly abrupt? When he sees the Shield (8.730), he will remain *rerum … ignarus* ("ignorant of history"), despite having witnessed the pageant of future heroes. No wonder, then, that the historian Fabius Pictor is said to have written that all Aeneas' future deeds and adventures appeared to him as a vision "in his sleep" (*secundum quietem*) (Q. Fabius Pictor fr. 1 Cornell = Cic. *Div.* 1.43):

> sint haec, ut dixi, somnia fabularum, hisque adiungatur etiam Aeneae somnium, quod +in numerum+ in Fabi Pictoris Graecis annalibus eius modi est, ut omnia quae ab Aenea gesta sunt quaeque illi acciderunt, ea fuerint, quae ei secundum quietem uisa sunt.

> Admittedly, these are dreams in myths, as I have said, and to these may also be added the Dream of Aeneas, which … in the Greek annals of Fabius Pictor, is of such a sort that everything that was done by Aeneas and everything that happened to him were things that appeared to him in his sleep.

Given this double framing – mystical secrecy and altered consciousness combined – it is unsurprising that Book 6 has a high concentration of the best-known puzzles of the *Aeneid*: some central, like the Gates and the Bough, some more minor, like the howlers picked out by Augustus' freedman, Hyginus.[12] When Palinurus, for example, instructs Aeneas to bury him near the port of Velia (366), Hyginus notes that it would not be founded for another six hundred years.[13] The absences of my title, and conversely the unexpected presences, can be approached in a number of different ways – none of them fully satisfying. Some readers are still troubled, for example, that, among the exclusive handful of earlier visitors who managed to go down to the underworld and come up again, Theseus is now in Tartarus, glued firmly to his seat (617–18), despite a previous resurfacing (122), while Orpheus is silent but living in Elysium (645). The likeliest explanation is that Vergil wants to count off the full set of individuals – mortal or semi-mortal – who initially survived the underworld (Hercules, Theseus, Pirithous, Orpheus, Castor, and Pollux), before indicating that his Aeneas will join the more exceptional group, destined as he is to rise skywards and become a god.[14] As for the Golden Bough, perhaps it persists in tugging back in order to tell us how precarious the path will be between Aeneas and his glorious starry future. Other characters are absent when we might expect them to be there: Paris, Priam, Hector, Eurydice, and Creusa, to name but a few. Some of these absences are compensated for by intertextuality. Eurydice and Creusa, for example, have a ghostly presence through verbal echoes of Vergil's other works: gazed at longingly by Aeneas as she recedes into the forest, Dido stands in for Orpheus' lost wife in *Georgics* 4, who in turn blurs with the lost Creusa of *Aeneid* 2.[15] Other absences are for reasons of economy. There is little need, for example, for a repeat encounter with Hector, who visited Aeneas in *Aeneid* 2 to hand over the mantle of Trojan power.[16] At least one is practical: Priam, last seen, had no head, which would have made it awkward for Aeneas to attempt a conversation with him.[17]

Flippancy aside, the question of my title is partly a provocation. In an obvious sense, Homer is everywhere in *Aeneid* 6: in the tree felling for Misenus' pyre, which recalls the tree-felling for Patroclus' funeral in *Iliad* 23; in Aeneas' encounter with a stony silent Dido, who repeats Odysseus' encounter with Ajax in *Odyssey* 11; in the souls waiting by the Styx, like a myriad leaves, birds, or bees; in the landscape of the underworld itself (Elysian Fields, Gates of Sleep, Tartarus, Tityos, Sisyphus, and Tantalus).[18] The entire world below is Homeric in its colouring. But the figure of Homer himself: why isn't he there? My special focus in this paper will be on the moment when Aeneas arrives at Poets' Corner in the Elysian Fields and asks for his father Anchises (669–71).[19] He has just encountered, in a blur of dead poets (*plurima turba*), a single named one: Musaeus, Orpheus' pupil or son and great-grandfather of the poetic tradition.[20] Conspicuously missing from the scene is the one poet we might be expecting Aeneas to meet, the one who had such a vital influence on Vergil's concept of the world below. The shade of Homer is visited in Lucian's *Menippus* and *True History* and, more reverentially, in Silius' *Punica*.[21] Vergil himself will be honoured with a place in Dante's *Inferno* (as will Homer). So why doesn't he pay homage to Homer in *his* underworld? There are a number of possible answers to the question, most of them reasonably straightforward. Less straightforward are their consequences for the *Aeneid* as a whole.

The fi st, most obvious answer: Homer is not yet dead. After all, the narrative has not come very far chronologically from the end of the Trojan War; only the seven-year period of Aeneas' wanderings lies in between. Perhaps Odysseus/Ulixes, whose footsteps Aeneas has been following around the Mediterranean (most notably in the Cyclops episode in *Aeneid* 3), has not yet returned to Ithaca; perhaps he is still telling his story to the Phaeacians. In other words, Homer has probably not yet finished singing the *Odyssey*. The situation this gives rise to is already strange enough: Vergil's characters speak in translations of Homer, while he himself engages with the Iliadic and Odyssean Homer at every turn in the underworld – rewriting him, correcting his accounts – and yet Homer is still at large singing his tales. Or rather, Homer's surrogate Demodocus is still unwittingly singing the *Iliad* (or its sequel, the Trojan Horse being fi st mentioned in his recital) to Odysseus, a central hero of those epics. But we may need to go further still. If Homer is alive, that notion endorses the fiction that he was a contemporary, even a witness of the Trojan War – a valid assumption, as far as Vergil's concept of poetic simultaneity goes. In the other Iliadic sequel that is *Aeneid* 2, Aeneas' role as eyewitness is particularly stressed. His *ipse uidi*, "I saw with my own eyes" (5, 279, 499), and *pars magna fui*, "I played a crucial part" (6), testify to a witness's active (or passive) participation in the events that provoke this longest of all tragic messenger speeches.[22] Yet autopsy as a narrative position is not pressed by Homer himself, who famously says at *Il.* 2.485–6, "Only the Muses know about the heroic past; we hear only report [*kleos*] and do not know anything" (ὑμεῖς γὰρ θεαί ἐστε, πάρεστέ τε, ἴστέ τε πάντα, | ἡμεῖς δὲ κλέος οἶον ἀκούομεν οὐδέ τι ἴδμεν). Similarly, his Demodocus is praised for singing of the past "as though he had been present or heard from someone who had been present" (ὥς τέ που ἢ αὐτὸς παρεὼν ἢ ἄλλου ἀκούσας, *Od.* 8.491).[23] Nor was this the suspicion of the majority of ancient writers, let alone modern ones.[24]

We need, in short, to confront a more drastic possibility. According to most ancient commentators, Homer was not even born when Aeneas went down to the underworld. In fact, he was usually thought to have been born at least one century later than the Trojan War, and consequently later than the timeline of the *Aeneid*. As Barbara Graziosi reports in *Inventing Homer*, antiquity produced no consensus on Homer's date. Indeed, ancient scholars often make a positive display of the range of different hypotheses.[25] Here is one version of the spread of views (Ps.-Plutarch *Life of Homer* 1.5):

οἳ μέν φασι κατὰ τὸν Τρωϊκὸν πόλεμον, οὗ καὶ αὐτόπτην γενέσθαι· οἳ δὲ μετὰ ἑκατὸν ἔτη τοῦ πολέμου· ἄλλοι δὲ μετὰ πεντήκοντα καὶ ἑκατόν.

Some say [Homer] lived at the time of the Trojan War and that he was a direct witness of it; others that he lived a hundred years after the war; others still 150 years after it.

The choice of date, as Graziosi points out, often depended on a particular writer's relationship to Homer as a rival authority. Herodotus, for example, puts him even later, at 850 BCE, and Thucydides "long after the Trojan War" – because both want to diminish his value as a historian.[26] Christian writers also tend to give Homer a late date, in their case to establish the priority of Moses (whom some Hebrew writers identified with Musaeus). Closer to Vergil's time, Nepos has his own opinion on the date of Homer's *floruit*: 905 BCE, 160 years before the foundation of Rome and nearly three hundred years after the Sack of Troy.[27] The element of authorial or national interest in these cases makes it worth thinking in advance about which of the various Homeric birthdates would have been most advantageous for Vergil's purposes.

As for the date of the Sack of Troy, this, too, was a movable event. But a standard date, 1184/3 BCE, had long ago been established by Eratosthenes.[28] A good example of a poet apparently making use of that set date is Homer's self-appointed successor Ennius, who in the *Annals* made Troy his chronological anchor and starting point. There is nothing unusual about that: the Sack of Troy was a watershed date for Rome, as well as Greece.[29] But Denis Feeney, following Adrian Gratwick, notes that Ennius puts the conventional date to a wonderfully personal use. The year 1184/3 BCE is exactly a thousand years before 184/3 BCE, the year when Ennius became a Roman citizen, Cato was censor, and Fulvius Nobilior dedicated the temple of Hercules Musarum, where the whole of Roman time was subsequently stored in the consular *fasti*.[30] Other surviving fragments indicate that Ennius was himself calendrically hyper-aware. For example, the speaker of *Ann*. 154–5 Skutsch alleges that Rome was founded seven hundred years before his own time; we also have Ennius' supposed thoughts on the cycle of reincarnation – which Feeney assumes is another cycle of a thousand years (*Ann*. I x Skutsch); and there is the poet's record of his own age, sixty-seven, at the time of finishing the *Annales* (*sed. inc*. lxx Skutsch).[31] Ennius thus hints at several thousand-year cycles, related both to his own age and to certain sliding landmark dates, such as the fall of Troy and the foundation of Rome. This is a model we might expect Vergil to want to follow, or to adapt.

There is plenty of evidence, meanwhile, to suggest that Vergil was equally calendrically aware:[32]

1) Jupiter's prophecy in Book 1, which predicts a sequence of three plus thirty plus three hundred years from the end of the *Aeneid* down to the birth of Romulus and Remus, making a random literary moment, the end of the poem, into something chronologically significant[33]
2) Anchises' thousand-year cycle of reincarnation (6.748) in the underworld, linked to the return of the Golden Age under Augustus (6.792–4) and specificall , Feeney thinks, to Augustus' inauguration of a new cycle of time in the Secular Games of 17 BCE.[34]
3) An apparent allusion to the exact calendrical date of the Sack of Troy as given by Eratosthenes – the seventh or eighth day of the month Thargelion, suggested in the detail about a clearly visible moon during Aeneas' last night in Troy (*Aen.* 2.255).[35]
4) An implied link, spotted by Servius (*ad* 6.69), between Aeneas' arrival at the Temple of Apollo at Cumae and Augustus' inauguration of the temple of Apollo on the Palatine, which would house the Sibylline books (on 9 October 28 BCE).
5) Most striking of all, the wholly disingenuous *forte*, "By chance, as it happened" (*Aen.* 8.102), which marks the perfect synchronicity of Aeneas' arrival at Pallanteum with the inauguration of the Ara Maxima of Hercules in the Forum Boarium (1177 BCE) and the annual rites there (celebrated on August 12) and then of his waking the next day in Evander's cottage to coincide with Augustus' no doubt strategically chosen dates for his Triple Triumph after Actium, celebrated on 13–14 August, 29 BCE. All these coincidences enable us to tumble down through chronological "wormholes," which channel Aeneas, Hercules, and Augustus in the same direction.[36]

Nor is it a coincidence that Aeneas meets his father immediately after he has met the poets. As a prophet (*uates*), Anchises qualifies as a recent supplement to the troupe of bards, whose main spokesman turns out to be not Orpheus (a close encounter with another member of the "survivors' club" was perhaps not desirable) but Musaeus, pointedly described as the supreme and preeminently tall member of the group (667–8).[37] Vergil's turn of phrase, *umeris exstantem suspicit altis*, "they looked up at him as he stood out with his lofty shoulders," might suggest Ennius' epitaph for himself, *uolito uiuos per ora uirum* ("I shall flit living, over the mouths of men," fr. 46 Courtney). Yet for Servius, Musaeus recalled Plato (nicknamed πλατύς "broad"), which suggests further sympathy with the idea that individuals in the underworld might reverberate with individuals not born, and makes the absence of a clear avatar of Homer all the more glaring.[38] At 669 Musaeus is hailed as *optime uates*, "best of bards," a form of address to which he is entitled in Homer's absence, at least. Socrates in the *Apology* had included among the consolations of death the chance to meet Orpheus, Musaeus, Hesiod, and Homer in the underworld.[39] Hellenistic intellectuals had grouped Orpheus, Musaeus, and Homer together as founders of Greek wisdom and *paideia*.[40] In short, someone is missing here. When the Sibyl asks Musaeus where in the underworld Anchises is to be found (*quae regio Anchisen, quis habet locus?* 670), this looks very like a substitute for the more obvious question to put to a group of dead poets: "Where can I find Homer? [41]

Anchises duly appears, a fitting substitute, particularly in the bearing he adopts – shedding tears and telling Aeneas that he has been expecting him (6.684–8):

> isque ubi tendentem aduersum per gramina uidit
> Aenean, alacris palmas utrasque tetendit,
> effusaeque genis lacrimae et uox excidit ore:
> 'uenisti tandem, tuaque exspectata parenti
> uicit iter durum pietas?'

When he saw Aeneas coming towards him across the grass, he stretched out both his hands in eagerness, and tears poured down his cheeks and he uttered these words: "Have you come at last, and has the devotion your father expected overcome the harsh journey?"

Here is a conspicuous reminder of the lost dream encounter of the weeping Homer with his Roman successor Ennius at the start of the *Annales*, as recorded by Lucretius (Lucr. *DRN* 1.120–6 = Enn. *Ann.* 4 Skutsch):

> etsi praeterea tamen esse Acherusia templa
> Ennius aeternis exponit uersibus edens,
> quo neque permanent animae neque corpora nostra
> sed quaedam simulacra modis pallentia miris.
> unde sibi exortam semper florentis Homer
> commemorat speciem lacrimas effundere salsas
> coepisse et rerum naturam expandere dictis.

Although in addition Ennius set forth in everlasting verse that the realm of Acheron exists, through which neither our souls nor our bodies pass, except for certain phantoms, strangely pale. Whence he related the sight of shining Homer, rising before him, who poured out salty tears and began to expound the nature of things in words.

The connection, in Michael Wigodsky's words, is "so obvious as to seem undeniable, if it had not been denied" (by Norden, in this case).[42] Indeed, we have to keep quite a few relationships in our heads at this point – Anchises and Aeneas, Homer and Ennius, Homer and Vergil, Ennius and Vergil.[43] Through various intertextual echoes, Vergil makes sure that all of them remain active.[44]

Yet even if Anchises in some sense fills the space vacated by a venerable poet, there is another way of looking at the encounter in Poets' Corner. It is equally possible that Musaeus and company are still expecting a newcomer to join their ranks. From their perspective, it might be *Aeneas* who arrives to stand in for a long-awaited Homer. After all, he, too, is weeping. In the middle of a book associated with tears at moments of remembering and loss, he responds to his father's sobs with tears of his own: "as he remembered this, his face flooded with tears" (*sic memorans largo fletu simul ora rigabat,* 699).[45] We will return to his tears later, in connection with another charged Homeric moment. For now, let us recall another master text that injects its own images of dreaming and weeping into Vergil's underworld: Cicero's *Somnium Scipionis*. Scipio Aemilianus dreams that he meets his adoptive grandfather Scipio Africanus, who tells him about the afterlife (the Scipios themselves will duly appear as figures in Aeneas' dream, in the Parade of Heroes). Young Scipio is also reunited with his father, which provokes another tearful outpouring: "When I saw him, I poured out a flood of tears; but he embraced and kissed me, forbidding me to weep" (*quem ut uidi, equidem uim lacrimarum profudi, ille autem me complexus atque osculans flere prohibebat,* 14). Alluding to Ennius' signature dream, Scipio suggests that it was because his grandfather was the last thing on his mind before he went to bed that he went on to dream about him – a phenomenon, he says, "similar to what Ennius writes about Homer, about whom no doubt he very often used to talk and think when awake" (*tale quale de Homero scribit Ennius, de quo uidelicet saepissime uigilans solebat cogitare et loqui,* 10). Perhaps this is just a passing observation, but it also looks like a generic marker that will in due course unite four separate authors on the afterlife in whom dreaming and weeping coincide: Homer, Ennius, Cicero, and Vergil.[46]

To return to Anchises: he is more than just a (poet-)prophet here. He is also something of a meta-chronicler, unusually obsessed with numbers and chronological relationships, in a way that draws attention to Vergil's own manipulation of the historical record. First, he tells his son that he has been waiting for him, literally "counting the times" (*tempora dinumerans,* 691); then he proceeds to enumerate (*enumerare,* 717) for him the long line of his future descendants. Vergil pointedly uses the lexicon associated with the activities of a censor – "he was doing the rounds" (*lustrabat*, 681), "he totted up" (*recensebat*, 682) – which, again, should sensitize us to numerical elements in the episode. Anchises counts the phantoms in a strict order: "he could count them all in a long line" (*omnis longo ordine posset | ... legere*, 754–5); "he led his son along each thing in turn" (*natum per singula duxit*, 888).[47] Indeed, Sergio Casali has demonstrated that Anchises will go on to do some serious correction, in the Parade of Heroes, of Ennius' implausible chronological links between the Trojan War, the foundation of Rome, and later history.[48] Casali draws particular attention here to the phrase *tempora dinumerans*, which, he says, means not just impatiently "counting the days" till Aeneas's arrival, but also "making a calculation of the times."[49] One might add that the phrase "Have you come at last?" (*uenisti tandem*, 685), following as it does another telltale "by chance" (*forte*, 682), drops a significant hint that Aeneas arrived in the underworld precisely on 9 October, the date of the foundation of the temple of Palatine Apollo, linked by Servius with Apollo's temple at Cumae. Even the similes of falling leaves and birds flying south (309–12) and the muted colours of the underworld landscape (303: *ferruginea*; 320: *liuida*; 410: *caeruleam*; 416: *glauca*) might support a notional autumnal date for his descent.

Between this encounter and the Parade comes Anchises' brief description of reincarnation (724–51), also arranged systematically: "he lays out everything in order" (*ordine singula pandit*, 723). Feeney, again, has convincingly reconciled this eschatological section with the worldlier Parade of Heroes that follows it, on the grounds that, for all its splendour, the Parade ultimately embodies the "evanescence of mortal aspirations" (Richard Tarrant's words).[50] Anchises tells his son about the various stages of a great cycle of purification in which each soul comes out whiter than white a thousand years later. This most Lucretian page of the *Aeneid*, brimming as it does with typical tics and archaisms (*principio, modis ... miris, ollis, aurai*), directly counters Epicurean materialism with an eclectic amalgam of Orphic, Platonic, Pythagorean, and Stoic thinking on the afterlife.[51] Even so, we might want to ask: why is it here at all?

There is much in Anchises' account that recalls not just Lucretius but also Ennius and his meaningful lost cycles of reincarnation – as many scholars have deduced.[52] But there may be another dimension, too. Is it not the case that Vergil also primes us to wonder what will happen exactly a thousand years from when Anchises speaks? If Aeneas visits the underworld in 1177–6 BCE, say, seven years after the Sack of Troy (1184–3 BCE) and one year after Anchises' death in 1178/7 BCE (given that Aeneas has just staged fi st-anniversary games for him in Sicily), then we might expect a spotlight on 177/6 BCE – admittedly, not the most exciting year in Rome's history.

The salient event, perhaps, was a population crisis in Rome's Latin colonies, whose inhabitants, drifting back to Rome, had to be forced to return to their depleted townships (Livy 41.8.6–8). We might see an allusion to this event in Aeneas' famous question to Anchises at 719–21, "Why would the souls of the dead have such a suicidal desire (*dira cupido*) to go back to the upper world?" – if the upper world in question were somehow equated with Rome. It would then be no coincidence that Andrew Feldherr has detected traces of colonizing language in the idea of allotting underworld territory. The falsely accused, we are told, have their domain assigned to them "by lot," this being how land in a new colony was usually distributed in Vergil's time: "nor are these homes given to them without lot, without judicial process" (*nec uero hae sine sorte datae, sine iudice, sedes*, 6.431).[53]

More promising are the heavy hints dropped about a connection between Anchises and Cato, who became censor in 184, exactly a thousand years after Troy fell.[54] Vergil would not just be paying homage to Ennius' supposed millennial tribute in the *Annals*. He would also be forging a stronger link between Cato and Augustus' Trojan ancestors. But Anchises will go on to spot a "great" Cato (Cato Maior?) in the Parade, *quis te, magne Cato, tacitum aut te, Cosse, relinquat?* ("Who would omit you, great Cato, in silence, or you, Cossus?" 841), just as Cato had mentioned Anchises in his own history of Rome.[55] Anchises' actual reincarnation as Cato thus seems unlikely. A further snag, beyond some arithmetical imprecision, is that Anchises is so exceptionally pious that he does not need to be reincarnated. As one of the favoured few who inhabit Elysium, he will eventually be rarefied into pure fire (744–7). Yet Musaeus' description of the flimsy community – "no one is of fixed abode" (*nulli certa domus*, 673) – keeps Vergil's options open: Anchises may not yet be permanently domiciled. In his answer to Aeneas' notorious query, why some exceptional souls (*sublimis animas*) would ever want to be reincarnated in the upper world (719–20), it is not clear whether Anchises distinguishes between these special cases and the greater mass of mankind who undergo a thousand-year cycle of purgation before forgetting everything and returning to human bodies (748–51).[56]

Instead, we might want to think harder about the exceptional poets among those "sublime souls" and their potential for rebirth. If the ancient tradition offers such a wide range of possibilities for Homer's birthdate, from before the Sack of Troy to several hundred years later, this in turn gives Vergil a wide range of possibilities for a further eventuality: Homer's future reincarnation in the body of another poet. Even if he made his *Annals* end with the thousandth anniversary of Troy's fall partly in order to praise Cato and his patron's artistic activities in Rome, Ennius had a likely ulterior motive: to demonstrate that he himself was Homer reborn.[57] As Waszink puts it, more cautiously, "[E]xactly one thousand years could be supposed to lie between

Homer's activity and the beginning of the composition of the *Annales* by Ennius."[58] Such a poetic aspiration would also help explain the prominence of Pythagorean lore at the outset of the *Annals*. In Skutsch's words: "[Only] with the help of the migration of souls could Ennius claim to be a second Homer."[59] All these calculations, of course, rely on Homer's *floruit* coinciding with the Trojan War, despite the fact that many authors put him later.

Might Vergil be using Anchises' thousand-year period, plus seven, plus a bit of unspecified leeway in Elysium, to hint at something similar for himself? Nearly 170 years separate the births of Ennius (b. c. 239 BCE) and Vergil (b. 70 BCE), 150 years their deaths (c. 169 and 19 BCE, respectively). In removing Homer from his underworld (whether he is alive and at large or still unborn), Vergil is giving himself room for two different scenarios, neither of them directly paraded but each one hanging in the air in this encounter with a weeping Ennian-Homeric father figur . Homer's contested birthdate gives him the potential to be reincarnated, a thousand years after his death, whenever that was, *either as Ennius or as Vergil*. Remember that Vergil traditionally had an October birthday (the fifteenth according to the ancient *Vita*), only a few days after our notional date for Aeneas' visit.[60] Remember, too, that the underworld river Eridanus, mentioned in an inconsequential-seeming detail as flowing upwards (658 *superne*) from the Elysian Fields, traditionally erupted into Vergil's home river, the Po – a signal, perhaps, that he is thinking of a specific geographical link between the poets and their future heir, as well as a specific calendrical moment.[61] By writing Homer out of the epic, or rather writing him in by eliding his weeping fi - ure alternately with Aeneas' father and Aeneas himself, Vergil is relieved of having to do anything so immodest as to choose in his own favour.[62]

What would a Homerless world do for the rest of the *Aeneid*? Perhaps its strangest consequences can be seen in the episode in Book 1 where Aeneas sees his recent past in the scenes in Dido's temple (*Aen.* 1.456–57): *uidet Iliacas ex ordine pugnas, | bellaque iam fama totum uulgata per orbem* ("He sees the battles of Troy in order and the war already broadcast through its fame across the world"). The natural assumption here is that the decorative scheme derives from the global renown of the Trojan War, which has ended up depicted on the walls of a temple in far-off Carthage, precisely thanks to the prior existence of the *Iliad*. Recognizing himself in the battle melee (*se quoque principibus permixtum agnouit Achiuis*, 488), Aeneas weeps, channelling Odysseus' reaction to his own name among the other warriors in Demodocus' song at the Phaeacians' banquet (*Od.* 8.93): ἐλάνθανε δάκρυα λείβων ("he shed secret tears") But the context here – the fi st, self-conscious ecphrasis of Vergil's epic – gives another meaning to those tears. Memories of its earliest model, the Shield of Achilles, are filtered through the viewer's response to more recent pictures (*Aen.* 1.465): *largoque umectat flumine uultum* ("He moistened his face with a broad river [of tears]"). According to Austin, the metaphor of a *flumen* of tears is Vergil's invention.[63] But another observation suggests itself: the broad stream that wets Aeneas' face and borders his experience is none other than an emotional counterpart to the mighty force of Ocean that encircles the microcosm of the Shield of Achilles, ἐν δ' ἐτίθει ποταμοῖο μέγα σθένος Ὠκεανοῖο ("he set in it the great strength of the stream of Ocean," *Il.* 18.607), an ocean which later came to symbolize the limitless influence of Homer on his poetic successors.[64] Alcinous will go on to remark of Odysseus' sorrow: μάλα πού μιν ἄχος φρένας ἀμφιβέβηκεν ("I think grief has encircled his heart," *Od.* 8.541). Thus Vergilian ecphrasis, with its particular stress on personal responses to the universality of Homeric narrative, provides its own tearful cosmic framing.[65]

In his landmark article "Future Reflexiv ," Alessandro Barchiesi uses the temple episode as a good example of the way allusion normally works: a newer text refers back to an older one, which is chronologically prior, both in and out of the fictional frame.[66] In its homage to the *Iliad,* for instance, the *Aeneid* creates a "feeling of a natural following-on"; what results is a "'smooth' kind of effect" (333). In other words, Vergil's deferential sequel can be read as a foil for all those artful Hellenistic or Ovidian poems that position themselves as chronological prequels to earlier master texts: Apollonius' *Argonautica* to Homer or to Euripides' *Medea,* Theocritus' "Song of the Cyclops" to the *Odyssey,* the *Heroides* to Greek tragedy, and so on. In a later essay on ecphrasis, Barchiesi notes that Vergil's *uulgata per orbem* ("broadcast across the globe," 1.457), suggests a pun on the Greek word for the epic cycle, κύκλος, from which, indeed, many of the temple scenes are taken, Vergil's description being a tissue of Homeric and post-Homeric narratives, compressed here because they are too well worn to be repeated in detail.[67] It also recalls the *orbis* Homer himself created, the round Shield that itself embraced a world. But if our current assumption is that Homer does not yet exist, we must ask: who has sung these stories and spread their fame? Can the post-Homeric exist without Homer? Are the facts thus conceived of as a pure entity, devoid of any singer?[68]

As for Vergil, he must be setting up the conditions for his own ghostly presence in the underworld. According to Anchises' specifications for the cleansing and eventual transmigration of souls, a prior version of himself – perhaps still contained within an unborn Homer? – is likely to be among those undergoing purification during Aeneas' visit, ready to be reincarnated a thousand years later (*mille … per annos,* 748) and destined to be every bit as forgetful (*immemor*) of his experience down there as Aeneas is. It is another of the dizzy-making thoughts typical of Vergil's underworld.

NOTES

1 Thanks to audiences at the Villa Vergiliana and Università degli Studi di Roma Tor Vergata for their comments on earlier versions of this paper, and to Bill Gladhill and Micah Myers for helping me to improve it. A special thank you also goes to Elena Giusti.

2 For suggested solutions to these problems, see Michels 1945 and West 1990 (Golden Bough); Tarrant 1982 (Gates of Sleep). See Zetzel 1989: 267 on Vergil's "radically different and mutually incompatible accounts of the afterlife and the nature of the soul" and O'Hara 2007: 91–5 for a concise overview of the puzzles of *Aeneid* 6.

3 For initiation as a framework in Aristophanes' *Frogs*, see Lada-Richards 1999; in Lucr. *DRN* 3: Reinhardt 2004; in Hor. *Sat*. 1.5: Cucchiarelli 2001. Lloyd-Jones 1967 reconstructs an ancient account of how Hercules underwent initiation before descending to the underworld. Servius points to the Bough's *quiddam mysticum*, noting that one could not participate in the rites of Proserpina without carrying a bough; cf. Bremmer 2009: 200: "In other words, by carrying the bough and offering it to Proserpina, queen of the underworld, Aeneas also acts as an Eleusinian initiate."

4 Zetzel 1989: 274–6. On the secrecy of the mysteries in relation to *Aen*. 6, see Luck 1973; Horsfall 1991: 130; Bremmer 1995: 71–8; Burkert 2006: 1–20; Bremmer 2009: 186n19 for a list of parallels for the Sibyl's words. Bremmer believes that Norden was on the right track in detecting mystery ritual here, even if this was not specifically the cry of the Eleusinian mysteries the Derveni papyrus confirms that the formula comes from the Orphic Theogony, from which non-initiates were excluded. See also Quiter 1984: 49–56, "Die Sibylle als Mystagogin"; Zetzel 1989: 377.

5 Cf. Pl. *Symp*. 218b.

6 See Casali 1995 on why the Sibyl moves Aeneas away from the temple doors. Vergil's underworld as *praeteritio*: Gowers 2005: 176.

7 Dream: Michels 1944; Otis 1957: 174–6. For the entire *Aeneid* as "a dream of Homer," see Oliensis 2001: 45.

8 Note how close the similes are in this book, above all, to their subjects: the misfit Golden Bough is "like mistletoe," a journey in the dark "like a journey through a dark wood." See also Barchiesi in this volume.

9 3.420, 424 (Scylla), 3.212 (Harpies), 5.118 (Chimaera), 5.122 (Centaur).

10 Just so, when Aeneas encounters Dido, it is in an uncertain half-light: "as when a man sees or thinks he sees the moon rise amid the clouds" (*qualem primo qui surgere mense | aut uidet aut uidisse putat per nubila lunam*, 453–4).

11 Hubaux 1939.

12 O'Hara 2007: 91–5. On the Bough, see Thomas 2001: 99–100.

13 Hygin. *apud* Gell. *NA* 10.16.

14 A list recollected at 119–23. A *synkrisis* between Theseus and Aeneas is the simplest explanation of the interrupted description of the scenes on the doors of the Temple of Apollo at Cumae: Vergil is consciously discarding a conventional Theseid in favour of relating Aeneas' more illustrious journey (Zarker 1967). See the crucial insight of Barchiesi 1997: 274 that ecphrasis is a form of *praeteritio*, a gesture towards an alternative story, now rejected; cf. ibid. 276–7: "The shield of Aeneas is a substitute for an alternative epic poem, a poem which could have been Ennian, historical, written in tableaux, in sequential order, and focused on praise."

15 Creusa was called "Eurydica" in Ennius (*Ann.* 36 Skutsch) and Vergil had already based the search for Creusa in *Aen.* 2 on Orpheus' backtracking in *G.* 4.

16 Hardie 1993: 101–3 and Kofler 2003 76–88 identify this specifically as a metapoetic transfer of pre-eminence from Homer and/or Ennius to Vergil.

17 For the belief that the dead continue to display the injuries they received in life, see Dodds *ad* Pl. *Gorg.* 524a–525a, cited Horsfall 2013a: 2.362, and cf. 446 (Eriphyle), 450 (Dido), 495–7 (Deiphobus), 2.278–9 (Hector); cf. Horsfall 2008: 244–5.

18 See Knauer 1964: 107–47 on Vergil's specific engagement with *Od.* 11.

19 On the Elysian Fields, see Curtis and Myers in this volume. For Augustine's rewriting in *Confessions* 9 of the Vergilian meeting with a parent, see Mackey in this volume.

20 Orpheus is a silent figur , submerged in periphrasis (645 *Thracius sacerdos*, where *sacerdos*, "priest," is a further allusion to the Orphic background). Horsfall 2013a: 2.458 surmises that as a fellow widower and wife deserter he cannot be seen talking to Aeneas ("too difficult and delicate")

21 Luc. *Men.* 1, *Hist. Ver.* 2.15, 20, 28 (see Kim 2010, esp. 162–8; Ni-Mheallaigh 2014 on Lucian's self-conscious games with Homeric tradition); Sil. *Pun.* 13.778–97. See Hardie 1993: 113–16 on Silius' Homer, a near-god but also a quasi-Marcellus (a glittering young man, surrounded by a crowd: compare *Pun.* 13.779–83 with *Aen.* 6.860–5) who died too soon to compose the national epic of Rome; cf. Hardie 2004a: 152. See further Casali 2006 and Van den Keur 2014 on Silius' negotiation of the Homeric/Ennian/Vergilian landscape. It is worth noting that at *Pun.* 13.781 Silius conflates two questions from Aeneas in *Aen.* 6 ("Where can I find Anchises?" and "Who is that young man?") and answers them both with "Homer," as if identifying his erasure from the earlier text.

22 Austin 1964 *ad* 2.5. Cf. Martin 1989 on the Iliadic Achilles as a stand-in for Homer.

23 Clay 1983: 12–20.

24 Graziosi 2002: 111–24.

25 Graziosi 2002: 90–124.
26 Herodotus' date is a halfway point four hundred years after Troy, four hundred years before his own time, which Graziosi 2002: 117 calls a "careful balancing act of distance and appropriation."
27 *FRH* I: Nepos F1.
28 Feeney 2007: 19.
29 Feeney 2007: 142.
30 And, as Bill Gladhill reminds me, the precise moment where Ovid ends his *Fasti*. See Feeney 2007: 143–4; Gratwick 1982: 63–5. Waszink 1979: 101 (following a suggestion by Franco Munari) had already detected the 1000-year interval between Homer's *floruit* and Ennius' inauguration of the *Annals*.
31 Feeney 2007: 143. Following Dreizehnter 1978, Feeney 2007: 100–1 suggests that Ennius' penchant for seven-hundred-year periods is connected with the tradition that this was the normal lifespan of a city (noting Livy's accommodation at *praef*. 4 of this precise gap in his own fi st-century distance from the foundation). This is to assume, with most scholars, that Camillus is Ennius' mouthpiece and that he speaks soon after the Sack of Rome in 387/6 BCE, i.e., seven hundred years from the foundation of Rome and eight hundred years after Eratosthenes' date for the Sack of Troy. See Elliott 2013: 65 on the lack of evidence for the (usual) ascription of these words to a fourth-century speaker; Var. *RR* 3.1.2, the source of the fragment, says nothing to suggest that Ennius himself is not speaking, which would suggest that Rome was founded at the start of the ninth century BCE, not the start of the tenth.
32 Cf. *Vita Donati* 15: *maxime mathematicae operam dedit* ("he gave the greatest attention to mathematics").
33 On Vergil's numerological instincts here, see Horsfall 1974 on 333 as halfway to the meaningful year 666 AUC (= 88 BCE), assuming a foundation in 754/3.
34 Feeney 2007: 133–4; cf. Zetzel 1989: 277–84. For further attempts to make dynastic capital out of links with the Sack of Troy, see Zetzel 1997.
35 Pfeiffer 1968: 51, 163.
36 Drew 1927: 16–17. Wormholes: Feeney 2007: 161–3.
37 Austin 1977 *ad* 667 finds it "odd" that the crowd surrounds Musaeus, not Orpheus; Lloyd-Jones 1967: 223–4 suggests that it is his connection with the Eleusinian Mysteries that gives him precedence.
38 Serv. *ad* 6.668: *quasi philosophum, ac si diceret Platonem* ("like a philosopher, as if he were speaking of Plato").
39 Pl. *Apol*. 41a. Ennius, who appears as a centurion at Sil. *Pun*. 12.393–416, is labelled by Apollo (12.410–13) the Roman heir to Hesiod, not Homer.
40 Zeitlin 2001: 204.
41 Bremmer 2009: 202 notes Norden's parallel (1957: 300) with Dionysus' question to the Eleusinian initiates about where to find Pluto at Ar. *Frogs* 431–3;

he proposes instead that, given the presence of Musaeus, the source is the *katabasis* of Orpheus (not that of Hercules).

42 Wigodsky 1972: 73–4, challenging Norden 1957: 21n3. Hardie 1986: 69–83 extends the Ennian similarities to the Parade of Heroes (which embraces the plot of the *Annals*) and, before it, the quasi-scientific doctrine of reincarnation (a topic also dear to Ennius). See also Kofler 2003 75–93 and Goldschmidt 2013: 166–8. Servius' comment *ad* Verg. *Aen.* 6.748, that *rotam uoluere per annos* sounds Ennian, has prompted editors to propose a specific link between *Aen.* 6.724–51 (Anchises on reincarnation) and Ennius' proem, which may well be correct: see Elliott 2013: 252n74. Most 1992 detects a similar metapoetic/intratextual dimension to the Odyssean *Nekyia* in relation to the epic tradition. See Casali 2007 on metapoetic succession in *Aeneid* 6 and Farrell 1999: 101–4 on Anchises in *Aeneid* 5 as a metaliterary father figur .

43 See Hardie 1993: 102–5 for a concise overview of Homer and Ennius as alternative and intertwined poetic forebears in Aeneas' visit from Hector in *Aeneid* 2 and Aeneas' encounter with Anchises in *Aeneid* 6.

44 Wigodsky 1972 in general has a hard time disentangling Homeric from Ennian allusion in Vergil, given Homer's influence on the plot and diction of the earlier poet. His solution is to say that Homer simply trumps Ennius where the two interfere with each other. But that interference must be deliberate if Vergil is constructing himself as successor to both poets at once. Compare Van de Keur 2014: 292: Silius' "status of epic successor to Vergil includes his incorporation of Vergil's (and Ennius') quality of being the Roman Homer." See Elliott 2013: 198–232, 246–63 on the intrinsic links between including the figure of Homer (or Homerizing traits) and the aspiration to universal history.

45 Cf. "So he spoke, weeping" (*sic fatur lacrimans,* 1); "he shed tears and spoke to her with tender affection" (*demisit lacrimas dulcique adfatus amore est,* 455); "he comforted her with these words and provoked tears" (*lenibat dictis animum lacrimasque ciebat,* 468); "he followed her at a distance, weeping, and pitied her as she went" (*prosequitur lacrimis longe et miseratur euntem,* 476).

46 See Hardie 1986: 69–83 on the speech of Anchises in relation to the *Somnium* and Ennius' dream of Homer.

47 The phrase *ordine perpetuo* ("in unbroken order") is used by another old man reciting a list of kings, this time Trojan ones, at Ov. *Met.* 11.755. For Feeney 1999: 20, the phrase is "a certain sign that some serious chronological dislocation is afoot"; Troy suddenly becomes a thing of the past.

48 If Camillus is the speaker of *Ann.* 154–5, Ennius has to make a mere seven kings span a seven-hundred-year period from the foundation of Rome to the present day.

49 Casali 2007: 126.

50 Feeney 1986; Tarrant 1982: 54.

51 Horsfall 2013a: 2.484; Hardie 1986: 77–83. In general, on Vergil's sources: Norden 1957: 3–48.
52 See Norden 1957.
53 Feldherr 1999: 94n26. See Norden 1957: 245–6 on legal terms in this passage. At Cic. *Somnium* 1, King Massinissa uses *migrare* of departing from life, a word more commonly used of moving house or migrating to a new colony. An intriguing coincidence is the foundation in 177 BCE of the Ligurian colony of Luna (Livy 41.13.5). Persius (*Sat.* 6.9) had quoted Ennius' line *Lunai portum, est operae, cognoscite, ciues* (= *op. inc.* 1 Skutsch), relating it specifically to the immediate aftermath of the dream-visit from Homer (*Sat.* 6.10–11); Kissel 1990: 776–87 deduced that *Lunai* in Ennius referred literally to the Moon, above which Pythagorean souls gathered to await reincarnation: thus the line might come after all from the *Annals*, rather than another work such as the *Satires*; see also Gildenhard 2007: 78. But there is still a chance that the annalist was referring to the terrestrial Luna.
54 Gratwick 1982: 63–5; Feeney 2007: 143–4.
55 See Feeney 1986: 13 on the ambiguity here. Cato's tendentious claim that Anchises did not die in Sicily but accompanied his son to Italy is corrected by Vergil's account: *Orig.* fr. 9 Peter = *F6 Cornell.
56 For Horsfall 2013a: 2.502–8, the distinction is clear and helps clarify the differences between the mass of souls and the elite; in his view, 720 *sublimis* means "exceptional" rather than simply "upwards." See Bremmer 2009: 204 on the tradition of millennial calculations: Empedocles' "thrice ten thousand seasons" (B 115 D–K), Plato's "ten thousand years" (*Phaedr.* 249a) and, for a philosophical life, "three times thousand years"; the myth of Er cites a period of a thousand years (Pl. *Rep.* 10.615b, 621d).
57 Waszink 1979: 100 calls Pythagorean lore "the indispensable base for the *figmentum poeticum* that Homer's soul (*thumos*) was actually present in the body of Ennius." See Elliott 2013: 75n 1: the most direct ancient evidence for this assumption comes from scholia, *commentum Cornuti ad* Pers. *Sat. prol.* 2 and Porph. *ad* Hor. *Ep.* 2.1.51. Aicher 1989 adds that the dream authorizes Ennius' stylistic Homerisms as well as making claims for his identity.
58 Waszink 1979: 101.
59 Skutsch 1968: 8.
60 But n.b. Feeney 2007: 150 on the meaninglessness of such a date.
61 Horsfall 2013a: 2.453, *ad* 658 *unde superne* dismisses Bremmer's parallel with 1 Enoch 28.2 (an elevated spring in heaven itself) in favour of Vergil's known interest in earthly rivers with subterranean origins (cf. *Aen.* 1.244–5, 3.694, *Georg.* 3.151).
62 Petrarch, by contrast, has no qualms about making his own future epic the one heralded by Homer (to Ennius) in *Africa* 9: see Hinds 2004: 171–3.

63 On *umectat,* Austin 1971 *ad loc.* cites *lacrimis salsis umectent ora genasque* ("they wet their faces and cheeks with salty tears," Lucr. 1.920, of the effects of laughter). This inevitably brings to mind other tears, those of Homer, *lacrimas effundere salsas* ("to pour out salty tears," Lucr. 1.125), where the language suggests not just a ghost's sorrow but an ocean of tragic inspiration.

64 Ps.-Plut. *Life of Homer* 2.93 cites *Il.* 14.246 ("Ocean who gave birth to all things") and proposes Homer as a predecessor to Thales, the philosopher who gave priority to water; cf. Eustath. *ad Il.* 14.202–4. Homer was often equated with Ocean as the source of all inspiration: see Brink 1972 and Morgan 1999: 32–3. Hardie 1986: 70 sees the opening of Anchises' speech, *principio caelum ac terras,* etc. (6.724–5), as an allusion to the opening "cosmic" description of the Shield of Achilles (*Il.* 18.483–5).

65 Barchiesi 1997: 275 speaks of the "non-chronological and emotional selection of the images." The *Somnium* uses repeated images of (sometimes tearful) embrace to suggest many kinds of microcosmic/macrocosmic connections, from generational contact to the grip of sleep to cosmological relationships: *complexus me senex collacrimauit* ("the old man *embraced* me, weeping," 9); *artior, quam solebat, somnus complexus est* ("sleep folded me in a tighter *embrace* than usual," 10); *quem ut uidi, equidem uim lacrimarum profudi, ille autem me complexus atque osculans flere prohibebat* ("when I saw him and spontaneously poured out a torrent of tears, he *embraced* me and, kissing me, forbade me to weep," 14); *nam terra nona immobilis manens una sede semper haeret complexa medium mundi locum* ("for the earth, which is ninth, stays still in one position and perpetually *embraces* the middle area of the universe," 18). Silius gives his Homer a similarly cosmic reach: *carmine complexus terram, mare, sidera, manes* ("*embracing* in his poetry the earth, the sea, the stars, the dead," *Pun.* 13.787). This echoes an earlier description of Achilles' all-encompassing shield: *clipeo amplexus terramque polumque | maternumque fretum totumque in imagine mundum* ("*embracing* on his shield the earth and the heavens and his mother's ocean – the whole world in one image," *Pun.* 7.121–2); Van den Keur 2014: 291.

66 Barchiesi 1993: 333.

67 Barchiesi 1997: 273.

68 As Micah Myers points out to me, Homer's use of Demodocus and Phemius as singers of Trojan War epic within the *Odyssey* provides a model for Vergil's "post-Homeric before Homer."

12

The Silence of *Aeneid* 6 in Augustine's *Confessions*[1]

JACOB L. MACKEY

This chapter's title reflects the fact that throughout the *Confessions,* Vergil's epic is often quite noisily audible. So the silence to which I shall advert is significant I shall offer examples of some of Augustine's Vergilian "noise" before showing how he silences the *Aeneid* – specificall , its sixth book – in the ninth book of his *Confessions.* My fundamental *demonstrandum* is this: in the ninth book of the *Confessions,* Augustine describes an *anabasis* or mystical ascent of the soul that he experienced with his mother Monnica at Ostia just before her death. He models their *anabasis* on Aeneas' *katabasis* in *Aeneid* 6. But he displaces and thus silences *Aeneid* 6 by substituting for Anchises' cosmological, psychological, and eschatological speech a Latin translation of a treatise from Plotinus' *Enneads.* In Augustine's Latin translation, the Neoplatonic text silences not only the *Aeneid* but *itself* as well. Indeed, in silencing itself, Augustine's Plotinus translation silences the very book into which it has been incorporated, the *Confessions.* Thus, the *Confessions* shuts down, or tries to shut down, verbal communication at its own most polyphonic moment, a moment that demands the most scrupulous act of reading.

Why? In order to answer this question, let us begin by surveying the various worlds of words in which Augustine moved. As a boy in Africa, he read the *Aeneid* and discovered a love of poetry and a talent for rhetoric (*Conf.* 1.13.20–2; 1.17.27). As a teen in Carthage, he read Cicero's now-lost *Hortensius* and heard its exhortation to philosophy (*Conf.* 3.4.7). This encounter threw him into a dilemma: the philosophers did not speak of Christ, and yet scripture, which did speak of Christ, lacked the sophistication of philosophy (*Conf.* 3.4.8–3.5.9). This led him to the Manichees, who combined a high-flown discursive style with talk of Christ (*Conf.* 3.6.10). Years later, in Milan, a decisive encounter with Neoplatonic philosophy (*Conf.* 7.9.13) caused him decisively to reject Manichaeism. Finally, Paul's *Epistle to the Romans* at last made him receptive of scripture (*Conf.* 8.12.29). Thus, we may discern in the

Confessions the intermingling and interaction of at least three literary traditions: fi st, classical Latin literature, second, Neoplatonic philosophy, and third, scripture.

The place of the *Aeneid* in the *Confessions* has been mapped by Hagendahl, Courcelle, O'Meara, Bennett, MacCormack, Müller, and others.[2] Here I merely rehearse a few well-known and salient points. I do wish to emphasize, however, that Augustine's references and allusions to the *Aeneid* almost always appear under the motif of *katabasis*, of death and descent. See, for example, Augustine's description of how in reading the *Aeneid*, he became a type not only of the lost Aeneas, but also of the dying Dido (*Conf.* 1.13.20):

tenere cogebar Aeneae nescio cuius errores oblitus errorum meorum et plorare Didonem mortuam quia se occidit ab amore cum interea me ipsum in his a te morientem, deus, uita mea, siccis oculis ferrem miserrimus.

I was forced to memorize the wanderings of some fellow Aeneas, forgetful of my own wanderings, and to cry for Dido, dead because she killed herself for love, while in the meantime, wretch that I was, I endured with dry eyes my own death in these stories, away from you, O God my life.

In school, so he says, he memorized the wanderings, *errores*, of Aeneas, while forgetful of his own wanderings (*oblitus errorum meorum*), and he cried for Dido's suicide. At the time, despite his empathetic response to their travails, he failed to recognize himself in Aeneas and Dido, or at least did not see how Aeneas' wandering and Dido's death reflected his true condition of remotion from God. His descent into Vergilian poetry was a *katabasis* of the soul. He was dying in this literature (*in his ... morientem*), as yet hermeneutically unprepared to access the revelations that his older self, a more mature reader, could find ther .

Yet, despite his misreadings, the *Aeneid* was furnishing him the narrative template that he needed to recount his own itinerary (*Conf.* 1.17.27):

proponebatur enim mihi negotium ... ut dicerem uerba Iunonis irascentis et dolentis quod non posset "Italia Teucrorum auertere regem," quae numquam Iunonem dixisse audieram. sed figmentorum poeticorum uestigia errantes sequi cogebamur, et tale aliquid dicere solutis uerbis quale poeta dixisset uersibus.

For the task was put to me ... to speak the words of Juno, angry and grieving because she could not "turn the king of the Trojans away from Italy" [*Aen.* 1.38], words which I had been given to know Juno had never said. But we were compelled to follow in our own wanderings the tracks of poetic fiction , and to express in prose whatever the poet had said in verse.

As Augustine discovers his rhetorical talents, we his readers discover that his youthful "wanderings," *errores*, will follow "the tracks of poetic fiction ," *figmentorum poeticorum uestigia*. Thus we anticipate Vergilian narrative structures in his autobiography.

In this, the *Confessions* does not disappoint. Soon enough, Augustine will abandon his mother, Monnica, at Carthage in order to sail for Rome to find his destiny, just as Aeneas had abandoned Dido on the same shore, headed for the same destination (*Conf.* 5.8.15):

sed ea nocte clanculo ego profectus sum, illa autem non; mansit orando et flend … flauit uentus et impleuit uela nostra et litus subtraxit aspectibus nostris, in quo mane illa insaniebat dolore, et querellis et gemitu implebat aures tuas … et tamen post accusationem fallaciarum et crudelitatis meae conuersa rursus ad deprecandum te pro me abiit ad solita, et ego Romam.

But that night I set out in secret. She [Monnica] did not, but stayed behind praying and weeping … The wind blew and filled our sails and the shore drew away from our sight. There the next morning she went mad with grief, and filled your [i.e., God's] ears with complaints and moaning … And nevertheless, after her accusations of my deceitfulness and cruelty, turning again to praying to you on my behalf, she went away to her home, and I to Rome.

This episode has stimulated the spilling of a fair amount of psychoanalytic ink.[3] But whether or not we should see here Augustine's life imitating Vergil's art, it is clear that at the very least Augustine has arranged his narrative of his own wanderings to recall pointedly the narrative of Vergil's poem.[4] And what follows, in Vergil's narrative, the flight of Aeneas and the death of Dido? What follows, after the funeral games for Anchises in Sicily, is Aeneas' landing in Italy, and his descent to the underworld.

With this, we are now in a position to see how *Aeneid* 6 figures in *Confessions* 9. Augustine recounts in this book a mystical ascent that he and his mother Monnica enjoyed at Ostia just before her death in 387 CE. Camille Bennett, who fi st noted and discussed at length this episode's dependence on the meeting of Aeneas and Anchises in Elysium, has written, "[a] last talk with a parent on the shores of Italy, by a son who has consciously identified himself with Vergil's hero, openly invites comparison with the last conversation of Aeneas and his parent" (1988, 65). Many parallels between Augustine's narrative of the episode at Ostia and Vergil's narrative of the meeting of Aeneas and Anchises in Elysium might be enumerated. I shall mention only a few of the more significant one .

First, as Kenneth Burke has pointed out, the Ostia episode is "written explicitly under the sign of [Monnica's] death" (1961: 121). He refers to the fi st words of the episode (*Conf.* 9.10.23):

impendente autem die, quo ex hac uita erat exitura ... prouenerat ... ut ego et ipsa soli staremus incumbentes ad quandam fenestram, unde *hortus* intra domum ... prospectabatur, illic apud *Ostia Tiberina* ...

When that day was drawing near, on which she [Monnica] was to depart from this life ... it came to pass ... that I and she were standing alone, leaning at a certain window, which looked upon the *garden* inside the house ... there at *Ostia on the Tiber* ...

In *Aeneid* 6, of course, Anchises stands already in the realm of the dead, in the verdant fields of Elysium. In the *Confessions*, Monnica stands at the threshold of death, looking out upon a garden[5] and enjoying a preview of the next life, as we are about to see.

At Ostia, Augustine and Monnica rest after a long trip from Milan and prepare to sail to Carthage. The following passage continues the one previously quoted (*Conf.* 9.10.23):

... ubi remoti a turbis post longi itineris laborem instaurabamus nos nauigationi. Conloquebamur ergo soli ualde dulciter et "praeterita obliuiscentes in ea quae ante sunt extenti," quaerebamus inter nos ... qualis futura esset uita aeterna sanctorum.

... where removed from the crowds [cf. *Conf.* 6.14.24: *remoti a turbis otiose uiuere* with O'Donnell *ad loc.*] we were refreshing ourselves for a sea passage after the toil of a long journey. So we were alone speaking together very pleasantly, and "forgetting the past, stretched out toward that which lay before us" [Phil. 3:13], we were asking ourselves ... what the eternal life of the saints would be like.

In this moment of solitude and peace – the last they will know together – the newly baptized Augustine and his piously Christian mother speculate about eschatology. Alone together in a garden, at the end of one journey, preparing themselves for another, forgetful of the past, mindful of the future, they ask themselves "what the eternal life of the saints would be like." A conversation that reorients parent and progeny away from past toils toward a glorious future along with eschatological speculations about the destiny of the soul: these features of the episode obviously invite comparison to *Aeneid* 6. For, of course, the conversation of Aeneas and Anchises had focused Aeneas on what lay ahead of him, in addition to vouchsafing eschatological revelations.

Let us pause over the conceit Augustine introduces here, by way of quoting Paul's letter to the Philippians, of "forgetting the past," *praeterita obliuiscentes*. We might note, with Bennett, that "a river of forgetfulness plays a role in both" narratives, the Vergilian and the Augustinian.[6] In the *Aeneid*, the souls of the dead, before returning from the underworld to live again in mortal bodies, "drink care-dispelling liquids and long oblivion at the waters of the

Lethean stream" (*Lethaei ad fluminis undam | securos latices et longa obliuia potant*, *Aen.* 6.713–715). Similarly, in preparation for their own brief ascent to the *uita aeterna*, Augustine relates of himself and Monnica that they drank at the *fons uitae*. The following words come closely after the ones in block quotation, above, and conclude the fi st sentence of the Ostia episode (*Conf.* 9.10.23):

sed inhiabamus ore cordis in superna fluenta fontis tui, fontis uitae, qui est apud te; ut inde pro captu nostro aspersi, quoquo modo rem tantam cogitaremus.

But we were opening wide the mouths of our hearts at the supernal streams of your fountain, the fountain of life, which resides with you, so that, sprinkled with its waters insofar as we could absorb them, somehow we might meditate on so great a matter.

While Lethe's waters cause souls to forget their past lives so that they will once again desire to assume bodies,[7] the *fons uitae* effects a forgetting of temporal existence and a longing for eternal life. Both waters cause cognitive changes in those who drink them. Both waters mark and contribute to their drinkers' transition to or from corporal embodiment to or from spiritual existence. Augustine adumbrates here, already, in a potatory recollection of his Vergilian subtext, the very forgetfulness of his Vergilian subtext, along with all the rest of the past, that he is about to describe.

So, from its very fi st words, Augustine's account of the Ostia episode primes us for a re-enactment of the meeting of Aeneas and Anchises in Elysium. Let us pause to recollect some relevant aspects of *that* underworld encounter before we delve further into Augustine's narrative. I present some lines from Anchises' fi st speech to his son (*Aen.* 6.724–32 & 743–7):

principio caelum ac terras camposque liquentis
lucentemque globum Lunae Titaniaque astra
spiritus intus alit, totamque infusa per artus
mens agitat molem et magno se corpore miscet.
inde hominum pecudumque genus, uitaeque uolantum,
et quae marmoreo fert monstra sub aequore pontus.
igneus est ollis uigor et caelestis origo
seminibus, quantum non noxia corpora tardant,
terrenique hebetant artus moribundaque membra […]
… exinde per amplum
mittimur Elysium, et pauci laeta arua tenemus,
donec longa dies, perfecto temporis orbe,
concretam exemit labem, purumque relinquit
aetherium sensum atque aurai simplicis ignem.

First of all, heaven and earth and flowing sea-fields | and the shining globe of the Moon and the Titanian Sun | an inward spirit makes thrive; and a mind, suffusing its members, | moves the entire mass, and mixes itself with the great body. | Hence the race of men and of beasts comes into being, and the lives of flying creatures, and the uncanny things | the sea bears beneath its marbled surface. | Fiery is the force and celestial origin of those seeds, | insofar as noxious bodies do not slow them, | and earthly limbs and mortal members dull them. […] … After that [i.e., punishment & purification] we are sent | through spacious Elysium, and a few of us hold these happy field , | until that distant day, the cycle of time fulfilled | has taken away our accreted stain, and left pure, | ethereal mind and fire of unmixed he ven.

Hardie 1986 has prepared us to note cosmological patterns in Vergil. Anchises begins his speech by twice distributing cosmic elements across four terms: fi st, we get heaven (*caelum*), earth (*terrae*), sea (*campi liquentes*), and the highest, fiery ether, in the guise of the moon and the sun; second, we get the forms of life proper to these four cosmological domains: men and beasts, birds, aquatic life, and finally the ethereal, fiery seeds, *semina,* that vivify all living creatures. In this last detail, Anchises adumbrates a psychology in which individual souls are as sparks derived from an ethereal World Soul, the *spiritus* or *mens* that suffuses the whole cosmos.[8] Anchises then turns from psychology to eschatology, assuring Aeneas that some individual souls will eventually be cleansed of corporeal pollution and will escape the cycle of death and reincarnation that the souls who drink at Lethe are about to repeat. These lucky few will reunite with the World Soul in the highest ether. After this quick lesson in cosmology, psychology, and eschatology, Anchises turns to historical prophecy, the *Heldenschau,* which begins at line 756, foretelling the fates of the souls who must take on bodies, famous Romans of the future chief among them.

With these aspects of Anchises' speech fresh in our minds, and recalling that Augustine and Monnica specifically seek a glimpse of the "eternal life of the saints," that is to say, a kind of Christian *Heldenschau,* let us turn to Augustine's account of the *anabasis* at Ostia. Note that where Vergil gives us a speech by Anchises, Augustine, too, gives us direct quotation, but he attributes the words to himself and his mother jointly (*Conf.* 9.10.23):

dicebamus ergo, "si cui sileat tumultus carnis, sileant phantasiae terrae et aquarum et aeris, sileant et poli *et ipsa sibi anima sileat, et transeat se non se cogitando, sileant somnia et imaginariae reuelationes, omnis lingua et omne signum* et quidquid transeundo fit si cui sileat omnino (quoniam … dicunt haec omnia, 'non ipsa nos fecimus, sed fecit nos qui manet in aeternum') … si iam taceant … et loquatur ipse solus … ut audiamus uerbum eius, non per linguam carnis neque per uocem angeli nec per sonitum nubis nec per aenigma similitudinis, sed ipsum … sicut nunc extendimus nos et rapida cogitatione attingimus aeternam sapientiam super omnia manentem, si continuetur hoc et subtrahantur aliae uisiones longe inparis generis, et haec una rapiat et absorbeat et recondat in interiora gaudia spectatorem suum, ut talis sit sempiterna uita, quale fuit hoc momentum intellegentiae, cui suspirauimus, nonne hoc est: 'intra in gaudium domini tui' [Matt. 25:21]? et istud quando? an cum 'omnes resurgimus, sed non omnes inmutabimur' [1 Cor. 15:51]?"

And so we were saying: "If for someone the tumult of the flesh should fall silent, silent the phantoms of the earth, and of the waters and of the air, silent also the heavens, *and if the very soul should fall silent to itself, and transcend itself by not thinking about itself; if dreams should fall silent, and imaginary revelations, every language and every sign,* and if for this person whatever comes to be by passing away should fall wholly silent (since … all these things are saying: 'we did not make ourselves, but He made us who remains in eternity'), if … now these things should fall silent … and if He alone should speak … so that we may hear His Word, not through the language of the flesh nor through the voice of an angel, nor from a cloud, nor through a mysterious symbolism, but He himself … just as now we extend ourselves and in a fleeting thought touch the eternal wisdom which abides beyond all things; if this should continue and other visions of a far inferior sort be taken away and this one vision seize and absorb and enfold its spectator in an inner joy so that the eternal life would be such a thing as was this moment of understanding for which we sighed, wouldn't this be 'enter into the joy of your Lord' [Matt. 25:21]? And when shall this be? When 'we all rise again, but shall not all be changed' [1 Cor. 15:51]?"

Now, this passage is far too subtle to unpack completely in the present chapter, but please indulge me a few blunt observations to get us going. First, Augustine makes good on his promise to preview the eternal life of the saints. The beatific vision presented here is in effect an eternal synesthesia without sensation: a *hearing* of God's eternal Word without speech, a *vision* of God's eternal wisdom beyond the realm of the visible. Second, as in the Vergilian underworld, so here the revelation is shared communally. This is important because Augustine's previous, ultimately unsatisfying mystical ascents, in *Confessions* 7, had been non-social. They were Plotinian moments of individual revelation: "the flight of the alone to the alone" (*Enneads* 6.9.11: 51). Third, note that the eschatology on offer here involves neither metempsychosis nor reabsorption into the World Soul, but rather, quoting from Paul's First Corinthians, the resurrection of the flesh or more specificall , a Pauline resurrection fleshed out *with* and interpreted *through* Plotinian mysticism, as we are about to see.

Now let us descend deeper into our Augustinian passage, to observe the Neoplatonic text by Plotinus that undergirds it. Augustine's *anabasis* at Ostia turns out, in the telling, to be in part a close translation of Plotinus, as Paul Henry (1938) long ago noted.[9] Plotinus writes (*Enneads* 5.1.2: 16–17):

ἥcυχον δὲ αὐτῇ ἔστω μὴ μόνον τὸ περικείμενον cῶμα καὶ ὁ τοῦ cώματος κλύδων, ἀλλὰ καὶ πᾶν τὸ περιέχον· ἥcυχος μὲν γῆ, ἥcυχος δὲ θάλαcca καὶ ἀὴρ καὶ αὐτοc οὐρανὸc ἀμείνων.

Let not only the soul's enveloping body and the sea of flesh be still [ἥcυχον], but also its entire surroundings: still [ἥcυχοc] the earth, and still [ἥcυχοc] the sea, and the air and greater heaven itself.

Our passage of the *Confessions* translates Plotinus as follows (I quote again from above):

si cui sileat tumultus carnis, sileant phantasiae terrae et aquarum et aeris, sileant et poli …

If for someone the tumult of the flesh should fall silent [*sileat*], silent [*sileant*] the phantoms of the earth, and of the waters and of the air, silent [*sileant*] also the heavens …

This is a close rendition, with the Latin verb *silere* translating the Greek adjective ἥcυχοc. Now let us read the bit of Plotinus that *precedes* the bit we just read (*Enneads* 5.1.2: 14–15):

cκοπείcθω δὲ τὴν μεγάλην ψυχὴν ἄλλη ψυχὴ οὐ cμικρὰ ἀξία τοῦ cκοπεῖν γενομένη ἀπαλλαγεῖcα ἀπάτης καὶ τῶν γεγοητευκότων τὰc ἄλλαc ἡcύχῳ τῇ καταcτάcει.

Let another soul, no small one, look upon the Great Soul [μεγάλη ψυχή], having become worthy to look upon it by having been released from deceit and the beguilements of the other souls by its own still quietude [ἡcύχῳ καταcτάcει].

Augustine translates these lines rather loosely, transposing their position relative to the previous lines from fi st place to second, as may be seen from the italicization in the full quotation of the *Confessions* passage, above. Here is Augustine again:

et ipsa sibi anima sileat, et transeat se non se cogitando, sileant somnia et imaginariae revelationes, omnis lingua et omne signum …

[if] the very soul should fall silent [*sileat*] to itself, and transcend itself by not thinking about itself; if dreams should fall silent [*sileant*], and imaginary revelations, every language and every sign …

It is central to the thesis of this chapter that Augustine translates Plotinus' adjective ἥσυχος, "quiet" or "still," with the verb *silere*, "to be silent." Augustine thus follows but significantly alters Plotinus in *silencing* rather than *stilling* the four cosmic elements: earth, water, air, and higher heaven. Both Plotinus and Augustine also *still* or *silence* the soul and the body it inhabits. Indeed, quietude of soul, in original and translation both, is the prerequisite for the soul's ascent. For Plotinus, the individual soul's quietude allows it to attend to the Great Soul, μεγάλη ψυχή, from which it derives, and thus to effect an eschatological *return* to it.[10] But for Augustine, as we saw, the soul ascends to God's Word, or Christ, and hears Him speaking silently in eternity. The silent speech of God's Word explains why Augustine adds to Plotinus' list of things to be silenced *omnis lingua et omne signum*. Indeed, Augustine's reorientation of Plotinus' passage away from the Great Soul and toward God's Word explains the replacement of the trope of stillness with the trope of silencing.[11]

I said above that this passage offers, in its citation of 1 Corinthians, a Pauline resurrection of the flesh interpreted through Plotinian mysticism. It is worth noting, very briefl , that Augustine's accomplishment here is more complex than that. For Plotinus and scripture are *mutually interpreting* here. Augustine redescribes the affective dimension of Plotinian ascent in terms of the beatific vision of Matthew 25:21: *intra in gaudium domini tui*. At the same time, the placement of Matthew's words at the climax of a Neoplatonic ascent reimagines the nature of the Evangelist's *gaudium*. Moreover, in a way that Plotinus could not possibly have done, Augustine places the eschatological moment of which his experience at Ostia was but a foretaste squarely in time, at the moment of the resurrection of the flesh when *omnes resurgimus, sed non omnes inmutabimur* (1 Cor. 15:51).[12]

Let us now refocus: What has all this to do with *Aeneid* 6? We may start with the fact that the Vergilian underworld, like the Augustinian ascent, was characterized by silence. In a remarkable verbal parallel, Augustine sums up his seven uses of the verb *silere*, in the passage quoted above, with the verb *tacere*: "if now these should fall silent" (*si iam taceant)*. A similar silence, signified by the same alteration of *silere* followed by *tacere*, is the aural mark of the Vergilian underworld, at 6.264 (*umbraeque silentes*) and 265 (*loca nocte tacentia late*).

Beyond the shared atmosphere and vocabulary of silence, let us note, too, the thematic parallels that the appropriated Plotinian passage shares with Anchises' speech. Anchises enumerates precisely the same four cosmological elements – earth, water, air, ethereal heaven – as do Plotinus (and Augustine). He also references, like Plotinus (but unlike Augustine), a cosmic soul, from which individual souls derive, and the bodies these souls animate. Anchises further specifie , as we have already seen, the forgetfulness of past incarnations required for these souls either to be reborn or to rejoin the cosmic soul. In Plotinus, this forgetfulness comes by way of the stilling of the soul's enveloping body, the beguilements to which it is otherwise subject, and of the physical cosmos.

The Stoic confluence of cosmology, psychology, and eschatology evinced in Anchises' speech is shared, *mutatis mutandis,* by Plotinus, as in these lines, which immediately precede those that Augustine has translated (*Enneads* 5.1.2: 1ff):

Ἐνθυμείcθω τοίνυν πρῶτον ἐκεῖνο πᾶcα ψυχή, ὡc αὐτὴ μὲν ζῷα ἐποίηcε πάντα ἐμπνεύcαcα αὐτοῖc ζωήν, ἅ τε γῆ τρέφει ἅ τε θάλαccα ἅ τε ἐν ἀέρι ἅ τε ἐν οὐρανῷ ἄcτρα θεῖα, αὐτὴ δὲ ἥλιον, αὐτὴ δὲ τὸν μέγαν τοῦτον οὐρανόν, καὶ αὐτὴ ἐκόcμηcεν, αὐτὴ δὲ ἐν τάξει περιάγει.

So let every soul fi st consider this, that it made all living things itself, breathing life into them, those the earth and those the sea nourishes and those in the air and the divine stars in heaven; soul itself made the sun, and it made this great heaven, and it gave it order, and soul drives it round in orderly movement.

As I have mentioned, these lines from Plotinus' treatise introduce the lines that Augustine has chosen to translate to narrate his *anabasis*. Their similarity to Anchises' cosmological and psychological doctrine is striking.[13] I submit that Augustine would have found this Plotinian treatise suggestively close to Anchises' speech, and thus ideally suited to gloss the Vergilian lines, and indeed an apposite substitute for them in his own inverted *imitatio* of the *Aeneid*'s *katabasis*.

What I propose, then, is that in Augustine's self-conscious rewriting of *Aeneid* 6 in the ninth book of his *Confessions,* the saint has *substituted* the Neoplatonic passage from Plotinus *in place of* Anchises' cosmological, psychological, and eschatological speech. I propose to call Augustine's strategy "hermeneutic substitution." Rather than quote Anchises' speech at this moment in his own narrative that parallels Aeneas' meeting with his father, Augustine instead quotes a Neoplatonic text that effectively *interprets* his Vergilian model in a way that is not only consonant with but also positively contributes to his Christian philosophy.[14] Plotinus' text is thus a hermeneutic substitution for Anchises' speech, interpreting the latter's doctrine even as it replaces its words. Or, put another way, it replaces or stands in for Anchises' speech by way of interpreting it.

At this point, we may fairly ask: Why did Augustine bother to use the *Aeneid* as a subtext in recounting this episode at all? Why not just get on with the business of offering a Neoplatonic vision of Christianity? Let me state the answer as plainly as I can: Vergil offered Augustine a *social* model of spiritual experience not available in Plotinus. In his earlier, ultimately unsatisfying spiritual ascent, at Milan, Augustine had felt himself admonished by Plotinus to undertake a solitary inward flight *admonitus redire ad memet ipsum, intraui in intima mea* (*Conf*. 7.10.16). At Ostia, Augustine and his mother, like Aeneas and Anchises, instead share intersubjectively in the revelatory experience. Indeed, the social dimension of Augustine's ascent at Ostia has received emphasis in recent scholarship, even if its essential debt to the *Aeneid* in this regard has gone unremarked.[15] In the words of J.P. Kenney (2005: 141): "The vision at Ostia is represented as being endemically social, involving two people as its subjects. It begins and ends in conversation. Both Monica and her son participate in the ascension and both are equal in visionary awareness."

Augustine took this social model for and social conception of mystical experience from the poignant encounter between father and son in Elysium. Just as *Aeneid* 6 offers a deeply social revelation about the future of the Roman community, so the vision at Ostia offered Augustine and Monnica a deeply social revelation about the future of the Christian community. Thus, the ascent at Ostia, like the revelation in Vergil's underworld, depicts not merely a vision shared *with* others but also a vision *about* others, about another community, whether of saints or of heroes, toward which the visionary, in one way or another, tends. The Augustinian vision is not – and neither, I would add, is the Vergilian vision – "in the end, about the self."[16] Rather, for Aeneas, the vision in Elysium pertains to the institution of the Roman community, while for Augustine, the vision at Ostia pertains to "the recovery of a transcendent community."[17] Here is Kenney again (2005: 143): "For Augustine vision led to a deepened sense of the larger community of souls into whose transcendent state the soul had been admitted and whose contemplation of Wisdom the soul had joined." If Augustine's ascent at Ostia "is no solitary flight of the alone to the alone,"[18] à la Plotinus, this is owed in part to *Aeneid* 6, which offered him a model of mystical experience as a social experience, and of revelation as the revelation of community.

We are now in a position to ask another question, one that is perhaps less pressing, but one that deserves an answer nonetheless: Why would Augustine choose a Neoplatonic text as a hermeneutic substitution for Anchises' speech? Permit me here a brief excursus on Augustine's tendency to interpret Vergil platonically, especially Anchises' speech in *Aeneid* 6. Consider fi st two Augustinian passages asserting the unique commensurability of Neoplatonism and Christian philosophy (*De uera religione* 4.7, c. 390 CE and *Ciu*. 8.5, after 413 CE, respectively):

ita si hanc uitam illi uiri nobiscum rursum agere potuissent, ... paucis mutatis uerbis atque sententiis christiani fierent sicut plerique recentiorum nostrorumque temporum Platonici fecerunt.

If those men were able to lead their lives again amongst us ... with the change of a few words and opinions they would become Christian, just as many Platonists of our own more recent times have done.

nulli nobis quam isti propius accesserunt.

None have more closely agreed with us (Christians) than those (Platonists).

Now, in this light, reflect upon a few remarks from *De ciuitate Dei* in which Augustine explicitly asserts that Vergil voices Platonic doctrine in Anchises' fi st speech:

- quod Platonice uidetur dixisse Vergilius ... (*Ciu.* 10.30, quoting *Aen.* 6.750–1)
  Vergil seems to have spoken in Platonic fashion ...
- Vergilius ex Platonico dogmate dixisse laudatur ... (*Ciu.* 13.19, quoting *Aen.* 6.750–1)
  Vergil is praised for having spoken in accord with Platonic doctrine ...
- Vergilius Platonicam uideatur ... explicare sententiam ... (*Ciu.* 14.3, quoting *Aen.* 6.730–4)
  Vergil may be seen ... to explain a Platonic doctrine ...
- Vergil is presented as *locutor nobilis* for a Platonic doctrine of body and soul (*Ciu.* 14.5, quoting *Aen.* 6.719–21)
- dixerunt quidem Platonici ... unde Vergilius ... (*Ciu.* 21.3, quoting *Aen.* 6.733)
  The Platonists have said ... whence Vergil (says) ...
- Vergil expresses *sententia* of *Platonici* regarding postmortem punishment (*Ciu.* 21.13, quoting *Aeneid* 6.733–42)

If the Platonists, in some of their doctrines, approach or are nearly commensurate with Christianity, and if Vergil can be seen so often to voice Platonic doctrines, then surely Vergil and Christianity need not be seen as intrinsically opposed.

Though the citations just adduced from *De ciuitate Dei* postdate the *Confessions,* we do have a *terminus ante quem* for Augustine's familiarity with a Platonizing hermeneutic for reading Vergil: the *De consensu*

Euangelistarum (*Cons. eu.*). This treatise was written c. 400, that is, around the same time as the *Confessions*.[19] In a passage from this text (1.22.30) that precedes the one quoted just below, Augustine discusses Varro's equation of the God of the Jews with Jupiter, a clear reference to the largely lost *Antiquitates rerum diuinarum*. He goes on to cite both Platonizing and Stoicizing interpretations of Vergil's Jupiter (*Cons. eu.* 1.23.31):

quid illud quod idem poeta dicit aethera? quomodo accipiunt? Sic enim ait: "tum pater omnipotens fecundis imbribus Aether | coniugis in gremium laetae descendit." aetherem quippe non spiritum, sed corpus esse dicunt sublime, quo caelum super aerem distenditur. An poetae conceditur nunc secundum Platonicos, ut non corpus, sed spiritus, nunc secundum Stoicos loqui, ut corpus sit deus?

What is that which the same poet [*sc.* Vergil] names *Aether*? How do they take the term? For he speaks thus: "Then the omnipotent father Aether, with fertilizing showers, | came down into the bosom of his fruitful spouse" [*G.* 2.325–6]. They say, indeed, that this Aether is not spirit, but a lofty body in which the heaven is stretched above the air. Is it granted to the poet to speak now like the followers of Plato, as if God was not body, but spirit, and now like the Stoics, as if God was a body?

This passage shows that around the time that he was writing the *Confessions*, Augustine knew a tradition of philosophical interpretation not only of the traditional gods but also of Vergil's poetry about the gods. We may therefore say with some confidence that the Augustine who wrote the *Confessions* could interpret Anchises' speech as a statement of Platonic doctrine. This should hardly surprise us. For Augustine mentions by name, in an earlier work, while arguing the necessity of expert guides for understanding scripture as much as for understanding the classics, three commentators on Vergil – Asper, Cornutus, and Donatus.[20] Moreover, the commentaries of Servius on Vergil and of Macrobius on Cicero's *Somnium Scipionis*, which feature Neoplatonic interpretations of the *Aeneid*, are both roughly contemporaneous with the *Confessions*. Indeed, Fabio Stok (this volume) has posited that these latter two commentators share a common Neoplatonizing source or sources. Whatever the identity of such sources, presumably their interpretations, or the reflexes of their interpretations in other authors, would have been available to Augustine.

It is worth noting here, in passing, that Vergil himself, perhaps in the wake of Cicero's *Somnium Scipionis*, constructed his *katabasis* in such a way that it easily afforded an anabatic interpretation to readers disposed to look for such things. On such an interpretation, Anchises and Aeneas meet in the superlunary heavens, rather than under the earth, just as in the *Somnium*, Scipio Africanus the Younger visited in a dream his father, Paullus, and his adoptive grandfather, Scipio Africanus the Elder, where their souls dwelt among the stars. Key lines for such an anabatic interpretation are 6.640–1 and 6.887. Servius, spurred by Anchises' mention of Elysium at 5.735 – *piorum concilia elysiumque colo* – quotes these lines in his comment (*ad Aen.* 5.735):[21]

Elysium est ubi piorum animae habitant post corporis animaeque discretionem … quod secundum poetas in medio inferorum est suis felicitatibus plenum, ut "solemque suum, sua sidera norunt" [*Aen.* 6.641] … secundum philosophos elysium est insulae fortunatae … secundum theologos circa lunarem circulum, ubi iam aër purior est: unde ait ipse Vergilius "aëris in campis" [*Aen.* 6.887].

Elysium is where the souls of the pious dwell after the separation of body and soul … According to the poets, it is in the midst of the infernal regions, and equipped with its own delights, so that the souls there "know their own sun, their own stars" [*Aen.* 6.641]… According to the philosophers, Elysium is the Isles of the Blessed … According to the theologians, it is around the lunar circle, where the air is purer: hence Vergil himself says, "in the fields of the air [*Aen.* 6.887].

Like Servius, Macrobius in his commentary on the *Somnium Scipionis* adduces line 6.641 and, in addition, 6.640. But unlike Servius, who was happy to consider without choosing between katabatic and anabatic interpretations of these lines, Macrobius presses both lines into service of an anabatic interpretation of Vergil's underworld (1.9.8):

Vergilius … licet argumento suo seruiens heroas in inferos relegauerit, non tamen eos abducit a caelo, sed "aethera" his deputat "largiorem" [*Aen.* 6.640], et "nosse eos solem suum ac sua sidera" [*Aen.* 6.641] profitetu , ut geminae doctrinae obseruatione praestiterit et poeticae figmentum et philosophiae ueritatem

Vergil … although he relegated his heroes to the underworld in service to his plot, nevertheless did not deprive them of heaven, but he assigned to them a "larger sky" [*Aen.* 6.640] and confesses they "know their own sun and their own stars" [*Aen.* 6.641], so that he has exhibited by observation of this twin teaching both the fiction of poetry and the truth of philosophy.

These commentators locate in the *Aeneid*, in addition to the patent "poetic" motif of descent, a latent "theological" or "philosophical" teaching about the soul's ascent. If we extend Stok's suggestion (this volume) and suppose that they share a common source (beyond Vergil's own suggestive words) for this idea, we nonetheless see their idiosyncrasy in its deployment. For Servius, line 6.641 refers to a "poetic" underworld, complete with its own sun and stars, whereas for Macrobius, the sun and stars of 6.641 evince a philosophical doctrine: the heroes dwell in the heavens.

Whatever the divergences in their interpretations of individual lines and clusters of words, we have seen that both commentators find that it is possible to read a doctrine of the soul's ascent into *Aeneid* 6. From this perspective, Augustine's Ostia episode may be seen to stand in a tradition of interpreting *Aeneid* 6 not only Neoplatonically, but also anabatically. In recounting the vision that he shared with his mother Monnica – a vision calculated to recall the eschatological vision shared by Aeneas and his father, a vision that partook of the anabatic interpretive affordances of Vergil's own poetry – Augustine glossed Anchises' revelations with up-to-date Neoplatonic philosophy. That is, he imitated and in so doing interpreted Vergil by an act of hermeneutic substitution.

It is this act of hermeneutic substitution that silences *Aeneid* 6 in the *Confessions*. But this act of substitution involves a series of double gestures. The fi st double gesture: the text of Plotinus interprets the cosmology, psychology, and eschatology of Anchises' speech, thus amplifying Vergil's words by disclosing their true Neoplatonic import even as it stands in for, displaces, and silences them. The second double gesture: Augustine so translates the Plotinian text that it, in turn, silences *itself* by calling for the silencing of all speech: *sileant omnis lingua et omne signum*. Indeed, Augustine could scarcely serve his readers Neoplatonism straight, no matter how congenial to his Christian philosophy he considered Platonism to be. So he chose a Plotinian passage that by a licit but scarcely innocent act of translation could be made to *silence itself*. By rendering Plotinus' Greek adjective ἥσυχος by means of the Latin verb *silere*, Augustine silenced the very text to which he was giving Latin voice. The third and final double gesture: to report, in direct quotation, a dialogue in which all language and every sign falls silent in the presence of God's ineffable Word is not only to flirt with silencing scripture, i.e., God's written word, but is also to indulge a paradox. For it is to ask the reader to mute the *Confessions* at the very pinnacle of the book's textual polyphony, when classical poetry, Neoplatonic philosophy, and Christian doctrine all merge in tremulous harmony.

Thus does Augustine's autobiography silence all the texts that it accumulates, or better, all the texts of which it, like Augustine's life itself, is an accumulation: the *Aeneid*, Plotinus, scripture, and the *Confessions* itself. Augustine has inscribed the story of his life like a palimpsest over Plotinus' treatise, with its doctrine of the soul's transcendence of the sensible cosmos, while in the same act inscribing Plotinus' text over Anchises' philosophical speech in *Aeneid* 6. In placing the *Aeneid's katabasis* at two removes and Plotinus' *anabasis* at one remove from the silence of his own climactic ascent, Augustine attempts to kick away, as it were, the textual scaffolding that brought him to his summit, the words upon which he climbed to God's Word. And yet this predicament – that he can only convey the spiritual silence of heaven through the cacophony of the carnal tongue – ensures the eternal audibility of the stubborn structures upon which the *Confessions* rests.

NOTES

1 I thank Matthew Keil, Vittorio Montemaggi, and Andrew M. Selby for discussing this material with me. I learned much from each of them. I dedicate this chapter to my late father, Louis H. Mackey, and to my late mentor in Classics, Douglass S. Parker. I began this work under their tutelage, though I did not know it at the time.

2 Hagendahl 1967 and Müller 2003 represent indispensable research tools. In addition, I have found the following studies useful in one way or another: Schelkle 1939; Courcelle 1955a, 1955b, 1984; O'Meara 1963, 1968, 1988; Ramage 1970; Currie 1974–5; Fichter 1982; Bennett 1988; Spence 1988; Springer 1989; Broeniman 1992–3; Ziolkowski 1995; MacCormack 1998; Lim 2004; Lafferty 2005; LaChance 2008; Hunink 2009; McCarthy 2009; Clark 2010a; Wills 2010; Pucci 2014. These works show how Augustine incorporated the *Aeneid* into his prose, but Christian epic poets of the fourth and fifth centuries could also make use of Vergil's poem, not least of all its underworld.

3 Kligerman 1957 is seminal in this regard (cf. Rudnytsky 1994). For more such references, and arguments against Kligerman and "psychohistorical" interpretation, see Schindler 1997.

4 Not only narrative patterns but verbal resonances may be found as well. For example, the passage on Monnica's abandonment quoted just above echoes Verg. *Aen.* 4.586–8: *regina e speculis ut primam albescere lucem | uidit et aequatis classem procedere uelis, | litoraque et uacuos sensit sine remige portus, | terque quaterque manu pectus percussa decorum | flauentisque abscissa comas* ... ("When from her tower the queen saw the fi st light | whitening, and the fleet setting forth sails set | in order, and she beheld the shore and its harbour, empty of rowers, | three times, four times she struck her ornamented breast with her hand | and she tore her golden hair ...").

5 Note the green places and the *ostia* common to both Vergil and Augustine. With Augustine's *hortus* cf. *Aen.* 6.638: *amoena uirecta*; 6.679: *conualle uirenti*; 6.704: *seclusum nemus et uirgulta sonantia siluae*. With Augustine's *Ostia Tiberina* cf. *Aen.* 1.13–14: *Tiberinaque* ... | *ostia*; 6.109: "*sacra ostia panda.*"

6 Bennett 1988: 65.

7 *Aen.* 6.751: after drinking at Lethe, the souls *incipiant in corpora uelle reuerti.*

8 See, e.g., D.L. VII.142–3.

9 See, too, Poque 1975.

10 See Blumenthal 1971.

11 Note that the one thing Augustine found lacking in the *Platonicorum libri* was the doctrine of the incarnation of the Word: *uerbum caro factus est et habitauit in nobis, non ibi legi* (*Conf.* 7.9.13). See Johnson 1972.

12 For Augustine's use of these passages and their relationship to Neoplatonic themes, see O'Donnell 1992 *ad loc.*

13 For Plotinus' discussion of Stoic psychology, see *Enn.* 4.7.

14 Cf. Soranzo and Stok in this volume on Christianizing approaches to *Aeneid* 6's golden bough and Tartarus, respectively.

15 See Soskice 2002: 455: "It is precisely Monica's presence which reveals the differences. In the fi st place the experience is shared, an impossibility in Plotinian union where the soul is no longer conscious that she is in the body, no longer conscious of herself as distinct from the One, and so could not be conscious of another person."

16 Kenney 2005: 143.

17 Kenney 2005: 143.

18 Kenney 2005: 145.

19 For the date, see O'Donnell 1992, 1.lxvii.

20 *De utilitate credendi* 17 and for mention of Vergil, 13.

21 Note also the superlunary interpretations at Servius *ad Aen.* 6.640 (*campi Elysii aut apud inferos sunt, aut in insulis fortunatis, aut in lunari circulo,* "The Elysian Fields are either in the underworld, in the Isles of the Blessed, or in lunar circle") and *ad Aen.* 6.887 (… *qui putant Elysium lunarem esse circulum,* "[there are people] who think Elysium is the lunar circle").

13

Spiritualism as Textual Practice

GRANT PARKER

I. The Gates of Sleep

Our key text, the Gates of Sleep, comes at the end of Book 6 and marks the midpoint of the poem (*Aen.* 6.893–9):

> sunt geminae Somni portae, quarum altera fertur
> cornea, qua ueris facilis datur exitus umbris,
> altera candenti perfecta nitens elephanto,
> sed falsa ad caelum mittunt insomnia Manes.
> his ibi tum natum Anchises unaque Sibyllam
> prosequitur dictis portaque emittit eburna,
> ille uiam secat ad nauis sociosque reuisit.

There are twin Gates of Sleep, of which one is said to be of horn, allowing an easy exit for shadows which are true. The other is all of shining white ivory, perfectly made; but the Spirits send visions which are false in the light of day. And Anchises having said this now escorted his son and the Sibyl with him on their way, and let him depart through the Gate of Ivory. Aeneas took a direct path along the shore to his ships and rejoined his comrades.

The lines that follow have the transitional character of a coda, bringing a point of closure, which also contains, by referring to ships, a note of expectation for that which will unfold in the second part of the poem (*Aen.* 6.900–1): *Tum se ad Caietae recto fert limite portum. | ancora de prora iacitur; stant litore puppes* ("Next he coasted along to Caieta's harbour. Anchors were cast from prows. Sterns stood along the beach"). The translation quoted is

W.F. Jackson Knight's; it appeared in 1956 and seems to have remained in print for more than six decades now despite the appearance of many rivals. To the translator we shall return in due course; for the present we might merely note the fact that he takes *falsa ad caelum* in immediate conjunction, rather than linking *ad caelum* with *mittunt*. Such an interpretation is eccentric, to say the least: for present purposes its interest value lies less in any explicatory value per se than in the critical practice underlying it.

Since ancient times, as we shall soon see, Vergil's readers have been faced with a logical problem: Aeneas departs via the Gate of Ivory, that is, the one associated with false dreams (*falsa … insomnia*, 896). How are we to understand the passage, and what are its implications for the work as a whole? *Insomnia* alone is troubling, since the word might variously connote sleep, or its opposite, or else dreams.[1] It is no exaggeration to say that the passage remains to this day an exegetical headache and, to judge from a major book on Vergilian studies, has become something of a cause célèbre.[2]

In these pages I begin with Servius' commentary on the passage in order to broadly characterize the kinds of critical approaches it has elicited since antiquity (section II). This is the background to the real subject of the essay, namely, the distinctive critical practice of Jackson Knight, whereby he and his associate Theo Haarhoff sought to make contact with Vergil's spirit (section III). Rather than merely writing off such an unorthodox approach, we find that in its very unorthodoxy it offers some telling insights into the way *Aeneid* 6 – or for that matter any revered text – can be analysed, and what is at stake with such textual exegesis. By understanding something of the evolution of Jackson Knight's approach and in particular his connection with Haarhoff we get more clues about what is at stake (section IV). The distinctiveness of Jackson Knight's exegesis emerges via selected comparanda, all involving other worlds (section V). Finally, all this allows us to identify the features of what may be called spiritualist philology, and to take stock of its unique appeal (section VI).

II. Servius Grammaticus

The commentary on Vergil's works surviving in a bifurcated textual tradition under the name of Servius (early fifth century CE) is easily the most substantial Latin work of its kind to survive from antiquity, and is usually thought to reflect the lost commentary of Aelius Donatus, the distinguished grammarian of the mid-fourth century.[3] The extant commentary is a teacher's instrument, as Robert Kaster has shown, intended to guide young learners through the poem, line by line, adducing textual and cultural material relevant to the understanding of Vergil's original. In terms of social status, such grammarians were generally humble compared to the more celebrated *rhetores*.[4] As regards the Vergilian text itself, Servius' exegesis is a good place to start:

[893] SUNT GEMINAE SOMNI PORTAE pro somniorum. est autem in hoc loco Homerum secutus, hoc tantum differt, quod ille per utramque portam somnia exire dicit, hic umbras ueras per corneam, per portam quas umbras somnia indicat uera. et poetice apertus est sensus: uult autem intellegi falsa esse omnia quae dixit. physiologia uero hoc habet: per portam corneam oculi significantu , qui et cornei sunt coloris et duriores ceteris membris: nam frigus non sentiunt, sicut et Cicero dicit in libris de deorum natura. per eburneam uero portam os significatur a dentibu . et scimus quia quae loquimur falsa esse possunt, ea uero quae uidemus sine dubio uera sunt. ideo Aeneas per eburneam emittitur portam. est et alter sensus: Somnum nouimus cum cornu pingi. et qui de somniis scripserunt dicunt ea quae secundum fortunam et personae possibilitatem uidentur habere effectum. et haec uicina sunt cornu: unde cornea uera fingitur porta ea uero quae supra fortunam sunt et habent nimium ornatum uanamque iactantiam dicunt falsa esse: unde eburnea, quasi ornatior porta, fingitur falsa

SUNT GEMINAE SOMNI PORTAE ["THERE ARE TWO GATES OF SLEEP"] Instead of "of dreams" [*somniorum*] In this passage he follows Homer, merely diverging in that Homer asserts that dreams depart through both gates, whereas Vergil says that true shades depart through the gate of horn: by these shades he means true dreams. In poetic terms the gist is clear: he wants it understood that everything he has said is false. In physiological terms this is what is going on: by the gate of horn the eyes are meant, which have the colour of horn and are tougher than other body parts, since they are insensitive to cold, as Cicero also writes in *On the Nature of the Gods* [2.57].[5] By the gate of ivory the mouth is meant, on account of the teeth. We know that what we say could be false whereas what we see is true without any doubt. For this reason Aeneas is let out by the gate of ivory. There is a further meaning: we know that sleep is depicted with a horn. And writers about dreams say that dreams which are commensurate with a person's fortune and ability will come true. And these are close to a horn. That's why the true gate is made from horn. On the other hand, as they say, dreams are false if they involve what is beyond one's fortunes and have too much decoration and inane showiness: hence the ivory gate, being more elaborate, is made the false one.

Servius' comments here are typical, in that they seem aimed at "the removal of 'difficulties' rather than their incorporation into a more complex reading."[6] So important a source for mythography in the Middle Ages, Servius here strikes a curious double note of self-confident unambiguous certainty on one hand (*poetice apertus est sensus*) and nihilism on the other (*falsa esse omnia quae dixit*). Breezily offering this assessment of radical implications, Servius diagnoses a problem to which centuries of scholars have applied their minds with different degrees of persuasiveness. Among the many solutions offered, some editors have doctored the text, engaging in what Richard Thomas has called "textual cleansing."[7] This is not the place to canvass all possible solutions; rather, there is value in reflecting on what is at stake in some of the solutions offered. At any rate, it is clear that Servius lays the groundwork by distinguishing between the human capacities of sight and speech, thus combining the logic of metaphor (horn ~ eyes, by virtue of colour) with that of metonymy (ivory, i.e., teeth ~ speech). Sight, according to Servius, has greater truth value compared to speech.[8]

III. Non-Suspicious Hermeneutics

However unsatisfactory Servius' account may seem, it does point to some of the main lines of interpretation. At the risk of painting with a broad brush, we shall proceed by indicating some of the larger trends. These should not be considered mutually exclusive.[9] Much of what we shall see differs from contemporary discourse analysis, which is more commonly characterized by the "hermeneutics of suspicion," namely, reading between the lines, against the grain, focusing on contradictions and omissions, gravitating towards power differentials.

(a) One kind of interpretation we have seen may be characterized as intratextual: the challenge of the critic is to understand the text in such a way as to minimize internal contradictions: "Intratextuality involves the principles on which any individual text might be organized, and thus recognized: structure, segmentation, and the relations between parts and the whole."[10] It is especially important, in such a framework, to trace Aeneas' journey into and out of the underworld.[11] Following the speech of the Sibyl, she and Aeneas are on the verge (*Aen.* 6.262–3): *tantum effata furens antro se immisit aperto; | ille ducem haud timidis uadentem passibus aequat* ("So much she said, and plunged madly into the opened cave; he, with fearless steps, keeps pace with his advancing guide").What comes after is an invocation of the underworld gods (*Aen.* 6.264–7):

> Di, quibus imperium est animarum, umbraeque silentes
> et Chaos et Phlegethon, loca nocte tacentia late,

sit mihi fas audita loqui; sit numine uestro
pandere res alta terra et caligine mersas.

You gods who hold the domain of spirits! You voiceless shades! You, Chaos, and you, Phlegethon, you broad, hushed tracts of night! Suffer me to tell what I have heard; suffer me of your grace to unfold secrets buried in the depths of darkness and of the earth!

When the reader sees Aeneas and the Sibyl again they are already *inside* "the empty halls of Dis and his phantom realm" (*Aen.* 6.268–72):

ibant obscuri sola sub nocte per umbram
perque domos Ditis uacuas et inania regna,
quale per incertam lunam sub luce maligna
est iter in siluis, ubi caelum condidit umbra
Iuppiter, et rebus nox abstulit atra colorem.

On they went dimly, beneath the lonely night amid the gloom, through the empty halls of Dis and his phantom realm, even as under the niggard light of a fitful moon lies a path in the forest, when Jupiter has buried the sky in a shade, and black Night has stolen from the world her hues.

Their slow pace is indicated with a spondaic line (6.268),[12] and darkness shrouds this atmosphere of foreboding. The descent into the underworld thus seems to turn on narratorial sleight of hand, in that the actual moment of entry is cloaked in an invocation of the gods. By the same token, there are similarities of phrasing between our passage and the Gates of War, suggesting that too deserves consideration.[13]

Consistency is typically a basis for textual scholarship; for example, it underlies the principle of *Homeron ex Homerou saphenizein*, a comment by Aristarchus that has been glossed as to "clarify Homer by way of Homer."[14] On the other hand, O'Hara (2007) has made a detailed study of what he calls inconsistency in Latin epic, arguing that this reflects not incompleteness, as was long believed, but alternative ways of understanding texts. The Gates of Sleep passage is one such example of critical doubt that the text arouses.

(b) Whereas the still novel term intratextuality focuses on connections and ruptures within the purview of a single text, the well-established concept of intertextuality stretches beyond. Among Vergil's many Homeric intertexts, there is a *prima facie* link with *Odyssey* 19.560–9, at the point where Penelope addresses Odysseus disguised as a beggar, having just recounted a dream in which twenty geese had been killed by an eagle (*Od.* 19.560–9):

ξεῖν', ἦ τοι μὲν ὄνειροι ἀμήχανοι ἀκριτόμυθοι
γίγνοντ', οὐδέ τι πάντα τελείεται ἀνθρώποισι.
δοιαὶ γάρ τε πύλαι ἀμενηνῶν εἰσὶν ὀνείρων·
αἱ μὲν γὰρ κεράεσσι τετεύχαται, αἱ δ' ἐλέφαντι·
τῶν οἳ μέν κ' ἔλθωσι διὰ πριστοῦ ἐλέφαντος,
οἵ ῥ' ἐλεφαίρονται, ἔπε' ἀκράαντα φέροντες·
οἱ δὲ διὰ ξεστῶν κεράων ἔλθωσι θύραζε,
οἵ ῥ' ἔτυμα κραίνουσι, βροτῶν ὅτε κέν τις ἴδηται.
ἀλλ' ἐμοὶ οὐκ ἐντεῦθεν ὀίομαι αἰνὸν ὄνειρον
ἐλθέμεν· ἦ κ' ἀσπαστὸν ἐμοὶ καὶ παιδὶ γένοιτο.

My friend, dreams are something mystifying and hard to construe, and do not always reach fulfilment in relation to humans. There are two gates for insubstantial dreams: one is composed of horn and the other of ivory. Dreams emerging from the gates of sawn ivory deceive people, conveying vain messages. But those that come through the gate of polished horn make true things come to pass for the dreamer. But it was not from there that my awful dream came, I think: it would have been welcome to my son and me if that had been the case.

Dramatic irony attends Penelope's comment that "dreams are hard to interpret," given that she is recounting the dream, in detail but also in generalizing terms, to the person who is its referent. The Homeric passage contains a twofold Greek pun, which defies attempts at translation: κέρας ("horn") with κραίνω ("fulfil") and ἐλέφας ("ivory") with ἐλεφαίρομαι ("deceive"). The passage contains interpretive questions of its own,[15] and beyond that the extent of its relevance to the *Aeneid* passage is open to debate. The etymological turn in these lines is a means of explaining words by ostensibly naturalizing them, a habit further developed by Vergil.[16] It is hard to explain why the Vergilian passage completely lacks etymological wordplay when its Greek intertext centres on it.

Whereas this Homeric intertext is the most obvious, it does not by any means preclude other possibilities. In Homer there is also a Gate of Hades (*Iliad* 23.62–76) and a Gate of the Sun (*Iliad* 24.11–14). However, the relevance of the passage quoted is surely placed beyond dispute by virtue of the *Aeneid*'s obvious and multifaceted dialogue with Homeric epic, and as we have seen is supported by Servius himself. To take a divergent example of interpretation, Tarrant (1982: 54) adduces Plato's *Phaedo* (66B–C) as the key intertext, so that Anchises (6.730–4) echoes Socrates in presenting the body, via its senses, as a hindrance to the soul's search for truth. All in all, Penelope's emphasis on the difficulty of interpreting dreams (ἀκριτόμυθοι) seems to cast a shadow of indeterminacy over not only her own dream but on the related Vergilian passage.

(c) Archaeology, both classical and beyond, provides for a third approach. An eminent example in relation to the Gates of Sleep is Highbarger (1940), who argues that the ivory gate is a uniquely Greek invention, for Egyptians and Babylonians used horn-shaped gates instead.[17] Because we have the adjective *cornea*, it is hypothetically possible that Vergil refers not to horn as a material but as a shape, i.e., the motif of double horns. In essence, Highbarger's approach and underlying assumptions are familiar enough in our field some element of material culture is adduced, like a rabbit out of a hat, and the resulting identification of text with object supposedly resolves questions about the interpretation of the text in question.[18] In this case the added complication of eastern origins, never a neutral part of classical studies, is part of the equation.

Taken together, these different approaches offer what we might call – with apologies to archaeologist colleagues – archaeologies of significanc , variously involving physical objects, locations, and texts. Semiotic value, it is clear, can be added in many different ways. Whatever the approach, in the textual problem about the Gates of Sleep the stakes are high: according to some explications, Aeneas' entire experience in the underworld, and in particular the pageant of Roman heroes (6.752–853), is under the threat of seeming false. In one variant, this reality check has played into the notion of Vergilian pessimism, the sense that Rome's triumph was a Pyrrhic victory; West here sees "man's uncertainty about the ordinances of god."[19] Here it is necessary to recognize what we might call deconstructive potential, the logic of the Derridean supplement; even Servius seems to point in that direction. Before we resign ourselves to critical aporia, following leads of Servius, Austin, and West, it is high time to ask the poet himself.

IV. Spiritualism between Johannesburg, Bloxham, and Exeter

When, in the translation quoted at the beginning, Jackson Knight offers "but the Spirits send visions which are false in the light of day" he is at one with his friend and lifelong supporter, T.J. ("Theo") Haarhoff, who for several decades occupied the Chair of Classics at the University of the Witwatersrand in Johannesburg. Haarhoff published a short piece in *Greece and Rome* (1948) in which he argued that *falsa ad caelum* should be taken closely together, "false to the world above," "false in the eyes of men." That reading seems counter-intuitive, given that *ad caelum* adjoins *mittunt*, and has not otherwise found favour.

Another surprising choice made by Jackson Knight concerns the opening lines of the poem, where he prints the supposititious four lines *ille ego qui quondam* as an epigraph. In this second case we do know from the scholars' correspondence that the choice follows Vergil's advice: in a Johannesburg séance with Mrs. Margaret Lloyd, Haarhoff had asked the author how the poem began, and *ille* was the clear reply.[20]

But just who was this scholar/translator? The life and works of W.F. Jackson Knight (1895–1964) have been the subject of an engaged yet critical essay by T.P. Wiseman.[21] After entering Hertford College, Oxford, on a scholarship in December 1913, his studies were interrupted by the war, in the course of which he suffered severe injury, including shellshock. After the war he taught at high schools before then returning to Oxford in September 1920, taking a second-class pass in Greats in 1922. He then spent ten years teaching at Bloxham School in Oxfordshire (1925–35) before gaining a junior appointment in Classics at University College of the South West of England at Exeter, now the University of Exeter. He retired from Exeter in 1961, after twenty-five years of service, and died three years later. It was at Exeter that his late-blossoming career saw a spate of publications on Vergil's *Aeneid.*

Though this is by no means an orthodox *cursus honorum,* he became widely known for his Penguin translation and also *Accentual Symmetry in Vergil's Aeneid* (1939) and *Roman Vergil* (1944), the latter a book aimed at general readers and hugely popular in its time. Composed in the darkest days of the Second World War, in its celebration of the poetry the book conveyed a message of optimism about the fate of civilization.[22] Jackson Knight was one of the founders of the Virgil Society. He was a real eccentric – dapper and formal in his manner, but also enormously warm and generous in his personal interactions. It is possible to gain insight into the man, warts and all, via the detailed biography written by his brother, G. Wilson Knight, himself one of the major Shakespearean scholars of the twentieth century.[23]

As Wiseman recounts, Jackson Knight and Haarhoff had fi st corresponded after admiring each other's short published notes on the *Aeneid.*[24] Later, when Haarhoff visited the UK, he was instrumental in securing the Exeter junior lectureship for Jackson Knight in 1936. Haarhoff was a convinced spiritualist, and it was through his influence that Jackson Knight turned increasingly in that direction, particularly from 1950: in that year his mother Caroline died – as a devout Anglo-Catholic she disparaged the evocation of spirits from the dead. On the other hand, Jackson Knight, like his brother, saw no contradiction. The year 1950 was also when Jackson Knight visited Johannesburg and personally took part in Mrs. Lloyd's circle.

In many ways, both intellectual and emotional, Jackson Knight differed hugely from his younger contemporary, R.G. Austin (1901–74).[25] Austin's Oxford red commentary on Book 6 was completed in his dying days, and was destined to be the route into the poem for many English-speaking readers of Vergil. Austin, who comes across, by contrast, as a model of British common sense, admits defeat over the Gates of Sleep: "The matter remains a Virgilian enigma and none the worse for that." Austin would rather resign himself to critical indeterminacy than pursue the kinds of connections that animate Jackson Knight's or Haarhoff's scholarship.[26]

Jackson Knight's interest in structures and their symbolic implications was clear from the start: his fi st article was "Vergil and the Maze" (1929). For Vergil, he argued, the maze was a "symbol of the state of earthly life in doubt and disintegration, which often precedes a revelation of religious truth."[27] Certainly Jackson Knight is not alone in his fascination with mazes, in the sense that Western medieval mazes have been subject to allegorical interpretation.[28] Despite the brevity of the piece, he makes dizzying interpretative leaps from Norden, via R.S. Conway to the medieval *Graphia aurea Urbis Romae,* to poetic symbolism à la Dante, Shelley, and Yeats, and finally Bishop Warburton, before reaching a "provisional" conclusion that Vergil in *Aeneid* 6 presents "moral and eschatological doctrines [that are] conveyed in the initiation ceremonies by action" (213).[29] Significantl , the same year he published reports on Romano-British excavations near Bloxham, where he taught in the Bloxham School, expressing an archaeological dimension of the same issue. In this early work he was interested in labyrinths for the control of access they offered, and as defensive structures whose integrity had to be kept mystically intact. Labyrinths are good to think with, within this framework – especially in comparative ethnology. Here Jackson Knight owed much to J.G. Frazer's work.[30] A look at Jackson Knight's footnotes and prefaces shows also the influence of his associate and sometime psychotherapist, John Layard, who in 1914 did fieldwork in the New Hebridean island of Malekula, now Vanuatu (Layard 1942). Hence Jackson Knight's interest in so-called stone people. Both Layard and Jackson Knight were influenced by Jung's idea of a collective unconscious. For Jackson Knight – and in a way for Wilson Knight too – it was these deep paradigmatic structures that were the true stuff of literary analysis. Another figure that might seem surprising in the footnotes is Jan Smuts, not as a political figure but as the author of a book on the philosophy of holism, something that was central also to Haarhoff's thought-world.[31] Haarhoff's Vergil was a figure of unity that resolved apparent antitheses.

By 1956, writing the preface to his Penguin translation, Jackson Knight had finally begun to own his residual spiritualist leanings, now that his mother had died six years previously. In the introductory thanks, there is a half-concealed pointer to supernatural sources of guidance: "There is no space to recognize the great number of written and spoken communications on which I have depended in the Introduction and throughout this book." The word "communications" is used here with pointed suggestiveness, carrying enormous weight. By the same token, the thanks he offers Haarhoff are telling: "special acknowledgement ... to Professor T.J. Haarhoff who has been helping and guiding me for nearly twenty-five years and has always sent me prompt answers to all my frequent enquiries; how authentic his direction has been must be left to appear hereafter." How authentic indeed.

V. Spirits, Authors, Critics

The story of Jackson Knight and Haarhoff's engagement with Vergil requires broader contextualization, starting in antiquity. Now it is well known that the status of Vergil and the *Aeneid* were well established by the time of the poet's death in 19 BCE. Less easy to understand is some of the tradition called the *sortes Virgilianae*. Since Comparetti's influential book this has been considered a widespread practice of ancient bibliomancy, reflecting not only the ubiquity of the *Aeneid* but also Vergil's quasi-magical power.[32] The earliest references are to be found in the *Historia Augusta*, a notoriously unreliable and salacious series of imperial biographies starting with Hadrian and dating to the late fourth century. However, Ekbom's thorough new study suggests that, far from being a product of Roman prophecy, such references are part of an elaborate literary conceit, comparable in this regard with the contemporary habit of writing Centos: a "quilt"-like stitching together of phrases from Vergil in order to make new poetry, which could be either pious (as in the *Cento Probae*) or obscene (Ausonius' *Cento Nuptialis*).[33] Such references to Vergil's role in prophecy cannot be taken at face value, Ekbom argues. This is all the more reason to exercise a healthy skepsis on the nature and importance of the so-called *sortes Virgilianae.* What a tome such as Ziolkowski and Putnam's *The Virgilian Tradition* overwhelmingly shows is Vergil's vast literary and cultural influence in antiquity and the Middle Ages; nor does the story of Vergilian tradition end there.

Nonetheless, Vergil's authority in antiquity is one thing; to link it to Jackson Knight's spiritualism is no easy task. And magic can mean very different things in relation to texts.[34] To be sure, much could be said concerning modern context, and here I can touch only on a few points. The concept of spiritualism, as expressed in the foundation of the Society for Psychical Research (SPR) in 1882, has been articulated in the publications of the Society ever since. While Jackson Knight and Haarhoff stand out in their willingness to communicate with the spirit of Vergil, spiritualism or paranormal psychology was by no means unique to them.[35]

One of the most famous, and controversial, practitioners of spiritualism in a literary context was Helena Blavatsky (1831–91), founder of the Theosophical Society (1875), and author of *Isis Unveiled* (1877), her theosophical manifesto that synthesizes science, philosophy, and religion. The work draws on Buddhism and other South Asian traditions as well as Neoplatonism and Hermeticism – a combination of several usable pasts from a wide range of ancient cultures. Her book is symptomatic of the eclecticism of Western esotericism, as well as its appetite for exoticism. Its dizzying eclecticism has a similar effect to some of Jackson Knight's writings, in which a wide array of texts is typically combined in the same argument.

Classics has played an unexpectedly significant role in the history of spiritualism. Oxford's successive Regius Professors in the years 1908–60 were both active in this sphere: Gilbert Murray (1866–1957) served as SPR president in the years 1915–16 and again in 1952; and E.R. Dodds (1893–1979) served 1960–3. Dodds' lifelong interest in the supernatural is immediately apparent in his scholarly output, notably *The Greeks and the Irrational.* His address to the Society remains a valuable overview of the subject:[36] at the time its main purpose was to explain philology and psychical research to each other. Nor are these two figures alone: Frederic (F.W.H.) Myers (1843–1901), one of the founders of the SPR in 1882, initially held a fellowship in Classics at Trinity College, Cambridge;[37] A.W. Verrall (1851–1912) and Andrew Lang (1844–1912) were also early presidents of the society.

That philology and ghosts may be compatible is evident in a famous lecture given by Ulrich von Wilamowitz-Moëllendorff, the eminent professor from Berlin, on the occasion of his visit to Oxford in June 1908:

> We know that ghosts cannot speak until they have drunk blood; and the spirits which we evoke demand the blood of our hearts. We give it to them gladly; but if they then abide our question, something from us has entered into them; something alien, that must be cast out, cast out in the name of truth![38]

The key difference in this reference, which has spawned considerable commentary in its own right, is that this is merely a passing metaphor, clearly signalled as such, coming here as the punchy coda to his much-anticipated lecture.[39] In fact, he is arguing for the radical otherness of that ghostly realm rather than its availability for human use, such as spiritualists might wish.

What is distinctive about the spiritualism of Jackson Knight and Haarhoff is that it is aimed not at poetic creation per se, drawing inspiration in the style of Coleridge or even Madame Blavatsky: rather, it is yoked to classical philology, in particular the explication of ancient texts. This brings to the fore not esteemed authors but their altogether more modest servants: classical philologists.[40] If Classics is a famously object-oriented discipline, it is hard to discuss scholars in the same breath. Yet the context of spiritualism is one that brings scholars into the picture. By a well-established classical principle, the author is the originator and thus ultimate arbiter of meaning. The *uitae* (biographies) of poets that survive from antiquity, many of them merely extrapolating details from the works themselves, are proof of the salience of this principle in antiquity. In such a setting authors are able to exercise "interpretive tyranny." Whereas post-structuralist and other literary theory is generally at pains to minimize the interpretive tyranny exercised by authors,[41] Jackson Knight and Haarhoff indulge that tyranny to an extreme degree.

Jackson Knight and Haarhoff address themselves to the inspiration infusing an author, in this case Vergil, whereas the scholar is not typically part of this matrix. Classical scholars who communicate with dead authors subordinate their own roles to those of an author of Vergil's prestige: their role is more closely comparable to that of a scribe or a secretary (see below), and invites comparison with the humble *grammaticus* rather than to that of a major poet.

VI. Features of Spiritualism

What is at stake with all this? First, a word of warning: if one focuses on the afterlife, suddenly many features of ancient religion come into play, including divination. It is hard to circumscribe the phenomenon. Recall Dodds' lecture to the SPR on the question of how to characterize links between spiritualism and the philological enterprise. By way of summing up I would like to offer five broad observations. Many of them involve some conflation of author and text: Vergil as author is assumed to be the gatekeeper of his text, which is by implication spiritually accessible via his shade.

(a) If there is such a thing as spiritualist philology, it focuses, not to say fixate , on objects that have symbolic potential, objects that are *semiotically overcharged.* All three modes of analysis discussed above play a part in the dynamics of meaning: other parts of the same text; different texts; and external phenomena of a physically visible nature, such as the ritual pattern supposedly underlying the megaliths of Malekula. The labyrinth is one such object, as Jackson Knight pursued in *Vergil's Troy* and *Cumaean Gates,* partly responding to Layard's work in Vanuatu. Jackson Knight's choice of topics responds to the allure of hidden knowledge. This kind of philology focuses on heightened signification In a self-fulfilling exercise, there is a sense that the stakes of interpretation or hermeneutics are raised – even to the level of humanity's shared unconscious, as Jung would have it.

This brings us to some ways in which we might consider some metapoetic aspects. To draw on a huge category, ancient dreams are the obvious focus for this sense of poetic language as a holder of secret knowledge. Thus when Penelope comments that dreams are 'impenetrable, hard to interpret' (ἀμήχανοι ἀκριτόμυθοι, *Od.* 19.560), there are many layers of irony given that, as noted above, she herself provides the initial interpretation, while speaking to the person whose presence and future actions constitute further interpretation. This comment has relevance to the epic narrative itself, with its multiple prolepses and retrospect.

To take up a different form of understanding the text: Jackson Knight's approach makes it a mandala of sorts, if we may broaden his own analysis of the Cumaean Gates. Here he draws both on comparative mythology and particularly on Carl Jung. This figure linking eastern and western thought-worlds is the key intertext for Jackson Knight's analysis of this other Vergilian interpretive crux. As a "'fortified city with walls and moats,' the mandala perfectly illustrates the supposed 'Initiation Pattern.'"[42]

(b) Spiritualist philology appears to be markedly *apolitical.* One might compare Haarhoff's *Stranger at the Gate,* ostensibly dedicated "to the spirit of racial co-operation" but in practice restricted in its purview to a white South Africa divided between English and Afrikaans speakers. Jackson Knight, by contrast, seems to have been interested in neither ancient nor modern politics. Wilson Knight knew his brother very well, and for some periods there were daily letters, yet when he wrote the biography even he did not know what Jackson Knight felt about the rival merits of Churchill and Attlee, the main statesmen of post-war Britain.[43] There is undoubtedly a certain historicism in Jackson Knight's work, especially if one looks at *Roman Vergil,* but this is superficial and stops short of scrutinizing its subject position. And perhaps any such expectation would be churlish in any case. In this respect Gilbert Murray is the exception, in that he was politically active for several phases of his life, and after the First World War, as a committed internationalist, was an early participant in organizations aligned to the fledgling League of Nation .[44]

For the younger men especially, the First World War does seem to have engendered implicit politics by the celebration of Vergil as all that is "civilized" in Western civilization amid the ravages of war. (And it will be remembered that Jackson Knight had served in the war and subsequently gained fame at both Bloxham School and at Exeter in the local Office s' Training Corps.) The irony of this martial context is that Germany, Britain's adversary in both world wars, was also the original home of classical philology in the modern period.

As noted above, in contrast to Jackson Knight, the "Harvard School" of pessimistic approaches to the *Aeneid* is framed by a post-war mindset: in the 1960s, in particular, there was a strong impetus to challenge authority via social institutions. Just as US imperialism generated self-doubt on the part of young Americans during the Korean and Vietnam Wars, so interpretations of the *Aeneid* focused on the troubling aspects of the narrative, especially the price paid for the founding of Rome. This line of thought found little resonance in Germany of the same period, nor was it in line with ancient interpretations.[45]

If, however, we seek to understand the spiritualism of Jackson Knight and Haarhoff, it is necessary to think of the evolution of the practice in the late nineteenth century. Certainly, by the end of the nineteenth century spiritualism had become an antidote to a widely felt sense of degeneration, in ways that might have had ongoing impact on Jackson Knight.[46] The case of Haarhoff is different, in that his underlying politics was demonstrably shaped by the traumatic experience of the Anglo-Boer War – something he experienced via his mother, who as a young Afrikaner woman spent time in a concentration camp. This led to a strong, if nebulous and ultimately myopic, dedication to "the spirit of racial co-operation": this definitively meant détente between Afrikaans- and English-speaking South Africans.[47]

(c) Spiritualist philology focuses on, or even creates, what we might call an *absolute text* – elevating the text in question to a level where it is deemed to answer all questions one might have. If a recent book on classical commentaries can speak of the "fetishizing of the source text,"[48] that term may be used so much more strongly of the textual practice of spiritualist classicists. The text gains this status because, as Jackson Knight writes, it acts as a repository of collective memory:

> [I]t is hard to refuse the conclusion that the Sixth *Aeneid* preserves a very ancient memory, now extant only, as in Malekula, on the periphery of megalithic influence a memory which was still alive in Italy in Vergil's day, retained for us by his poetic insight and by his knowledge of the inherent meaning of tradition.[49]

Outside the Judaeo-Christian tradition, the *Aeneid* might be unique in this respect.[50] In the case of Jackson Knight, it is clear that the spiritualist approach goes hand in hand with close attention to language and style: it is no coincidence that the author of *Cumaean Gates* also wrote *Accentual Symmetry.* Here it is worth emphasizing again Jackson Knight's astute grasp of literary texture in relation to metre. To return to the emphasis on human senses in the Homeric passage quoted above, it is the sense of hearing that matters in spiritualism, and this seems to be reflected in Jackson Knight's attentiveness to the sound of the *Aeneid.* While it is true, as we have seen, that Servius prefers sight over sound as an index of truth, we may be critical of his statement on that score.[51]

(d) The link between *Aeneid* 6 and spiritualist philology might be described as *overdetermined*. By integrating séances into their exegesis, Jackson Knight and Haarhoff have replicated, in their textual practice, the very narrative of that book. They perform a *katabasis* of their own in their efforts, spiritualist and philological, to explicate the text. The scholars are emulating the hero of the story: like Aeneas, they consult with key figures in the underworld. In this respect a book like *Cumaean Gates* outdoes Frazer's *Golden Bough*, in which in essence Frazer riffs comparatively on the seventeen original words of Strabo 5.3.12.[52] Frazer's comparative impulse in the *Golden Bough* grew ever stronger as successive editions swelled it from two volumes to twelve. In the process the ostensible original question about the Arician priesthood literally disappeared from view. A loquacious answer to a non-existent question, as J.Z. Smith shows; "Balderdash," thunders D.A. West, in a wittily dismissive reference to the Scandinavian Balder.[53] By contrast, Jackson Knight never lost sight of the *Aeneid* even when he took a comparative turn, and even if the fi st chapter of *Cumaean Gates* takes the reader straight from Vergil to Vanuatu. Yet it is hard to imagine a major Nordenesque or even Austinesque commentary ever coming from Jackson Knight's pen.

(e) Spiritualist philology seems to involve *charismatic transference*: by this I mean a sense of being at one with the author. This is most evident when Haarhoff communes with Vergil via his spirit media in Johannesburg, Mrs. Margaret Lloyd and Mrs. Emmy Verwey.[54] As Wiseman recounts, sometimes this contact is very general, on other occasions it is very specific such as when the supposititious fi st four lines *ille ego qui quondam* ... are supposedly approved by the author himself. At some level, the desire to hear the poet's voice is a natural desire for any commentator, any critic. Charismatic transference is something we see at the end of the biography, when Jackson Knight and Vergil appear together to Wilson Knight at a séance. Indeed, it may be significant that in his thoughtful and measured biography, Wilson Knight gives only some hints of spiritualism in the bulk of the book, and only goes into detail for Jackson Knight's last years and his life after death. By turning only at the end to the spirit realm, Wilson Knight may be consoling himself at his beloved older brother's death.

Since the work of the church historian Rudolph Sohm and the sociologist Max Weber, charisma has been considered a human attribute, a source of legitimacy.[55] But in some of what we have seen the text itself takes on the qualities usually associated with an author. In the present context it is reasonable to speak about the charisma of the *Aeneid* itself. Meanwhile, spiritualism holds the promise of privileged access to a text via its author or, more precisely, its author's shade.

VII. Secretaries of the Invisible (Conclusion)

I am a writer, and what I write is what I hear. I am a secretary of the visible, one of the many secretaries over the ages. That is my calling: dictation secretary. It is not for me to interrogate, to judge what is given me. I merely write down the words and then test them, test their soundness, to make sure I have heard right.[56]

With these words, Elizabeth Costello in J.M. Coetzee's eponymous novel describes her role as a writer: this eighth and final vignette of *Elizabeth Costello* is called "At the gate." (Whether this is a coincidence, given Coetzee's classical engagements since student days at the University of Cape Town, is an apt question, though one that is unlikely to be resolved, given his famous reticence.) In the novel Elizabeth is in a waiting room hoping for an interview with a petty bureaucrat who could presumably provide access to an undefined world beyond that gate. Essentially this scenario reverses Haarhoff's perspective in *Stranger at the Gate*: Haarhoff had chosen the perspective from within, looking outside, whereas Elizabeth seeks entry. At a point when Elizabeth has faced intrusive bureaucratic questions, she exasperatedly yet resolutely describes herself as "Secretary of the invisible: not my own phrase, I hasten to say. I borrow it from a secretary of a higher order, Czeslaw Milosz, a poet, perhaps known to you, to whom it was dictated long ago."[57] However many are the levels of Coetzee's irony and narrative frames, the phrase does suggest that a mystified sense of writing lives on in our own cynical age. As distant descendants of Servius and other ancient grammarians, Jackson Knight and Haarhoff come across as philologists par excellence: secretaries who are unambitious in their subordination to"powers beyond us,"[58] which in their case are centred on Vergil's shade.

NOTES

1 Thus Servius *ad loc.*: see section II of the current essay. On *insomnia*, see *TLL* VII 1.1935.75–1936.62. Conington *ad loc.* canvasses the suggestion that *somni* stands for the metrically inadmissible *somnii*, but this is merely one of many unconvincing explanations.

2 Thomas 2001: 100–1, 103–8. Thomas' account is unusual in being a survey of solutions that does not argue for its own solution to the textual problem; the current essay follows suit.

3 On Servius and the cultural authority he enjoyed, see Kaster 1988: 169–98; cf. Ziolkowski and Putnam 2008: 628–36; Fowler 1997a. See also Stok in this volume.

4 Kaster 1988: 99–134, gives a detailed account of the livelihood of grammarians, which he describes as *mediocritas* (middling range).

5 Servius botches this detail in that Cicero refers instead to ears at this point of the *De natura deorum*. See further Copeland and Sluiter 2012.

6 Fowler 1997a: 73–4.

7 Thomas 2001 is most concerned by the willingness of scholars, notably two eminent nineteenth-century textual critics, Otto Ribbeck (1827–98) and August Nauck (1822–92), to emend the text: the logic is typically circular, he shows, in that a scholar's overall interpretation causes details to be changed – while at the same time the overall interpretation rests on significant detail . Both Ribbeck and Nauck are notoriously trigger-happy in this regard. Thomas notes that such emendations, from the eighteenth century up to contemporary times, are typically contingent on the idea of the *Aeneid* fulfilling a pro-Augustan program; Thomas, on the other hand, follows the "pessimist" school.

8 Cf. Nightingale 2016, who shows that Plato is deeply contradictory concerning sight: on the one hand he is outwardly dismissive of the seeing, on the other hand the sense of sight pervades his theories of knowledge and understanding.

9 For example, Highbarger's 1940 archaeological approach is buttressed by an intratextual element (positing that Aeneas must have entered and left the underworld by the same gate) and an intertextual one (the Homeric gate is considered important in decoding the Vergilian one).

10 Laird 2000: 145; compare other essays in the same collection. For Laird, the term specifically ci cumvents the issue of authorial design and is useful for that reason. It must be said that the term "intratextual" has not necessarily found wide currency, and has not (yet) received the blessing of the *Oxford English Dictionary*.

11 On movement in and through the underworld of *Aeneid* 6, see also Herrero in this volume.

12 Edwards 2002: 104.

13 Note esp. the opening, 7.607: *Sunt geminae belli portae* ("there are twin gates of war").

14 Nagy 2003: x; contrast Dawe 2006: 6. Alexander Pope in his *Essay on Criticism* elegantly sums up this Aristarchan principle, as well as Vergilian intertextuality, with the following injunction concerning Homer: "Still with itself compar'd, his text peruse; / And let your comment be the Mantuan Muse."

15 See, e.g., Levaniouk 2011: chapter 13: as she points out, Penelope does not request explication but provides it herself.

16 Vergil's use of this practice in the *Aeneid* is spelled out by O'Hara 2017; see 182–3 on our passage.

17 Jackson Knight 1946: 136 affirms Highbarger s approach to this question.

18 Some scholars use material culture unreflectivel , to explain away problems in an ancient text, Martin 2008.

19 West 1990: 238; cf. Minson 2003–4.
20 Wiseman 1992: 199–206.
21 "Talking to Virgil," the eponymous essay of Wiseman's book, 1992: 171–209.
22 Clark 2017 interestingly contrasts this optimism with the pessimism of the "Harvard School."
23 Wilson Knight 1975.
24 In the *Rand Daily Mail*, a Johannesburg newspaper, Haarhoff published one of the most enthusiastic reviews of Jackson Knight's early work, *Vergil's Troy*. See Wilson Knight 1975: 145.
25 Henderson 2006: 37–69.
26 Austin's distaste for Jackson Knight's excesses is apparent in reviews of his books: one that appeared after Jackson Knight's death mixes scepticism about his approach with admiration for the enthusiasm with which it is pursued: "He seems, in his Vergilianism, always to be stretching out his hands in longing for some further shore; he makes us conscious that such a shore exists, even though we may not travel in his company." Austin 1977: 163. See further Henderson 2006: 38.
27 Jackson Knight 1929: 212.
28 Delaney 1994: 210–11.
29 Cf. Kilgour in this volume.
30 On Frazer, see also Barchiesi and Soranzo in this volume.
31 Smuts 1926.
32 Comparetti 1895: 48; cf. Ziolkowski and Putnam 2008: 829–30. It is possible that the early modern tradition about the *sortes Virgilianiae* may have contributed to misunderstandings about the ancient phenomenon.
33 Ziolkowski and Putnam 2008: 471–85; Ekbom 2013.
34 For example, E.K. Rand, Pope Professor of Latin at Harvard and co-founder of the Harvard Servius project, in a major book speaks of Vergil's "magical power," which in effect seems to mean the transmutation of older elements into a new poetic whole: Rand 1931. Compare Jackson Knight's review 1935: 146, itself characteristic of an inability to sustain an argument.
35 Haarhoff appears to have been more aware of the limits of the process than was Jackson Knight: Wiseman 1992: 202.
36 Dodds 1946.
37 Kripal 2010: chapter 1, "The Book as Séance." Kripal emphasizes the role of personal experience in the spiritualist leanings of Murray and other key figure . Compare Gauld 2011 and Taylor 2007: 26, "his intense, idealistic Hellenism never really left him."
38 Wilamowitz-Moellendorff 1908: 25.
39 Note the title of Sir Hugh Lloyd-Jones' book of essays, *Blood for the Ghosts* (1983), which we may take to indicate both reverence for Wilamowitz and

distance from his two predecessors as Regius Professor of Greek. Ironically, it was Murray that translated the lecture from German into English. Lloyd-Jones held the chair from 1960 to 1989, succeeding Dodds.

40 A possible exception here is Myers. A proficient composer of Latin ve se, which was at the time a staple of the Oxbridge classical curriculum, he won the prestigious Camden Medal in 1862, but was later found to have copied verses wholesale from Vergil and forced to resign the award. In this intriguing case the boundary between scholarship and creative composition was blurred by one of the most flamboyant of all spiritualist , who was also a distinguished classicist. See Gauld 2011. This intriguing episode also challenges the paradigm often used in literary theory of a relationship between author, text and reader. Contrast Kilgour in this volume on the prominence of a key figure in the *Aeneid* (the Sibyl) as opposed to the text itself.

41 Note especially the famous essays by Roland Barthes ("The Death of the Author") and Michel Foucault ("What Is an Author?"), the latter of which may be a response to the former. Both essays would have considerable impact on literary studies in Europe and the English-speaking world.

42 Jackson Knight 1967: 271.

43 Wilson Knight 1975: 474.

44 Stray 2008.

45 Kallendorf 1999.

46 Taylor 2007.

47 Parker 2010 emphasizes the link between Haarhoff and the politics of General Smuts.

48 Kraus and Stray 2015: 8.

49 Jackson Knight 1936: 272–3.

50 Note, however, Ekbom 2013: 65–78 on the so-called *sortes biblicae*: this phenomenon seems to have been more limited. For the relation of Vergil's text to the Bible, explicitly or otherwise, compare the diverging material of Kilgour and Soranzo in this volume.

51 *ad Aen.* 6.893: *et scimus quia quae loquimur falsa esse possunt, ea uero quae uidemus sine dubio uera sunt* ("We know that what we say could be false whereas what we see is true without any doubt"). On the sounds of Latin verse, see also Edwards 2002: 102–24.

52 Again Servius (*ad Aen.* 6.136) fulfils a subordinate but important role in explicating the text. Two of Frazer's early modern forebears in this respect are discussed in Soranzo's contribution to the current book. On Frazer, see also Barchiesi in this volume.

53 West 1990: 228.

54 At the risk of making my own unwelcome emendation, it does seem that Wiseman's reading of "Vermey" in the correspondence is incorrect, since that

name is not otherwise known. More common, and surely more plausible here, is "Verwey": *w* could easily be misread as *m* in mid-twentieth-century cursive.

55 Feuchtwang 2008.

56 Coetzee 2003: 199.

57 Coetzee 2003: 199. Milosz' poem, "Secretaries," in the point of reference (2001: 343): "I am no more than a secretary of the invisible thing | That is dictated to me and a few others. | Secretaries, mutually unknown, we walk the earth | Without much comprehension. Beginning a phrase in the middle | Or ending it with a comma. And how it all looks when completed | Is not up to us to inquire, we won't read it anyway." The last line adds a note of bathos.

58 Coetzee 2003: 200.

WORKS CITED

Ableitinger, D. 1972. "Die Aeneassage im *Carmen Saeculare* des Horaz (Verse 37–44)." *Wiener Studien* 6: 33–44.

Ahl, F.M. 1984. "The Rider and the Horse: Politics and Power in Roman Poetry from Horace to Statius." *ANRW* II 32.1: 40–124.

Aicher, P. 1989. "Ennius' Dream of Homer." *AJP* 110: 227–32.

Aiello, L. 2013. *After Reception Theory: Fedor Dostoevskii in Britain, 1869–1935*. New York.

Alexander, C. 2011. "Out of Context." *The New York Times*. 7 April 2011.

Allen, T.W., ed. 1917. *Homeri Opera*. Oxford.

Anderson, W.S. 1963. "Multiple Change in the *Metamorphoses*." *TAPA* 94: 1–27.

Andrews, F. 2006. *The Other Friars: The Carmelite, Augustinian, Sack and Pied Friars in the Middle Ages*. Woodbridge, UK.

Ariosto, L. 1974. *Orlando Furioso*. Edited by E. Sanguineti, introduction and notes by M. Turchi. 2 vols. Milan.

– 1963. *Ariosto's* Orlando Furioso*: Selections from the Translation of Sir John Harrington*, edited by R. Gottfried. Bloomington.

Armisen-Marchetti, M. 2003. *Macrobe: Commentaire au Songe de Scipion*. Paris.

Austin, R.G. 1964. *P. Vergili Maronis* Aeneidos *Liber Secundus*. Oxford.

– 1967. "Mystic Guide to Virgil." *The Classical Review* 17: 161–2.

– 1971. *P. Vergili Maronis* Aeneidos *Liber Primus*. Oxford.

– 1977. *P. Vergili Maronis* Aeneidos *Liber Sextus*. Oxford.

Bacon, H.H. 1994–5. "The Chorus in Greek Life and Drama." *Arion* 3: 6–24.

Bailey, C. 1947. *Titi Lucreti* De Rerum Natura. 3 vols. Oxford.

Ball, R. 1983. *Tibullus the Elegist: A Critical Survey*. Göttingen.

Barchiesi, A. 1979. "Palinuro e Caieta: Due 'epigrammi' virgiliani (*Aen.* V.870 sg.; VII.1–4)." *Maia* n.s. 31: 3–11.

– 1993. "Future Reflexive Two Modes of Allusion and Ovid's *Heroides*." *HSCP* 95: 333–65.

– 1994. "Immovable Delos: *Aeneid* 3.73–98 and the Hymns of Callimachus." *CQ* 44: 438–43.

– 1997. "Virgilian Narrative: Ecphrasis." In *The Cambridge Companion to Virgil*, edited by C. Martindale, 271–81. Cambridge.

– 2000. "Rituals in Ink: Horace on the Greek Lyric Tradition." In *Matrices of Genre: Authors, Canons and Society*, edited by M. Depew and D. Obbink, 167–82. Cambridge, MA.

– 2002. "The Uniqueness of the *Carmen Saeculare* and Its Tradition." In *Traditions and Contexts in the Poetry of Horace*, edited by A.J. Woodman and D. Feeney, 107–23. Cambridge.

– 2005. "Centre and Periphery." In *A Companion to Latin Literature*, edited by S. Harrison, 394–405. Malden, MA; Oxford.

– 2017. "Colonial Readings in Vergilian Geopoetics: The Trojans at Buthrotum." In *Imagining Empire*, edited by V. Rimell and M. Asper, 151–65. Heidelberg.

Barolini, T. 1984. *Dante's Poets: Textuality and Truth in the Comedy*. Princeton.

Barrett, Sir William. 1918. *On the Threshold of the Unseen: An Examination of the Phenomena of Spiritualism and of the Evidence for Survival after Death*. New York.

Barthes, R. 1977 [1967]. "The Death of the Author." Reprinted in *Image Music Text*, translated by Stephen Heath, 142–8. New York.

Bausi, F. 2001. "Poésie et religion au Quattrocento." In *Poétiques de la Renaissance*, edited by F. Hallyn et al., 219–38. Geneva.

Beard, M. 1993. "Frazer et ses bois sacrés." In *Les bois sacrés*, 171–80. Naples.

Beard, M., J. North, and S. Price. 1998. *Religions of Rome. Volume 1: A History*. Cambridge.

Bennett, C. 1988. "The Conversion of Vergil: The *Aeneid* in Augustine's *Confessions*." *Revue des Études Augustiniennes* 34: 47–69.

Bernabé, A., and A.I. Jiménez. 2008. *Instructions for the Netherworld: The Orphic Gold Tablets*. Boston and Leiden.

Berry, D.H. 1992. "The Criminals in Vergil's Tartarus: Contemporary Allusions in *Aeneid* 6.621–4." *CQ* 42: 416–20.

Bettini, M. 1991. *Anthropology and Roman Culture: Kinship, Time, Images of the Soul*. Baltimore.

Blavatsky, H.P. 1919. *Isis Unveiled: A Master-Key to the Mysteries of Ancient and Modern Science and Technology*. Rev. ed. Point Loma, CA.

Blumenthal, H.J. 1971. "Soul, World-Soul, and Individual Soul in Plotinus." *Le Neoplatonisme, colloque de Royaumont, 9–13 juin 1969*. Paris: 55–66.

Bodel, J.P. 1994. "Trimalchio's Underworld." In *The Search for the Ancient Novel*, edited by J. Tatum, 237–59. Baltimore.

– 1997. "Monumental Villas and Villa Monuments." *JRA* 10: 5–35.

Bolisani, E. 1958. "Una curiosa interpretazione allegorica del *ramus aureus* di Virgilio (*Aen.* VI *passim*)." *Atti e Memorie dell'Accademia Patavina* 71: 157–70.

Bömer, F., ed. 1976. *P. Ovidius Naso,* Metamorphosen*: Kommentar Buch IV-V.* Heidelberg.

Bordone, F. 2007–8. "L'inferno secondo Paolino di Nola: le figure mitologiche dell'Oltretomba pagano nel carm. 31." *ITFC* 7: 261–92.

Borgeaud, P. 1974. "The Open Entrance to the Closed Palace of the King: The Greek Labyrinth in Context." *History of Religions* 14: 1–27.

Boucher, J.-P. 1965. *Caius Cornélius Gallus.* Paris.

Bowen, A., and P. Garnsey. 2003. *Lactantius*: Divine Institutes. Liverpool.

Boyd, B.W. 1997. *Ovid's Literary Loves: Influence and Innovation in the* Amores. Ann Arbor.

Boyle, A.J. 1985 "In Nature's Bonds: A Study of Seneca's *Phaedra.*" *ANRW* II 32.2: 1284–1347.

– 1997. *Tragic Seneca: An Essay in the Theatrical Tradition.* London and New York.

– 2011. *Seneca:* Oedipus. Oxford.

Braund, S. 1997. "Virgil and the Cosmos: Religious and Philosophical Ideas." In *The Cambridge Companion to Virgil,* edited by C. Martindale, 204–21. Cambridge.

– 2006. "A Tale of Two Cities: Statius, Thebes, and Rome." *Phoenix* 60.3–4: 259–73.

Brazouski, A. 1990. "Lovers in Elysium." *CB* 66: 35–6.

Bremmer, J.N. 1987. "Oedipus and the Greek Oedipus Complex." In *Interpretations of Greek Mythology,* edited by J.N. Bremmer, 41–59. Routledge.

– 1991. "Walking, Standing and Sitting in Ancient Greek Culture." In *A Cultural History of Gesture,* edited by J.N. Bremmer and H. Roodenburg, 15–35. Cambridge.

– 1995. "Religious Secrets and Secrecy in Classical Greece." In *Secrecy and Concealment,* edited by H.G. Kippenberg and G.G. Stroumsa, 61–78. Leiden.

– 2009. "*The Golden Bough*: Orphic, Eleusinian, and Hellenistic-Jewish Sources of Virgil's Underworld in *Aeneid* VI." *Kernos* 22: 183–208.

– 2014. *Initiation into the Mysteries of the Ancient World.* Berlin and New York.

– 2015. "Theseus and Peirithous' Descent into the Underworld." *Les Etudes Classiques* 83: 35–49.

Bremmer, J.N., and N.M. Horsfall. 1987. *Roman Myth and Mythography.* London.

Bright, D. 1971. "A Tibullan Odyssey." *Arethusa* 4.2: 197–214.

– 1978. *Haec Mihi Fingebam: Tibullus in His World.* Leiden.

Brink, C.O. 1972. "Ennius and the Hellenistic Worship of Homer." *AJP* 93: 547–67.

Brockliss, W., P. Chaudhuri, A.H. Lushkov, and K. Wasdin, eds. 2012. *Reception and the Classics.* Cambridge.

Broeniman, C.S. 1992–3. "The *Confessions* of St. Augustine and Virgil's Aeneas: A Study in Narrative Design." *Proceedings of the Patristic, Medieval & Renaissance Conference* 16–17: 23–38.

Burke, K. 1961. *The Rhetoric of Religion: Studies in Logology.* Boston.

Burkert, W. 1987. *Ancient Mystery Cults*. Cambridge, MA.

– 2006. *Kleine Schriften* III: *Mystica, Orphica, Pythagorica*, edited by F. Graf. Göttingen.

Burrow, C. 1999. "'Full of the Maker's Guile': Ovid on Imitating and on the Imitation of Ovid." In *Ovidian Transformations*, edited by P. Hardie, A. Barchiesi, and S. Hinds, 271–87. Cambridge.

Busch, A. 2007. "*Versane Natura Est?*' Natural and Linguistic Instability in the Extispicium and Self-Blinding of Seneca's *Oedipus*." *CJ* 102.3: 225–67.

Bush, D. 1969. *Mythology and the Romantic Tradition in English Poetry*. Cambridge, MA.

Cahoon, L. 1984. "The Poet and the Parrot: The Function of Ovid's Funeral Elegies." *CJ* 80: 27–35.

Cairns, F. 1979. *Tibullus: A Hellenistic Poet at Rome*. Cambridge.

– 2006. *Sextus Propertius: The Augustan Elegist*. Cambridge.

Cameron, A. 1995. *Callimachus and His Critics*. Princeton.

– 2011. *The Last Pagans of Rome*. Oxford.

Caruso, C., and A. Laird. 2009. *Italy and the Classical Tradition: Language, Thought and Poetry, 1300–1600*. London.

Carver, R.H. 2007. *The Protean Ass: The* Metamorphoses *of Apuleius from Antiquity to the Renaissance*. Oxford.

Casali, S. 1995. "Aeneas and the Doors of the Temple of Apollo." *CJ* 91: 1–9.

– 2006. "The Poet at War: Ennius on the Field in Silius's *Punica*." *Arethusa* 39: 569–93.

– 2007. "Killing the Father: Ennius, Naevius, and Vergil's Intertextual Imperialism." In *Ennius Perennis: The* Annals *and Beyond*, edited by W. Fitzgerald and E. Gowers, 103–28. Cambridge.

Casali, S., and F. Stok, eds. 2008. *Servio: stratificazioni esegetiche e modelli culturali / Servius: Exegetical Stratifications and Cultural Models*. Brussels.

Claassen, J.-M. 1996. "Exile, Death and Immortality: Voices from the Grave." *Latomus* 55: 576–85.

Clark, G. 2010a. "Augustine's Varro and Pagan Monotheism." In *Monotheism between Pagans and Christians in Late Antiquity*, edited by P. van Nuffelen and S. Mitchell, 181–201. Leuven.

– 2010b. "Paradise for Pagans? Augustine on Virgil, Cicero and Plato." In *Paradise in Antiquity: Jewish and Christian Views*, edited by M. Bockmuehl and G.G. Stroumsa, 166–78. Cambridge.

Clark, R. 1979. *Catabasis: Vergil and the Wisdom Tradition*. Amsterdam.

– 1992. "Vergil, *Aeneid* 6: The Bough by Hades' Gate." In *The Two Worlds of the Poet*, edited by R.M. Wilhelm and H. Jones, 167–78. Detroit.

– 2017. "Optimism and Pessimism of the Harvard School: Contrasting Perspectives." *CW* 111.1: 57–61.
Clausen, W. 1994. *Virgil:* Eclogues. Oxford.
Clay, J.S. 1983. *The Wrath of Athena*. Princeton.
Cockburn, G.T. 1992. "Aeneas and the Gates of Sleep." *Phoenix* 46: 362–5.
Coetzee, J.M. 2003. *Elizabeth Costello: Eight Lessons*. London.
Coleman, K.M. 1988. *Statius* Siluae *IV*. Oxford.
Coleman, R. 1962. "Gallus, the *Bucolics*, and the Ending of the Fourth *Georgic*." *AJPh* 83: 55–71.
Collins, A.L. 2001. "The Etruscans in the Renaissance: The Sacred Destiny of Rome and the 'Historia Viginti Saeculorum' of Giles of Viterbo (c. 1469–1532)." *Historical Reflections/Réflexions Historiques* 27.1: 107–37.
Comparetti, D. 1895. *Vergil in the Middle Ages.* New York.
Conington, J. 1876. *P. Vergili Maronis Opera. The Works of Virgil, with a Commentary.* Online ed.
Connors, C. 2011. "Eratosthenes, Strabo, and the Geographer's Gaze." *PCP* 46: 139–52.
Conte, G.B. 1994. *Latin Literature: A History.* Translated by J.B. Solodow. Baltimore.
– 2009. *Vergilius Maro* Aeneis. Berlin.
Copeland, R., and I. Sluiter. 2012. *Medieval Grammar and Rhetoric: Language Arts and Literary Theory, AD 300–1475.* Oxford.
Corbeill, A. 2004. *Nature Embodied: Gesture in Ancient Rome*. Princeton.
Cornell, T.J., ed. 2013. *The Fragments of the Roman Historians.* 3 vols. Oxford.
Courcelle, P. 1943. *Les Lettres grecques en Occident: De Macrobe à Cassiodore.* Paris.
– 1955a. "Les Pères de l'Église devant les enfers Vergiliens." In *Archives d'histoire doctrinale et littéraire du Moyen Age* 30: 5–74.
– 1955b. "Interprétations néo-platonisantes du livre VI de l'*Enéide*." In *Entretiens sur l'Antiquité classique, Tome III: Recherches sur la tradition platonicienne,* 95–136. Geneva.
– 1984. *Lecteurs païens et lecteurs chrétiens de l'*Énéide, 2 vols. Paris.
Courtney, E. 1981. "The Formation of the Text of Vergil." *BICS* 28: 13–29.
– 1987. "Petronius and the Underworld." *AJP* 108: 408–10.
– 1993. *The Fragmentary Latin Poets.* Oxford.
Cowley, A. 1905. *Abraham Cowley: Poems: Miscellanies, The Mistress, Pindarique Odes, Davideis, Verses Written on Several Occasions.* Edited by A.R. Waller. Cambridge.
Cucchiarelli, A. 2001. *La satira e il poeta: Orazio tra* Epodi *e* Sermones. Pisa.
Cuche, V. 2014. "Le coureur et le guerrier: Anthropologie de la course à pied et de ses vertus militaires." *Kernos* 27: 9–50.
Cumont, F. 1920. "Lucrèce et le symbolisme pythagoricien des enfers." *RPh* 44: 229–40.

– 1949. *Lux perpetua*. Paris.

Curran, L. 1966. "Vision and Reality in Propertius 1.3." *YCS* 19: 189–207.

Currie, H.M. 1974–5. "St. Augustine and Virgil." *Proceedings of the Virgil Society* 14: 6–16.

Curtis, L. 2017. *Imagining the Chorus in Augustan Poetry.* Cambridge.

Dante. 1971–5. *The Divine Comedy*. Translated by C.S. Singleton. 6 vols. Princeton.

Dawe, R.D. 2006. *Sophocles,* Oedipus Rex. Cambridge.

Debrohun, J.B. 1994. "Redressing Elegy's *Puella*: Propertius IV and the Rhetoric of Fashion." *JRS* 84: 41–63.

Delaney, S. 1994. *The Naked Text: Chaucer's Legend of Good Women.* Berkeley.

De Ley, H. 1967. "Le traité sur l'emplacement des enfers chez Macrobe." *AC* 36: 190–208.

Della Corte, F. 1985. *La mappa dell'Eneide*. Florence.

Delvigo, M.L. 1995. "Ambiguita dell'*emendatio:* edizioni, riedizioni, edizioni postume." In *Formative Stages of Classical Traditions: Latin Texts from Antiquity to the Renaissance,* edited by O. Pecere and M. Reeve. Spoleto. 14–30.

Deramaix, M. 1990. "La genèse du *De partu Virginis* de Jacopo Sannazaro et trois eglogues inédites de Gilles de Viterbe." *Mélanges de L'Ecole Française de Rome. Moyen-Age, Temps Modernes* 102.1: 173–276.

Deschamps, L. 1999. "Les citations de *De rerum natura* de Lucrèce dans le commentaire de Servius à l'oeuvre de Vergile." In *Présence de Lucrèce,* edited by R. Poignault, 199–216. Tours.

Dietz, D.B. 1995. "*Historia* in the Commentary of Servius." *TAPA* 125: 61–97.

Dinter, M. 2005. "Epic and Epigram: Minor Heroes in Virgil's *Aeneid.*" *CQ* 55: 153–69.

– 2011. "Inscriptional Intermediality in Latin Elegy." In *Latin Elegy and Hellenistic Epigram: A Tale of Two Genres at Rome,* edited by A. Keith, 7–18. Newcastle.

Doblhofer, E. 1978. "Ovids Spiel mit Zweifel und Verzweiflung Stilistische und literaturtypologische Betrachtungen zu *Tristia* und *Ex Ponto.*" *WJA* 4: 137–8.

– 1987. *Exil und Emigration: Zum Erlebnis der Heimatferne in der Römischen Literatur*. Darmstadt.

Dodds, E.R. 1928. "Augustine's *Confessions*: A Study of Spiritual Maladjustment." *The Hibbert Journal* 26: 459–73.

– 1946. "Telepathy and Clairvoyance in Classical Antiquity." *Journal of Parapsychology* 10.4: 290–309.

– 1960. "Numenius and Ammonius." In *Les Sources de Plotin: Dix exposés et discussions.* , 3–32. Geneva.

– 1972. "Gilbert Murray's Last Experiments." *Proceedings of the Society for Psychical Research* 55: 371–402.

Doob, P. 1990. *The Idea of the Labyrinth: From Classical Antiquity to the Middle Ages*. Cornell.
Doody, A. 2010. *Pliny's Encyclopedia: The Reception of the* Natural History. Cambridge.
Dougherty, C. 1993. *The Poetics of Colonization*. Oxford.
Dreizehnter, A. 1978. *Die rhetorische Zahl. Quellenkritische Untersuchungen anhand der Zahlen 70 und 700*. Munich.
Drew, D.L. 1927. *The Allegory of the* Aeneid. Oxford.
Dunlap, D.W. 2014. "A Memorial Inscription's Grim Origins." *The New York Times*. 3 April 2014.
Dyson, J.T. 2001. *King of the Wood: The Sacrificial Victor in Virgil's* Aeneid. Norman, OK.
Edmonds, R.G. 2010. "The Bright Cypress of the Orphic 'Gold' tablets: Direction and Illumination in Myths of the Underworld." In *Light and Darkness in Ancient Greek Myth and Religion*, edited by M. Christopoulos et al., 221–34. Lanham, MD.
– 2011. "Festivals in the Afterlife: A New Reading of the Petelia Tablet (*OF* 476.11)." In *Tracing Orpheus. Studies of Orphic Fragments*, edited by M. Herrero de Jáuregui et al., 185–8. Berlin, New York.
Edmondson, J. (forthcoming) "Towards a Reconstruction of the *Elogium* of Aeneas from the Forum Augustum in Rome: Reflections on th Copies from Augusta Emerita and Pompeii."
Edwards, M.W. 2002. *Sounds, Sense, and Rhythm: Listening to Greek and Latin Poetry*. Princeton.
Eisenberger, H. 1960. "Der innere Zusammenhang der Motive in Tibulls Gedicht I, 3." *Hermes* 88: 188–97.
Ekbom, M. 2013. *The* Sortes Vergilianae*: A Philological Study*. Uppsala.
Eliot, T.S. 1957. "Virgil and the Christian World (1951)." In *On Poetry and Poets*, 121–31. London.
Elliott, J. 2013. *Ennius and the Architecture of the* Annales. Cambridge.
Evans, H.B. 1983. *Publica Carmina: Ovid's Books from Exile*. Lincoln.
Fagiolo, M., and C.A. Luchinat. 1981. *Natura e artificio: l'ordine rustico, le fontane, gli automi nella cultura del Manierismo europeo*. Rome.
Fairclough, H.R. 1999. *Virgil*. 2 vols. Revised by G.P. Goold. Cambridge, MA.
Fantham, E. 2009. *Latin Poets and Italian Gods*. Toronto.
Faraone, C. 2011. "Magical and Medical Approaches to the Wandering Womb in the Ancient Greek World." *CA* 30: 1–23.
Farrell, J. 1999. "*Aeneid* 5: Poetry and Parenthood." In *Reading Vergil's Aeneid*, edited by C. Perkell, 96–110. Norman, OK.
Farrell, J., and M.C.J. Putnam, eds. 2010. *A Companion to Vergil's* Aeneid *and Its Tradition*. Malden, MA.

Fedeli, P. 1980. *Il primo libro delle* Elegie*: Sesto Properzio.* Florence.
– 1985. *Il Libro Terzo delle* Elegie. Bari.
Feeney, D.C. 1986. "History and Revelation in Vergil's Underworld." *PCPhS* 32: 1–24.
– 1993. "Horace and the Greek Lyric Poets." In *Horace 2000: A Celebration. Essays for the Bimillennium,* edited by N. Rudd, 41–63. Ann Arbor.
– 1998. *Literature and Religion at Rome.* Cambridge.
– 1999. "*Mea Tempora*: Patterning of Time in the *Metamorphoses.*" In *Ovidian Transformations,* edited by P. Hardie, A. Barchiesi, and S. Hinds, 13–30. Cambridge.
– 2007. *Caesar's Calendar: Ancient Time and the Beginnings of History*. Berkeley.
– 2016. *Beyond Greek*. Cambridge, MA.
Feldherr, A. 1999. "Putting Dido on the Map: Genre and Geography in Vergil's Underworld." *Arethusa* 32: 85–122.
Feuchtwang, S. 2008. "Suggestions for a Redefinition of Charism" *Nova Religio* 12.2: 90–105.
Fichter, A. 1982. *Poets Historical: Dynastic Epic in the Renaissance*. New Haven.
Firpo, G. 2002. "Il monosandalismo degli Ernici (Verg. *Aen.* 7.678–690)." In *Guerra e diritto nel mondo greco e romano,* edited by M. Sordi, *Scienze storiche* 80 = *Contributi dell'Istituto di Storia Antica* 28: 185–200. Milan.
Fitch, J.G. 1987. *Seneca's* Hercules Furens: *A Critical Text with Introduction and Commentary.* Ithaca.
Fitzgerald, W. 1984. "Aeneas, Daedalus and the Labyrinth." *Arethusa* 17.1: 51–65.
Flamant, J. 1977. *Macrobe et le néo-platonisme latin à la fin du IVe siècle.* Leiden.
Fogazza, D. 1981. *Domiti Marsi Testimonia et Fragmenta*. Rome.
Folch, M. 2015. *The City and the Stage: Performance, Genre, and Gender in Plato's Laws.* Oxford.
Force, P. 1993. "Les Signes marginaux et la mise en page des poèmes." In Groupe de Recherches sur l'Afrique Antique (G.R.A.A.). *Les Flavii de Cillium: étude architecturale, épigraphique, historique et littéraire du mausolée de Kasserine* (CIL VIII, 211–16), 96–110. Rome.
Ford, P. 2007. *De Troie à Ithaque: réception des épopées homériques à la Renaissance.* Geneva.
Foucault, M. 1977 [1969]. "What Is an Author?" In *Language, Counter-Memory, Practice,* edited by D.F. Bouchard, 113–38. Oxford.
Fowler, D. 1997a. "The Virgil Commentary of Servius." In *The Cambridge Companion to Virgil,* edited by C. Martindale, 73–8. Cambridge.
– 1997b. "Virgilian Narrative: Story-Telling." In *The Cambridge Companion to Virgil,* edited by C. Martindale, 259–70. Cambridge.
– 2002. "Masculinity Under Threat? The Poetics and Politics of Inspiration in Latin Poetry." In Spentzou and Fowler 2002: 141–59.

Fraenkel, E. 1945. "Some Aspects of the Structure of *Aeneid* VII." *JRS* 35: 1–14.
– 1957. *Horace.* Oxford.
Frazer, J.G. 1922. *The Golden Bough: A Study in Magic and Religion*. New York.
Feeney, D. 2007. *Caesar's Calendar: Ancient Time and the Beginnings of History*. Berkeley.
Furley, W.D., and J.M. Bremer. 2001. *Greek Hymns: Selected Cult Songs from the Archaic to the Hellenistic Period.* 2 vols. Tübingen.
Ganiban, R.T. 2007. *Statius and Virgil. The* Thebaid *and the Reinterpretation of the* Aeneid. Cambridge.
García, L.R. 2008. "Vergil *Aeneid* 6.445–446: A Critical Note." *HSCP* 104: 273–87.
Garvey, J.X.K. 1995. "City Limits: Reading Gender and the Urban Spaces in *Ulysses*." *TCL* 41: 108–23.
Gauld, A. 2011. "Myers, Frederic William Henry (1843–1901)." *Oxford Dictionary of National Biography*. Revised online edition: https://doi.org/10.1093/ref:odnb/35177.
Gildenhard, I. 2007. "Vergil vs. Ennius, Or: The Undoing of the Annalist." In *Ennius Perennis: The* Annals *and Beyond,* edited by W. Fitzgerald and E. Gowers, 73–102. Cambridge.
Giles (Aegidius) of Viterbo and D.J. Nodes. 2010. *The Commentary on the Sentences of Petrus Lombardus*. Leiden.
Ginzburg, C. 1989. *Storia notturna: una decifrazione del Sabba*. Milan.
Godwin, W. 1965. "Of the Study of Classics." In *The Enquirer: Reflections on Education, Manners, and Literature in a Series of Essays: 1797,* 36–55. New York.
Goldberg, S. 1996. "The Fall and Rise of Roman Tragedy." *Transactions of the American Philological Society* 126: 265–86.
Goldschmidt, N. 2013. *Shaggy Crowns: Ennius'* Annales *and Vergil's* Aeneid. Oxford.
Goldstein, P., and J.L. Machor 2008. *New Directions in American Reception Study*. Oxford.
Goodman, K. 2004. *Georgic Modernity and British Romanticism: Poetry and the Meditation of History*. Cambridge.
Goold, G.P. 1967. "*Noctes Propertianae*." *HSCP* 71: 59–106.
Gotoff, H. 1985. "The Difficulty of the Ascent from Avernus." *CP* 80: 35–40.
Gowers, E. 1993. "Horace, *Satires* 1.5: An Inconsequential Journey." *PCPhS* 39: 48–66.
– 2005. "Virgil's Sibyl and the 'Many Mouths' Cliché (*Aen*. 6.625–7)." *CQ* 55: 170–82.
– 2011. "The road to Sicily: Lucilius to Seneca." *Ramus* 40: 168–97.
– 2012. *Horace:* Satires *Book 1*. Cambridge.

Graf, F., and S.I. Johnston. 2013. *Ritual Texts for the Afterlife: Orpheus and the Bacchic Gold Tablets*. 2nd ed. London and New York.

Grafton, A., G.W. Most, and S. Settis. 2010. *The Classical Tradition*. Cambridge, MA.

Gransden, K.W. 1984. "The *Aeneid* and *Paradise Lost*." In *Virgil and His Influence: Bimillennial Studies*, edited by C. Martindale, 95–116. Bristol.

Gratwick, A. 1982. "Ennius' *Annales*." In *Cambridge History of Classical Literature: Vol. 2: Latin Literature*, edited by E.J. Kenney, 60–76. Cambridge.

Graver, B.E. 1991. "Wordsworth's Georgic Beginnings." *Texas Studies in Literature and Language* 33. 2: 137–59.

Graziosi, B. 2002. *Inventing Homer: The Early Reception of Epic*. Cambridge.

Graziosi, B., and E. Greenwood. 2007. *Homer in the Twentieth Century: Between World Literature and the Western Canon*. Oxford.

Grebe, S. 2010. "Why Did Ovid Associate His Exile with a Living Death?" *CW* 103.4: 491–510.

Grimal, P. 1954. "Le livre VI de l'*Enéide* et son actualité en 23 av. J.-C." *REA* 56: 40–60.

Haarhoff, T.J. 1948. *Stranger at the Gate: Aspects of Exclusiveness and Co-operation in Ancient Greece and Rome, with Some Reference to Modern Times*. Oxford.

Habinek, T.N. 1989. "Science and Tradition in *Aeneid* 6." *HSCP* 92: 223–55.

Hagendahl, H. 1967. *Augustine and the Latin Classics*, 2 vols. Gothenburg.

Hanegraaff, W.J. 2012. *Esotericism and the Academy: Rejected Knowledge in Western Culture*. Cambridge.

Hanslik, R. 1970. "Tibulls Elegie I 3." In *Forschungen zur römischen Literatur*, edited by W. Wimmel, 138–45. Wiesbaden.

Hardie, A. 1983. *Statius and the* Siluae*: Poets, Patrons and Epideixis in the Graeco-Roman World*. Liverpool.

Hardie, P. 1986. *Vergil's* Aeneid*: Cosmos and Imperium*. Oxford.

– 1990. "Ovid's Theban History: The First 'Anti-*Aeneid*'?" *The Classical Quarterly* 40.1: 224–35.

– 1993. *The Epic Successors of Virgil: A Study in the Dynamics of a Tradition*. Cambridge.

– 1994. *Vergil,* Aeneid *Book IX*. Cambridge.

– 1997. "Closure in Latin Epic." In *Classical Closure: Reading the End in Greek and Latin Literature*, edited by D.H. Roberts, F.M. Dunn, and D. Fowler, 139–62. Princeton.

– 1998. "Horace, the Paean and Roman *Choreia* (*Odes* 4.6)." *Papers of the Leeds International Latin Seminar* 10: 251–93.

– 2002. *Ovid's Poetics of Illusion*. Cambridge.

– 2004a. "In the Steps of the Sibyl: Tradition and Desire in the Epic Underworld." *MD* 52: 143–56.
– 2004b. "Vergilian Imperialism, Original Sin, and Fracastoro's *Syphilis.*" In *Latin Epic and Didactic Poetry,* edited by M. Gale, 223–34. Swansea.
– 2012. *Rumour and Renown: Representations of* Fama *in Western Literature.* Cambridge.
– 2014. *The Last Trojan Hero: A Cultural History of Virgil's* Aeneid. London.
Hardwick, L., and C. Stray. 2007. *A Companion to Classical Receptions.* Malden, MA.
Harrison, R.P. 2009. *Forests: The Shadows of Civilization.* Chicago.
Harrison, S.J. 2007. *Generic Enrichment in Vergil and Horace.* Oxford.
Hawkins, P.S. 2003. "For the Record: Rewriting Virgil in the *Commedia.*" *Studies in the Literary Imagination* 36.1: 75–97.
Heaney, S. 2016. Aeneid *Book VI: A New Verse Translation.* New York.
Heil, A. 2002. *Studien zur Vergil- und Statiusrezeption Dante Alighieris.* Frankfurt am Main.
Heinzelman, K., ed. 1991. *Texas Studies in Literature and Language* 33, no. 2.
Henderson, J. 1998. *A Roman Life: Rutilius Gallicus on Paper & in Stone.* Exeter.
– 2006. *Oxford Reds: Classic Commentaries on Latin Classics.* London.
– 2007. "Bringing It All back Home: Togetherness in Statius *Siluae* 3.5." *Arethusa* 40.2: 245–77.
Henkel, J. 2014. "Metrical Feet on the Road of Poetry: Foot Puns and Literary Polemic in Tibullus." *CW* 107.4: 451–75.
Henrichs, A. 1994–5. "Why Should I Dance? Choral Self-referentiality in Greek Tragedy." *Arion* 3: 56–111.
– 1996. *"Warum soll ich denn tanzen?": Dionysisches im Chor der griechischen Tragödie.* Stuttgart.
Henry, P. 1938. *La Vision d'Ostie: Sa place dans la vie et l'oeuvre de Saint Augustin.* Paris.
Herrero de Jáuregui, M. 2013. "*Emar Tode:* Recognizing the Crucial Day in Early Greek Poetry." *CA* 32.1: 35–77.
– 2015a. "Traditions of Catabatic Experience in *Aeneid* 6." *Les Études classiques* 83: 329–49.
– 2015b. "The Construction of Inner Religious Space in Wandering Religion of Classical Greece." *Numen: International Review for the History of Religions* 62: 667–97.
– 2016. "Trust the God: *Tharsein* in Ancient Greek Religion." *Harvard Studies in Classical Philology* 108: 1–52.
Heyworth, S.J. 2007. *Cynthia: A Companion to the Text of Propertius.* Oxford.
Highbarger, E.L. 1940. *The Gates of Dreams: An Archaeological Examination of Virgil's* Aeneid *6.893–899.* Baltimore.

Hinds, S. 1998. *Allusion and Intertext: Dynamics of Appropriation in Roman Poetry.* Cambridge.

– 2004. "Petrarch, Cicero, Virgil: Virtual Community in *Familiares* 24, 4." *MD* 52: 157–75.

– 2005. "Defamiliarizing Latin Literature, from Petrarch to Pulp Fiction." *TAPA* 135: 49–81.

Hollander, R. 1969. *Allegory in Dante's Commedia.* Princeton.

Hollis, A. 1970. *Ovid:* Metamorphoses *Book VIII.* Oxford.

– 1977. *Ovid.* Ars Amatoria. *Book I.* Oxford.

– 2007. *Fragments of Roman Poetry c. 60 BC–AD 20.* Oxford.

Holmes, D. 2008. "Practicing Death in Petronius' *Cena Trimalchionis* and Plato's *Phaedo.*" *CJ* 104: 43–57.

Hölscher, U. 1988. *Die Odyssee.* Munich.

Horsfall, N. 1974. "Vergil's Roman Chronography: A Reconsideration." *CQ* 24: 111–15.

– 1989. "Aeneas the Colonist." *Vergilius* 35: 8–27.

– 1991. *L'epopea in alambicco.* Naples.

– 1993. "*Odoratum lauris nemus* (Virgil, *Aeneid* 6.658)." *SCI* 12: 156–8.

– 2000. *Virgil,* Aeneid *7: A Commentary.* Leiden.

– 2006. *Virgil,* Aeneid *3: A Commentary.* Leiden.

– 2008. *Virgil,* Aeneid *2: A Commentary.* Leiden.

– 2013a. *Virgil,* Aeneid *6: A Commentary.* 2 vols. Berlin.

– 2013b. "Poets and Poetry in Virgil's Underworld." *Vergilius* 59: 85–90.

– 2014. "Poetic Immortality and Virgil's Elysium." *Paideia* 69: 363–5.

– 2015. "*Exempla* in Virgil's Underworld." *WS* 128: 63–7.

Houghton, L. 2007. "Tibullus' Elegiac Underworld." *CQ* 57: 153–65.

Hubaux, J. 1939. "Déiphobe et la Sibille." *AC* 8: 97–109.

Hübner, U. 1968. *Elegisches in der* Aeneis. Dissertation. Gießen.

Hulls, J.-M. 2010. "Replacing History: Inaugurating the New Year in Statius, *Siluae* 4.1." In *Latin Historiography and Poetry in the Early Empire: Generic Interactions,* edited by J.F. Miller and A.J. Woodman, 87–103. Leiden.

Hunink, V. 2009. "Hating Homer, Fighting Vergil: Books in Augustine's *Confessions.*" In *Readers and Writers in the Ancient Novel,* edited by M. Paschalis, S. Panayotakis, and G.L. Schmeling, 254–67. Eelde.

Hunter, R. 2001 "Vergil and Theocritus. A Note on the Reception of the Encomion to Ptolemy Philadelphus." *Seminari Romani* 4: 159–63.

Huskey, S.J. 2005. "In Memory of Tibullus: Ovid's Remembrance of Tibullus 1.3 in *Amores* 3.9 and *Tristia* 3.3." *Arethusa* 38.3: 367–86.

Idel, M. 2002. "*Prisca Theologia* in Marsilio Ficino and in some Jewish Treatments." In *Marsilio Ficino: His Theology, His Philosophy, His Legacy,* edited by M.J.B. Allen et al., 143–56. Leiden.

Ingold, T., and J.L. Vergunst, eds. 2008. *Ways of Walking: Ethnography and Practice on Foot.* Aldershot.

Irvine, M. 1994. *The Making of Textual Culture: "Grammatica" and Literary Theory, 350–1100.* Cambridge.

Jacoff, R., and J.T Schnapp, eds. 1991. *The Poetry of Allusion: Virgil and Ovid in Dante's* Commedia. Stanford.

Jauss, H.R. 1982. *Toward an Aesthetic of Reception.* Translated by Timothy Bahti. Minneapolis.

Jenkyns, R. 1998. *Vergil's Experience.* Oxford.

Jeunet-Mancy, E. 2012. *Servius, Commentaire sur l'*Énéide *de Vergile: Livre VI.* Paris.

Johnson, D.W. 1972. "*Verbum* in the Early Augustine (386–397)." *Recherches Augustiniennes* 8: 25–53.

Johnson, W.A. 2004. *Bookrolls and Scribes in Oxyrhynchus.* Toronto.

Jones, J.W., Jr. 1986. "The Allegorical Traditions of the *Aeneid.*" In *Vergil at 2000. Commemorative Essays in the Poet and his Influence,* edited by J.D. Bernard, 107–32. New York.

Kallendorf, C. 1989. *In Praise of Aeneas: Virgil and Epideictic Rhetoric in the Early Italian Renaissance.* Hannover, NH.

– 1999. "Historicizing the 'Harvard School': Pessimistic Readings of the *Aeneid* in Italian Renaissance Scholarship." *HSCP* 99: 391–403.

– 2007a. *A Companion to the Classical Tradition.* Malden, MA.

– 2007b. *The Other Virgil: Pessimistic Readings of the* Aeneid *in Early Modern Culture.* Oxford.

Käppel, L. 1992. *Paian: Studien zur Geschichte einer Gattung.* Berlin.

Kaster, R.A. 1988. *Guardians of Language.* Berkeley.

– 2012. *The Appian Way: Ghost Road, Queen of Roads.* Chicago.

Kaufmann, H. 2010. "Vergil's Underworld in the Mind of Roman Late Antiquity." *Latomus* 69: 150–60.

Keith, A.M. 1994. "*Corpus Eroticum*: Elegiac Poetics and Elegiac *Puellae* in Ovid's *Amores.*" *CW* 88: 27–40.

– 1999. "Slender Verse: Roman Elegy and Ancient Rhetorical Theory." *Mnemosyne* 52: 41–62.

Kennedy, D.F. 1997. "Modern Receptions and their Interpretive Implications." In *The Cambridge Companion to Virgil,* edited by C. Martindale, 38–55. Cambridge.

Kenney, E.J., ed. 1981. *Lucretius:* De rerum natura *Book III.* Cambridge.

– ed. 1994. *P. Ovidi Nasonis,* Amores, Medicamina Faciei Feminae, Ars Amatoria, Remedia Amoris. Oxford.

Kenney, J.P. 2005. *The Mysticism of Saint Augustine: Rereading the* Confessions. New York.

Kenyon, F.G. 1932. *Books and Readers in Ancient Greece and Rome.* Oxford.

Ker, J. 2015. "Seneca and Augustan Culture." In *The Cambridge Companion to Seneca,* edited by S. Bartsch and A. Schiesaro, 109–21. Cambridge.

Khayyam, Omar, and P.B. Caldéron. 1928. *The Rubaiyat of Omar Khayyam (First and Second Editions) and Six Plays of Calderon.* Translated by Edward Fitzgerald. London.

Kilgour, M. 2005. "'One immortality': The Shaping of the Shelleys in *The Last Man." European Romantic Review* 16.5: 563–88.

– 2013. "Dante's Ovidian Doubling." In *Dantean Dialogues: Engaging with the Legacy of Amilcare Iannucci,* edited by M. Kilgour and E. Lombardi, 174–214. Toronto.

– 2016. "Growing Up with Virgil." In *With Wandering Steps: Generative Ambiguity in Milton's Poetics,* edited by M. Fenton and L. Schwartz, 83–96. Duquesne.

Kim, L. 2010. *Homer between History and Fiction in Imperial Greek Literature.* Cambridge.

King, P. 2005. "Augustine's Encounter with Neoplatonism." *The Modern Schoolman* 82.3: 213–26.

Kissel, W. 1990. *Aulus Persius Flaccus*: Satiren. Heidelberg.

Kligerman, C. 1957. "A Psychoanalytic Study of the *Confessions* of St. Augustine." *Journal of the American Psychoanalytic Association* 5: 469–84.

Knauer, G. 1964. *Die* Aeneis *und Homer: Studien zur poetischen Technik Vergils, mit Listen der Homerzitate in der* Aeneis. Göttingen.

Knight, G.W. 1975. *Jackson Knight: A Biography.* Oxford.

Knight, W.F.J. 1929. "Vergil and the Maze." *Classical Review* 43.6: 212–13.

– 1935. Review of *The Magical Art of Virgil* by Edward Kennard Rand. *The Classical Weekly* 28.19: 145–8.

– 1936. "A Prehistoric Ritual Pattern in the Sixth *Aeneid." TAPA* 66: 256–73.

– 1939. *Accentual Symmetry in Vergil.* Oxford.

– 1946. *Roman Vergil.* 2nd ed. London.

– 1967. *Vergil, Epic and Anthropology: Comprising Vergil's Troy, Cumaean Gates, and The Holy City of the East.* New York.

Knox, P.E. 2005. "Milestones in the Career of Tibullus." *CQ* 55: 204–16.

Kofle , W. 2003. *Aeneas und Vergil: Untersuchungen zur poetologischen Dimension der* Aeneis. Heidelberg.

Kraggerud, E. 1965. "Caeneus und der Heroinenkatalog, *Aeneis* VI.440ff." *SO* 40: 60–71.

Kraus, C.S., and C. Stray. 2015. "Form and content." In *Classical Commentaries: Explorations in a Scholarly Genre,* edited by C.S. Strauss and C. Stray, 1–15. Oxford.

Krell, D.F. 1975. "Female Parts in *Timaeus. Arion* 2: 400–21.

Kripal, J.J. 2010. *Authors of the Impossible: The Paranormal and the Sacred.* Chicago.

Kristeller, P.O. 1967. *Le Thomisme et la pensée italienne de la renaissance.* Montreal.

Kurke, L. 2012. "The Value of Chorality in Ancient Greece." In *The Construction of Value in the* Ancient *World,* edited by J.K. Papadopoulos and G. Urton, 218–35. Los Angeles.

Kyriakidis, S. 1998. *Narrative Structure and Poetics in the* Aeneid*: The Frame of Book 6.* Bari.

LaChance, P.J. 2008. "A Christian *Aeneid*: Pagan and Christian Education in the *Confessions.*" In *Augustine and World Religions,* edited by B. Brown, J. Doody, and K. Paffenroth, 71–96. Lanham, MD.

Lada-Richards, I. 1999. *Initiating Dionysus: Ritual and Theatre in Aristophanes'* Frogs. Oxford.

Ladianou, K. 2005. "The Poetics of *Choreia*: Imitation and Dance in the *Anacreontea.*" *QUCC* 80: 47–58.

Lafferty, M. 2005. "Augustine, the *Aeneid* and the Roman Family." In *Hoping for Continuity: Childhood, Education and Death in Antiquity and the Middle Ages,* edited by K. Mustakallio et al., 105–18. Rome.

Laird, A. 2000. "Design and Designation in Virgil's *Aeneid,* Tacitus' *Annals* and Michelangelo's *Conversion of Saint Paul.*" In *Intratextuality: Greek and Roman Textual Relations,* edited by A. Sharrock and H. Morales, 143–70. Oxford.

– 2007. "Figures of Allegory from Homer to Latin Epic." In *Metaphor, Allegory, and the Classical Tradition: Ancient Thought and Modern Revisions,* edited by G.R. Boys-Stones, 151–76. Oxford.

Layard, J. 1942. *The Stone Men of Malekula: Vao.* London.

Lazzarini, C. 1984. "*Historia/fabula*: forme della costruzione poetica Vergiliana nel commento di Servio all'*Eneide.*" *MD* 12: 117–44.

Lee, G., ed. 1990. *Tibullus:* Elegies. Revised by R. Maltby. Leeds.

Lee-Stecum, P. 1998. *Powerplay in Tibullus: Reading* Elegies *Book One.* Cambridge.

Leigh, M. 2010. "Lucan's Caesar and the Sacred Grove: Deforestation and Enlightenment in Antiquity." *Lucan: Oxford Readings in Classical Studies,* edited by C. Tesoriero, 201– 38. Oxford.

Lennartz, K. 1999. "Fliegen oder flattern? Zu Epitaph des Ennius (frg. var. 17f. Vahlen 2)." *Philologus* 143: 181–2.

Levaniouk, O. 2011. *Eve of the Festival: Making Myth in* Odyssey *19.* Washington, DC.

Lim, R. 2004. "Augustine, The Grammarians and The Cultural Authority of Vergil." In *Romane Memento: Vergil in the Fourth Century,* edited by R. Reed, 112–27. London.

Lloyd-Jones, H. 1967. "Heracles at Eleusis: P. Oxy. 2622 and P.S.I. 1391." *Maia* 19: 206–29.
– 1983. *Blood for the Ghosts: Classical Influences in the Nineteenth and Twentieth Centuries.* Baltimore.
Lovatt, H. 2007. "Statius, Orpheus, and the post-Augustan *vates.*" *Arethusa* 40.2: 145–63.
Lowes, J.L. 1927. *The Road to Xanadu: A Study in the Ways of the Imagination.* Princeton.
Lowrie, M. 2009. *Writing, Performance, and Authority in Augustan Rome.* Oxford.
– 2010. "Rom immer wieder gegründet." In *Übertragene Anfänge: imperiale Figurationen um 1800,* edited by T. Döring et al., 23–50. Munich.
Luck, G. 1973. "Vergil and the Mystery Religions." *AJP* 94: 147–66.
Lyne, R.O.A.M. 1980. *The Latin Love Poets: From Catullus to Horace.* Oxford.
– 1998a. "Propertius and Tibullus: Early Exchanges." *CQ* 48: 519–44.
– 1998b. "Love and Death: Laodamia and Protesilaus in Catullus, Propertius, and Others." *CQ* 48: 200–12.
MacCormack, S. 1998. *The Shadows of Poetry: Vergil in the Mind of Augustine.* Berkeley.
Macdonald, R.R. 1987. *The Burial-Places of Memory: Epic Underworlds in Vergil, Dante, and Milton.* Amherst.
MacPhail, E.M. 2014. *Dancing Around the Well: The Circulation of Commonplaces in Renaissance Humanism.* Leiden.
Maguinness, W.S. 1956. "Seneca and the Poets." *Hermathena* 88: 81–98.
Maltby, R. 2002. *Tibullus:* Elegies*: Text, Introduction and Commentary.* Cambridge.
Mantuanus, B. 1497. *De patientia libri tres.* Brescia.
Mantuanus, B., and A. Severi. 2010. *Adolescentia.* Bologna.
Mantuanus, B., and L. Piepho. 1989. *Adulescentia: The Eclogues of Mantuan.* New York.
Mariotti, S. 1963. "Intorno a Domizio Marso." In *Miscellanea di studi alessandrini in memoria di Augusto Rostagni,* 588–614. Turin.
Martelli, F. 2009. "Plumbing Helicon: Poetic Property and the Material World of Statius' *Siluae.*" *MD* 62: 145–77.
Martin, R.P. 1989. *The Language of Heroes: Speech and Performance in the* Iliad. Ithaca.
– 2008. "Words Alone Are Certain Good(s): Philology and Greek Material Culture." *TAPA* 138.2: 313–49.
Martindale, C. 1993. *Redeeming the Text: Latin Poetry and the Hermeneutics of Tradition.* Cambridge.
– 1997. *The Cambridge Companion to Virgil.* Cambridge.
Martindale, C., and R.F. Thomas, eds. 2006. *Classics and the Uses of Reception.* Blackwell.

Masaracchia, E. 1982. "Tantalo nell'oltretomba di Tibullo. 1, 3, 67–80." *RFIC* 110: 429–34.

Masters, J. 2007. *Poetry and Civil War in Lucan's* Bellum Civile. Cambridge.

McCarthy, M.C. 2009. "Augustine's Mixed Feelings: Vergil's *Aeneid* and the Psalms of David in the *Confessions*." *Harvard Theological Review* 102.4: 453–79.

McCullough, A. 2007/8. "Heard But Not Seen: Domitian and the Gaze in Statius' *Siluae*." *CJ* 104.2: 145–62.

McGann, M.J. 1970. "The Date of Tibullus' Death." *Latomus* 29: 774–80.

McKeown, J.C. 1989. *Ovid:* Amores*: Vol. II: A Commentary on Book One.* Leeds.

– 1998. *Ovid:* Amores*: Vol. III: A Commentary on Book Two.* Leeds.

McNelis, C. 2007. *Statius'* Thebaid *and the Poetics of Civil War*. Cambridge.

Méndez Dosuna, J.V. 2009. "¿Un nuevo testimonio de αἶζα, 'cabra', en una lámina órfica? In *Estudios de Epigrafía Griega*, edited by A. Martínez Fernández, 369–75. La Laguna, Spain.

Merkelbach, R. 1961. "Aeneas in Cumae." *MH* 18: 83–99.

– 1971. "Aeneia Nutrix." *RhM* 114: 349–51.

Michels, A.K. 1944. "Lucretius and the Sixth Book of the *Aeneid*." *AJP* 65: 135–48.

– 1945. "The Golden Bough of Plato." *AJP* 66: 59–63.

Miller, J.F. 2009. *Apollo, Augustus, and the Poets*. Cambridge.

Mills, D. 1974. "Tibullus and Phaeacia: A Reinterpretation of 1.3." *CJ* 69: 226–33.

Milosz, C. 2001. *New and Collected Poems, 1931–2001*. New York.

Milton, J. 2007. *Paradise Lost*. Edited by Barbara K. Lewalski. Oxford.

Minson, R.A. 2003–4. "A Century of Extremes: Debunking the Myth of Harvard School Pessimism (A Reinterpretation of Twentieth Century Criticism of Virgil's *Aeneid*)." *Iris: Journal of the Classical Association of Victoria* 16–17: 46–63.

Molyviati-Toptsis, U. 1995. "*Sed Falsa ad Caelum Mittunt Insomnia Manes* (*Aeneid* 6.896)." *AJP* 116.4: 639–52.

Momigliano, A. 1942. "*Terra Marique*." *JRS* 32: 53–64.

Morgan, L. 1999. *Patterns of Redemption in Virgil's* Georgics. Cambridge.

– 2000. "Metre Matters: Some Higher-level Metrical Play in Latin Poetry." *PCPhS* 46: 99–120.

– 2010. *Musa Pedestris: Metre and Meaning in Roman Verse*. Oxford.

Morzadec, F. 2004. 'Stace et la Sibylle: rivalité littéraire autour de la louange de Domitien. La Silve, IV, 3." In *La sibylle, parole et representation*, edited by M. Bouquet and F. Morzadec, 85–98. Rennes.

Most, G.W. 1992. "Il poeta nell'Ade: catabasi epica e teoria dell'epos tra Omero e Vergilio." *SIFC* 10: 1014–26.

Mozley, J.H., ed. and trans. 1967. *Statius*. 2 vols. Rev. ed. Cambridge, MA.

Müller, G.A. 2003. *Formen und Funktionen der Vergilzitate bei Augustin von Hippo*. Paderborn.

Murgatroyd, P. 1980. *Tibullus I*. Pietermaritzburg.

– 1994. *Tibullus:* Elegies *II*. Oxford.
Murgia, C. 2004. "The Truth About Vergil's Commentators." In *Romane Memento: Vergil in the Fourth Century*, edited by R. Rees, 189–200. London.
Myers, K.S. 2000. "*Miranda fides:* Poets and Patrons in Paradoxographical Landscapes in Statius' *Siluae.*" *MD* 44: 103–38.
– 2009. *Ovid,* Metamorphoses *Book XIV.* Cambridge.
Mynors, R.A.B., ed. 1969. *P. Vergili Maronis Opera*. Oxford.
– 1990. *Virgil:* Georgics. Oxford.
Nagle, B.R. 1980. *The Poetics of Exile: Program and Polemic in the* Tristia *and* Epistulae ex Ponto. Brussels.
Nagy, G. 2003. *Homeric Responses.* Austin.
Nash, J. 2006. *James Joyce and the Act of Reception: Reading, Ireland, Modernism.* Cambridge.
Nauta, R.R. 2002. *Poetry for Patrons: Literary Communication in the Age of Domitian*. Leiden.
– 2008. "Statius in the *Siluae.*" In *The Poetry of Statius*, edited by J.J.L. Smolenaars, H.-J. van Dam, and R.R. Nauta, 143–74. Leiden.
Nelis, D. 2004. "La Sibylle et Medee: Vergile et la tradition argonautique." In *La Sibylle: Parole et representation*, edited by M. Bouquet and F. Morzadec, 61–8. Rennes.
Newlands, C.E. 2002. *Statius'* Siluae *and the Poetics of Empire*. Cambridge.
– 2012. *Statius, Poet between Rome and Naples*. London.
Nicoll, W.S.M. 1988. "The Sacrifice of alinurus." *CQ* 38.2: 459–72.
Nightingale, A.W. 2016. "Sight and the Philosophy of Vision in Classical Greece: Democritus, Plato and Aristotle." In *Sight and the Ancient Senses*, edited by M. Squire, 54–67. Milton Park.
ní Mheallaigh, K. 2014. *Reading Fiction with Lucian: Fakes, Freaks and Hyperreality.* Cambridge.
Nisbet, R.G.M., and M. Hubbard. 1978. *A Commentary on Horace:* Odes *Book II.* Oxford.
Norden, E. 1957. *P. Vergilius Maro:* Aeneis *Buch VI*. 4th ed. Stuttgart.
Öberg, J. 1987. "Some Interpretative Notes on Vergil's *Aeneid*, Book VI." *Eranos* 83: 105–9.
O'Donnell, J.J. 1992. *Augustine* Confessions. *Introduction, Text, and Commentary*, 3 vols. Oxford.
O'Hara, J.J. 1996. "An Unconvincing Etymological Argument about Aeneas and the Gates of Sleep." *Phoenix* 50.3/4: 331–4.
– 2007. *Inconsistency in Roman Epic*. Cambridge.
– 2017. *True Names: Vergil and the Alexandrian Tradition of Etymological Wordplay.* New and expanded ed. Ann Arbor.
Oliensis, E. 2001. "Freud's *Aeneid.*" *Vergilius* 47: 39–63.

O'Malley, J.W. 1968. *Giles of Viterbo on Church and Reform: A Study in Renaissance Thought.* Leiden.
– 1969. "Fulfillment of the Christian Golden Age Under Pope Julius II: Text of a Discourse of Giles of Viterbo, 1507." *Traditio* 25: 265–338.
O'Meara, J.J. 1963. "Augustine the Artist and the *Aeneid*." In *Mélanges offerts à Mademoiselle Christine Mohrmann*, 252–61. Utrecht-Anvers.
– 1968. "Virgil and Saint Augustine: The Roman Background to Christian Sexuality." *Augustinus* 13: 307–26.
– 1988. "Virgil and Augustine: The *Aeneid* in the *Confessions*." *The Maynooth Review/Revieú Mhá Nuad* 13: 30–43.
O'Neil, E. 1967. "Tibullus 2.6: A New Interpretation." *CPh* 62: 163–8.
Ossa-Richardson, A. 2008. "From Servius to Frazer: The Golden Bough and Its Transformations." *IJCT* 15: 339–68.
O'Sullivan, T. 2011. *Walking in Roman Culture.* Cambridge.
Otis, B. 1959. "Three problems of *Aeneid* 6." *TAPA* 90: 165–79.
Owen, S.G., ed. 1915. P. *Ovidi Nasonis,* Tristium Libri Quinque, Ibis, Ex Ponto Libri Quattuor, Halieutica Fragmenta. Oxford.
Paley, M.D. 1993. "*The Last Man*: Apocalypse Without Millenium." In *The Other Mary Shelley: Beyond* Frankenstein, edited by A.A. Fisch, A.K. Mellor, and E. Schor, 107–23. New York.
Pandey, N.B. 2014. "Reading Rome from the Farther Shore: *Aeneid* 6 in the Augustan Urban Landscape." *Vergilius* 60: 85–116.
– 2017. "Sowing the Seeds of War: The *Aeneid's* Prehistory of Interpretive Contestation and Appropriation. *CW* 111.1: 7–25.
Papanghelis, T.D. 1987. *Propertius: A Hellenistic Poet on Love and Death.* Cambridge.
Parke, H.W. 1988. *Sibyls and Sibylline Prophecy in Classical Antiquity.* London.
Parker, G. 2010. "Heraclitus on the Highveld: The Universalism (Ancient and Modern) of T.J. Haarhoff." In *Classics and National Cultures,* edited by S.A. Stephens and P. Vasunia, 217–34. Oxford.
Paschalis, M. 1994. "The Bull and the Horse: Animal Theme and Imagery in Seneca's *Phaedra*." *TAJPh* 115.1: 105–28.
Peponi, A.E., ed. 2013. *Performance and Culture in Plato's Laws.* Cambridge.
Pérez-Gómez, A. 1985. "The Myth of Daedalus." *AASA* 10: 49–52.
Perkins, C.A. 1993. "Love's Arrow's Lost: Tibullan Parody in *Amores* 3.9." *CW* 86: 459–66.
Perret, J. 1964. "Les compagnes de Didon aux enfers." *REL* 42: 247–61.
– 1984. "L'ordre de successione des vers dans *Énéide*, 6, 602–620." *RPh* 58: 19–33.
Pfeiffer, R. 1968. *History of Classical Scholarship: From the Beginnings to the End of the Hellenistic Age.* Oxford.
Pichon, R. 1902. *De sermone amatorio apud latinos elegiarum scriptores.* Paris.

Piepho, L. 1994. "Erasmus on Baptista Mantuanus and Christian Religious Verse." *Erasmus Studies* 14: 46–54.

Pighi, G. 1965. *De ludis saecularibus*. Amsterdam.

Pillinger, E. 2013. "*Inventa est blandae rationis imago:* Visualizing the Mausoleum of the Flavii." *TAPA* 143: 171–211.

– 2019. *Cassandra and the Poetics of Prophecy in Greek and Latin Literature.* Cambridge.

Poque, S. 1975. "L'expression de l'anabase plotinienne dans la prédication de saint Augustin et ses sources." *Recherches Augustiniennes* 10: 187–215.

Porter, J.I. 2016. *The Sublime in Antiquity*. Cambridge.

Powell, A. 1998. "The Peopling of the Underworld: *Aeneid* 6.608–627." In *Vergil's* Aeneid: *Augustan Epic and Political Context,* edited by H.P. Stahl, 85–100. London.

Prauscello, L. 2015. *Performing Citizenship in Plato's* Laws. Cambridge.

Pucci, J.M. 2014. *Augustine's Virgilian Retreat: Reading the Auctores at Cassiciacum.* Toronto.

Purcell, N. 1990. "The Creation of Provincial Landscape: the Roman Impact on Cisalpine Gaul." In *The Early Roman Empire in the West,* edited by T. Blagg and M. Millett, 7–29. Oxford.

– 1996. "The Ports of Rome." In *Roman Ostia Revisited* (Festschrift Russell Meiggs), edited by A. Claridge and A. Gallina Zevi, 267–79. London.

– 1998. "Discovering a Roman Resort-coast: The *litus Laurentinum* and the Archaeology of *otium.*" https://intranet.royalholloway.ac.uk/classics/research/laurentine-shore-project/documents/pdf/litus-laurentinum-english-version.pdf.

– 2012. "Rivers and the Geography of Power." *Pallas* 90: 373–87.

Purves, A. 2006. "Falling into Time in Homer's *Iliad.*" *CA* 25.1: 179–209.

– 2013. "Thick Description: Auerbach and the Boar's Lair (*Od.* 18. 388–475)." In *Topography, Geography, Landscape. Configurations of Space in Greek and Roman Epic,* edited by M. Skempis and I. Ziogas, 37–62. Berlin.

Putnam, M.C.J. 1990. "Vergil's Lapiths." *CQ* 40: 562–6.

– 1992. "Umbro, Nireus and Love's Threnody." *Vergilius* 38: 12–23.

– 2000. *Horace's* Carmen Saeculare: *Ritual Magic and the Poet's Art.* New Haven.

– 2005. "Virgil and Tibullus 1.1." *CPh* 100: 123–41.

Quint, D. 1993. *Epic and Empire: Politics and Generic Form from Virgil to Milton.* Princeton.

– 2014. *Inside* Paradise Lost: *Reading the Designs of Milton's Epic.* Princeton.

Quiter, R.J. 1984. *Aeneas und die Sibylle: Die rituellen Motive im sechsten Buch der* Aeneis. Königstein.

Ramage, C.L. 1970. "The Confessions of St. Augustine: The *Aeneid* Revisited." *Pacific Coast Philology* 5: 54–60.

Rand, E.K. 1931. *The Magical Art of Virgil.* Cambridge, MA.

Redpath, I.D. 2010. "Plato in Petronius: Petronius *in Platanona*." *CQ* 60: 577–95.

Reed, J. 1997. "Ovid's Elegy on Tibullus and Its Models." *CP* 92: 260–9.

Rees, R. ed. 2004. *Romane memento: Vergil in the Fourth Century*. London.

Reeves, M. 1969. *The Influence of Prophecy in the Later Middle Ages: A Study in Joachimism*. Oxford.

Reinhardt, T. 2004. "Readers in the Underworld: Lucretius, *De Rerum Natura* 3.912–1075." *JRS* 94: 27–46.

Reitz, B. 2012. "*Tantae molis erat*: On Valuing Roman Imperial Architecture." In *Aesthetic Value in Classical Antiquity*, edited by I. Sluiter and R.M. Rosen, 315–44. Leiden.

Riedweg, C. 2011. "Initiation–Death–Underworld: Narrative and Ritual in the Gold Leaves." In *The Orphic Gold Tablets and Greek Religion: Further Along the Path*, edited by R.G. Edmonds III, 213–50. Cambridge.

Robertson, N. 1980. "Heracles' 'Catabasis'." *Hermes* 108: 274–300.

Robichaud, D. 2006. "Marsilio Ficino's *De vita Platonis, Apologia de moribus Platonis*." *Accademia* 8: 23–59.

Roller, D. 2014. *The* Geography *of Strabo*. Cambridge.

– 2018. *A Historical and Topographical Guide to the* Geography *of Strabo*. Cambridge.

Rollin, C., and J.B.L. Crevier. 1768. *The Roman History from the Foundation of Rome to the Battle of Actium: That is, to the End of the Commonwealth*. 10 vols. 3rd ed. London.

Roman, L. 2010. "Martial and the City of Rome." *JRS* 100: 88–117.

Rosa, R. 1976. "Tomismo e antitomismo in Battista Spagnoli Mantovano (1447–1516)." *Memorie domenicane* 7: 227–64.

Rosati, G. 2002. "Muse and Power in the Poetry of Statius." In Spentzou and Fowler 2002: 229–51.

– 2011. "I tria corda di Stazio, poeta Greco, Romano e Napoletano." In *Filellenismo e Identità Romana in Età Flavia*, edited by A. Bonadeo, A. Canobbio, and F. Gasti, 15–34. Pavia.

Ross, C.S. 2004. *Publius Papinus Statius: The Thebaid: Seven Against Thebes*. Baltimore.

Rossi, A. 2002. "The Fall of Troy: Between Tradition and Genre." In *Clio and the Poets: Augustan Poetry and the Traditions of Ancient Historiography*, edited by D.S. Levene and D.P. Nelis, Mnem. Supp. 224, 231–51. Leiden.

Rudnytsky, P.L. 1994. "Freud and Augustine." In *Freud and Forbidden Knowledge*, edited by P.L. Rudnytsky and E.H. Spitz, 128–52. New York.

Ruppert, T. 2009. "Time and the Sibyl in Mary Shelley's *Last Man*." *Studies in the Novel* 41.2: 141–56.

Rutherford, I. 2001. *Pindar's* Paeans: *A Reading of the Fragments with a Survey of the Genre*. Oxford.

Sachs, J. 2010. *Romantic Antiquity: Rome in the British Imagination, 1789–1832.* Oxford.

Saggi, L. 1954. *La congregazione mantovana dei Carmelitani sino alla morte del B. Battista Spagnoli (1516).* Rome.

Santamaría, M.A. 2011. "I Have Reached the Desired Crown with Swift Feet (*OF* 488.6)." In *Tracing Orpheus: Studies of Orphic Fragments in Honour of Alberto Bernabé,* edited by M. Herrero de Jáuregui et al., 213–18. Berlin.

– 2014. "Las zancadas de Aquiles: un raro momento de alegría en el Hades homérico (*Od.* 11.538–540)," *Helmantica* 65: 279–92.

Schafer, J.K. 2017. "Authorial pagination in the *Eclogues* and *Georgics.*" *TAPA* 147.1: 135–78.

Schelkle, K.H. 1939. *Virgil in der Deutung Augustins.* Stuttgart.

Schiesaro, A. 1994. "Seneca's Thyestes and the Morality of Tragic Furor." In *Reflections of Nero: Culture, History, and Representation,* edited by J. Elsner and J. Masters, 196–210. Chapel Hill.

– 2003. *The Passions in Play: Thyestes and the Dynamics of Senecan Drama.* Cambridge.

Schindler, A. 1997. "Verifying or Falsifying Psychohistorical Observation: The Case of Dido's Suicide in Augustine's Confessions." In *Augustine and His Opponents, Jerome, Other Latin Fathers After Nicaea, Orientalia,* edited by E.A. Livingstone, 239–43. Leuven.

Schnapp, J.T. 1991. "'Sì pïa l'ombra d'Anchise si porse': *Paradiso* 15.25." In *The Poetry of Allusion: Virgil and Ovid in Dante's* Commedia, edited by R. Jacoff and J.T. Schnapp, 145–56. Stanford.

Schnegg-Köhler, B. 2002. *Die augusteischen Säkularspiele.* Munich.

Schwartz, R. 1988. "From Shadowy Types to Shadowy Types: The Unendings of *Paradise Lost.*" *MS* 24: 123–39.

Segal, C. 1983. "Boundary Violation and the Landscape of the Self in Senecan Tragedy." *Antike und Abendland* 29.2: 172–87.

– 1984. "Senecan Baroque: The Death of Hippolytus in Seneca, Ovid, and Euripides." *TAPA* 114: 311–25.

Setaioli, A. 1995. *La vicenda dell'anima nel commento di Servio a Vergilio.* Frankfurt.

Shackleton Bailey, D.R. 1967. *Propertiana.* Cambridge.

– 1995. *Q. Horati Flacci: Opera.* 3rd ed. Stuttgart.

– 2003. *Statius:* Siluae. Cambridge, MA.

Shanzer, D. 2012. "Augustine and the Latin Classics." In *A Companion to Augustine,* edited by M. Vessey, 161–74. Malden, MA.

Sharrock, A. 1994. *Seduction and Repetition in Ovid's* Ars Amatoria II. Oxford.

Shelley, M. 1985. *The Last Man.* Introduced by Brian Aldiss. London.

– 1996. *The Last Man.* Edited and introduced by Anne McWhir. Peterborough, ON.

– 1987. *The Journals of Mary Shelley 1814–1844*. Edited by P.R. Feldman and D. Scott-Kilvert. 2 vols. Oxford.
– 1980–8. *The Letters of Mary Wollstonecraft Shelley*. Edited by Betty T. Bennett. 3 vols. Baltimore and London.
Shelley, P.B. 1927. *The Complete Poetical Works of Percy Bysshe Shelley.* Edited by T. Hutchison. Oxford.
Shelton, J. 1978. *Seneca's* Hercules Furens: *Theme, Structure and Style.* Göttingen.
Skutsch, O. 1968. *Studia Enniana*. London.
– 1985. *The Annals of Quintus Ennius*. Oxford.
Smith, J.Z. 1973. "When the Bough Breaks." *History of Religions* 12.4: 342–71.
– 2004. *Relating Religion: Essays in the Study of Religion*. Chicago.
Smith, K.F. 1913. *The* Elegies *of Albius Tibullus.* New York.
Smith, R.A. 2005. *The Primacy of Vision in Virgil's* Aeneid. Austin.
Smolenaars, J.J.L. 1994. *Statius,* Thebaid VII*: A Commentary.* Leiden and New York.
– 1998. "The Vergilian Background of Seneca's *Thyestes* 641–682." *Vergilius* 44: 51–65.
– 2006. "Ideology and politics along the Via Domitiana." In *Flavian Poetry,* edited by R.R. Nauta, H.-J. van Dam, J.J.L. Smolenaars, 223–44. Leiden.
Smuts, J.C. 1926. *Holism and Evolution.* New York.
Solmsen, F. 1982. *Kleine Schriften* III. Hildescheim.
– 1990. "The World of the Dead in Book 6 of the *Aeneid*." In *Oxford Readings in Vergil's Aeneid,* edited by S.J. Harrison, 208–23. Oxford.
Solnit, R. 2000. *Wanderlust: A History of Walking*. Chicago.
Solodow, J. 1988. *The World of Ovid's Metamorphoses*. Chapel Hill.
Soranzo, M. 2013. "Words of Conversion: Poetry and Religious Identity in Early Modern Italy." *Journal of Religion in Europe* 6.2: 229–6.
– 2014. *Poetry and Identity in Quattrocento Naples*. Burlington, VT.
– 2015. "A New Look at Spirituality: Knowledge and Transformation in Early Modern Italy." *Journal of Religion in Europe* 8.2: 185–209.
Soskice, J.M. 2002. "Monica's Tears: Augustine on Words and Speech." *New Blackfriars* 83.980: 448–58.
Spence, S. 1988. *Rhetorics of Reason and Desire: Vergil, Augustine, and the Troubadours.* Ithaca.
– 2001. *Poets and Critics Read Virgil.* New Haven.
Spenser, E. 1977. *The Faerie Queene*. Edited by A.C. Hamilton. London.
Spentzou, E., and D. Fowler, eds. 2002. *Cultivating the Muse: Struggles for Power and Inspiration in Classical Literature*. Oxford.
Springer, C.P.E. 1989. "Augustine on Vergil: The Poet as *Mendax Vates*." *SP* 22: 337–43.
Stärk, E. 1995. *Kampanien als geistige Landschaft*. Munich.
Stahl, W.R. 1990. *Macrobius: Commentary on the Dream of Scipio.* New York.

Staley, G.A. 2010. *Seneca and the Idea of Tragedy.* Oxford.
Steiner, D. 2011. "Dancing with the Stars: *Choreia* in the Third Stasimon of Euripides' *Helen.*" *CP* 106: 299–323.
Stock, B. 1996. *Augustine the Reader: Meditation, Self-Knowledge and the Ethics of Interpretation.* Cambridge.
Stok, F. 2010. "The Life of Vergil Before Donatus." In *A Companion to Vergil's* Aeneid *and Its Tradition,* edited by J. Farrell and M.C.J. Putnam, 107–20. Malden, MA.
– 2013. "Servio e la metempsicosi." In *Totus scientia plenus: Percorsi dell'esegesi Vergiliana antica,* edited by F. Stok, 165–92. Pisa.
– 2016. "Servio, l'epica e la storia." *Rationes rerum* 8: 99–117.
Stray, C. 2008. "Murray, (George) Gilbert Aimé." *Oxford Dictionary of National Biography.* Revised online edition. https://doi.org/10.1093/ref:odnb/35159.
Strzelecki, W. 1964. *Cn. Naevii* Belli Punici *Carmen.* Lipsiae.
Suerbaum, W. 1981. *Vergils* Aeneis. *Beiträge zu ihrer Rezeption in Geschichte und Gegenwart.* Bamberg.
– 2008. *Handbuch der illustrierten Vergil-Ausgaben 1502–1840.* Hildesheim.
Swift, E., and A.M. Kinney, 2010. *The Vulgate Bible: The New Testament.* Cambridge, MA.
Tarrant, R.J. 1978. "Senecan Drama and its Antecedents." *HSCP* 82: 213–63.
– 1982. "Aeneas and the Gates of Sleep." *CP* 77.1: 51–5.
– 1995. "Greek and Roman in Seneca's Tragedies." *HSCP* 97: 215–30.
– ed. 2004. *P. Ovidi Nasonis* Metamorphoses. Oxford.
Tatum, J. 1984. "Allusion and Interpretation in *Aeneid* 6.440–76." *AJPh* 105: 434–52.
Taylor, J.B. 2007. "Psychology at the Fin de Siècle." In *The Cambridge Companion to the Fin de Siècle,* edited by G. Marshall, 13–30. Cambridge.
Thalmann, W. 2011. *Apollonius of Rhodes and the Spaces of Hellenism.* Oxford.
Theodorakopoulos, E. 1997. "Closure: The Book of Virgil." In *The Cambridge Companion to Virgil,* edited by C. Martindale. 155–65. Cambridge.
Thilo, G. 1886. *P. Virgilis Maronis Carmina.* Leipzig.
Thomas, R.F. 1988. *Virgil:* Georgics. 2 vols. Cambridge.
– 1999 [1985]. "From *Recusatio* to Commitment: The Evolution of the Virgilian Program." In *Reading Virgil and His Texts: Studies in Intertextuality,* 101–13. Ann Arbor.
– 2001. *Virgil and the Augustan Reception.* Cambridge.
– 2011. *Horace,* Odes 4 *and* Carmen Saeculare. Cambridge.
Thomas, R.F., and J.M. Ziolkowski, eds. 2014. *The Virgil Encyclopedia.* Chichester, UK.
Tissol, G. 1993. "Ovid's Little *Aeneid* and the Thematic Integrity of the *Metamorphoses.*" *Helios* 20: 69–79.

Treichel, T. 2009. *"And so Hell's Probable": Herman Melville's* Moby-Dick *and* Pierre *as Descent Narratives*. Trier.

Trinacty, C. 2014. *Senecan Tragedy and the Reception of Augustan Poetry*. Oxford.

– 2016. "Catastrophe in Dialogue: *Aeneid* 2 and Seneca's *Agamemnon*." *Vergilius* 62: 99–114.

Ulrich, R.B., and C.K. Quenemoen. 2014. *A Companion to Roman Architecture*. Malden, MA.

Ustinova, Y. 2009. *Caves and the Ancient Greek Mind: Descending Underground in the Search for Ultimate Truth*. Oxford.

Van den Keur, M. 2014. "*Meruit deus esse videri*: Silius' Homer in Homer's *Punica* 13." In *Flavian Poetry and Its Greek Past*, edited by A. Augoustakis, 287–304. Leiden.

Van Sickle, J. 1980. "The Book-Roll and Some Conventions of the Poetic Book." *Arethusa* 13.1: 5–42.

Vernant, J.P. 1982. "From Oedipus to Periander: Lameness, Tyranny, Incest in Legend and History." *Arethusa* 15: 19–39.

Videau-Delibes, A. 1991. *Les* Tristes *d'Ovide et l'élégie romaine: une poétique de la rupture*. Paris.

Von Stuckrad, K. 2005. "Western Esotericism: Towards an Integrative Model of Interpretation." *Religion* 35.2: 78–97.

– 2010. *Locations of Knowledge in Medieval and Early Modern Europe: Esoteric Discourse and Western Identities*. Leiden.

Wallace, E.O. 1938. *The Notes on Philosophy in the Commentary of Servius on the* Eclogues, *the* Georgics, *and the* Aeneid *of Vergil*. Dissertation. Columbia. New York.

Warden, J. 1980. Fallax Opus: *Poet and Reader in the Elegies of Propertius*. Toronto.

Ware, C. 2018. "The Ashplant and the Golden Bough: Heaney in Vergil's Labyrinth." *CRJ* 10: 229–48.

Waszink, J.H. 1979. "Ennianum." In *Opuscula Selecta*, 99–106. Leiden.

Watkins, J. 1995. *The Specter of Dido: Spenser and Virgilian Epic*. New Haven.

Weber, C. 2008. "Amor the Great in Propertius 1.19.12." *CPh* 103: 184–8.

Weeber, K.-W. 1974. "*Troiae lusus:* Alter und Entstehung eines Ritterspiels." *Ancient Society* 5: 171–96.

Wells, R.H. 1997. "Shakespeare, Virgil and the Politics of Violence." *Sederi* VIII: 149–62.

West, D.A. 1987. "The Bough and the Gate." Jackson Knight Memorial Lecture, University of Exeter. Exeter. [Reprinted in *Oxford Readings in Vergil's* Aeneid, edited by S.J. Harrison, 224–38. Oxford, 1990.]

– 1995. *Cast Out Theory: Horace Odes 1.4 and 4.7*. Classical Association. London.

West, G.S. 1980a. "Caenus and Dido." *TAPA* 110: 315–24.

– 1980b. "The Significance of Vergil's Eriphyle (*Aeneid* 6.445–446)." *Vergilius* 26: 52–4.

Wetherbee, W. 2008. *The Ancient Flame: Dante and the Poets.* South Bend, IN.

White, P. 1993. *Promised Verse: Poets in the Society of Augustan Rome.* Cambridge, MA.

Wigodsky, M. 1972. *Vergil and Early Latin Poetry*. Wiesbaden.

Wilamowitz-Moellendorff, U. 1895. *Euripides,* Herakles. 2 vols. Berlin.

– 1908. *Greek Historical Writing, and Apollo: Two Lectures Delivered before the University of Oxford, June 3 and 4, 1908.* Translated by G. Murray. Oxford.

Wilde, O. 1989. "The Decay of Lying." In *The Complete Works of Oscar Wilde,* edited by Vyvyan Holland, 970–92. New York.

Williams, G. 1994. *Banished Voices.* Cambridge.

Williams, M.F. 2010. "Virgil's *Aeneid* and the Historical Imagination in *Macbeth.*" *SSRN Electronic Journal* 10.2139/ssrn.1598019.

Williams, R.D. 1990. "The Sixth Book of the *Aeneid.*" In *Oxford Readings in Vergil's Aeneid,* edited by S.J. Harrison, 191–207. Oxford.

Willis, I. 2011. *Now and Rome: Lucan and Vergil as Theorists of Politics and Space.* London.

Wills, G. 2010. "Vergil and St. Augustine." In *A Companion to Vergil's* Aeneid *and Its Tradition,* edited by J. Farrell and M.C.J. Putnam, 123–32. Malden, MA.

Wilson, P. 2003. "The Politics of Dance: Dithyrambic Contest and Social Order in Ancient Greece." In *Sport and Festival in the Ancient Greek World,* edited by in D. Phillips, and D. Pritchard, 163–96. Swansea.

Wilson-Okamura, D.S. 2010. *Virgil in the Renaissance.* Cambridge.

Winden, J.C.M. van. 1959. *Calcidius on Matter: His Doctrine and Sources: A Chapter in the History of Platonism.* Leiden.

Winsbury, R. 2009. *The Roman Book: Books, Publishing and Performance in Classical Rome.* London.

Wiseman, T.P. 1992. *Talking to Virgil: A Miscellany*. Exeter.

Woolf, G. 2003. "The City of Letters." In *Rome the Cosmopolis,* edited by C. Edwards and G. Woolf, 203–21. Cambridge.

Wray, D. 2003. "What Poets Do: Tibullus on 'Easy' Hands." *CPh*: 98: 217–50.

– 2007. "Wood: Statius' *Siluae* and the Poetics of Genius." *Arethusa* 40.2: 127–43.

Wyke, M. 2002. *The Roman Mistress: Ancient and Modern Representations.* Oxford.

Zanker, P. 1988. *The Power of Images in the Age of Augustus.* Translated by A. Shapiro. Ann Arbor.

Zarker, J.W. 1967. "Aeneas and Theseus in *Aeneid* 6." *CJ* 62: 220–6.

Zeitlin, F.I. 2001. "Visions and Revisions of Homer." In *Being Greek Under Rome: Cultural Identity, the Second Sophistic and the Development of Empire,* edited by S. Goldhill, 195–266. Cambridge.

Zetzel, J.E.G. 1989. "*Romane Memento*: Justice and Judgment in *Aeneid* 6." *TAPA* 119: 263–84.
– 1997. "Rome and Its Traditions." In *The Cambridge Companion to Virgil*, edited by C. Martindale, 188–203. Cambridge.
Ziolkowski, E.J. 1995. "St. Augustine: Aeneas' Antitype, Monica's Boy." *Literature & Theology* 9: 1–23.
Ziolkowski, J.M., and M.C.J. Putnam. 2008. *The Virgilian Tradition: The First Fifteen Hundred Years*. New Haven.
Zissos, A. 2009. "Shades of Virgil: Seneca's *Troades*." *MD* 61:191–210.

INDEX

PHOENIX SUPPLEMENTARY VOLUMES

1 *Studies in Honour of Gilbert Norwood* edited by Mary E. White
2 *Arbiter of Elegance: A Study of the Life and Works of C. Petronius* Gilbert Bagnani
3 *Sophocles the Playwright* S.M. Adams
4 *A Greek Critic: Demetrius on Style* G.M.A. Grube
5 *Coastal Demes of Attika: A Study of the Policy of Kleisthenes* C.W.J. Eliot
6 *Eros and Psyche: Studies in Plato, Plotinus, and Origen* John M. Rist
7 *Pythagoras and Early Pythagoreanism* J.A. Philip
8 *Plato's Psychology* T.M. Robinson
9 *Greek Fortifications* F.E. Winter
10 *Comparative Studies in Republican Latin Imagery* Elaine Fantham
11 *The Orators in Cicero's* Brutus: *Prosopography and Chronology* G.V. Sumner
12 Caput *and Colonate: Towards a History of Late Roman Taxation* Walter Goffart
13 *A Concordance to the Works of Ammianus Marcellinus* Geoffrey Archbold
14 *Fallax opus: Poet and Reader in the Elegies of Propertius* John Warden
15 *Pindar's* Olympian One: *A Commentary* Douglas E. Gerber
16 *Greek and Roman Mechanical Water-Lifting Devices: The History of a Technology* John Peter Oleson
17 *The Manuscript Tradition of Propertius* James L. Butrica
18 Parmenides of Elea *Fragments: A Text and Translation with an Introduction* edited by David Gallop

19 *The Phonological Interpretation of Ancient Greek: A Pandialectal Analysis* Vít Bubeník
20 *Studies in the Textual Tradition of Terence* John N. Grant
21 *The Nature of Early Greek Lyric: Three Preliminary Studies* R.L. Fowler
22 Heraclitus *Fragments: A Text and Translation with a Commentary* edited by T.M. Robinson
23 *The Historical Method of Herodotus* Donald Lateiner
24 *Near Eastern Royalty and Rome, 100–30 BC* Richard D. Sullivan
25 *The Mind of Aristotle: A Study in Philosophical Growth* John M. Rist
26 *Trials in the Late Roman Republic, 149 BC to 50 BC* Michael Alexander
27 *Monumental Tombs of the Hellenistic Age: A Study of Selected Tombs from the Pre-Classical to the Early Imperial Era* Janos Fedak
28 *The Local Magistrates of Roman Spain* Leonard A. Curchin
29 Empedocles *The Poem of Empedocles: A Text and Translation with an Introduction* edited by Brad Inwood
30 Xenophanes of Colophon *Fragments: A Text and Translation with a Commentary* edited by J.H. Lesher
31 *Festivals and Legends: The Formation of Greek Cities in the Light of Public Ritual* Noel Robertson
32 *Reading and Variant in Petronius: Studies in the French Humanists and Their Manuscript Sources* Wade Richardson
33 *The Excavations of San Giovanni di Ruoti, Volume I: The Villas and Their Environment* Alastair Small and Robert J. Buck
34 *Catullus Edited with a Textual and Interpretative Commentary* D.F.S. Thomson
35 *The Excavations of San Giovanni di Ruoti, Volume 2: The Small Finds* C.J. Simpson, with contributions by R. Reece and J.J. Rossiter
36 The Atomists: Leucippus and Democritus *Fragments: A Text and Translation with a Commentary* C.C.W. Taylor
37 *Imagination of a Monarchy: Studies in Ptolemaic Propaganda* R.A. Hazzard
38 *Aristotle's Theory of the Unity of Science* Malcolm Wilson
39 Empedocles *The Poem of Empedocles: A Text and Translation with an Introduction, Revised Edition* edited by Brad Inwood
40 *The Excavations of San Giovanni di Ruoti, Volume 3: The Faunal and Plant Remains* M.R. McKinnon, with contributions by A. Eastham, S.G. Monckton, D.S. Reese, and D.G. Steele
41 *Justin and Pompeius Trogus: A Study of the Language of Justin's* Epitome *of Trogus* J.C. Yardley
42 *Studies in Hellenistic Architecture* F.E. Winter

43 *Mortuary Landscapes of North Africa* edited by David L. Stone and Lea M. Stirling
44 Anaxagoras of Clazomenae *Fragments and Testimonia: A Text and Translation with Notes and Essays* by Patricia Curd
45 *Virginity Revisited: Configurations of the Unpossessed Body* edited by Bonnie MacLachlan and Judith Fletcher
46 *Roman Dress and the Fabrics of Roman Culture* edited by Jonathan Edmondson and Alison Keith
47 *Epigraphy and the Greek Historian* edited by Craig Cooper
48 *In the Image of the Ancestors: Narratives of Kinship in Flavian Epic* Neil W. Bernstein
49 *Perceptions of the Second Sophistic and Its Times – Regards sur la Seconde Sophistique et son époque* edited by Thomas Schmidt and Pascale Fleury
50 *Apuleius and Antonine Rome: Historical Essays* Keith Bradley
51 *Belonging and Isolation in the Hellenistic World* edited by Sheila L. Ager and Riemer A. Faber
52 *Roman Slavery and Roman Material Culture* edited by Michele George
53 *Thalia Delighting in Song: Essays on Ancient Greek Poetry* Emmet I. Robbins
54 *Stymphalos: The Acropolis Sanctuary, Volume 1* Gerald Schaus with contributions by Sandra Garvie-Lok, Christopher Hagerman, Monica Munaretto, Deborah Ruscillo, Peter Stone, Mary Sturgeon, Laura Surtees, Robert Weir, Hector Williams, Alexis Young
55 *Roman Literary Cultures: Domestic Politics, Revolutionary Poetics, Civic Spectacle* edited by Alison Keith and Jonathan Edmondson
56 Fides *in Flavian Literature* edited by Antony Augoustakis, Emma Buckley, and Claire Stocks
57 *Maternal Conceptions in Classical Literature and Philosophy* edited by Alison Sharrock and Alison Keith
58 *Celebrity, Fame, and Infamy in the Hellenistic World* edited by Reimer Faber
59 *Walking through Elysium: Vergil's Underworld and the Poetics of Tradition* edited by Bill Gladhill and Micah Young Myers

www.ingramcontent.com/pod-product-compliance
Lightning Source LLC
LaVergne TN
LVHW090152080826
844660LV00013B/769/J

* 9 7 8 1 4 8 7 5 0 5 7 7 6 *